The Legal and Institutional Framing of Collective Bargaining in CEE Countries

Bulletin of Comparative Labour Relations

VOLUME 101

Founding Editor

The series started in 1970 under the dynamic editorship of Professor Roger Blanpain (Belgium), former President of the International Industrial Relations Association. Professor Blanpain, Professor Emeritus of Labour Law, Universities of Leuven and Tilburg, was also General Editor of the International Encyclopedia of Laws (with more than 1,600 collaborators worldwide) and President of the Association of Educative and Scientific Authors Authors. He passed away in October 2016.

General Editor

In 2015 Frank Hendrickx, Professor of labour law at the Faculty of Law of the University of Leuven (Belgium) joined as a co-Editor. Frank Hendrickx has published numerous articles and books and regularly advises governments, international institutions and private organisations in the area of labour law as well as in sports law. He is the Editor-in-Chief of the European Labour Law Journal and General Editor of the International Encyclopaedia of Laws.

Introduction

The Bulletins constitute a unique source of information and thought-provoking discussion, laying the groundwork for studies of employment relations in the 21st century, involving among much else the effects of globalization, new technologies, migration, and the greying of the population.

Contents/Subjects

Amongst other subjects the Bulletins frequently include the proceedings of international or regional conferences; reports from comparative projects devoted to salient issues in industrial relations, human resources management, and/or labour law; and specific issues underlying the multicultural aspects of our industrial societies.

Objective

The Bulletins offer a platform of expression and discussion on labour relations to scholars and practitioners worldwide, often featuring special guest editors.

The titles published in this series are listed at the end of this volume.

BULLETIN OF COMPARATIVE LABOUR RELATIONS – 101

The Legal and Institutional Framing of Collective Bargaining in CEE Countries

Between Europeanisation and Decentralisation

Author

Ivana Palinkaš

General Editor

Frank Hendrickx

Founding Editor

Roger Blanpain

Published by:
Kluwer Law International B.V.
PO Box 316
2400 AH Alphen aan den Rijn
The Netherlands
E-mail: international-sales@wolterskluwer.com
Website: lrus.wolterskluwer.com

Sold and distributed in North, Central and South America by:
Wolters Kluwer Legal & Regulatory U.S.
7201 McKinney Circle
Frederick, MD 21704
United States of America
Email: customer.service@wolterskluwer.com

Sold and distributed in all other countries by:
Air Business Subscriptions
Rockwood House
Haywards Heath
West Sussex
RH16 3DH
United Kingdom
Email: international-customerservice@wolterskluwer.com

Printed on acid-free paper.

ISBN 978-90-411-9199-1

e-Book: ISBN 978-90-411-9200-4
web-PDF: ISBN 978-90-411-9201-1

© 2018 Kluwer Law International BV, The Netherlands

All rights reserved. No part of this publication may be reproduced, stored in a retrieval system, or transmitted in any form or by any means, electronic, mechanical, photocopying, recording, or otherwise, without written permission from the publisher.

Permission to use this content must be obtained from the copyright owner. More information can be found at: lrus.wolterskluwer.com/policies/permissions-reprints-and-licensing

Printed in the United Kingdom.

Notes on Author

Ivana Palinkaš obtained law degree from University in Belgrade in Serbia, after which she obtained a master degree (LLM) in International and European Law at University of Amsterdam in the Netherlands in 2007. In 2016, she defended her PhD dissertation at Tilburg University, where she previously worked as doctoral researcher at Reflect institute (The Research Institute for Flexicurity, Labour Market Dynamics and Social Cohesion). Ivana Palinkaš is currently working at the Ministry of Foreign Affairs of the Republic of Serbia, and at the time of publishing this book is on her diplomatic post at the Mission of the Republic of Serbia to the EU in Brussels.

Table of Contents

Notes on Author	v
Preface and Acknowledgements	xv
List of Abbreviations	xvii
List of Figure and Tables	xix

CHAPTER 1
Introduction: Framing the Study on the Legal and Institutional Framework of Decentralised Collective Bargaining in CEE 1
1 Introduction 1
2 Decentralised Collective Bargaining in CEE 3
3 Questions 7
    3.1 Research Aim, Approach and Questions 7
    3.2 Relevance 10
4 Framing the Study: Normative Model of Articulated Multi-employer Bargaining 13
    4.1 Decentralisation of Collective Bargaining: Concept and Rationale 13
    4.2 Articulated Multi-employer Bargaining Model 16
    4.3 The Legal Architecture of the Model of Articulated Collective Bargaining 19
        4.3.1 Nature and Role of Labour Law 19
        4.3.2 Nature and Role of Collective Agreements 21
        4.3.3 Articulation 22
5 Research Methodology and Country Selection 23
6 Structure of the Study 26

Table of Contents

PART I
General Reflections on the Legal and Institutional Framework ... 29

CHAPTER 2
Capitalism, Welfare and Industrial Relations in CEE ... 31
1 Introduction ... 31
2 Explaining Capitalism, Welfare and Industrial Relations in CEE ... 34
    2.1 Capitalism in CEE ... 34
        2.1.1 Varieties of Capitalism ... 34
        2.1.2 Explaining CEE Capitalism ... 36
    2.2 Welfare Regimes in CEE ... 38
    2.3 Industrial Relations in CEE ... 40
3 Four CEE Countries: Major Traits ... 43
    3.1 Slovenia ... 43
    3.2 Slovakia ... 45
    3.3 The Czech Republic ... 47
    3.4 Poland ... 49
4 Conclusion: Comparative Remarks ... 50

CHAPTER 3
The Genesis and Positioning of Collective Agreement in CEE Labour Laws ... 53
1 Explaining the Genesis of Modern CEE Labour Laws ... 53
2 Deconstructing Labour Law Development in CEE ... 54
    2.1 Factors Pertinent to Labour Law Transformation ... 54
    2.2 In Search of a Leading Paradigm of Labour Law Transformation ... 56
3 The Development of Labour Law in the Four Countries ... 60
    3.1 Slovenia ... 60
    3.2 Slovakia ... 63
    3.3 The Czech Republic ... 64
    3.4 Poland ... 65
4 The Emancipation of Collective Agreements in CEE ... 67
    4.1 Collective Agreements: Defining the Legal Nature ... 67
    4.2 The Scope of Collective Bargaining Freedom ... 70
        4.2.1 Widening the Substantive Scope of Collective Agreement ... 70
        4.2.2 Collective Autonomy ... 74
5 Conclusion ... 75

CHAPTER 4
From Accession to the Economic and Financial Crisis: What Role for the EU? ... 79
1 Introduction ... 79
2 The EU Accession Process ... 81
    2.1 The Message of the EU During the Accession Process ... 81
        2.1.1 The ESM and the EU Model of Industrial Relations ... 81
        2.1.2 Social Acquis Related to the Accession Process ... 85

	2.2	Transferring the Message: The Mechanism	88
		2.2.1 The Role of the European Commission	88
		2.2.2 Europeanisation: Notion and Mechanism	89
	2.3	Assessing the Effects of Europeanisation	92
3	The Role of the EU During the Crisis	95
	3.1	The Context of the Crisis: A Changed Legal and Industrial Relations Environment	95
	3.2	EU Responses to the Crisis	96
4	Conclusions	99

PART II
Levels   101

CHAPTER 5
National Level: The Role of Tripartism   103
1   Introduction   103
2   Legal and Institutional Framework in the Four Countries   105
    2.1   Slovenia   105
          2.1.1   The Tripartite Body: Power and Functioning   105
          2.1.2   Representativeness   106
          2.1.3   History of Social Pacts   106
          2.1.4   Crisis   107
          2.1.5   Cross-Sectoral Agreements   108
    2.2   Slovakia   108
          2.2.1   The Tripartite Body: Power and Functioning   108
          2.2.2   Representativeness   110
          2.2.3   History of Social Pacts   110
          2.2.4   Crisis   111
          2.2.5   Regional Tripartite Social Dialogue   112
    2.3   The Czech Republic   112
          2.3.1   The Tripartite Body: Power and Functioning   112
          2.3.2   Representativeness   113
          2.3.3   History of Social Pacts   114
          2.3.4   Crisis   114
          2.3.5   Regional Tripartite Social Dialogue   115
    2.4   Poland   115
          2.4.1   The Tripartite Body: Power and Functioning   115
          2.4.2   Representativeness   116
          2.4.3   History of Social Pacts   117
          2.4.4   Crisis   118
          2.4.5   Regional Tripartite Social Dialogue   119
3   Comparative Overview of Legal and Institutional Traits   119
    3.1   Social Pacts: Weak Instruments of Standard Setting in CEE   119
    3.2   Institutionalisation of Tripartite Bodies   123

Table of Contents

4	Concluding Remarks		125
	4.1	Explaining the Development of the Legal and Institutional Framework for Tripartite Social Dialogue	125
	4.2	Standard Setting at National Level	127

CHAPTER 6
Evolution of Sectoral Collective Agreement   129

1	Introduction		129
2	Four Countries: Overview of Their Legal and Institutional Framework		132
	2.1	The Sectoral Collective Agreement: Definition and Origin	132
		2.1.1 Slovenia	132
		2.1.2 Slovakia	134
		2.1.3 The Czech Republic	135
		2.1.4 Poland	136
	2.2	Content of Sectoral Collective Agreements	138
		2.2.1 Slovenia	138
		2.2.2 Slovakia	139
		2.2.3 The Czech Republic	140
		2.2.4 Poland	141
	2.3	The Articulation of Sectoral Collective Agreements	141
		2.3.1 Slovenia	141
		2.3.2 Slovakia	142
		2.3.3 The Czech Republic	143
		2.3.4 Poland	144
	2.4	The Parties and Rules on Representativeness	144
		2.4.1 Slovenia	144
		2.4.2 Slovakia	146
		2.4.3 The Czech Republic	147
		2.4.4 Poland	148
	2.5	Mechanism of Erga Omnes Extension (General Applicability of Collective Agreements)	150
		2.5.1 Slovenia	150
		2.5.2 Slovakia	151
		2.5.3 The Czech Republic	153
		2.5.4 Poland	154
	2.6	Other Issues	154
		2.6.1 Personal Scope of Collective Agreements: To Whom Do the Collective Agreements Apply?	154
		2.6.1.1 Slovenia	154
		2.6.1.2 Slovakia	155
		2.6.1.3 The Czech Republic	155
		2.6.1.4 Poland	155

x

		2.6.2	Registration and Duration	155
		2.6.3	Procedure for Collective Bargaining	156
3	Comparative Overview: Sectoral Collective Agreements in CEE			156
	3.1	The Concept of Sectoral Collective Agreement in CEE		157
		3.1.1	Definition of Sectoral Collective Agreement in the Legal Framework	157
		3.1.2	The Content of Sectoral Collective Agreement	158
		3.1.3	Mechanism of Erga Omnes Extension (General Applicability of Collective Agreements)	160
	3.2	Sectoral Collective Agreement as an Instrument for Articulation		161
	3.3	Parties and Representativeness		164
4	Conclusions			166
	4.1	Development of Sectoral Collective Agreement		166
	4.2	Sectoral Collective Agreements: The Legal and Institutional Framework in CEE		167

CHAPTER 7
Company Level: Collective Bargaining and Other Forms of Standard Setting 171

1	Introduction				171
2	Four Countries: Overview of Legal and Institutional Framework				175
	2.1	Explaining Company Collective Agreements			175
		2.1.1	Definition and Origin		175
			2.1.1.1	Slovenia	175
			2.1.1.2	Slovakia	176
			2.1.1.3	The Czech Republic	176
			2.1.1.4	Poland	177
		2.1.2	Content of Company-Level Agreements and Articulation with Other Standard-Setting Sources		178
			2.1.2.1	Slovenia	178
			2.1.2.2	Slovakia	179
			2.1.2.3	The Czech Republic	180
			2.1.2.4	Poland	180
	2.2	Collective Bargaining Parties			181
		2.2.1	Who Can Conclude Collective Agreements?		181
			2.2.1.1	Slovenia	181
			2.2.1.2	Slovakia	182
			2.2.1.3	The Czech Republic	182
			2.2.1.4	Poland	182
		2.2.2	Organisation of Trade Unions and Competences		183
			2.2.2.1	Slovenia	183
			2.2.2.2	Slovakia	183
			2.2.2.3	The Czech Republic	184
			2.2.2.4	Poland	185

Table of Contents

	2.3	Other Issues			187
		2.3.1	Procedure of Collective Bargaining		187
		2.3.2	Duration		187
		2.3.3	To Whom Does the Company Collective Agreement Apply?		187
	2.4	Beyond Collective Bargaining			188
		2.4.1	Employers' Unilateral Standard-Setting		188
			2.4.1.1	Slovenia	188
			2.4.1.2	Slovakia	188
			2.4.1.3	The Czech Republic	188
			2.4.1.4	Poland	189
		2.4.2	Other Forms of Employee Representation: Works Councils		189
			2.4.2.1	Slovenia	189
			2.4.2.2	Slovakia	191
			2.4.2.3	The Czech Republic	191
			2.4.2.4	Poland	192
3	Comparative Overview: Company Collective Agreements and the Company as the Locus of Standard Setting in CEE				193
	3.1	Introduction: Explaining the Legal and Institutional Framework for Company Standard Setting			193
	3.2	Company Collective Agreements: Notion and Articulation			196
	3.3	Parties to Company Collective Agreements			198
	3.4	Procedure			199
	3.5	Beyond Collective Bargaining			200
		3.5.1	Works Councils		200
		3.5.2	Managerial Powers: Individualisation of Terms and Conditions of Work		200
4	Conclusions				202
	4.1	Notes on Development			202
	4.2	Assessing the Legal Framework for Company Collective Bargaining			203

CHAPTER 8
Conclusions 207
1 Introduction 207
2 Summary of Findings of the Study 207
3 Interpreting the Findings 213
   3.1 Normative Model of Articulated Multi-employer Bargaining 213
      3.1.1 Country Variations 213
      3.1.2 The Legal Architecture of the Normative Model: Three Analytical Elements 215

	3.2	Sketching Answers to the Research Questions	217
4		Limits, Outlooks and Future Challenges	221

Bibliography	223
List of Interviewees	245
Index	249

Preface and Acknowledgements

This book is a follow up of my PhD dissertation which I defended at Tilburg University in December 2016. Minor changes were inserted into the original text and tables. The research for this study has been funded by Tilburg University. The views expressed in this study are written in my personal capacity and may not necessarily represent the official position of my current employer.

I would like to express my sincere gratitude to all those who have in various ways contributed to this study. In the first place, I am greatly indebted to my supervisors, Prof. Dr Ton Wilthagen and Prof. Dr Linda Senden, whose guidance in conducting the research was invaluable. I am deeply grateful for the feedback and constructive comments received from the members of the PhD committee, Prof. Dr Csilla Kollonay-Lehoczky, Prof. Dr Frank Hendrickx, Prof. Dr Frans Pennings, Prof. Dr Maarten Keune, Prof. Dr Mijke Houwerzijl, and Dr Sonja Bekker. Moreover, I would also like to thank Prof. Dr Aukje van Hoek for helpful encouragement during the research beginnings. This study has also greatly benefited from stimulating discussions and support in various forms from many other people. I wish to particularly thank to Nuna Zekic, Irmgard Borghouts-van de Pas, Marta Kahancova, Monika Martiskova and Valentina Franca. I am sincerely thankful to all interviewees in Poland, the Czech Republic, Slovakia and Slovenia, whose dedication, knowledge and insights were invaluable in conducting this research. Conducting these interviews would not be possible without kind effort of people who assisted in establishing contacts in these countries.

Finally, my family has been the most supportive through all my journeys these years, to them I owe my deepest gratitude for completing this book.

Brussels, January 2018

List of Abbreviations

Alternativa	Slovenian Association of Trade Unions
ASO ČR	Association of Autonomous Trade Unions of the Czech Republic
AZZ SR	Federation of Employers' Associations of the Slovak Republic
BCC	Business Centre Club of Poland
CEE	Central and Eastern Europe
CMEs	Coordinated Market Economies
ČMKOS	Czech-Moravian Confederation of Trade Unions
ECHOZ	Energy and Chemical Sectors Trade Union Association of Slovakia
EMU	European Monetary Union
ESM	European Social Model
EU	European Union
FZZ	Trade Union Forum in Poland
GSZ	Chamber of Commerce and Industry of Slovenia
ILO	International Labour Organisation
IMF	International Monetary Fund
K-90	Confederation of Trade Unions of Slovenia
KNSS	New Trade Union Confederation of Slovenia
KOZ SR	Confederation of the Trade Unions of Slovak Republic
KPP	Confederation of Polish Employers
KUK	Confederation of Art and Culture of Slovakia
KZPS ČR	Confederation of Employers' and Entrepreneurs' Associations of the Czech Republic
LMEs	Liberal Market Economies
MIP	Macroeconomic Imbalance Procedure

List of Abbreviations

NACE	General Industrial Classification of Economic Activities
NKOS	Independent Christian Trade Unions of Slovakia
NSZZ Solidarnosc	Independent Self Governing Trade Union 'Solidarity'
OECD	Organisation for Economic Co-operation and Development
OPZZ	All-Poland Alliance of Trade Union
OS KOVO	Czech Metalworkers' Federation KOVO
OZS	Chamber of Crafts of Slovenia
Pergam	Confederation of Trade Unions Slovenia
PKPP Lewiatan	Polish Confederation of Private Employers Lewiatan
Pracodawcy RP	Employers of Poland
RUZ SR	National Union of Employers of the Slovak Republic
SMEs	Small and Medium Enterprises
Solidarnost	Association of Workers' Trade Unions of Slovenia
SP ČR	Confederation of Industry of the Czech Republic
SSS	Association of Free Trade Unions of Slovenia
TFEU	Treaty on Functioning of the European Union
UK	United Kingdom
VoC	Varieties of Capitalism
VSOZ	General Free Trade Union Association of Slovakia
ZDODS	Small Companies and Crafts Association of Slovenia
ZDS	Slovenian Employers' Association
ZMOS	Association of Cities and Municipalities of Slovakia
ZRP	Polish Crafts Union

List of Figure and Tables

Figure 1	Coverage Rates in Four CEE Countries
Table 1	Collective Bargaining Levels in CEE
Table 2	Dominant Bargaining Levels in Four Countries
Table 3	Collective Bargaining Coverage Before and after the Economic and Financial Crisis
Table 4	Industrial Relations at Sectoral Level
Table 5	Slovakia – Number of Extended Agreements
Table 6	Use of Extension Mechanisms
Table 7	Overview of Legal Possibilities for Derogations *in peius* from Statutory Law
Table 8	Industrial Relations at Company/Single-Enterprise Level
Table 9	Trends in Percentage Rates of Trade Union Density

CHAPTER 1
Introduction: Framing the Study on the Legal and Institutional Framework of Decentralised Collective Bargaining in CEE

1 INTRODUCTION

The pressures on collective bargaining posed by the recent economic and financial crisis raise questions about the ways in which standards for labour and work are set in the new Member States. For more than twenty-five years, the countries of Central and Eastern Europe (hereinafter 'CEE')[1] have witnessed a profound transformation of their labour laws. While the hope was that European Union (EU) membership would bridge the social gap between the new and old Member States, the reality is that the previous rounds of enlargements have brought greater diversity to the landscape of industrial relations in the EU. More than a decade after the enlargement round in 2004, in comparison to the other Member States, the CEE countries still have weak trade unions and employer' associations and an underdeveloped system of collective bargaining. The recent economic and financial crisis has illuminated the growing polarisation between the new and old Member States and the need to revitalise the industrial relations systems in the former group, in order to ensure the sustainability of the economic and social reforms.[2]

This study scrutinises the current legal and institutional framework for collective bargaining in CEE and the ways in which it has been developing in the past two

---

1. For the purpose of this study, the notion of Central and Eastern Europe shall refer to the countries that have joined the EU in the three previous enlargements; namely, Bulgaria, Croatia, the Czech Republic, Estonia, Hungary, Latvia, Lithuania, Poland, Romania, Slovakia, Slovenia.
2. As underlined in the report by the European Commission, *see* European Commission, Industrial Relation in Europe 2012, Luxembourg, Publications Office of the European Union, 2013, p. 53. Similar concerns were expressed by Kohl, H., 'Convergence and Divergence – Ten Years since EU Enlargement', *Transfer: European Review of Labour and Research*, 2015, vol. 21, no. 3, pp. 285–311.

decades. The decentralisation of industrial relations, amounting to vaguely developed sectoral and cross-sectoral standard setting in CEE, was addressed as problematic in the literature and expert reports more than a decade ago,[3] but the concerns remain valid.[4]

With these concerns in mind, this study aims to analyse the ways in which the legal and institutional framework in CEE actually supports and provides stimulus for collective bargaining at different collective bargaining levels. Ultimately, the study aims to reach a conclusion on whether the reasons for less developed centralised collective bargaining structures can be attributed to the legal environment. To streamline the analysis, the study concentrates on four CEE countries with different models of industrial relations: Slovakia, Slovenia, the Czech Republic and Poland.

The aim of this chapter is to further explain the research problem, the research questions and the structure and design of the study. To that end, this chapter begins with an explanation of decentralised collective bargaining in CEE (section 2), which is followed by a statement of the research aim, the research questions, and the approach and relevance of the study (section 3). Section 4 poses and explains the normative model which will guide the research and serve as a benchmark to analyse the legal and institutional framework of the CEE countries. Finally, section 5 explains the methodology of the study and the country selection, while section 6 explains the structure of the study.

Some terminological clarifications should be offered at this point. In this study, collective bargaining will be broadly understood as negotiations between trade unions or organisations of workers, and individual employers or employers' associations, with a view to determining terms and conditions of work and employment or relationship among them, by concluding a collective agreement. Social dialogue will be understood as all types of negotiations and consultations regarding all possible issues of common interest between state authorities, representatives of employers and representatives of employees.[5]

---

3. The issues of underdeveloped sectoral and cross-sectoral structures in CEE have been particularly addressed in: Vaughan-Whitehead, D., *EU Enlargement versus Social Europe? The Uncertain Future of the European Social Model*, Cheltenham, Edward Elgar, 2003; Pollert, A., 'Ten Years of Post-Communist Central Eastern Europe: Labour's Tenuous Foothold in the Regulation of the Employment Relationship', *Economic and Industrial Democracy*, 2000, vol. 21, no. 2, pp. 183–210; Ghellab, Y. and Vaughan-Whitehead, D., *Sectoral Social Dialogue in Future EU Member States: The Weakest Link*, Budapest, ILO, 2003; Kohl, H., Lecher, W. and Platzer, H.-W., 'Transformation, EU Membership and Labour Relations in Central Eastern Europe: Poland – Czech Republic – Hungary –Slovenia', *Transfer: European Review of Labour and Research*, 2000, vol. 6, no. 3, pp. 399–415.
4. Perez-Solorzano Borragan, N. and Smismans, S., 'The EU and Institutional Change in Industrial Relations in the New Member States' in S. Smismans (ed.), *The European Union and Industrial Relations: New Procedures, New Context*, Manchester, Manchester University Press, 2012, pp. 116–138; Meardi, G., *Social Failures of EU Enlargement: A Case of Workers Voting with Their Feet*, New York, Routledge, 2012a.
5. These definitions of social dialogue and collective bargaining are based on ILO understandings, see Olney, S. and Rueda, M., *Convention No 154: Promoting Collective Bargaining*, Geneva, ILO, 2005, pp. 5–6.

2 DECENTRALISED COLLECTIVE BARGAINING IN CEE

In most CEE countries, the industrial relations are decentralised. Around a decade ago, a study by Ghellab and Vaughan-Whitehead warned against a low number of sectoral collective agreements and weak structures for centralised (sectoral and cross-sectoral) collective bargaining arrangements.[6] A more recent data by the European Commission reconfirmed these weaknesses.[7] As Table 1 demonstrates, collective bargaining predominantly takes place at company level in CEE countries. The mechanisms for broadening the coverage of concluded collective agreements to third parties are not widely used in CEE.[8] The cross-sectoral collective activity is virtually non-existent in the CEE countries. At the same time, although tripartite structures are in place, there is limited output in terms of concluded social pacts.[9] The weakness of collective bargaining structures is accompanied by persistently falling trade union density rates on average from 59%, in 1990, to 19% in 2008.[10]

Nevertheless, collective bargaining practices are not uniform among the CEE countries and the four countries on which this study focuses – Slovenia, Slovakia, Czech Republic and Poland – have different models of collective bargaining. Slovenia has the most developed tradition of sectoral collective bargaining and in the past decades it has also had cross-sectoral collective agreements.[11] Slovakia has a fairly well-developed sectoral activity and sectoral standard setting predominates.[12] Poland and the Czech Republic have more decentralised collective bargaining than Slovenia and Slovakia. The Czech Republic has a certain level of sectoral activity, but Poland has almost no collective agreements concluded at this level.[13]

---

6. Ghellab and Vaughan-Whitehead 2003.
7. European Commission 2013, pp. 53–91.
8. Ibid., p. 64.
9. Ibid., pp. 74–75 and p. 80. Even though social pacts may not be labelled as collective agreements in a strict sense, given that they still represent a form of collective accord which arose in post-transitional CEE context and consequently shaped the industrial relations of these countries, their regulatory importance will be duly addressed in this study in Chapter 5.
10. Ibid., p. 62.
11. A concise overview of industrial relations trends in Slovenia can be found in: Kanjuo Mrčela, A., *Living and Working in Slovenia – Collective Bargaining*, Dublin, Eurofound, 2017.
12. See Czíria, L., *Living and Working in Slovakia*, Dublin, Eurofound, 2017.
13. For an overview of industrial relations trends in the Czech Republic and Poland, *see* Czarzasty, J. and Mrozowicki, A., *Living and Working in Poland – Collective Bargaining*, Dublin, Eurofound, 2017; Kyzlinkova, R., Lehmann, S., Pojer, P. and Veverková, S., *Living and Working in Czech Republic – Collective Bargaining*, Dublin, Eurofound, 2017.

Table 1   Collective Bargaining Levels in CEE

Country	National/Cross-Sectoral	Sector	Company
Poland	3	3	1
Czech Republic	-	3	1
Hungary	3	2	1
Croatia	3	2	1
Slovakia	-	1	2
Slovenia	2	1	2
Bulgaria	2	1	2
Romania	1	2*	2
Estonia	3	3	1
Latvia	3	3	1
Lithuania	-	3	1

Source: Kohl 2009, p. 29; see also Visser 2016.
Notes: 1 – predominant level of collective bargaining; 2 – important level, but not predominant; 3 – existing level.
*Since 2011, the predominant level is company, according to ICTWSS database 5.1 (Visser 2016).

The industrial relations data for these countries underpin the arguments presented. As demonstrated in Figure 1,[14] the coverage rates of collective agreements have been generally decreasing since the early 1990s. Except for Slovenia, these data lead to the conclusion that collective agreements have limited regulatory power as a source of standard setting. It can also be established that a large percentage of employees in the labour markets in the Czech Republic, Slovakia and Poland are not covered by the terms and conditions of collective agreements. This means that conditions of work and employment are for a large percentage of employees regulated by statutory legal rules only, and where applicable, by internal regulation issued unilaterally by employers at workplace level.

---

14. Coverage can be defined as a proportion of all employees, wage earners, with the right to collective bargaining, calculated as percentage, adjusted for the possibility that some sectors or occupations are excluded from the right to bargain, as in: Visser, J., *The ICTWSS Database: Institutional Characteristics of Trade Unions, Wage Setting, State Intervention and Social Pacts in 51 Countries between 1960 and 2014*, version 5.1, Amsterdam, Amsterdam Institute of Advanced Labour Studies, 2016.

Chapter 1: Introduction

Figure 1 Coverage Rates in Four CEE Countries

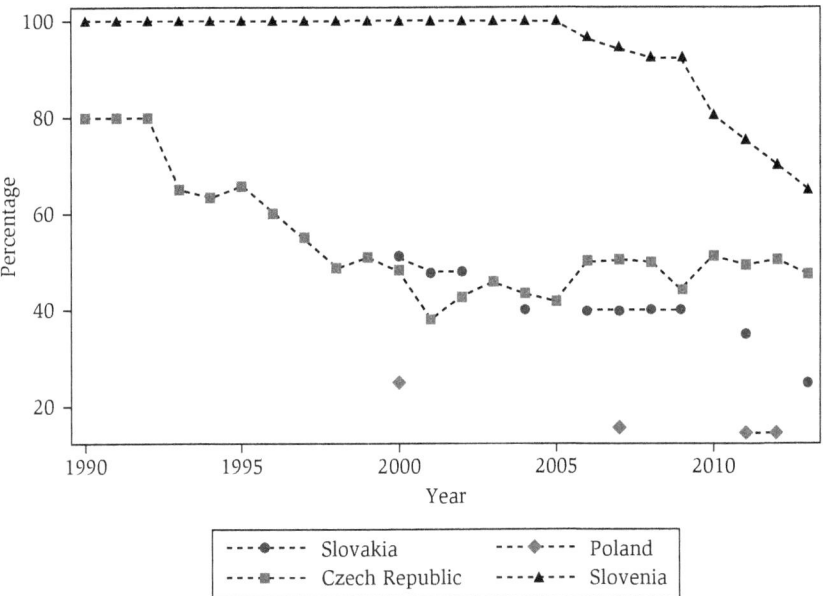

Source: ICTWSS database 5.1 (Visser 2016).
Notes: Coverage rate is defined as in ICTWSS database 5.1 (Visser 2016), as a proportion of all employees, wage earners, with the right to collective bargaining, calculated as percentage, adjusted for the possibility that some sectors or occupations are excluded from the right to bargain. Data covering the period 1990–2013; for Poland and Slovakia data not available for all years, as shown in this figure.

At the same time, as Table 2 demonstrates, collective bargaining has predominantly taken place at company level in the Czech Republic and Poland since the early transition period, while Slovakia has been subject to some degree of decentralisation since the late 1990s. It seems that Slovenia's collective bargaining have been the least subjected to trends of decentralisation.

Given that collective bargaining practices had only a marginal role in the communist setting, CEE industrial relations had to undergo a major transformative process from the 1990s. In an effort to enhance the standard-setting role of trade unions and employers' associations, the post-1990s legal and institutional developments sought to reinstate a culture of social dialogue. This task was particularly challenging since the trade unions were inexperienced at collective bargaining, while the employers' associations were mostly being established from scratch in the early 1990s.

Table 2 Dominant Bargaining Levels in Four Countries

	Slovenia	Slovakia	Czech Republic	Poland
1990	3	n/a	n/a	1
1991	3	n/a	2	1
1992	3	n/a	2	1
1993	3	3	2	1
1994	5	3	2	1
1995	5	3	1	1
1996	5	3	1	1
1997	3	3	1	1
1998	3	3	1	1
1999	5	2	1	1
2000	3	2	1	1
2001	5	2	1	1
2002	3	2	1	1
2003	5	2	1	1
2004	3	2	1	1
2005	3	2	1	1
2006	3	2	1	1
2007	5	2	1	1
2008	3	2	1	1
2009	3	2	1	1
2010	3	2	1	1
2011	3	2	1	1
2012	3	2	1	1
2013	3	2	1	1
2014	3	2	1	1

Source: ICTWSS database 5.1 (Visser 2016).
Notes: 1 – bargaining predominantly takes place at the local or company level, 2- intermediate or alternating between sector and company bargaining, 3 – bargaining predominantly takes place at the sector or industry level, 4 – intermediate or alternating between central and industry bargaining, 5 – bargaining predominantly takes place at central or cross-industry level and there are centrally determined binding norms or ceilings to be respected by agreements negotiated at lower levels. Data available until 2014.

The salience of boosting social dialogue has been recognised by the EU. The European Commission, which was guiding the accession negotiations with the CEE countries, consistently warned against low social dialogue culture and insisted upon boosting social partners' involvement in the socio-economic transformation of the CEE societies.[15] At the same time, the industrial relations reform was accompanied by a legal transformation which was aiming to align the CEE legal systems with the *acquis communautaire*. The refashioning of labour law was also taking place against the background of a wider market reform agenda in the CEE. The market reforms were by and large understood as an emanation of individual economic freedoms, which would replace the rigidity of the previous communist setting. In many CEE countries, the spirit of individual freedom brought radical macroeconomic restructuring and inspired labour law reform.[16] This provided a stimulating climate for decentralised industrial relations by reinforcing and promoting standard-setting arrangements at local level.

3 QUESTIONS

3.1 Research Aim, Approach and Questions

In the 1990s a fundamental transformation of CEE labour law commenced. Voluntary organisation of social partners and free and voluntary industrial relations, which had played only a marginal role in the previous system, had to be properly enshrined in law. Unlike the continental European countries, where the institutionalisation of industrial relations arose from a long-standing tradition, the CEE collective bargaining practices did not have time to establish a firm foothold. And yet, with their markets now open, CEE labour laws had to cope with the same set of international and transnational pressures as the other countries in Europe, from globalisation and competitiveness, to the recent economic and financial crisis.

More than two decades since the beginning of the economic and political transition, it is time to reflect on the current state of CEE labour laws and to assess their legal and institutional foundations of collective bargaining. How did CEE labour laws fare with respect to the regulation of collective bargaining and collective agreements? Have the labour laws enabled an adequate institutionalisation of industrial relations to allow free and voluntary collective bargaining at all bargaining levels? Or, has the decentralisation of collective bargaining been in some way underpinned by a lack of legal institutionalisation, particularly with respect to collective bargaining above company level? These questions are the core of the present study. In other words, the research aim is to scrutinise whether the legal and institutional frameworks of the selected countries have been conducive to collective bargaining taking place at various bargaining levels. This research task goes beyond checking whether the principles related to the social partners' independence and free and voluntary collective bargaining are formally accepted in law – these legal principles were formally inserted in law already in the early 1990s, when the CEE countries ratified the relevant International

---

15. The archives of yearly assessment reports can be accessed at the European Commission webpage: https://ec.europa.eu/neighbourhood-enlargement/countries/package_en (accessed 1 December 2017).
16. Kollonay Lehoczky, C., 'European Enlargement: A Comparative View of Hungarian Labour Law' in G.A. Bermann and K. Pistor (eds), *Law and Governance in an Enlarged European Union*, Oxford, Hart Publishing, 2004, pp. 210-211.

Labour Organisation (ILO) treaties.[17] The research task in this study requires a comprehensive scrutiny of the entire legal framework. To the fullest extent possible, the study will strive to point out legal shortcomings in the institutionalisation of collective bargaining in the four countries and to pinpoint how the existing legal frameworks can be enhanced in order to facilitate collective bargaining at three major levels.

This study takes a legal approach, and it is focused on investigating the role and content of law in the context of ongoing industrial relations developments. The study is focused on a specific time frame. It is understood that process of economic, social and political transition commenced in the early 1990s, with the collapse of centrally planned economies. The developments which have taken place since the early 1990s, after the onset of the transitional period, and up until mid-2015, are taken into consideration. Where possible, events taking place before the 1990s are taken into account. The data regarding the four selected countries have been collected to include events up to mid-2015.

Two research questions arise from the research aim:

(1) To what extent does the current legal and institutional framework in the four selected countries support and promote collective bargaining at different levels (cross-sectoral, sectoral and company)?
(2) How can the development of the legal and institutional framework of rules for collective bargaining in the selected CEE countries be explained? What role does the EU play in this respect?

The first research question aims at scrutinising the current state of play regarding the legal and institutional framework for collective bargaining. The assessment starts from the legal provisions pertinent to the entire collective bargaining system, followed by the legal provisions pertinent to collective bargaining at the three main levels (cross-sectoral, sectoral and company). Ultimately, answering this research question gives insights into whether the overall legal system is conducive to collective bargaining taking place at different levels.

To answer the first research question, it is necessary to set a normative benchmark against which the legal and institutional framework of CEE countries can be scrutinised. Setting the benchmark *first* requires defining the normative function of labour law vis-à-vis collective bargaining system. In this respect, the study understands that the role of labour law should be one of supporting and promoting collective bargaining and autonomous legal regulation by social partners. Section 4.3 will elaborate further on this topic.

Second, in order to be able to scrutinise legal and institutional rules at three major collective bargaining levels, this study establishes a normative model against which

---

17. ILO Freedom of Association and Protection of the Right to Organise Convention No 87, 1948 and ILO Right to Organise and Collective Bargaining Convention, No 98, 1949. Slovakia ratified these two conventions in 1993, Slovenia in 1992, the Czech Republic in 1993. Poland has been considered a party to these two conventions since 1957.

CEE laws will be assessed. However, there are inherent limits in defining such a model: fundamental principles of collective agreements and collective bargaining are differently understood across the Member States of the EU, and they usually reflect the country-specific tradition of collective bargaining. There is no uniform formula on how laws should look and how they can be transferred from one national setting to another. The normative model proposed in this study is therefore not based on a firm set of legal rules, but rather on a set of principles and traits. This model, to be referred to as an *articulated multi-employer bargaining model*, will be proposed and further explained in section 4.

The answer to the first research question will be delivered from different angles throughout the first and second part of this study. Some general insights on major labour law issues pertinent to collective bargaining in the four countries will be provided in Chapter 3. Chapters 5, 6 and 7 will provide answers to the research question from the perspective of the different collective bargaining levels. The final answer to this research question will be given in the concluding chapter of this book.

The second research question arises from the fact that the transformation on labour laws in CEE did not occur in isolation, but as a reference to the wider, multidimensional context. Since the opening up of the CEE economies in the early 1990s, the economic, welfare and industrial relations systems began a process of profound transformation. Answering the second research question therefore requires two steps. *First*, it is necessary to explain the environment which provided a pretext for labour law transformation in CEE. To do that, Chapter 2 will look into the existing theoretical knowledge that explains models of capitalism, welfare and industrial relations in CEE. Chapter 2 will also provide insights into economic, welfare and industrial relations processes in the four selected CEE countries.

The second step in dealing with this research question will be to evaluate the development of the legal and institutional framework for collective bargaining in each of the four countries, following the events which have unfolded in the past twenty-five years. This will take into account the beginning of the economic transition, the process of accession to the EU and the recent economic and financial crisis. This evaluation entails accounting for the explanatory weight of the different factors in shaping legal provisions during this time. Given the immense scale of labour law transformation in the CEE countries, it would be unsurprising to find that certain legacies, originating from the communist-based legal rules and legal principles, have continued to play a role in these countries. Additionally, part of the second research question is dedicated to influences coming from the EU, which the four CEE countries joined in 2004. A major source of EU influences originated in the accession process, under which the CEE countries were engaged in transposing and implementing social *acquis,* including the *acquis* on social dialogue. At the same time, the recent economic and financial crisis raises questions about the EU's competence over national collective bargaining systems, ultimately deeming necessary further (re)appraisal of the EU's pre-accession role in boosting social dialogue in CEE. As far as other international organisations are concerned, the study takes into account the role of the ILO to some extent, given that these countries were transposing and ratifying landmark ILO treaties, particularly in the 1990s. The role of external financial organisations in shaping CEE labour laws, such as the International Monetary Fund (IMF) and the OECD, will not be the focus of the study, given that their influence was less direct than the one of the EU. The EU seems to have had more comprehensive and pronounced impact on CEE, especially because these countries had to align their legal systems with the *acquis communautaire*. Yet, because of the dependence of CEE economies on international capital in the past decades, the pressures coming from the international financial institutions cannot be underestimated.[18]

The second research question is addressed from different angles throughout this study. How the economic, welfare and industrial relations environment presented a pretext for labour law transformation in the CEE will be assessed in Chapter 2. Further analytical identification of the factors which were pertinent to labour law transformation is given in Chapter 3, which also provides general insights into how the legal framework for collective bargaining developed in these four countries. Chapter 4 provides insights about the role of the EU. Chapters 5, 6 and 7 approach the second research question from the angle of different levels of collective bargaining respectively. Chapter 8 provides concluding answers and thoughts on the second research question.

3.2 Relevance

The issue of outstanding differences between 'new' and 'old' Member States in the social sphere was accentuated first and foremost on the eve of accession of the CEE countries to the EU. This issue was documented by observes who underlined that the EU should play a substantial role in order to help boosting social dialogue in the future Member States.[19] Since the very beginning of the accession process, the EU has recognised the importance of the difference between the social models in the CEE countries and those existing in the Member States. It was the European Council that prescribed tackling the social challenges of accession policies and making 'success of enlargement in the social field' in 2000.[20] Closing the 'gap' in industrial relations was deemed important not only for the sake of social and labour standards in the accession countries, but also because the functioning of several EU policies and agendas depended on meaningful collective bargaining mechanisms at national level.[21] More than ten years after the four countries entered the EU, the issue of the 'gap' between CEE countries and the rest of Europe remains topical, provoking pessimistic observations, such as that expressed by Meardi, that the rounds of enlargement have debunked

---

18. As argued by Cook, these international actors did not directly impose pressures on governments, but were setting flexibility agendas, *see* Cook, L.J., 'More Rights, Less Power: Labour Standards and Labour Markets in East European Post-Communist States', *Studies in Comparative International Development*, 2010, vol. 45, no. 2, p. 171.
19. Such views were expressed by Mailand, M. and Due, J., 'Social Dialogue in Central and Eastern Europe: Present State and Future Development', *European Journal of Industrial Relations*, 2004, vol. 10, no. 2, p. 195 and Meardi, G., 'The Trojan Horse for the Americanisation of Europe? Polish Industrial Relations towards the EU', *European Journal of Industrial Relations*, 2002, vol. 8, no. 1, pp. 77–99.
20. European Council, *Presidency Conclusions, Nice, 7–9 December 2000*.
21. This thesis is particularly underlined by Perez-Solorzano and Smismans 2012.

'the myth of a socially cohesive Europe'.[22] So far, at least in the area of industrial relations, existing knowledge of CEE prompts the conclusion that their industrial relations in no way resemble the existing models of continental European countries.[23] This study approaches the concern over the 'gap' between new and old Member States from a legal perspective, which has so far not been the predominant focus of the discussions. The ambition of this study to provide new insights into the debate over the existing 'gap' is furthermore reflected in the design of the normative model, which will be presented in section 4 of this chapter. This normative model will reflect, to the fullest extent possible, the reality of labour law systems in continental Europe and their collective bargaining practices.

More than two decades after the onset of transition and after several profound challenges to their collective bargaining systems – including EU accession and recent economic and financial crisis – it is the time to evaluate how CEE labour laws developed and the direction in which they are expected to further develop. The legal aspects of industrial relations in CEE countries have not had sufficient study in the past two decades, while the industrial relations aspects of collective bargaining decentralisation and industrial relations in CEE countries attracted considerably more attention in the empirical studies and academic literature. A few large-scale comparative studies undertaken on the eve of, and for a few years after the accession of the CEE countries to the EU, whilst primarily addressing industrial relations concerns, drew attention to the salience of a supportive legislative framework for collective bargaining.[24] The academic literature on CEE industrial relations has been flourishing in the past two decades, and in some instances this literature has also offered valuable legal insights. Likewise, it has been particularly underlined that inadequate implementation of existing legal provisions represents a worrying tendency.[25] There are authors who claimed that sectoral collective agreements have poor content and do not seem to be effective regulatory instruments.[26] Otherwise the scholarship was mostly focused on

---

22. Meardi 2012a, p. 184.
23. Kohl, H. and Platzer, H.-W., 'The Role of the State in Central and Eastern European Industrial Relations: The Case of Minimum Wages', *Industrial Relations Journal*, 2007, vol. 38, no. 6, pp. 616–620; Perez-Solorzano Borragan and Smismans, 2012, p. 117.
24. Parissaki, M. and Vega Vega, S., *Capacity Building for Social Dialogue at Sectoral and Company Level in the New Member States, Croatia and Turkey*, Dublin, Eurofound, 2008; Welz, C. and Kauppinen, T., *Social Dialogue and Conflict Resolution in the Acceding Countries*, Dublin, Eurofound, 2004; Kohl, H., *Freedom of Association, Employees' Rights and Social Dialogue in Central and Eastern Europe and the Western Balkans: Results of a Survey of 16 Formerly Socialist Countries in Eastern Europe*, Berlin, Friedrich Ebert Stiftung, 2009; Ghellab and Vaughan-Whitehead, 2003.
25. Bluhm, K., 'Resolving Liberalisation Dilemma: Labour Relations in East-Central Europe and the Impact of European Union', in M.A. Moreau and M.E. Blas-López (eds), *Restructuring in the New EU Member States: Social Dialogue, Firms Relocation, and Social Treatment of Restructuring*, Brussels, Peter Lang, 2008, pp. 59–79; Mailand and Due 2004; Treib, O. and Falkner, G., 'Conclusions – The State of EU Standards in Central and Eastern European Practice', in G. Falkner, O. Treib and E. Holzleithner (eds), *Compliance in the Enlarged European Union: Living Rights Or Dead Letters?*, Aldershot, Ashgate Publishing, 2008, pp. 157–182.
26. Lado, M. and Vaughan-Whitehead, D., 'Social Dialogue in Candidate Countries: What For?', *Transfer: European Review of Labour and Research*, 2003, vol. 9, no. 64, p. 76; also, Mailand and Due 2004, p. 187.

describing general features in all CEE countries or in several of them. In discussing decentralised industrial relations, scholarship has described the general weaknesses of collective bargaining, especially at sectoral and cross-sectoral level.[27] Trade unions have been identified as particularly weak, lacking collective bargaining experience and having a declining membership base.[28] The tripartite level has probably been the most researched aspect of industrial relations literature, with well-documented analysis of the emergence of tripartite bodies in the CEE. The literature, overall, pointed out the weaknesses of tripartite institutions in CEE and expressed expectations of playing a more prominent role in social and economic transformation.[29] Given the dependency of CEE economies on international capital, the ways in which the EU and international organisations in different ways affected the CEE policy making and industrial relations, was also a point of concern in the literature.[30]

Yet, so far the scholarship has not given a comprehensive comparative overview of the legal and institutional frameworks for collective bargaining in CEE, although in several instances the scholars called for their evaluation. Bronstein, likewise, noted that while the rules and legislation concerning social partners and industrial relations are in place, they have not been yet consolidated and, as such, might easily come under review in years that follow.[31] Moreover, different rules might come to the attention of law-makers, for example, rules on representativeness or on extending collective agreements to third parties.[32] In 2003, Casale provided a comparative overview of legislative trends in the CEE countries, including relevant mechanisms and institutions of collective bargaining and collective agreements.[33] Concluding that there is a positive trend in legislation promoting collective bargaining, Casale underlined that efficient implementation of provisions still remains a challenge in CEE countries.[34] Several ideas

---

27. For example Crowley, S., 'Explaining Labor Weakness in Post-Communist Europe: Historical Legacies and Comparative Perspective', *East European Politics and Societies*, 2004, vol. 18, no. 3, pp. 394–429; Meardi, G., 'More Voice after More Exit? Unstable Industrial Relations in Central Eastern Europe', *Industrial Relations Journal*, 2007, vol. 38, no. 6, pp. 503–523; Pollert, A., 'Trade Unionism in Transition in Central and Eastern Europe' *European Journal of Industrial Relations*, 1999, vol. 5, no. 2, pp. 209–234; Meardi 2012a; Pollert 2000.
28. Among many sources, *see* e.g. Ost, D., 'Illusory Corporatism in Eastern Europe: Neoliberal Tripartism and Postcommunist Class Identities', *Politics & Society*, 2000, vol. 28, no. 4, pp. 503–530; Crowley 2004; Meardi 2012a.
29. *See* e.g. Ost 2000; also, Avdagic, S., 'Tripartism and Economic Reforms in Slovenia and Poland' in L. Fraile (ed.), *Blunting Neoliberalism: Tripartism and Economic Reforms in the Developing World*, Basingstoke, Palgrave Macmillan, 2010a, pp. 39–84; Iankova, E.A., *Eastern European Capitalism in the Making*, Cambridge, Cambridge University Press, 2002. *See* Chapter 5 for further literature overview on tripartism.
30. For example *see* Bohle, D. and Greskovits, B., *Capitalist Diversity on Europe's Periphery*, Ithaca, Cornel University Press, 2012; Marginson, P. and Meardi, G., 'European Union Enlargement and the Foreign Direct Investment Channel of Industrial Relations Transfer', *Industrial Relations Journal*, 2006, vol. 37, no. 2, pp. 92–110.
31. Bronstein, A., 'Trends and Challenges of Labour Law in Central Europe' in J.D.R. Craig (ed.), *Globalisation and the Future of Labour Law*, Cambridge, Cambridge University Press, 2006, p. 214.
32. *Ibid.*
33. Casale, G., 'Evolution and Trends in Industrial Relations in Central and Eastern European Countries', *The International Journal of Comparative Labour Law and Industrial Relations*, 2003, vol. 19, no. 1, pp. 5–32.
34. *Ibid.*, pp. 31–32.

expressed in the legal scholarship have particularly inspired the design of current study. In Bronstein's opinion, the legal reform on collective bargaining in CEE has involved the processes of 'enrichment' of the existing legal framework with concepts which were previously unknown to the communist systems, for example industrial action or freedom of association.[35] Another process which Bronstein saw as important was the liberalisation of industrial relations, which necessitated review of individual labour laws with the aim of bringing them closer to the 'accepted wisdom in market economies'.[36] What Bronstein labelled as market wisdom was, for Kollonay-Lehoczky, essentially the process of restoration of contractual freedom – the contract-void communist labour laws were replaced with post-transitional legislation inspired by logic of entrepreneurial freedoms, private property and the '*laissez faire* mantra' which was undermining employee protection.[37]

4 FRAMING THE STUDY: NORMATIVE MODEL OF ARTICULATED MULTI-EMPLOYER BARGAINING

4.1 Decentralisation of Collective Bargaining: Concept and Rationale

Decentralisation is a generic term describing the process of shifting the focus of collective bargaining from higher to lower levels. The idea of decentralisation merely indicates that such downward movement exists, but it does not provide precise information about the substantive context of collective bargaining. Thus, the precise context of decentralisation can be given only in relation to national industrial relations practices. The downward movement may indicate decentralisation from sectoral to company level, as well as decentralisation from cross-sectoral to sectoral level. Also, the mere notion does not explain the extent to which the different collective bargaining levels are involved in standard setting. It also does not clarify the relationship between different bargaining levels, which is vital for explaining the national-specific context, as collective bargaining normally takes place at more than one level in any country.

In most of the countries in Europe, collective bargaining is predominantly developed at one particular level (the national or cross-sectoral, sectoral or branch and company or enterprise), while the other levels can play a more or less prominent role. Which collective bargaining level will be dominant is a complex question, the answer to which is determined in accordance with a range of social, political and economic factors, and can be also a matter of tradition. In countries such as the United Kingdom (UK) and the CEE countries, industrial relations take place predominantly at local level. In the case of the UK, centralised collective bargaining has disintegrated due to downward pressures, but in the CEE countries, centralised collective bargaining had to be built from scratch in the post-transitional period.

---

35. Bronstein 2006, pp. 194–198.
36. *Ibid.*, p. 197.
37. Kollonay Lehoczky 2004, p. 211.

In most of continental Europe, sectoral collective bargaining has traditionally formed a cornerstone of the collective bargaining systems.[38] Nevertheless, in previous decades, many European systems have been experiencing a trend towards decentralisation, moving the standard setting downwards in various forms and degrees and thereby shifting the centre of gravity from cross-sectoral to sectoral, and from sectoral to company level.[39] Yet, the picture of decentralisation has not been uniform in Europe – in some countries, in parallel to the top-down decentralisation movement, an opposite process took place, involving centralisation in the form of social pacts concluded between national organisations of trade unions and employers' organisations (e.g., in Spain, Italy, France and the Netherlands).[40] The recent economic and financial crisis has further underpinned decentralisation trends across European countries, affecting the ways in which standards are set, albeit to varying degrees.[41]

The division between the UK and the other continental European countries largely corresponds to the dichotomy between 'disorganised' and 'organised' decentralisation as coined by Traxler.[42] The systems of organised decentralisation are based on local level bargaining taking place under conditions and rules from higher (multi-employer) bargaining levels. In other words, the power and authority of lower bargaining levels derives from higher-level arrangements. In unorganised systems, the predominant local level arrangements do not take place under the framework of higher-level collective bargaining. A legal framework can facilitate organised decentralisation in various ways – for example, by stipulating the possibility of derogation from a number of statutory provisions to the detriment of employees (*in peius*).[43] Moreover, organised decentralisation can be facilitated by national (peak) level social partners in form of social pacts determining cross-sectoral rules and conditions under which collective bargaining can take place at lower bargaining levels.[44]

The general pattern of CEE decentralisation is unique when contrasted to other countries in continental Europe. In the first place, the CEE style of decentralisation does not entail downward movement. Specifically, the decentralised industrial relations in

---

38. Marginson, P., 'Coordinated Bargaining in Europe: From Incremental Corrosion to Frontal Assault?' *European Journal of Industrial Relations*, 2015, vol. 21, no. 2, pp. 97–114.
39. Marginson 2015, p. 99; Jacobs, A., 'Collective Labour Relations' in B. Hepple and B. Veneziani (eds), *The Transformation of Labour Law in Europe: A Comparative Study of 15 Countries 1945-2004*, Oxford, Hart Publishing, 2009, pp. 201–231.
40. Marginson, P. and Sisson, K., *European Integration and Industrial Relations: Multi-Level Governance in the Making*, Basingstoke, Palgrave Macmillan, 2006, p. 16 and p. 118.
41. Jacobs, A., 'Decentralisation of Labour Law Standard Setting and the Financial Crisis' in N. Bruun, K. Lörcher and I. Schömann (eds), *The Economic and Financial Crisis and Collective Labour Law in Europe*, Oxford, Hart Publishing, 2014, pp. 171–192.
42. Traxler, F., 'Farewell to Labour Market Associations? Organised versus Disorganised Decentralisation as a Map for Industrial Relations' in F. Traxler and C. Crouch (eds) *Organised Industrial Relations in Europe: What Future?*, Aldershot, Avebury, 1995, pp. 3–19. The notion of organised decentralisation has been often referred to as centrally coordinated decentralisation, *see* Ferner A. and Hyman R., 'Introduction: Industrial Relations in the New Europe – Seventeen Type of Ambiguity' in Ferner A. and Hyman R. (eds), *Industrial Relations in the New Europe*, Blackwell, Oxford, 1992.
43. Some country examples of legal frameworks facilitating organised decentralisation can be found in Jacobs 2014.
44. Marginson and Sisson 2006, p. 16 and p. 118.

CEE result from the general underdevelopment of higher-level bargaining levels. This originates in the pre-1990s systems when sectoral collective bargaining had not existed (or it was not free and voluntary), and where, for the same reason, social dialogue culture could not yet establish a foothold. The sectoral level weaknesses described have paved the way for the company-level bargaining to occupy a dominant position, as well as for strengthening managerial prerogatives at company level. In any case, the downward movement has not necessarily developed in CEE in the past two decades, but as Table 2 demonstrated, some form of decentralisation has been visible in Slovenia and Slovakia. Bearing in mind the absence of genuine downward movement in the Czech Republic and Poland, these two countries should be labelled as 'decentralised', rather than following the trend of 'decentralisation'.

There are many factors driving the decentralisation trend across Europe. The most obvious explanation is that it is a necessary by-product of competitive pressures and quests for flexible labour relations, as the local levels can most appropriately reflect the needs and conditions of the local labour market.[45] Growing market internationalisation has additionally underpinned decentralisation.[46] It has been furthermore underpinned by a combination of the other factors, among which technological changes, changes in economic demands, shifts in trade union powers and the ideological shift of many governments towards the free market narrative.[47] Statutory legal rules may only set broad provisions, and as such, are the most appropriate locus for setting minimum standards, even though it is not unimaginable that certain sectors and companies would not be able to comply.[48] Similarly, sectoral and cross-sectoral arrangements may not be able to reflect local level needs.[49] However, cross-sectoral and sectoral standard setting may have other benefits. Sectoral and cross-sectoral agreements, given their comprehensive scope, can set the floor for competition, particularly on wages or working time.[50] This benefit is particularly visible from the legal and social perspective, as synchronisation of rights and conditions of work can be used to prevent a 'race to the bottom' and the lowering of overall social standards.[51]

Yet, the question whether centralised or decentralised systems score better in terms of economic performance does not have a single answer. For a long time scholarship has been dominated by the work of Calmfors and Driffill,[52] who claimed that the best performing systems are those fully centralised or fully decentralised,

---

45. *Ibid.*, p. 146.
46. Particularly EMU, *ibid.*, p. 15.
47. As summarised by Soskice, D., 'Wage Determination: The Changing Role of Institutions in Advanced Industrialised Countries', *Oxford Review of Economic Policy*, 1990, vol. 6, no. 4, p. 52.
48. Jacobs 2014, p. 172.
49. Marginson and Sisson 2006, p. 146.
50. *Ibid.*, p. 145.
51. Traxler notes that these negotiations are by default so encompassing that the macroeconomic perspective cannot be avoided; in Traxler, F., 'Bargaining (De)centralisation, Macroeconomic Performance and Control over the Employment Relationship', *British Journal of Industrial Relations*, 2003a, vol. 41, no. 1, p. 3.
52. Calmfors, L. and Driffill, J., 'Bargaining Structure, Corporatism and Macroeconomic Performance', *Economic Policy*, 1988, vol. 3, no. 6, pp. 13–61.

unlike systems which occupy the middle position – neither fully centralised nor fully decentralised. However, the findings of Calmfors and Driffill have been mitigated by newer studies.[53]

This study presupposes the existence of three major bargaining levels across European countries: (a) national or cross-sectoral level; (b) sectoral, industry or branch level; and (c) company or enterprise level. To streamline the discussion, the study uses the generic term 'sectoral collective bargaining' to denote the bargaining level which takes place at a level intermediate to the national/cross-sectoral level and the local (company or enterprise) levels, without further designation of industry or branch structure. Similarly, the term 'company collective bargaining' is employed regardless of whether the bargaining takes place at the level of the entire company or in one of its units. Furthermore, the current study focuses on collective bargaining in private sector only, given that public sector – not being subject to same degree of market pressures, internationalisation and return to entrepreneurial freedoms in post-transitional years – may not adequately reflect the challenges of the decentralisation in CEE.

The following section sets out the analytical framework for further research, by putting forward a model that will serve as a benchmark against which CEE systems will be scrutinised.

4.2 Articulated Multi-employer Bargaining Model

This section presents the model of articulated multi-employer bargaining as a normative benchmark against which the legal and institutional framework in the four selected countries will be scrutinised in this study. The elements of the model come from industrial relations: in a nutshell, the term 'multi-employer bargaining' is widely used by industrial relations scholars to describe the collective bargaining models of most of the countries of Europe.[54] Multi-employer bargaining essentially denotes the type of collective bargaining in which employer organisations can generate binding decisions for their constituents, after they have joined the associations and obtained the mandate to negotiate.[55] Thus, this term implies the existence of collective bargaining structures at levels above company: sectoral and cross-sectoral. This multi-employer bargaining has remained the cornerstone of industrial relations across Europe despite being under strain because of several decades of the downward decentralisation pressures. For the purpose of this study, the concept of multi-employer bargaining will be further

---

53. The most influential argument involved the notion of coordinated bargaining, which can be roughly understood as the synchronisation between the bargaining levels and various bargaining parties. It has been claimed that coordination must be accounted for when discussing the economic performance of different models, as the coordinated decentralised systems, may be equal to fully centralised systems. Also, systems that are highly centralised may not necessarily be coordinated. For explanations over the role of coordination as well as the other critiques of Calmfors and Driffil thesis, *see* e.g. Traxler 2003a; also, Soskice 1990.
54. Among many sources, e.g. Marginson 2015; Marginson and Sisson 2006; Sisson, K. and Marginson, P., 'Coordinated Bargaining: A Process for Our Times?', *British Journal of Industrial Relations*, 2002, vol. 40, no. 2, pp. 197-220.
55. Visser, J., 'Wage Bargaining Institutions – from Crisis to Crisis', No. 488, Directorate General Economic and Financial Affairs (DG ECFIN), European Commission, 2013, p. 9.

analytically deconstructed and translated to the extent possible into the legal sphere. As a contrast to multi-employer bargaining, single-employer bargaining takes place when employers negotiate individually, as is the case in those countries with dominant company-level bargaining. Traxler explained that, as opposed to single-employer bargaining, multi-employer bargaining follows the *inclusive* pattern: it is associated with higher coverage rates, extension practices (allowing the extensions of powers of collective agreements to the third parties) and bargaining coordination at sectoral or central level.[56] Moreover, Traxler delineated three preconditions for functional multi-employer bargaining practices: strong trade unions, strong employer' associations and a supportive state.[57] Traxler also underlined the salient role of the legal framework underpinning multi-employer bargaining systems, noting that it is a decisive determinant of the collective bargaining structure in a country.[58]

Moreover, as underlined by Marginson, the effectiveness of multi-employer bargaining arrangements rests on *articulation or coordination*, which can be facilitated vertically across levels or horizontally across the bargaining units.[59] Coordination can be broadly explained as 'the extent to which the different levels are integrated so as to prevent them from mutually blocking their respective purposes'.[60] In this sense, coordination is an inherent element of multi-employer bargaining models. Biagi has underlined that the paradox of effective decentralised systems is that a certain degree of coordination is needed.[61]

In the context of this study, *articulation* will be the preferred term, and it will be used in a vertical sense to denote a procedural mechanism defining the relationship between higher and lower levels of standard setting. Therefore, articulation will be used to determine the relationship between collective agreements and statutory labour law; but also the relationship between collective agreements at different collective bargaining levels. The reason for using the term *articulation* rather than coordination is that it captures more adequately the two-way relationship, as explained by Marginson.[62] Moreover, this study will also follow the explanation of articulation by Marleau:

> If globalisation means that pressures and readjustments downward are unavoidable, there is a need for structural adjustment or articulation that would allow existing systems to continue to serve the purpose for which they were designed. In a fully decentralised regime, no such articulation is possible because there is no

---

56. Traxler, F., 'Collective Bargaining in the OECD: Developments, Preconditions and Effects', *European Journal of Industrial Relations*, 1998, vol. 4, no. 2, pp. 207–226.
57. Ibid., p. 213.
58. Traxler, F., 'Coordinated Bargaining: A Stocktaking of its Preconditions, Practices and Performance', *Industrial Relations Journal*, 2003b, vol. 34, no. 3, pp. 194–209.
59. Marginson 2015, p. 98, citing Crouch, C., *Industrial Relations and European State Traditions*, Oxford, Oxford University Press, 1993. and Traxler F., Blaschke S. and Kittel B., *National Labour Relations in Internationalised Markets*, Oxford, Oxford University Press, 2001.
60. Traxler, F., *Collective Bargaining: Levels and Coverage*, Employment Outlook, Paris, OECD, 1994.
61. Biagi, M., 'Changing Industrial Relations' in M. Biagi and M. Tiraboschi (eds), *Marco Biagi: Selected Writings*, The Hague, Kluwer Law International, 2003, p. 34.
62. Marginson 2015, p. 98.

central power or level vested with a power to intervene (nor even coordinated strategies between jurisdictions) to contain existing debasing pressures.[63]

Connected to the above understanding of articulation is the mechanism of complementarity – its purpose is to facilitate shared competences between different standard-setting venues and levels.[64] By using the complementarity mechanism, a balance between broad and narrow, central and local is reached with a view to establishing the 'checks and balances' of the entire model.[65]

This section has so far sketched the major analytical traits and objectives of the model which will be guiding the current study. Defined in this way, the analytical traits bear close resemblance to the model which was proposed by Lafoucriere and Green entitled a *concerted regulation model*. The ways in which the authors have defined this model with the aim of presenting it to CEE countries conform to the objectives of the proposed model in the current study:

> [Concerted regulation model] aims at triggering a process of competition and deregulation at the national level but with a view to integrating and re-regulating at all other possible levels, thereby ensuring the participation of all social forces, including wider involvement of workers...[66]

The authors explain that this model focuses more on 'process' than 'content'.[67] It is based on active involvement of social partners in standard setting and therefore it represents an alternative to state legislation. While Lafoucriere and Green did not aim to present its analytical elements, this study aims to go one step further. It will analytically deconstruct the *model of articulated multi-employer bargaining*, translate it to the legal realm and use it as a benchmark for scrutiny of the selected CEE countries.

Before doing so, it is also important to stress the underlying rationale for claiming that this model can benefit CEE countries. The articulated multi-employer bargaining model is used as a normative benchmark, not only to reflect the reality of most of the systems in Europe, but also because it offers certain advantages and as such can help to close the 'social gap' between the Member States. The advantages of (multi-employer) sectoral and cross-sectoral collective agreements were already explained in section 4.1 of this chapter. In addition, it is useful to add that the articulation offers certain benefits. As explained by Marleau, the advantage of the articulation between different standard-setting levels, is that it may offset the negative effects on working conditions generated by decentralisation which can lead to a regulatory 'race to the bottom'.[68] Moreover, the benefit of the model is that by its very nature, it promotes the

---

63. Marleau, V., 'Globalisation, Decentralisation and the Role of Subsidiarity in the Labour Setting' in J.R. Craig and M. Lynk (eds), *Globalisation And the Future of Labour Law*, Cambridge, Cambridge University Press, 2006, p. 120.
64. Marleau further develops her arguments by establishing subsidiarity as the articulating device; *ibid.*, p. 117.
65. *Ibid.*, pp. 108–109, 120.
66. Lafoucriere, C. and Green, R., 'Social Dialogue as a Regulatory Mode of the ESM: Some Empirical Evidence from the New Member States' in M. Jepsen and A. Serrano Pascual (eds), *Unwrapping the European Social Model*, Bristol, The Policy Press, 2006, pp. 234–235.
67. *Ibid.*, p. 234.
68. Marleau 2006, pp. 119–120.

active role of social partners and enhances the legitimacy of industrial relations. As underlined by Lafoucriere and Green, greater involvement of a wider set of actors assures that standard setting is based not only on economic needs but also on social factors.[69]

4.3 The Legal Architecture of the Model of Articulated Collective Bargaining

There are some legal traits that are easily detectable from the above description of the proposed analytical model. Essentially, since this model is anchored on the standard-setting role of social partners, the collective agreements represent the predominant substantive source of rules, rights and conditions of work and employment. The model is furthermore based on complementarity between collective agreements and statutory law as two different forms of standard setting, as well as complementarity between collective agreements at different levels. The legal definition of such a model comes with inherent limits. Bearing in mind the variety of legal solutions across European continental countries on even fundamental concepts pertinent to collective bargaining, such as the definition of collective agreements or the way in which freedom of association and collective autonomy is inserted into the legal systems,[70] this model cannot bring a clearly defined set of rules for the CEE countries. The model is therefore based on shared features of the existing models in continental Europe, which will form guiding principles for further research. To further explain the model, what follows is presentation of three analytical elements which this study will understand to represent the cornerstone of articulated multi-employer bargaining. Starting from the premise that standard setting in this model arises from two different sources: (a) statutory labour law; and (b) collective agreements; their nature and role in this process will be duly examined. After that, as a third element (c) it will be necessary to explain how the *articulation* between the two sources, as well the articulation between collective agreements at different levels is reached. The notion of articulation will be based on the principles of complementarity and shared competences in a multi-level system, as explained above in section 4.2.

4.3.1 *Nature and Role of Labour Law*

It has already been noted in this chapter that the role of labour law is to support and promote collective bargaining and autonomous regulation by social partners.[71] The ILO framework also underlined the role of the state in promoting collective bargaining although it has been emphasised that 'promotion' may not translate into imposition of

---

69. Lafoucriere and Green 2006, p. 235.
70. For example, agreeing on the meaning of basic principles, such as collective autonomy, is notoriously difficult – as noted by Le Friant, this concept is rarely used in some countries (France), but more frequently in the others (Germany and Italy). For comprehensive overview of the comparative dimension of collective autonomy in Europe, *see* Le Friant, M., 'Collective Autonomy: Hope or Danger?', *Comparative Labour Law and Policy Journal*, 2013, vol. 34, pp. 627–654.
71. As posed in section 2.

collective bargaining.[72] Although the basic function of labour law has been traditionally seen as one of protecting employees, in recent decades, there has been a growing understanding that labour law should also serve the economic objectives of productivity, efficiency and competitiveness.[73] The protective function of labour law – the function of protecting the employee as a weaker party – has therefore been increasingly challenged, but it has never ceased to play a vital role.[74] The protective function of labour law is in the first place exercised through what Kahn-Freund termed regulatory legislation – the set of statutory legal rules giving rise to individual rights and obligations on the part of workers and employers, observation of which is mandatory.[75] Labour law can also exercise a protective function by setting a legal minimum standard that can be further upgraded by collective agreements or individual contracts of employment. Apart from protective function, labour law should promote autonomous regulation by social partners. This function is more procedural in nature and refers to what Kahn-Freund termed as *auxiliary legislation*, which has the following aim:

> to promote collective bargaining, to ensure the observance of collective agreements, to define and to delineate the freedom of organisation and the freedom to strike, and the right to promote union interests at the level of the plant or enterprise, for instance, by means of the closed shop.[76]

Kahn-Freund further explicated that *auxiliary legislation* should promote and support: (a) the process of collective bargaining; (b) the conclusion of collective agreements (c) the application and observance of collective agreements.[77] This auxiliary function of labour law is corollary to the general tendency of law which according to Supiot is:

---

72. Gernigon, B., Odero, A. and Guido, H., 'ILO Principles Concerning Collective Bargaining' *International Labour Review*, 2000b, vol. 139, no. 1, p. 40. Otherwise, of the four countries examined in this study, the ILO Convention No. 154 concerning the promotion of collective bargaining of 1981 has been ratified only by two – Slovenia (2006) and Slovakia (2009).
73. Likewise, Hepple explained that different variations of regulatory theory appeared since the 1980s with the aim of shifting the focus away from the protective role of labour law, *see* Hepple, B., 'Factors Influencing the Making and Transformation of Labour Law in Europe' in G. Davidov and B. Langille (eds), *The Idea of Labour Law*, Oxford, Oxford University Press, 2011, pp. 30–42. For example Deakin and Wilkinson argued that economic assessment of social legislation should be a part of policy making, *see* Deakin, S. and Wilkinson, F., 'Rights vs Efficiency? The Economic Case for Transnational Labour Standards', *Industrial Law Journal*, 1994, vol. 23, no. 4, pp. 289–310.
74. Even more, the interventionist nature of the state, in the sense of directly regulating matters and substituting for collective bargaining has been on the rise in some European countries since the 1980s; *see* Howell, C., 'The Changing Relationship Between Labour and the State in Contemporary Capitalism', *Law, Culture and the Humanities*, 2012, vol. 11, no. 1, pp. 6–16.
75. Davies, P. and Freedland, M., *Kahn Freund's Labour and the Law*, 3rd edition, London, Stevens & Sons, 1983, p. 60.
76. *Ibid.*
77. Three elements were substantiated by Kahn Freund, *ibid.*, p. 87.

to be devoid of substantive provisions and to be supplemented by procedural rules designed to guarantee right to collective bargaining.[78]

Following this argument, Supiot explained that the role of a general legal framework is to establish the overall principles and objectives of the system of social policy, to ensure balance between parties to collective bargaining, and to encourage bargaining to favour its extension to areas reluctant to undertake dialogue.[79] Corollary to the presented legal thinking is three types of labour law standards delineated by Deakin and Wilkinson: (a) substantive standards, directly regulating labour relations; (b) procedural standards, regulating terms and condition of collective bargaining; (c) promotional standards, underpinning various forms of active labour policies.[80]

The transformation of the CEE labour laws which commenced in the early 1990s was profound, involving the process of transformation from the overly protective and regulatory role of the state, to one which supports and promotes the regulatory importance of collective agreements. It is questionable to what extent this process has been accomplished. The arguments presented above thus suggest the need to investigate whether CEE labour laws have indeed managed to transform their role during the last twenty-five years. This study will examine whether CEE countries managed to change the overwhelming regulatory role of labour law (while not losing the core protective role), and at the same time assess whether they managed to develop *auxiliary* approach towards self-regulation by social partners. This assessment will be made from different angles in several chapters: Chapter 3 will provide more general remarks while Chapters 5, 6 and 7 will contribute from the different angles of particular collective bargaining levels.

4.3.2 *Nature and Role of Collective Agreements*

The changing nature of collective agreements has been at the heart of debates on modernisation of labour law in most countries in Europe. With top-down decentralisation pressures, collective agreements underwent significant transformation, and according to Supiot acquired new functions.[81] One of the most prominent changes involved the introduction of the 'flexibilisation function' of collective agreements, allowing adaptation of their provisions to the needs of company competiveness. Supiot

---

78. Supiot, A., *Beyond Employment: Changes in Work and the Future of Labour Law in Europe*, Oxford, Oxford University Press, 2001, p. 98. There are views that such tendencies led to weakening of labour law. Goldin claims that such weakening occurs because collective agreements are assigned competence that used to be within the purview of the statutory law; *see* Goldin, A., 'Global Conceptualisations and Local Constructions of the Idea of Labour Law' in G. Davidov and B. Langille (eds), *The Idea of Labour Law*, Oxford, Oxford University Press, 2011, p. 74.
79. Supiot 2001, p. 99.
80. Deakin, S. and Wilkinson, F., 'Rights vs Efficiency? The Economic Case for Transnational Labour Standards', *Industrial Law Journal*, 1994, vol. 23, no. 4, pp. 290–292.
81. Supiot 2001, pp. 97–100.

has also added that collective agreements have become a company management tool and that they have started implementing legal regulations and performing legislative functions.

The collective agreements' functions presented by Supiot largely correspond to Bruun's delineation. Bruun observed the greater responsibility of collective agreements in implementing legal provisions ('regulatory function') and their increased role in becoming an instrument of adaptability ('flexibility function') and involving employees in policy making ('management function').[82] Given that in the past decades, and particularly with the recent economic and financial crisis, the pressures for decentralisation have increased, the function and role of sectoral collective agreement has been particularly challenged. Hence, Visser noticed the tendency for sectoral level agreements in Europe to be redesigned 'as a menu rather than a norm'.[83] In other words, sectoral agreements have a tendency to becoming predominantly concerned with providing rules and conditions for company-level bargaining, rather than setting universal sectoral standards. Modern CEE laws emerged from the previous communist system in which collective agreements have played only a marginal role and were not considered free and voluntary. It is therefore vital for this study to investigate the current function of collective agreements in the selected countries. There are practical limitations as to the extent to which this task can be performed, given that it would require thorough analysis of the contents of concluded collective agreements. Given the lack of comprehensive and comparative data, this study will therefore primarily focus on investigating the current legal framework and how it regulates collective agreements in CEE countries and on what functions it allows them to develop. This task will be performed from a general perspective in Chapter 3, but Chapters 5, 6, and 7 will also contribute to the discussion.

4.3.3 Articulation

As explained above, the articulated multi-employer bargaining model rests on procedural mechanisms which ensure the complementarity between various sources of standard setting. Articulation facilitates relationship between: (1) statutory legal rules and collective agreements as two distinct systems of regulation and sources of standard setting; and (2) collective agreements concluded at different levels (cross-sectoral, sectoral and company). The labour laws of the European countries share an important common trait in this respect. First of all, the laws of all the European countries are based on the hierarchical top-down relationship between different sources of labour

---

82. Bruun, N. 'The Autonomy of Collective Agreement' in R. Blanpain (ed.), *Collective Bargaining, Discrimination, Social Security and the European Integration*, Bulletin of Comparative Labour Relations, no. 48, The Hague, Kluwer Law International, 2003, p. 9.
83. Visser, J., 'Beneath the Surface of Stability: New and Old Modes of Governance in European Industrial Relations', *European Journal of Industrial Relations*, 2005, vol. 11, no. 3, p. 297.

regulation.[84] Thus, statutory labour law has priority over collective agreements, while collective agreements at a higher level (broader agreements) prevail over collective agreements at a lower level (narrower).[85]

In a formal legal sense, there are two different ways in which the described legal ordering can be upset:[86]

(1) By applying the principle of the most favourable rule, allowing the provisions of lower collective agreements to prevail over the rules which are applied at the higher level.
(2) Allowing lower sources to deviate to the detriment of employee (*in peius*), by using different legal techniques.

The latter legal possibility has been widely used by many European countries. A specific example is France, where the 2004 *Loi Fillon* introduced the principle that lower collective agreements can deviate from the standards set out in the agreements at higher level, even when they are less favourable.[87] There are many other legal possibilities allowing such deviation; for example, since the 1980s in Germany it has been possible to include opening clauses in sectoral collective agreements, which define the terms under which less favourable rules can be set at a lower bargaining level.[88] The role of these mechanisms described is to provide checks and balances for uncontrolled decentralisation, by defining conditions or upper boundaries for derogations at lower (company) level.

As long as the substantive regulation of work and employment is in practice set at local levels, the described legal ordering across European countries do not run counter to the logic of decentralisation of industrial relations. Otherwise, if the standards are being drawn (predominantly) from higher-level agreements, then the system is centralised.

The aim of the study is to identify the legal principles which keep the system articulated in selected countries, as well as the rules that play a procedural role in stimulating standard setting at lower levels.

5 RESEARCH METHODOLOGY AND COUNTRY SELECTION

Four countries are selected for in-depth analysis. The selection process aimed at reflecting different collective bargaining practices at various levels. As a first step, a

---

84. Jacobs underlined that the principle of hierarchy dominates the labour laws in most economies, *see* Jacobs 2014, p. 171.
85. *Ibid.*
86. Based on Jacobs, *ibid.*, pp. 172–181.
87. Freedland, M. and Kountouris, N., *The Legal Construction of Personal Work Relations*, Oxford, Oxford Monographs on Labour Law, 2011, p. 71.
88. Jacobs 2014, p. 177.

delineation presented in one study by Eurofound was taken into account. It outlined two groups of CEE countries:[89]

(1) the countries where sectoral collective agreements have higher coverage rates, combined with the practice of concluding company level agreements (Hungary, Romania, Slovakia and Slovenia);
(2) a second group of countries where company agreements prevail and sectoral collective agreements have a less prominent role. As a result, collective bargaining has lower coverage in general (Bulgaria, the Czech Republic, Estonia, Latvia, Lithuania and Poland).

As a second step, after a closer examination of industrial relations trends within both groups, four countries with the following distinct features were selected:[90]

(1) *Slovenia's* model of collective bargaining is unique in comparison to the other CEE countries. This country has the most developed practice of bargaining at sectoral level and the organisational capacities of social partners at this level are comparatively more developed than in the other CEE countries. Moreover, Slovenia has nurtured a tradition of concluding legally binding cross-sectoral collective agreements (at least, until the mid-2000s), for which it is also unique.
(2) *Slovakia* also has a relatively developed sector-level activity when compared to the other CEE countries, even though not all sectors have collective agreements in place. An additional argument for its selection is that Slovakia has been going through numerous labour law reforms in the past two decades, potentially suggesting that labour law transformation is still ongoing.
(3) *The Czech Republic* has predominantly company-level bargaining, with sectoral collective bargaining playing a certain role in industrial relations, but not as much as in Slovakia. The Czech Republic has also gone through a number of legislative reforms in the past two decades. Moreover, Slovakia and the Czech Republic share common legal and cultural legacies from the former federal state of Czechoslovakia. Bearing in mind that these two countries have different industrial relations trends today, the comparative analysis of their laws could yield useful insights regarding the two research questions.

---

89. The division of two groups of countries has been suggested in Parissaki and Vega 2008, p. 8. The data presented in this report largely correspond to the data from the ICTWSS database presented in Table 1. However, the two sources diverge with respect to Hungary and Bulgaria, and one may also add that Croatia was not included in the division presented by the Eurofound.
90. More detailed industrial relations overview per country can be found in: Czíria, L., *Capacity Building for Social Dialogue at Sectoral and Company Level-Slovakia*, Dublin, Eurofound, 2007a; Kajankova, M., *Capacity Building for Social Dialogue at Sectoral and Company Level – the Czech Republic*, Dublin, Eurofound, 2007; Luzar, B., *Capacity Building for Social Dialogue at Sectoral and Company Level-Slovenia*, Dublin, Eurofound, 2007; Sroka, J., *Capacity Building for Social Dialogue at Sectoral and Company Level – Poland*, Dublin, Eurofound, 2007.

(4) *Poland* is an example of a country where sectoral bargaining is less developed than in the other three countries and where sectoral agreements cover a marginal percentage of the labour market. Its labour law has also undergone a great number of revisions in the past two decades – it is noteworthy that the Labour Code originates back to 1974 (after being amended a number of times) and that Poland never underwent a thorough, complete recodification of its labour law.[91]

This research is based on two data sources: the analysis of existing literature and interviews. The former consists of available English language academic studies and policy data on law and industrial relations in the four countries, including the available English translations of the relevant legal acts. Interviews were conducted with legal and policy experts from social partners' organisations and with staff within the ministries for social affairs in the selected countries. The aim was to gain deeper insights into country-specific legal and collective bargaining issues at different bargaining levels. Sometimes different specialists in the same organisation were in a position to provide answers from the perspective of their specific expertise. In these cases, interview meetings were attended by more than one specialist. In total, twenty-five interviews were conducted in the four selected countries in 2012; these interviews are listed in the annex. While the majority of interviews were conducted during visits to the capital cities of the chosen countries, one interview was conducted by telephone and one was based on the completion of the questionnaire in writing. Most of the meetings were conducted in English, with translators attending some of the meetings in Slovakia, the Czech Republic and Poland.

While designing the interviews, the initial idea was to target experts from the ministries of social affairs and experts among social partners on both sides, at central and sectoral level. Ideally, these interviews would have comprised of seven interviews per country: one from the ministry of social affairs, two from the social partners organisations at the central (peak) level on both sides and two from the social partners organisations on both sides of the metals and the construction sectors. In practice, it proved impossible to conduct or schedule interviews with all of the organisations initially anticipated. This is reflected in the number and composition of the interview participants, as listed in the annex of this book. For example, data from the construction sector are particularly scarce. Also, in Slovakia one interview was held with specialists on the trade union side in the energy and chemical sector. In addition, useful information on Polish industrial relations was retrieved from an academic interview.

The interviews conducted were semi-structured. A general questionnaire was prepared containing questions about the legal regulation of collective agreements and collective bargaining, in general, and at different levels; tripartite social dialogue; recent legal and industrial relations developments; the relationship between collective agreements and statutory legal rules; the relationship between collective agreements at different levels; EU influences on collective bargaining; any other issue which the

---

91. As noted in Czarzasty, J., *Capacity Building for Social Dialogue in Poland*, Dublin, Eurofound, 2006, p. 4.

interviewees considered relevant, including, if applicable, wage bargaining. The questionnaire was designed in a general fashion in order to stimulate open-ended discussions on issues seen as relevant from the viewpoint of each interviewee. Each interview data, thus, largely reflected viewpoints pertinent to each collective bargaining level and the organisations represented by the interviewees.

The interview data has been used in two ways. First, the interviews conducted furthered the knowledge of the researcher on country-specific legal and industrial relations issues. Second, the interviewees' perceptions and interpretations of legal and industrial relations issues were used to build conclusions on the two research questions of this study. Moreover, this study relied on the interviewees' interpretations and perceptions, especially in those areas where precise data are not to be found – this is particularly the case regarding the content of collective agreements (matters covered by collective agreements) and the regulatory importance of company versus sectoral collective agreements.

The study has been designed to cover developments within a specific time frame. Principally, it focuses on developments which took place after the onset of the transitional period (the late 1980s and the beginning of 1990s), but also, where possible, the post-transitional developments are considered against the backdrop of the legal and institutional framework that had existed before the 1990s. The study takes into account developments up until mid-2015.

6 STRUCTURE OF THE STUDY

This study is divided in two parts. The first part is devoted to topics which are pertinent to the general legal and institutional framework, including the interlinked relevant aspects of industrial relations, economic and welfare models, and the EU-related issues (Chapters 1, 2, 3 and 4) while the second part of the study is focused on the legal and institutional aspects of collective bargaining at three major bargaining levels (Chapters 5, 6 and 7).

This chapter aimed at introducing the research topic, questions and research design.

Chapter 2 takes a non-legal approach and explains how the specific economic climate, welfare reforms and the corresponding industrial relations landscape provided a pretext for decentralised collective bargaining in these countries. This chapter relies on existing theoretical knowledge explaining models of capitalism, welfare and industrial relations in CEE, permitting deeper understanding of the general environment in which labour law transformation has been taking place in the past decades.

Chapter 3 discusses the development of labour law in the four selected countries. In this sense, it contributes towards the second research question, by looking into the national-specific responses to issues and challenges surrounding the development of a legal and institutional collective bargaining framework in these four countries in the past two and half decades. At the same time, given that such analysis provides insights into major national labour law traits and issues pertinent to collective bargaining, it represent a useful ground for further level-specific analysis in the second part of the book.

Chapter 4, in an effort to provide tentative answers to the second research question, aims to deconstruct the ways in which the EU has affected the development of legal and institutional framework for collective bargaining in the four countries. The chapter first scrutinises the role of the EU during the accession process, and then re-appraises this role in view of the developments that took place during the recent economic and financial crisis.

Chapters 5, 6 and 7, respectively, provide comparative country analysis of the legal and institutional framework of rules at cross-sectoral, sectoral and company collective bargaining level. These chapters contribute to answering both research questions from the perspective of specific bargaining levels.

Chapter 8 summarises the answers reached in the different chapters of the study and provides concluding thoughts about the two research questions.

PART I   General Reflections on the Legal and Institutional Framework

CHAPTER 2
Capitalism, Welfare and Industrial Relations in CEE

1 INTRODUCTION

The institutional configuration of communist systems was not identical throughout the CEE countries, but several key traits were common, including centralised decision-making on all relevant aspects of working life (including wages), and state ownership of the means of productions.[92] In addition, terms and conditions of work and employment were centrally set and the employees enjoyed high (at least *de iure*, prescribed by law) protection in a one-size-fits-all manner. With the demise of communist ideology in the early 1990s, the CEE countries began a profound transition to new economic, political and social systems. Building markets and boosting economic growth represented the overarching aim of the post-communist period. Centrally planned economics had to be reconstructed on the basis of free market principles, which involved becoming internationally competitive and undertaking privatisation of public (state-owned) property. However, the CEE countries came increasingly under the influence of transnational and international actors, including international financial institutions, EU and multinational corporations, given that foreign investments had started playing a vital role in building post-transitional economies. The post-transitional policies also had to deal with the large social costs of economic reforms due to rapidly increasing unemployment and inflation,[93] posing a question about which type of social policies should accompany the economic transformation.

---

92. Aslund provides one of the most comprehensive lists of traits and description of the previous communist systems, *see* Aslund, A., *How Capitalism Was Built: The Transformation of Central and Eastern Europe, Russia and Central Asia*, Cambridge, Cambridge University Press, 2007, pp. 11–29.
93. For the description of the economic and social environment surrounding post-transitional transformation in CEE, *see* e.g. Keune, M., 'The European Social Model and Enlargement' in M. Jepsen and A. Serrano Pascual (eds), *Unwrapping the European Social Model*, Bristol, The Policy

The pace and content of the reforms, however, differed significantly from one country to another. For many CEE countries, transition from command-and-control systems to free market economies involved radical macroeconomic changes, seen as an antipode to the previously controlled systems. These radical policies, as one observer explained, advocated the move towards a 'market on all fronts, and as quickly as possible' with the aim of catching up with the western countries.[94] Such a radical and comprehensive agenda was pursued in Poland, under the Balcerowicz programme invented in 1989 and often referred to as 'shock therapy'.[95] An even more radical programme was launched in Czechoslovakia in 1991.[96] *Neoliberalism* became a catchphrase to describe the interpretative framework for carrying out these reforms in CEE.[97] Such policy orientation has been embodied in the already-seminal quote of the former Czech Prime Minister, Vaclav Klaus, who called for building capitalism 'without adjectives'.[98] Yet, not all countries adopted this radical approach, or at least, not to the fullest possible extent. At the other end of spectrum, there was Slovenia, which adopted a more gradual approach towards economic transformation, with a low level of international investments, generous welfare and slow privatisation.[99]

It is in the midst of these political, social and economic reforms that the institutionalisation of industrial relations began. The transformation of industrial

---

Press, 2006, pp. 170–171; Standing, G., 'Social Protection in Central and Easter Europe: A Tale of Slipping Anchors and Torn Safety Nets' in G. Esping-Andersen (ed.), *Welfare States in Transition: National Adaptations in Global Economies*, London, SAGE, 1996, pp. 225–255; Martin, R., *Constructing Capitalisms: Transforming Business Systems in Central and Eastern Europe*, Oxford, Oxford University Press, 2013. Unemployment was also underlined as one of the factors determining current working and employment conditions in CEE, *see* Vaughan-Whitehead, D., 'The World of Work in the New EU Member States: Diversity and Convergence' in D. Vaughan-Whitehead (ed.), *Working and Employment Conditions in New EU Member States*, Geneva, ILO, 2005, pp. 1–43.

94. King, L., 'Postcommunist Divergence: A Comparative Analysis of the Transition to Capitalism in Poland and Russia', *Studies in Comparative International Development*, 2002, vol. 37, no. 3, p. 4.
95. Aslund 2007, p. 83, pp. 29–56; King 2002.
96. Aslund 2007, p. 85.
97. The notion of neoliberalism has been often used to describe the ideological framework of the CEE's post-1990s system restructuring; *see* e.g.: Bohle, D. and Greskovits, B., 'Neoliberalism, Embedded Neoliberalism and Neocorporatism: Towards Transnational Capitalism in Central-Eastern Europe', *West European Politics*, 2007, vol. 30, no. 3, pp. 443–466; Iankova, E. and Turner, L., 'Building the New Europe: Western and Eastern Roads to Social Partnership', *Industrial Relations Journal*, 2004, vol. 35, no. 1, pp. 76–92. While understanding that neoliberalism can be conceptually contested, this study will not use it in an either affirmative or critical manner, but rather as a means to denote the firm inclination of policy makers towards market-oriented reforms. In this sense, this study conforms to the explanation of neoliberalism provided by Baccaro and Howell, understood as a general process involving market liberalisation and disorganisation; and as a macroeconomic strategy involving, *inter alia*, trade and financial liberalisation; *see* Baccaro, L. and Howell, C., 'A Common Neoliberal Trajectory: The Transformation of Industrial Relations in Advanced Capitalism', *Politics & Society*, 2011, vol. 39, no. 4, p. 526.
98. Orenstein, M., 'Transitional Social Policy in the Czech Republic and Poland', *Czech Sociological Review*, 1995, vol. 3, no. 2, p. 180.
99. As explained by Crowley, S. and Stanojević, M., 'Varieties of Capitalism, Power Resources, and Historical Legacies: Explaining the Slovenian Exception', *Politics & Society*, 2011, vol. 39, no. 2, p. 269.

relations was country-specific, developing in relation to the pace and content of economic and social reforms. To some extent, legacies from the communist period also played a role. The Polish trade unions emerged as influential actors in the post-1990s developments, mainly thanks to the legacy of the trade union movement Solidarity which was formed after a massive wave of strikes in 1980.[100] Moreover, the Polish trade union movement managed to play a vital role in the privatisation process, by gaining concessions from the political elites at the beginning of the 1990s.[101] The trade union landscape in the former country of Czechoslovakia was completely different. The Czech Republic and Slovakia could not benefit from such favourable legacies as Polish trade unions and their role in policy making was not so pronounced in the 1990s.[102] Finally, there was Slovenia, which, following the philosophy of gradualism and a balanced approach between social and economic gains, shaped the post-transitional industrial relations on the basis of favourable paradigmatic legacy of 'self-management' and somewhat pro-market orientation which had existed in the pre-transitional socialist Slovenia.[103]

This chapter builds on the fact that post-communist labour laws did not develop in isolation, but as a response to the complex post-transitional setting. Hence, the content of labour laws developed in relation to a number of interlinked elements, including, but not limited to, market transformation, type of privatisation of state ownership, industrial relations developments and attitudes towards welfare. Furthermore, this chapter understands that processes guiding economic, welfare and industrial relations transformation were country-specific. Hence, the aim of the chapter will be to elaborate on how the specific economic climate and corresponding welfare reforms affected the industrial relations landscape, particularly decentralised collective bargaining, and provided a pretext for legal regulation of collective bargaining. The chapter therefore takes a non-legal approach and draws on existing theoretical knowledge explaining models of capitalism, welfare and industrial relations in CEE. At the same time, it provides a closer explanation of the relevant processes in the four countries selected for this study by providing deeper understanding of the country-specific traits and issues. It offers useful ground for the subsequent analysis that will be provided within the framework of the study.

The chapter is structured in the following manner. General explanations about the type of capitalism (section 2.1), welfare (section 2.2) and industrial relations (section 2.3) in CEE are provided at the outset. Following that, an overview of national

---

100. The role of Solidarity in transitional transformation has been particularly the focus of work of David Ost, see Ost, D., *Defeat of Solidarity: Anger and Politics in Postcommunist Europe*, Cornell, Cornell University Press, 2005; Ost, D., *Solidarity and the Politics of Anti-Politics: Opposition and Reform in Poland Since 1968*, Philadelphia, Temple University Press, 1990. Also, see Paczynska, A., *State, Labor, and the Transition to a Market Economy – Egypt, Poland, Mexico, and the Czech Republic*, Pennsylvania, The Pennsylvania State University Press, 2009, pp. 48–55.
101. As underlined by Paczynska, A., 'Confronting Change: Labor, State, and Privatisation' *Review of International Political Economy*, 2007, vol. 14, no. 2, p. 346; Paczynska 2009, pp. 129–161.
102. For description of trade unionism in the former country of Czechoslovakia, as well as comparison with trade union experiences in Poland, see Paczynska 2009.
103. Crowley and Stanojević 2011.

developments in the four countries (section 3) is given. Finally, some concluding thoughts of the chapter are given in section 4.

2 EXPLAINING CAPITALISM, WELFARE AND INDUSTRIAL RELATIONS IN CEE

2.1 Capitalism in CEE

So far, the literature has recognised that there can be more than one type of capitalism. Yet, more than two decades after the start of the transitional processes involving transformation from state-commanded to open market systems, judging from the volume of scholarship which this topic attracted, how to explain and classify the CEE economies remains unclear. The ambiguity is further exacerbated by some views that the CEE countries are still in a 'transiting' phase, and hence, the discussion should revolve less around the type of capitalism, but more around the scale of capitalism in CEE.[104] Thus, in an effort to explain capitalism in CEE, a list of questions appears relevant: what type of economies have the CEE countries developed more than two decades after the demise of centrally coordinated communist regimes? Do the modern CEE economies resemble the existing models of capitalism in Europe? Above all, have these economies managed a complete transformation to a market system? What follows aims to provide a concise overview of the flourishing literature on CEE capitalism. The ambition of the section is not to provide a comprehensive overview of existing literature, but to focus on those approaches offering analyses relevant to the four countries that are the subject of this study.

The next subsection starts with a brief analysis of the most influential approach in comparative political economy, Varieties of Capitalism (hereinafter 'VoC'). A large volume of CEE literature uses VoC as an analytical framework to explain the CEE countries. Thus, the ways in which scholars have applied the VoC approach to explain CEE capitalism will be subsequently presented. Yet, the VoC approach has not been universally accepted by authors dealing with capitalism in CEE – in this category, the regime classification of Bohle and Greskovits will be presented as the most influential.

2.1.1 Varieties of Capitalism

The approach of VoC was originally developed by Hall and Soskice in 2001,[105] after which it was widely accepted, in integral or modified form, by other scholars. This approach distinguished two major national production regimes with distinct institutional features: (a) liberal market economies (LMEs); and (b) coordinated market economies (CMEs). Hall and Soskice based the VoC classification on formal and

---

104. Lane, D., 'Emerging Varieties of Capitalism in Former State Socialist Societies', *Competition & Change*, 2005, vol. 9, no. 3, p. 231.
105. Hall, P.A., Soskice, P., 'An Introduction to Varieties of Capitalism' in A.P. Hall and P. Soskice (eds), *Varieties of Capitalism: The Institutional Foundations of Comparative Advantage*, Oxford, Oxford University Press, 2001, pp. 1–67.

informal rules which companies develop with other actors in the market, by taking into account several market areas, including industrial relations, vocational training and education, corporate governance, inter-firm relations, as well as the interaction between managers and employees. The two authors reached the following conclusions. In LMEs, the competitive market mechanism is the key coordinating tool and firm behaviour is determined on the basis of conditions of demand and supply.[106] In CMEs, non-competitive market institutions determine firm behaviour in the form of strategic interactions between firms and other actors.[107] Hall and Soskice designated the UK as a typical model of LMEs, while Germany represents an archetypal model of CMEs.

In the field of industrial relations, the difference between the two models is easy to spot. As a rule of thumb, because the market functions on the basis of competition, in LMEs the role of social partners is generally less prominent, there are substantial managerial prerogatives, and there is a lack of an economy-wide wage coordination.[108] On the other hand, CMEs have comparatively more developed social dialogue mechanisms, particularly at the sectoral level. Centralised collective bargaining in CMEs represents a coordinating mechanism and the social partners are more powerful and better organised when compared with LMEs.[109]

Hall and Soskice's approach on VoC is one of the most influential views in comparative political economy, and it has inspired a large volume of alternative explanations and classifications of capitalism.[110] This chapter will not present these views, but what matters here is that neither VoC nor subsequent approaches included CEE countries in the research. At best, the existence of CEE countries has been acknowledged under broad concepts, such as 'emerging market economies' by Hancké, Rhodes and Thatcher.[111] Such broad and general conceptualisations have been designed with the aim of demonstrating the presence of some form of capitalism in CEE, obviously different from the existing models in Europe and unable to be explained using the existing classification. Further research on CEE capitalism has been left entirely within the competence of CEE scholarship, which will be examined in the following section.

---

106. *Ibid.*, pp. 8–9.
107. *Ibid.*
108. *Ibid.*, p. 29.
109. *Ibid.*, pp. 24–25.
110. Yet, the original VoC approach was also criticised in the general (non-CEE centred) literature. In summary of the post-VoC literature, Hancké noted that the critics were directed either towards its institutionally driven basis, its elements; or the scholars were simply offering alternative explanations of capitalism; see Hancké, B., *Debating a Varieties of Capitalism: A Reader*, Oxford, Oxford University Press, 2009, pp. 5–6.
111. Hancké, B., Rhodes, M., Thatcher, M., 'Introduction: Beyond Varieties of Capitalism' in B. Hancké, M. Rhodes and M. Thatcher (eds), *Beyond Varieties of Capitalism: Conflict, Contradictions, and Complementarities in the European Economy*, Oxford, Oxford University Press, 2007, pp. 3–38.

2.1.2 Explaining CEE Capitalism

In seeking ways to explain the economic transformation and the type of economic models that developed in CEE, some attempts were made to adapt the existing VoC approach to CEE. However, no consensus has been reached among the scholars that this is viable or, to be more precise, whether the CEE countries can fit the VoC dichotomy, or whether alternative categories need to be invented. It has been claimed that the CEE economies might not fit the VoC dichotomy, given their specific traits and development in the past decades. This statement has been further underpinned with various arguments. For example, Crowley and Stanojević demonstrated that not only firm behaviour, but also role of labour should be accounted for.[112] Other authors, such as Nölke and Vliegenthart, as well as Bohle and Greskovits, stated that, unfortunately, VoC does not account for the role of external actors in explaining the development of capitalism, while the role of international financial organisations and multinational companies has been vital for shaping the CEE economies.[113] King argued that, in principle, it is possible to extend VoC to CEE, but that this would also require adaptation and contextualisation of this classification to the historical and structural features of these countries.[114]

There are views in the literature claiming that, despite the criticism, VoC can be applied to the CEE countries, in integral or modified form. However, there is no consensus in the literature on how to classify these countries. Two strands of literature can be found here:

(a) First, there are scholars who extend the VoC approach to the CEE countries by developing alternative categories to LME and CME. Likewise, Nölke and Vliegenthart developed a notion of 'dependent market economy' as a third VoC category, with the major trait being the dependence on international capital.[115] Yet, these authors have not provided further explanations within this general cluster that could demonstrate country variations. In a similar fashion, King designated the CEE countries as 'liberal dependent', a category which represents an extension of the VoC dichotomy – but which contains elements of both LMEs and CMEs – and with the major trait of being dependent on foreign direct investment.[116] Lane labelled Poland, Slovakia, the Czech Republic and Slovenia as being close to the continental type of market capitalism, yet more state-led, having in mind their reasonably well-developed welfare state, which contrasts them sharply with the other

---

112. Crowley and Stanojević 2011.
113. Bohle, D. and Greskovits, B., 'Varieties of Capitalism and Capitalism *"tout court"*', *European Journal of Sociology*, 2006, vol. 50, no. 3, p. 380; Nölke, A. and Vliegenthart, A., 'Enlarging the Varieties of Capitalism: The Emergence of Dependent Market Economies in East Central Europe', *World Politics*, 2009, vol. 61, no. 4, p. 673.
114. King, L., 'Central European Capitalism in Comparative Perspective' in B. Hancké, M. Rhodes and M. Thatcher (eds), *Beyond Varieties of Capitalism: Conflict, Contradictions, and Complementarities in the European Economy*, Oxford, Oxford University Press, 2007, pp. 313–327.
115. Nölke and Vliegenthart 2009.
116. King 2007.

post-transitional countries that have more hybrid forms of capitalism.[117] Moreover, as noted in this chapter, Hancké, Rhodes and Thatcher invented the notion of 'emerging market economies'.[118]

(b) Second, there are authors who follow the VoC approach and classify the CEE countries as either LME or CME. Based on the institutional legacies and policy choices, Feldmann established two archetypal models of VoC in Eastern Europe: Slovenia as CME (having institutionalised coordination) and Estonia as LME (having market-based coordination). However, other countries were not explored in this study, even though the author noted that they belong on a continuum between these two archetypical models.[119] In a similar fashion, Crowley and Stanojević designated Slovenia as CME, although claiming that VoC may not be sufficient in explaining CEE capitalism.[120]

As this brief overview of approaches demonstrates, it is not possible to unambiguously designate the CEE countries under the VoC classification and this is why some scholars proposed their own typologies. Possibly the most comprehensive theoretical framework by far has been provided by Bohle and Greskovits. Moving away from the VoC logic, these authors were inspired by Polanyi's seminal understanding of the market society based on conflicts and compromises between the economic liberalism and social protection.[121] Bohle and Greskovits defined regimes as capitalist political economies where marketisation and social protection were institutionalised with differing degrees of vigour and explained that they develop in relation to several different factors.[122] *First*, the authors have argued that the role of the initial policy choices at the beginning of the transitional period mattered, including the role of the legacies and the ways they have been perceived by the policy makers. *Second*, Bohle and Greskovits claimed that the role of the external influences in shaping the CEE economies must be accounted for, including pressures originating from the EU and multinational corporations. Following these arguments, the authors have differentiated three types of regime:

(a) *Neoliberal* in the Baltic countries, featuring a strong neoliberal economic trajectory and less pronounced social protection.

---

117. Lane, D., 'Post-State Socialism: A Diversity of Capitalisms?' in D. Lane and M. Myant (eds), *Varieties of Capitalism in Post-Communist Countries*, Basingstoke, Palgrave Macmillan, 2007, p. 35; the state-led model has been juxtaposed to the hybrid forms that had developed in other post-transitional countries, which are not part of the EU, such as Russia or Moldova.
118. Hancké, Rhodes and Thatcher 2007.
119. Feldmann, M., 'Emerging Varieties of Capitalism in Transition Countries: Industrial Relations and Wage Bargaining in Estonia and Slovenia', *Comparative Political Studies*, 2006, vol. 39, no. 7, pp. 829–854.
120. Crowley and Stanojević 2011.
121. Bohle, D. and Greskovits, B., 'Neoliberalism, Embedded Neoliberalism and Neocorporatism: Towards Transnational Capitalism in Central-Eastern Europe', *West European Politics*, 2007, vol. 30, no. 3, p. 445, citing Polanyi, K., *The Great Transformation: The Political and Economic Origins of Our Time*, Boston, Beacon Press, 1957.
122. Ibid., pp. 444–445.

(b) *Embedded neoliberal*, existing in the Visegrad countries (Poland, the Czech Republic, Slovakia and Hungary) featuring a balancing act between social and neoliberal policies.
(c) *Neocorporatist*, which can be found in Slovenia, with the institutionalised balance between economic and social policies, including decision-making, based on consensus between the state and social actors, including social partners.

In a subsequent publication, the two authors have examined the effects which the recent economic and financial crisis had on the three types of regime.[123] While noting that embedded neo-liberal regimes and neocorporatist Slovenia were, in principle, less affected by the crisis, Bohle and Greskovits demonstrated that all three regime types showed signs of erosion and that the crisis managed to emphasise already existing social and political tensions.[124] The crisis has moved all three regimes further in the direction of markets, rather than towards social protection, and exposed the weaknesses of institutional foundations and capabilities in solving the ensuing tensions and preventing social disintegration.[125]

The delineation of regimes presented by Bohle and Greskovits represents perhaps the most comprehensive overview of post-transitional traits in CEE that exists. The current study largely builds on these observations. In the first place, these observations provide useful insight into the type of transformation undertaken by the four countries examined in this study. Furthermore, this study takes on board the factors which Bohle and Greskovits deemed essential for explaining post-transitional developments (policy choices, including the legacies, and external factors) as part of the explanatory framework for the second research question which will be further explained and elaborated in Chapter 3. Specifically, these factors will be adapted and translated into the realm of labour law and used for analytical purposes in the context of this study.

2.2 Welfare Regimes in CEE

During the communist period, the CEE welfare states resembled each other, given their common underlying features including, amongst others, guaranteed employment, subsidised prices and free health and education services.[126] The welfare provision was universal and wage inequalities were rather marginal. However, after 1989, the question of post-transitional welfare transformation in CEE became topical, given that it implied the reform of one of the lynchpins of the communist systems, namely, the extensive welfare provision. The quest for welfare transformation involved two challenges. In the first place, it was questionable to what extent the CEE countries

---

123. Bohle, D. and Greskovits, B., *Capitalist Diversity on Europe's Periphery*, Ithaca, Cornel University Press, 2012.
124. *Ibid.*, pp. 223-258.
125. *Ibid.*
126. Deacon, B., 'Eastern European Welfare States: The Impact of the Politics of Globalisation', *Journal of European Social Policy*, 2000, vol. 10, no. 2, p. 147.

could afford the all-encompassing extensive welfare provision, particularly in a context of neoliberal policy orientation. The second challenge involved dealing with the social cost of the economic transition – growing unemployment, inflation and poverty, with gross domestic product declining sharply in all countries.[127]

The literature explaining the post-transitional CEE welfare development evolved in two major phases, which will be briefly presented in the following lines. *First*, in the early 1990s, it was too soon to cluster the welfare regimes in CEE. Thus, the early scholarship restricted itself to enumerating and describing what was seen as the common characteristics of emerging welfare models. Deacon noted that transformation had just commenced and that it was not yet evident how the CEE welfare regimes would evolve, and that this prevented clustering these countries.[128] Deacon therefore presented a catalogue of the common characteristics of emerging welfare models, including, *inter alia*, trends of ad hoc welfare policies, privatisation of some health and social provisions, a shift in the nature of social inequalities and deconstruction of social security systems.[129]

Second, although explaining welfare models turned out to be just as challenging as explaining models of capitalism in CEE, welfare literature has flourished in the 2000s. The Esping-Andersen's typology of welfare regimes emerged as the most influential in the general welfare literature, and it has also inspired debates on CEE welfare regimes.[130] By taking into account the criteria of decommodification (understood as the degree to which individuals are emancipated in the market), stratification (social citizenship that includes the class structure in the society) and employment, Esping-Andersen distinguished three regimes:[131] (a) *liberal*, characterised by means-tested and modest social assistance; (b) *conservative-corporatist*, characterised by prioritisation of welfare provision over market pressures; (c) *social-democratic*, inspired by the ideas of social democracy and the universal provision of social services.

Although the Esping-Andersen typology served as a source of inspiration, the post-2000s CEE literature has not reached a consensus about explaining and classifying welfare and whether mainstream approaches can be applied to these countries. Even though the literature was not so much focused on clustering the existing CEE regimes, there were views that the CEE regimes can be clearly distinguished from the traditional welfare regimes,[132] and that they represent institutional hybrids which in no way

---

127. *See* fn 93.
128. *See* Deacon, B., 'Developments in East European Social Policy' in C. Jones (ed.), *New Perspectives on the Welfare State in Europe*, London, Routledge, 1993, pp. 163–184.
129. Deacon 1993, pp. 174–175.
130. Esping-Andersen defined welfare regimes as: 'the institutional arrangements, rules and understandings that guide and shape concurrent social policy decisions, expenditure developments, problem definitions, and even the respond-and-demand structure of citizens and welfare consumers', *see* Esping-Andersen, G., *Three Worlds of Welfare Capitalism*, New Jersey, Princeton University Press, 1990, p. 80.
131. *Ibid.*, pp. 26–27.
132. According to Fenger, who claimed that there are clear differences between post-communist welfare countries and traditional Western welfare states; *see* Fenger, H.J.M., 'Welfare Regimes in Central and Eastern Europe: Incorporating Post-Communist Countries in a Welfare Regime Typology', *Contemporary Issues and Ideas in Social Sciences*, 2007, vol. 3, no. 2.

resemble the typology of Esping-Andersen.[133] Possibly the most comprehensive comparative overview so far that involves the four countries selected for analysis in this study has been offered by Lendvai[134] who distinguished three clusters of countries:

(a) *Neoliberal*, in Slovakia and in the Baltic countries, with low welfare spending and radical neoliberal reforms.
(b) *Dual welfare*, in Poland and Hungary, combining neoliberalism and welfare populism, the latter being used as a counteracting tool for neoliberal policies.
(c) *Social corporativist welfare regime*, Slovenia and the Czech Republic, as 'Scandinavian islands' in CEE, with the most comprehensive social protection and favourable economic situation inherited from the previous system.

In a similar fashion, Potucek provided a summary of the state of the art of welfare regimes in CEE – Slovenia most resembles the traditional welfare state models in Europe, while the Czech Republic has a less generous welfare state. Poland and Hungary have residual restrictive policies in some areas, while Slovakia moves closer to a liberal welfare state.[135]

Another comprehensive comparative insight into the CEE countries has been provided by Inglot, who observed the development of welfare states in the Visegrad countries (Czech Republic, Slovakia, Poland and Hungary) in a historical context, from the early twentieth century until the modern post-communist period. By describing the evolution of social security systems in these countries, Inglot underlined the role of legacies, as these countries were seeking ways to reinstitute their historically rooted welfare provision honed under German and Austrian-Hungarian tradition at the beginning of the twentieth century.[136] While demonstrating that these countries exerted strong commitment to social spending, Inglot showed that they share some common features which originate from the 'Bismarck-style' of their legacies.[137]

2.3 Industrial Relations in CEE

Industrial relations in the CEE countries share more than a few common features. In addition to what has been already presented in Chapter 1, the common features involve

---

133. Cerami, A. and Vanhuysse, P., 'Introduction: Social Policy Pathways, Twenty Years after the Fall of the Berlin Wall' in A. Cerami and P. Vanhuysse (eds), *Post-Communist Welfare Pathways – Theorising Social Policy Transformations in Central and Eastern Europe*, Basingstoke, Palgrave Macmillan, 2009, p. 5.
134. Lendvai, N., 'EU Integration and Post-Communist Welfare: Catch-up Convergence Before and After the Economic Crisis' in I.E. Vural (ed.), *Converging Europe: Transformation of Social Policy in the Enlarged European Union and in Turkey*, Farnham, Ashgate, 2011, p. 183.
135. Potucek, M., 'Metamorphoses of Welfare States in Central and Eastern Europe' in M. Seeleib-Kaiser (ed.), *Welfare State Transformations: Comparative Perspectives*, Basingstoke, Palgrave Macmillan, 2008, p. 85.
136. See Inglot, T., *Welfare States in East Central Europe, 1919-2004*, Cambridge, Cambridge University Press, 2008, p. 23.
137. *Ibid*., pp. 1–20.

weaknesses of social partners, a rapid fall in the trade union membership base during the past two decades and weak sectoral and cross-sectoral bargaining structures.[138] Wage bargaining coordination is fragmented and decentralised and there is a trend of declining coverage rates of collective agreements, which can be linked to the lower degree of bargaining coordination, weak enforcement, and a failure to use available legal instruments for extension of collective agreement to enlarge its coverage to the sector or economy.[139] In reality, the CEE countries remain heterogeneous even when one takes into account all these parameters, particularly collective bargaining coverage and the relative regulatory importance of sectoral collective bargaining in relation to company level, as demonstrated in Chapter 1.[140] Yet, it remains unclear whether it is possible to establish any meaningful comparison of the industrial relations regimes in CEE.

The discipline of industrial relations, as Meardi noted, has not so far offered 'any integrated effort at understanding industrial relations comparatively',[141] given the lack of large-scale studies involving a greater number of countries and comparable dimensions. As much as there is no comprehensive classification in general literature, there are no comprehensive typologies of CEE industrial relations. As a matter of fact, in the scholarship the CEE countries are usually denoted as a single group with loosely defined common characteristics. This has been also the case in, so far, the most comprehensive typology of comparative industrial relations as presented by Visser, who delineated the four following regimes: social partnership in continental (Western) Europe, Nordic organised corporatism (in Scandinavian countries), liberal pluralism in the UK and the polarised or state-centred regime found in Southern Europe.[142] Visser stated it is a matter of debate whether the CEE group of countries can form a separate regime. In trying to explain the CEE countries, Visser set out the mixed character of their industrial relations – because of the underdeveloped sectoral collective bargaining and low bargaining coverage rates, these industrial relations tend to resemble the 'liberal model', but because of the strong role of the state, the CEE countries resemble the 'state-centred' model of southern Europe. But the CEE fragmented or state-centred model differs from the state centred model in the south because of the weak role of trade unions and the confrontational relationship between social partners.[143]

In the CEE-focused literature there have been very few attempts to classify the existing industrial relations regimes. Such an attempt has been made by Kohl and Platzer, who on the basis of the attitudes towards works councils, sectoral level

---

138. As demonstrated in the report of the European Commission published in 2013, in its dedicated section on CEE industrial relations; *see* European Commission, *Industrial Relations in Europe 2012*, Luxembourg, Publications Office of the European Union, 2013, pp. 53–91.
139. *Ibid.*, p. 66.
140. *See* Tables 1 and 2 and Figure 1 in Chapter 1.
141. Meardi, G., 'Industrial Relations *after* European State Traditions?' in L. Burroni, M. Keune and G. Meardi (eds), *Economy and Society in Europe: A Relationship in Crisis*, Cheltenham, Edward Elgar, 2012b, p. 105.
142. Visser, J., 'The Quality of Industrial Relations and the Lisbon Strategy' in European Commission, *Industrial Relations in Europe 2008*, Luxembourg, Publications Office of the European Union, 2009, pp. 45–73.
143. *Ibid.*, p. 50.

dialogue developments and the role of tripartite dialogue distinguished between: (a) the transitional northern group (Poland and Baltic states); (b) the southern group consisting of Slovenia and Hungary, being the most advanced in terms of meeting the standards of continental Europe; and (c) the countries in the middle, the Czech Republic (having similar traits to the northern group) and Slovakia (having similar traits to the southern group).[144] Yet, Kohl and Platzer noted that CEE industrial relations do not fit any existing model of EU-centred classifications, even though Slovenia to some extent resembles the continental social partnership model. As a matter of fact, the CEE countries do exhibit certain similarities to some of the traits of the existing models in Europe, such as the degree of state influence and involvement as in the Latin systems and the underdevelopment of sectoral collective bargaining in the Anglo-Saxon systems.[145]

One can note that the literature on CEE industrial relations has rather focused on the analysis of general traits than on proposing any classifications. Pollert emphasised the hybridised character of industrial relations in CEE, which stems from the combination of 'formal neocorporatist structures, with heavy leanings on the German model, and voluntarism and fragmentation' and the emphasis on local standard settings and local trade union branches.[146] Moreover, creeping sectoral deregulation leads to trade union fragmentation and decline.[147] In addition to what has been already stated, Kohl and Platzer observed that CEE countries share unstable structures of fragmented employee representation, as well as a tension between deregulation and the development of social rights.[148] Meardi, as well as Ghellab and Vaughan-Whitehead, have noted that in the CEE system of industrial relations, sectoral collective bargaining represents the 'weakest link',[149] with sectoral collective agreements having meagre content and poor coverage.[150] The general weaknesses of trade unions and the ambiguous role of the state failing to promote collective autonomous bargaining have been amongst others stressed as the factors contributing towards the underdevelopment of sectoral dialogue.[151] The company level dialogue is described as featuring fractured and decentralised trade union representation, which is a trait further underpinning the decentralisation of collective bargaining.[152] Much of the CEE literature has focused on tripartite bargaining, which has been described as being too weak and

---

144. Kohl, H. and Platzer, H.-W., 'The Role of the State in Central and Eastern European Industrial Relations: The Case of Minimum Wages', *Industrial Relations Journal*, 2007, vol. 38, no. 6, pp. 616–620.
145. *Ibid.*, when it comes to the Latin systems, the authors particularly refered to France.
146. Pollert, A., 'Ten Years of Post-Communist Central Eastern Europe: Labour's Tenuous Foothold in the Regulation of the Employment Relationship', *Economic and Industrial Democracy*, 2000, vol. 21, no. 2, p. 186; in a similar fashion *see* explanations in Pollert, A., 'Trade Unionism in Transition in Central and Eastern Europe' *European Journal of Industrial Relations*, 1999, vol. 5, no. 2, p. 214.
147. Pollert 2000, *ibid.*, pp. 192–197.
148. Kohl and Platzer 2007, p. 617.
149. Meardi 2012a, p. 58; Ghellab, Y. and Vaughan-Whitehead, D., *Sectoral Social Dialogue in Future EU Member States: The Weakest Link*, Budapest, ILO, 2003.
150. Ghellab and Vaughan-Whitehead 2003, pp. 8–14.
151. *Ibid.*, pp. 15–26.
152. Pollert 2000, pp. 194–198.

unable to generate meaningful negotiated outcomes, despite the fact that all CEE countries established tripartite institutions early in the transition period. Likewise, in now-famous words, Ost labelled it as 'illusory corporatism',[153] and Pollert as a 'fragile shell of tripartism'.[154] On a more general level, Bluhm saw CEE countries as facing the liberalisation dilemma – states risking strengthening managerial unilateralism to cover for the weaknesses of social partners and collective bargaining.[155]

3 FOUR CEE COUNTRIES: MAJOR TRAITS

In addition to what has been said already about the four countries, the following sections provide a brief introduction to their key economic, welfare and industrial relations traits in an effort to provide understanding of major processes surrounding their labour law transformation.

3.1 Slovenia

Slovenia came into being in 1991 after the dissolution of the former country of Yugoslavia. In more than twenty years of transition, Slovenia has developed a substantially specific economic and social landscape in comparison to the other CEE countries. The current literature describes Slovenian economic and welfare model in a variety of terms. Bohle and Greskovits consider Slovenia as a neocorporatist state.[156] Some authors designate it as a coordinated market economy (CME).[157] According to Lendvai, in terms of its social development Slovenia is a social corporativist state and a 'Scandinavian island' in the CEE countries.[158] Unlike the other CEE countries, Slovenia did not resort to neoliberal policy making in the 1990s. As the country embarked on economic and social transformation with a relatively favourable economic situation at the beginning of the 1990s,[159] the policy makers could afford slow privatisation and gradual economic reforms. This gradual approach facilitated economic stability and avoided the high social costs of transition, such as high rates of unemployment.[160] Slovenia also entered the transitional period with a more favourable industrial relations situation – trade union density figures and collective bargaining coverage rates were higher than in the other CEE countries.[161] A specific feature of Slovenian industrial relations has been the active involvement of employers'

---

153. Ost, D., 'Illusory Corporatism in Eastern Europe: Neoliberal Tripartism and Postcommunist Class Identities', *Politics & Society*, 2000, vol. 28, no. 4, pp. 503–530.
154. Pollert 2000.
155. Bluhm, K., 'Resolving Liberalisation Dilemma: Labour Relations in East-Central Europe and the Impact of European Union', in M.A. Moreau and M.E. Blas-López (eds), *Restructuring in the New EU Member States: Social Dialogue, Firms Relocation, and Social Treatment of Restructuring*, Brussels, Peter Lang, 2008, p. 60.
156. Bohle and Greskovits 2012.
157. Crowley and Stanojević 2011; Feldmann 2006.
158. Lendvai 2011.
159. As noted by Crowley and Stanojević 2011.
160. *Ibid.*
161. *Ibid.*, p. 272. For coverage rates trends in the four CEE countries, *see* Figure 1 in Chapter 1.

organisations in collective bargaining during the past decades. This active involvement through mandatory membership of the Chamber of Commerce and Industry for individual employers, something which was in force until 2006, contributed towards exceptionally high coverage rates of collective agreements. That is, since the Chamber was the main bargaining partner on the employers' side, the collective agreements it concluded were binding upon its constituencies. A further feature, specific to Slovenian industrial relations and contributing to higher coverage rates, were the legally binding cross-sectoral collective agreements, regularly concluded until the mid-2000s.

The specific traits of Slovenian industrial relations as described above can be explained with two key elements:

(a) Legacies: The specific type of communism, honed in the former Yugoslavia, provided a vital pretext in developing market institutions. The Yugoslav variation of communism, which developed outside the Soviet bloc, was built on the paradigm of 'self-management'. Under this paradigm, the workers were considered to be the owners of the means of production and the decision-makers in the enterprises, and the property of the enterprises was not considered to belong to the 'state' but to 'society'.[162] Even though these systems were practically considered devoid of real influence on the part of the workers,[163] the self-management represented a useful legacy for organised labour in the post-communist period. Another factor contributing to post-transitional developments was the relative openness of the self-management economy and its pro-market orientation.[164]

(b) Policy choices: Slovenia did not introduce extreme liberal economic reforms and 'shock therapy', but opted for gradual policy transformation, combined with slow privatisation and low dependency on international capital. This also helped creating inclusive and centralised bargaining structures.[165] At the same time, Slovenian policy making was based on a balanced combination of social and economic principles.[166]

---

162. Explanation of the self-management paradigm and the role it played for industrial relations and labour law can be found in several sources, e.g. see Končar, P., 'Changes and Adaptations of Labour Law and Industrial Relations in Slovenia' in R. Blanpain and L. Nagy (eds), *Labour Law and Industrial Relations in Central and Eastern Europe (from Planned to Market Economy)*, Bulletin of Comparative Labour Relations, no. 31, The Hague, Kluwer Law International, 1996, pp. 157–172; Stanojević, M., 'Avoiding Shock Therapy: Trade Unions' Role in the Transition to a Market Economy in Slovenia' in D. Dimitrova and J. Vilrokx (eds), *Trade Union Strategies in Central and Eastern Europe: Towards Decent Work*, Budapest, ILO, 2005, pp. 201-229; Grdesic, M., 'Mapping the Paths of the Yugoslav Model: Labour Strength and Weakness in Slovenia, Croatia and Serbia', *European Journal of Industrial Relations*, 2008, vol. 14, no. 2, pp. 133–151; also, Crowley and Stanojević 2011.
163. Feldmann explains that workers did not act as genuine owners, Feldmann 2006, p. 844; Končar notes that the overall system was inefficient see Končar 1996, p. 158.
164. Crowley and Stanojević 2011, p. 275.
165. Crowley and Stanojević 2011, p. 269; Stanojević, M. and Vehovar, U., 'Slovenia's Integration into the European Market Economy: Gradualism and Its Rigidities' in P. Leisink, B. Steijn and U. Veersma (eds), *Industrial Relations in the New Europe: Enlargement, Integration and Reform*, Cheltenham, Edward Elgar, 2007, p. 82.
166. Crowley and Stanojević 2011.

The Slovenian industrial relations have been exposed to certain changes since the mid-2000s, including decentralisation from cross-sectoral to sectoral level.[167] There were a few reasons driving this decentralisation, in the first place, the legally binding cross-sectoral collective agreements, which otherwise ensured wide coverage rates, had ceased to exist and were no longer being concluded.[168] In addition, around this time, the mandatory membership of the Chamber of Commerce and Industry was abolished. As the result of the ongoing decentralisation, coverage rates dropped significantly after the mid-2000s, as evidenced in Chapter 1.[169]

With the recent economic and financial crisis, the industrial relations structures in Slovenia have further weakened and the policy making has shifted to some extent in a neoliberal direction.[170] Whilst the coverage of collective agreements is still estimated to be considerably higher than in the other CEE countries, the interview participants estimated that the incidence of collective bargaining has substantially dropped since the crisis. The major industrial relations trend has been decentralisation, although sector remains a prominent standard-setting level.[171]

3.2 Slovakia

Slovakia was formed following the dissolution from the federal country of Czechoslovakia in 1993. As already noted in this chapter, Bohle and Greskovits labelled Slovakian type of capitalism as an 'embedded neoliberal'.[172] Claiming that certain neoliberal features prevail in Slovakia, Miklos puts forward the view that Slovakia has fully achieved a transition from a predominantly continental socio-economic model to a predominantly Anglo-Saxon economic model.[173] Bohle and Greskovits held that two factors were pertinent to the specific shape of the capitalism formed in Slovakia:

---

167. As explained by Stanojević, M. and Klarič, M., 'The Impact of Socio-Economic Shocks on Social Dialogue in Slovenia', *Transfer: European Review of Labour and Research*, 2013, vol. 19, no. 2, pp. 217–226; *see also* Feldmann, M., 'Coalitions and Corporatism: The Slovenian Political Economy and the Crisis', *Government and Opposition*, 2014, vol. 49, no. 1, pp. 70–91.
168. Stanojević and Klarič 2013, p. 223.
169. *See* Figure 1 in Chapter 1.
170. Guardiancich, I., 'The Uncertain Future of Slovenian Exceptionalism', *East European Politics & Societies*, 2011, vol. 26, no. 2, pp. 380–399; Stanojević, M., 'Conditions for a Neoliberal Turn: The Cases of Hungary and Slovenia', *European Journal of Industrial Relations*, 2014, vol. 20, no. 2, pp. 97–112.
171. Recent studies show pressures towards decentralisation since the recent crisis period, but that it is still early to detect an entirely new industrial relations patterns in terms of complete shift from sector to company level, *see* Stanojević, M. and Kanjuo Mrčela, A., 'Social Dialogue during the Economic Crisis: The Impact of Industrial Relations Reforms on Collective Bargaining in the Manufacturing Sector: Slovenia', *Project: The Impact of Industrial Relations Reforms on Collective Bargaining in the Manufacturing Sector*, Brussels, European Commission, 2014; Stanojević, M. and Kanjuo Mrčela, A., 'Slovenia at the Crossroads: Increasing Dependence on Supranational Institutions and the Weakening of Social Dialogue', *European Journal of Industrial Relations*, 2016, vol. 1, no. 14, pp. 1–14.
172. Bohle and Greskovits (2007).
173. Miklos, I., 'Slovakia: A Story of Reforms' in W. Bienkowski, J. Brada and M. Radlo (eds), *Growth versus Security: Old and New EU Members – Quest for a New Economic and Social Model*, Basingstoke, Palgrave Macmillan, 2011, p. 75.

accentuated nationalist policy making and exclusion from the international arena at the beginning of transitional process.[174] More specifically, the economic and welfare reform went through different phases.

The beginning of the transitional period was marked by international isolation, economic exclusion and a difficult economic situation.[175] The government, however, kept a close relationship with the trade unions, as the result of which basic social dialogue institutions were formed during this period. Also, the policy making in the early 1990s was labelled as a version of social democratic ideology.[176]

With the new government formed in the late 1990s, economic and welfare policies altered. The policy making in this 'Dzurinda era' (from 1998 to 2006) was characterised by neoliberal features, aiming at structural economic reforms and involving restrictive welfare policies.[177] This period also marked an end to the political and economic isolation of the country internationally.[178] To boost economic growth, the government was promoting flexible labour relations. As a result, major legislative change took place in this period – the new Labour Code was promulgated in 2003, leading to a deregulated labour market.[179] Nonetheless, according to some views, 'the Dzurinda era' was not a complete turning towards neoliberalism since the welfare state had not been completely wiped out.[180]

After 2006 (the 'Fico era'), more balanced policy making took place, and also involved coordination with trade unions.[181] Building a social state had been declared as one of the objectives of the policy making.[182]

Overall, Slovakian post-transitional developments majorly varied in relation to the political constellation in the past two decades. As interviews with the Slovak social partners demonstrated, the actual powers of trade unions depended greatly on the political set up of the moment, although the basic collective bargaining institutions had been established in the early 1990s. In comparison with the other CEE countries, and despite the market-oriented economic policies, Slovak industrial relations are based on a relatively high degree of coordination,[183] with a reasonably well-organised central

---

174. Bohle and Greskovits 2012, p. 179.
175. The country was internationally excluded and economically on the brink of collapse, as described by Miklos 2011, pp. 54–56, also, Bohle and Greskovits, *ibid*.
176. Inglot, T., 'Czech Republic, Hungary, Poland and Slovakia: Adaptation and Reform of the Post-Communist 'Emergency Welfare States' in A. Cerami and P. Vanhuysse (eds), *Post-Communist Welfare Pathways – Theorising Social Policy Transformations in Central and Eastern Europe*, Basingstoke, Palgrave Macmillan, 2009, pp. 88–89.
177. Miklos 2011, p. 54.
178. Bohle and Greskovits 2012, p. 180.
179. Duman, A. and Kureková, L., 'The Role of State in Development of Socio-Economic Models in Hungary and Slovakia: the Case of Industrial Policy', *Journal of European Public Policy*, 2012, vol. 19, no. 8, p. 1217; Fisher, S., Gold, J. and Haughton, T., 'Slovakia's Neoliberal Turn', *Europe-Asia Studies*, 2007, vol. 59, no. 6, pp. 982–983.
180. Fisher, Gold, Haughton 2007, p. 978.
181. Bohle and Greskovits 2012, p. 245.
182. Miklos 2011, p. 83.
183. Bulla, M., Czíria, L. and Kahancová, M., 'Impact of Legislative Reforms on Industrial Relations and Working Conditions in Slovakia', ILO Background Study, 2013, p. 2.

representation of social partners.[184] As demonstrated by Table 2 in Chapter 1, some level of decentralisation can nevertheless be observed from sectoral to company level since the beginning of the 2000s. Such decentralisation has been additionally underpinned with declining trade union and employers' organisations density rates.[185]

As the recent studies have demonstrated, the reasonably well-developed industrial relations at sectoral level had an important mitigating effect on the economic and financial crisis, helping the recovery of the economy and industrial relations were not substantially affected by the crisis.[186] However, the crisis has deeply affected the economy, particularly wages and employment rates.[187]

3.3 The Czech Republic

The Czech Republic emerged from the former state of Czechoslovakia in 1993. As this chapter already demonstrated, Bohle and Greskovits have identified this country as belonging to embedded neoliberal economic systems. The style of capitalism that has developed in the Czech Republic can to a great extent be attributed to the pro-market legacy of former Prime Minister Vaclav Klaus, who closely followed neoclassical approaches, and criticised the pre-1990s overwhelmingly paternalistic and overregulated policies.[188] This style of capitalism enjoyed wider societal support, which led to fewer strikes than in other post-communist countries.[189] Moreover, the Czech model of capitalism did not exclude social policies. The inclination of the Czech Republic to liberal market policies was also combined with universal approach to welfare.[190] Overall, the welfare provision was mixed – in some areas, it resembled a liberal market approach, while in other areas, social-democratic elements prevailed.[191]

---

184. Duman and Kureková 2012; Kahancová, M., 'From Bargaining to Advocacy: A Trade-off Between Improved Working Conditions and Trade Union Fragmentation in Slovakia' in M. Bernaciak and M. Kahancová (eds), *Innovative Union Practices in Central-Eastern Europe*, Brussels, ETUI, 2017.
185. Bulla et al. 2013, pp. 7–8.
186. Kahancová, M., 'The Demise of Social Partnership or a Balanced Recovery? The Crisis and Collective Bargaining in Slovakia', *Transfer: European Review of Labour and Research*, 2013, vol. 19, no. 2, p. 173, citing Czíria, L., 'Collective Bargaining and Balanced Recovery: The Case of the Slovak Republic', Bratislava, Institute for Labour and Family Research, 2013a.
187. Czíria, L., 'Collective Bargaining and Balanced Recovery: The Case of the Slovak Republic', Bratislava, Institute for Labour and Family Research, 2013a, retrieved from http://www.ivpr.gov.sk/IVPR/images/IVPR/2013/collective.pdf (accessed 1 December 2017), pp. 9–11, also, Bulla et al. 2013.
188. Bohle and Greskovits 2012, p. 140.
189. Orenstein, M., 'The Czech Tripartite Council and Its Contribution to Social Peace', *Druzboslovne razprave*, 1994, vol. 17–18, p. 193.
190. Saxonberg, S. and Sirovatka, T., 'Neoliberalism by Decay? The Evolution of the Czech Welfare State', *Social Policy and Administration*, 2009, vol. 43, no. 2, pp. 186–203; Orenstein 1995.
191. Myant, M., 'The Czech Republic: From 'Czech' Capitalism to 'European' Capitalism' in D. Lane and M. Myant (eds), *Varieties of Capitalism in Post-Communist Countries*, Basingstoke, Palgrave Macmillan, 2007, p. 105.

One can observe two major phases in the development of the economy and welfare:[192]

(a) Unlike some CEE countries that already begun reform during the communist period, the Czech Republic started post-transitional reform from scratch in the 1990s.[193] Between 1992 and 1997, policy making was inspired by neoclassical and neoliberal approach, advocated by then Prime Minister, Vaclav Klaus.[194] Nevertheless, the country set the basic social policy principles in the early 1990s, when the Parliament of the country of Czechoslovakia endorsed a programme of social reforms. [195] After 1992, the social policy had become more market oriented and some restrictive social policies were introduced. [196]

(b) The government elected in 1998 showed increased attention towards social policies, but the implementation was constrained because of budgetary limits.[197] Nevertheless, the formal orientation of policy makers towards the social sphere sufficed to label the Czech welfare state as exhibiting typical features of the continental, Bismarckian and corporatist welfare model.[198]

A few remarks about Czech industrial relations can be made. First, the development of industrial relations was greatly affected by the continuous decline of the trade union membership base since 1989.[199] Also, it was affected by inconsistent support to tripartite social dialogue.[200] Also, the trade union picture in the Czech Republic can be described as decentralised and fragmented, which can be ascribed to the legacy of the communist principle of organising one single trade union per workplace.[201] Sectoral collective bargaining was in continuous decline since the 1990s.[202] However, available data for the recent crisis period show that the collective bargaining system has not experienced substantial change,[203] and that the area of welfare was not affected by radical liberal reforms.[204]

---

192. The delineation based on Potucek, M., 'Accession and Social Policy: The Case of the Czech Republic', *Journal of European Social Policy*, 2004, vol. 14, pp. 253–266, although the author considered the beginning period of transition (1989–1992) as a distinct (third) phase.
193. Bohle and Greskovits mentioned that, unlike Czechoslovakia, countries like Poland and Hungary executed some reforms in the last period of communism, see Bohle and Greskovits 2012, p. 141.
194. Myant 2007, pp. 106–107. The economic and political developments in the early 1990s have been also discussed in Potucek, M., 'Current Social Policy Developments in the Czech and Slovak Republics', *Journal of European Social Policy*, 1993, vol. 3, pp. 209–226.
195. Saxonberg and Sirovatka 2009, p. 191; Orenstein 1994, p. 193.
196. Orenstein 1995, p. 186.
197. Potucek 2004, pp. 255–256; Potucek 2008, p. 87.
198. Potucek 2008, p. 93.
199. Myant, M., 'Trade Unions in the Czech Republic', Report 115, Brussels, ETUI, 2010, pp. 53–54.
200. Bohle and Greskovits 2007, p. 454.
201. Myant 2010, p. 12.
202. *Ibid.*, pp. 18–19.
203. Myant, M., 'The Impact of the Economic Crisis on Collective Bargaining in the Czech Republic', *Transfer: European Review of Labour and Research*, 2013, vol. 19, no. 2, p. 194.
204. Bohle and Greskovits 2012, pp. 237–248.

3.4 Poland

The size of the country and its unique trade union legacy dating back from the 1980s are the reasons that Poland attracted comparatively more attention in the literature than the other CEE countries. This chapter has already noted that Bohle and Greskovits labelled Poland as an 'embedded neoliberal regime'. Unlike Slovenia which honed a gradual model of transformation, Poland went through a resolute liberalisation of its economy from the early years of transition, embodied in a macroeconomic 'shock therapy' approach. In contrast to the Slovenian gradualism, the main objective of the Polish economic policy in the early 1990s was to create a free market as quickly as possible.[205] However, the downside of this 'shock therapy' was a sharp deterioration of the social conditions, including large unemployment and inflation rates and a fall in production.[206] This has led to the development of what Inglot explained as an 'emergency welfare state' – welfare policies aimed to respond to acute and emergent needs in the 1990s, and to mitigate the harsh social effects of the 'shock therapy'.[207] In this spirit, Lendvai described the Polish welfare state as dual and incongruous – shaped by duality of pressures and institutionalised responses to political, social and economic challenges.[208]

Industrial relations in Poland are highly decentralised since collective bargaining predominantly takes place at company level. As Chapter 1 demonstrated, the coverage rates are the lowest among the four countries selected. At the same time, as the interviews have demonstrated, in the past two decades the state has provided only modest support for building the industrial relations infrastructure, which represents one of the reasons behind the weaknesses of central bargaining levels. Another reason has been the fragmentation of the trade union movement itself since the 1990s, with the 'competitive pluralism' between large numbers of trade unions coexisting in the same companies and competing with each other.[209]

The shape of modern industrial relations in Poland can to a great extent be ascribed to the pre-transitional industrial relations legacy. The year 1980 marked the establishment of the trade union movement Solidarnosc (in English 'Solidarity'), which had a vital role in facilitating the post-1990s transitional developments.[210] In 1982, the Trade Union Act was enacted, setting out the basis for a decentralised trade union landscape. Specifically, this Act allowed trade union formation at company level with

---

205. See e.g. Aslund 2007, pp. 29–56; King 2002.
206. King 2002, p. 13.
207. Inglot defines emergency welfare states as temporary creations which have in reality become permanent structures, and labels them as 'no less resistant to reform than the commonly recognized welfare regimes', and inherently unstable, see Inglot 2009, p. 75 and p. 87.
208. Lendvai 2011, p. 187, citing Mykhenko, V., 'Strengths and Weaknesses of "Weak" Coordination: Economic Institutions, Revealed Comparative Advantages, and Socio-Economic Performance of Mixed Market Economies in Poland and Ukraine' in B. Hancké, M. Rhodes and M. Thatcher (eds), *Beyond Varieties of Capitalism: Conflict, Contradictions, and Complementarities in the European Economy*, Oxford, Oxford University Press, 2007, pp. 351–378.
209. Gardawski, J., Mrozowicki, A. and Czarzasty, J., *Trade Unions in Poland*, Brussels, ETUI, 2012, p. 11.
210. See fn 100.

a high level of autonomy vis-à-vis associations of trade unions at federal and confederal level.[211] Also, in the mid-1980s, another large trade union was formed – a confederation All-Poland Alliance of Trade Union (OPZZ). Politically motivated competition between Solidarity and OPZZ in subsequent years contributed towards the fragmentation of trade union movement in the country.[212]

Polish scholarship distinguished three phases of industrial relations developments in the post-transitional period:[213]

(a) the period between 1989 and 1993 has been characterised by trade union pluralism, the establishment of tripartite structures and increased strike activity;
(b) after 1993, the collective bargaining landscape was characterised by a weakly unionised private sector;
(c) the third phase took place after 2001 and was characterised by stronger institutionalisation of the tripartite institutions and increased trade union activity in the private sector.

There are two specific traits which delineate Polish industrial relations from the other three countries. First, unlike the other CEE examples, Polish industrial relations have not undergone a process of decentralisation from sectoral to company level in the past two decades (as described in Chapter 1, section 4.1). This would not be possible, given the marginal importance which sectoral collective bargaining has had since the beginning of the 1990s. Second, another specific feature of the Polish landscape was the support of the trade union movement for the neoliberal transformation,[214] a feature that further underpinned the trend to decentralised industrial relations.

On a final note, it seems that in comparison with the other three countries, Polish industrial relations have been the least affected by the recent economic and financial crisis, having in mind the evidence of increased tripartite activity in this period.[215]

4 CONCLUSION: COMPARATIVE REMARKS

This chapter demonstrated that industrial relations in the CEE countries, as well as their economic and welfare models, substantially differ from those in other European countries. At the same time, this chapter demonstrated that the CEE group is extremely heterogeneous and that using the general term 'CEE industrial relations' alongside the terms 'CEE economies' or 'CEE welfare' can be fairly misleading, since it is vital to account for country-specific characteristics. However, despite obvious national differences, in the area of collective bargaining, the four CEE countries share some important

---

211. Gardawski et al. 2012, p. 17.
212. *Ibid.*, p. 12.
213. *Ibid.*, p. 20.
214. As described in the work of David Ost and Agnieszka Paczynska, *see* fn 100.
215. For the overview of tripartite developments during the crisis period, *see* Bernaciak, M., 'Social Dialogue Revival or "PR Corporatism"? Negotiating Anti-Crisis Measures in Poland and Bulgaria', *Transfer: European Review of Labour and Research*, 2013, vol. 19, no. 2, pp. 239–251.

traits. These traits have been depicted in section 2.3, in addition to what has been already presented on this topic in Chapter 1. The key common feature which distinguishes the CEE countries from most of the industrial relations systems in Europe is decentralised collective bargaining coupled with weak sectoral and cross-sectoral infrastructure. Slovenia is somewhat an exception to this trend, even though this country has also experienced some trend towards decentralisation since the mid-2000s.

Furthermore, this chapter demonstrated that the peculiar economic style of reforms undertaken in the 1990s underpinned the decentralisation of industrial relations in CEE. This is more evident in the countries that opted for a shock-therapy style of macroeconomic reform, because the ideological orientation towards individualism and personal freedoms provided a pretext for decentralisation, sectoral deregulation and emphasis on company-level collective bargaining. Unfortunately, a comprehensive understanding of the factors conducive to collective bargaining decentralisation is somewhat hindered by the lack of a clear and sophisticated comparative classification of the CEE economic and welfare models, as well as models of industrial relations. Nonetheless, the approaches on capitalism and welfare presented in sections 2.1 and 2.2 of this chapter lead to the conclusion that the liberal style of economic reform in CEE was not rendered incompatible with the reform of welfare and institutionalisation of industrial relations and the idea of 'welfare state' was not wiped out.

In addition, section 2.3 demonstrated that the literature has not yet been able to present a comprehensive framework for classifying and contrasting CEE industrial relations. Notwithstanding the lack of such theoretical framework, this chapter delineated several common characteristics of CEE industrial relations, and presented the major country-specific developments in the four countries.

While understanding that the factors driving the institutionalisation of industrial relations are multifaceted and complex, and that their comprehensive analysis would go well beyond the scope of this study, there are certain remarks that can be made at this point about the four countries. These remarks subsume the country elements and findings presented in section 3, as well as the country regime clustering proposed by Bohle and Greskovits in section 2.1 of this chapter. These remarks furthermore build upon the collective bargaining features depicted in Chapter 1, namely that Poland has the most decentralised collective bargaining, followed by the Czech Republic, while, at the opposite end of the spectrum, Slovenia has the most centralised collective bargaining system, followed by Slovakia. Out of the four countries, *Slovenia*'s industrial relations resemble most the style of continental European industrial relations, because of the favourable role of legacies, gradual approaches to policy making and the more favourable market position of the country in contrast to the other CEE countries at the beginning of the transformation period.[216] At the other end of the spectrum, *Poland*'s economic reforms have emanated from a resolute 'shock therapy' approach which was combined with the 'emergency' welfare policies. At the same time, industrial relations developed in close relation to the legacies of the 1980s, in the first

---

216. As explained by Crowley and Stanojević 2011.

place aided by the establishment of the trade union movement Solidarity, but also by the legacy of a fragmented trade union landscape which was legally postulated in 1982. The *Slovak* and *Czech* examples come somewhere between the other two countries. Slovakia has managed to develop more centralised collective bargaining structures than the Czech Republic, despite the fact it is unique among the Visegrad countries for having developed a more pro-liberal and pro-market orientation on economic reforms. The Czech Republic was pursing resolute market-oriented reforms in the early 1990s, but after 1998, the policies included more socially oriented reforms.

On the basis of the country-specific characteristics depicted in this chapter, the task of the following chapter will be to further explore processes of labour law transformation in the four countries.

CHAPTER 3
The Genesis and Positioning of Collective Agreement in CEE Labour Laws

1 EXPLAINING THE GENESIS OF MODERN CEE LABOUR LAWS

No labour law systems have undergone such dramatic transformation as those in the CEE countries, following the demise of communism in the early 1990s. That transformative process essentially challenged the very foundation of labour laws because communist legal regulations were deemed incompatible with the needs and functions of open economies. Specifically, communist labour laws were founded on the ideology of maintaining full employment, and they applied work standards with a rather comprehensive, 'one-size-fits-all' approach to the entire economy. The trade unions were subservient to the ideology of the regime. Collective bargaining was not widespread, and in any case played a negligible role. The transformation and internationalisation of markets and economies therefore inevitably raised questions about the rationale of CEE labour laws. From the earliest stages of economic transition, CEE policy makers were faced with the fundamental issue of how labour law might be conceptualised. The major predicament facing the policy makers was clarification of the regulatory role and function of collective agreement, and its position and relationship with statutory labour laws. Determining the status and role of collective agreement went hand in hand with reclarifying the regulatory role and function of the state in industrial relations – having in mind its all-encompassing role in determining working life standards in the communist period.

The responses of the CEE countries to these fundamental challenges were shaped in a nation-specific context. The national pathways were all but identical, having been developed as a result of various influences, ranging from internal to external factors, and from policy choices to legalistic path-dependant solutions. In an effort to obtain guidance for labour law transformation, the CEE countries were looking towards continental European countries, hoping that mimicking the economically developed models would bring a comparable level of economic development and welfare within a reasonable time frame. Nevertheless, this has not been an easy task, given that the international setting in which this transformation was taking place was a dynamic one – continental European labour laws themselves were evolving in an effort to accommodate the pressures of international competition and globalisation. The recent economic and financial crisis exemplifies this point, because it has particularly challenged the industrial relations across the EU.[217]

This chapter is not built on the premise that CEE labour law transformation has been accomplished. However, the challenges that CEE labour laws have had to confront during the last two decades, starting from the onset of transition and economic transformation, accession to the EU and the recent economic and financial crisis, justify critical appraisal of the current CEE labour laws and an understanding of the processes surrounding their development. Bearing this in mind, this chapter has a twofold aim. *First*, it will explain national responses to common challenges surrounding CEE labour law transformation. By seeking explanations for the development of the legal and institutional framework for collective bargaining in the four countries, the chapter contributes to the second research question of this study. However, this chapter does not aim to provide a conclusive answer to that research question – to that end the analysis in the second part of this study will also be taken into account. *Second*, this chapter provides valuable insights on labour laws in the four countries. In this context, it also represents a useful introduction to the analysis which will be conducted in the second part of the study.

This chapter proceeds as follows. The following section 2 explains the common factors and triggers driving labour law transformation in CEE, and aims at identifying the leading paradigm of the transformation of labour law. The chapter then presents the overview of processes in the four CEE countries (section 3). Based on the analysis and data presented, section 4 sets out to explore how collective agreements emerged as the standard-setting instruments in CEE. Section 5 provides concluding notes on the genesis of labour law in the four countries and offers a guide to the further analysis contained in the second part of this book.

2 DECONSTRUCTING LABOUR LAW DEVELOPMENT IN CEE

2.1 Factors Pertinent to Labour Law Transformation

Although shaped under nation-specific mixes of circumstances, the underlying issues and challenges driving labour law transformation were similar across the CEE countries. In an effort to group the factors driving labour law transformation into distinct

---

217. The process of 'modernisation' and 'transformation' of labour laws in continental Europe inspired a number of scholarly debates, e.g. *see* Hendrickx, F., 'The Future of Collective Labour Law in Europe', *European Labour Law*, 2010, vol. 1, 59–79; Hepple, B., 'Factors Influencing the Making and Transformation of Labour Law in Europe', in G. Davidov and B. Langille (eds), *The Idea of Labour Law*, Oxford, Oxford University Press, 2011, pp. 30–42. The recent economic and financial crisis has further spurred debate on the topic, *see* Coutu, M., Le Friant, M. and Murray, G., 'Broken Paradigms: Labour Law in the Wake of Globalisation and the Economic Crisis', *Comparative Labour Law and Policy Journal*, 2013, vol. 34, pp. 565–584.

Chapter 3: The Genesis and Positioning of Collective Agreement

categories, this study builds on the elements which Bohle and Greskovits considered crucial for explaining capitalism diversities in CEE,[218] and translates them into the vocabulary of labour law:

(a) The policy choices undertaken by policy makers in the last two decades, including the stances taken and support put in place for the building of the legal and institutional framework for collective bargaining.

(b) Labour law legacies originating in the communist setting. While Bohle and Greskovits understood that legacies, being perceived as threats or assets, may represent an element influencing policy making, this study considers them as a distinct category driving labour law transformation. Moreover, this study understands that legacies can inspire specific legal solutions or represent a source of inspiration in formulating labour law principles. The idea of legal legacies originates from path dependency – legal ideas can be deeply embedded in the shared knowledge of the legal community and, as such, can create a preference of law-makers towards more 'familiar' choices.[219]

(c) External influences, coming from the EU and other international organisations.

It is reasonable to assume that the weight of each element has differed across the countries examined. To the extent that it is possible, this study, and this chapter in particular, will aim to account for the weight of each factor in explaining the processes of legal developments in the four selected countries. The role of the EU as an external influence will be specifically addressed in Chapter 4.

Apart from being subject to similar sets of issues and challenges, the transformation of the CEE labour laws was triggered by the same events:

(i) *First*, transition from command to open economy per se questioned the very legal foundation of the communist labour setting. Already at the onset of transitional period, the CEE countries had started introducing the first 'modern' labour law provisions, which were salient in allowing, for the first time, free and voluntary collective bargaining and free operation of trade unions and employers' associations. All four CEE countries examined in this study saw the first legal provisions on collective bargaining during this period. The former state of Czechoslovakia introduced the Collective Bargaining Act in 1991, Poland introduced Labour Code amendments in 1994,

---

218. As presented in Chapter 2, Bohle and Greskovits explained regime diversity in CEE by taking into account two major factors; first, initial policy choices, including the legacies of the past and their perception as threats or assets by policy makers, and second, the formative role of the transnational and international influences; see Bohle, D. and Greskovits, B., 'Neoliberalism, Embedded Neoliberalism and Neocorporatism: Towards Transnational Capitalism in Central-Eastern Europe', *West European Politics*, 2007, vol. 30, no. 3, pp. 443–444.

219. As explained by Chirico, F. and Larouche, P., 'Conceptual Divergence, Functionalism, and the Economics of Convergence' in S. Prechal and B. Roermund (eds), *The Coherence of EU Law: The Search for Unity in Divergent Concepts*, Oxford, Oxford University Press, 2008, p. 469.

containing rules on collective bargaining, and Slovenia regulated collective bargaining matters in the Act on Basic Rights of Employment Relationship of 1989 and the Employment Relationship Act of 1990. Another landmark feature of this initial transformation period was the institutionalisation of tripartite bodies, which took place in the Czech Republic and Slovakia in 1993, and in Poland and Slovenia in 1994. Many of the legal changes that occurred at the beginning of the 1990s were inspired by ILO architecture. As a matter of fact, the beginning of the transitional period was marked by transposition of ILO Conventions Nos 87 and 98, which brought the introduction of free and voluntary collective bargaining into their legislative systems.[220]

(ii) *Second*, the accession to the EU brought specific challenges to CEE labour laws, given that the EU requires candidate countries to build meaningful social dialogue infrastructure. Social dialogue also represents part of the *acquis communautaire* which the candidate countries are asked to transpose and implement. Yet, the ability of the EU to initiate and inspire changes pertinent to the institutionalisation of collective bargaining is challenged, as Chapter 4 will demonstrate in more detail.

(iii) *Third*, the recent economic and financial crisis challenged the European labour law systems, affecting mechanisms for setting working conditions, and inducing changes to the collective bargaining systems across the continent.[221] The existing data demonstrate that those systems which already possessed centralised collective bargaining mechanisms at the onset of the crisis could more easily generate collective agreements in response to the detrimental effects of the crisis.[222] From this viewpoint, the recent crisis period represented a genuine test for the CEE countries, questioning whether the overall legal framework is conducive to promoting and supporting centralised collective bargaining.

2.2 In Search of a Leading Paradigm of Labour Law Transformation

The CEE countries originally belonged to the European civil law tradition – their legal systems had deeply-entrenched German and Austrian-Hungarian roots before being

---

220. ILO Freedom of Association and Protection of the Right to Organise Convention No. 87, 1948 and Right to Organise and Collective Bargaining Convention, No. 98, 1949. As noted in Chapter 1, Slovakia ratified these two conventions in 1993, Slovenia in 1992, the Czech Republic in 1993. Poland has been considered a party to these two conventions since 1957.
221. For the overview of ways in which the recent economic and financial crisis affected labour law systems across Europe, *see* Countouris, N. and Freedland M. (eds), *Resocialising Europe in a Time of Crisis*, Cambridge, Cambridge University Press, 2013; Bruun, N., Lörcher, K. and Schömann, I. (eds), *The Economic and Financial Crisis and Collective Labour Law in Europe*, Oxford, Hart Publishing, 2014.
222. *See* Glassner, V., 'Central and Eastern European Industrial Relations in the Crisis: National Divergence and Path-Dependent Change', *Transfer: European Review of Labour and Research*, 2013, vol. 19, no. 2, p. 156.

substantially transformed by communist ideology.[223] With the inception of communist rule in the mid-twentieth century, labour laws underwent dramatic transformation. Despite the fact that the common trait in all communist systems was large-scale state intervention in all matters relating to work, it would be misleading to claim that the labour laws were identical in CEE. To begin with, the variation of Slovenian communism, grounded on the paradigm of 'self-management', differed starkly from the other Soviet-based models. Unlike in the other communist systems, self-management was the model in which employees were considered to be the owners of the 'socialist property', rather than the political party or the state. According to this principle, they were entitled to organise production and to decide on relevant conditions of work.[224] At the same time, the Slovenian pre-transitional system was particular in being the most market-oriented in comparison to the other three CEE countries.[225] Conversely, the variation of communist ideology honed in Czechoslovakia and Poland was comparatively more state-commanded, and conceptually tied to the notion of state property rather than the engagement of employees.

With the beginning of economic transition, the CEE countries embarked on yet another dramatic transformation of labour laws. In that respect, the following vital features of the communist systems were particularly subjected to post-transitional scrutiny:

(a) The function of communist law was to support socialism and a planned economy.[226]
(b) There was a lack of autonomous regulation of working conditions, as collective agreements were not a predominant form of standard setting, and the major regulator was the state, delivering statutory law and administrative regulations.[227] The lack of contractual relationship, either collective or individual, was a distinct feature of these systems.[228] For instance, as

---

223. Bronstein, A., 'Trends and Challenges of Labour Law in Central Europe' in J.D.R. Craig (ed.), *Globalisation and the Future of Labour Law*, Cambridge, Cambridge University Press, 2006, p. 201. How the German and Austrian Hungarian roots of CEE countries influenced today's CEE welfare settings has been addressed by Inglot, T., *Welfare States in East Central Europe, 1919-2004*, Cambridge, Cambridge University Press, 2008.
224. See fn 162 for sources explaining self-management.
225. Crowley and Stanojević 2011, p. 275.
226. Sajo, A., 'New Legalism in East Central Europe: Law as an Instrument of Social Transformation', *Journal of Law and Society*, 1990, vol. 17, no. 3, pp. 330–331.
227. Which derived from the overall regulatory style, whereby the state role was perceived as one of securing broad rights for all citizens. Conversely, the post-communist task was to ensure that the state may set only minimum rights, beyond which the citizens could set their own rules, as explained by Sewerynski, M., 'Prospects for the Development of Labour Law and Social Security Law in Central and Eastern Europe in the Twenty-First Century', *Comparative Labour Law and Policy Journal*, 1997, vol. 18, pp. 184–185.
228. As pointed out by Kollonay, C., 'The Future of Labour Law: Insights from an East European Country', *European Labour Law Journal*, 2010, vol. 1, no. 1, pp. 33–43; Kollonay Lehoczky, C., 'European Enlargement: A Comparative View of Hungarian Labour Law' in G.A. Bermann and K. Pistor (eds), *Law and Governance in an Enlarged European Union*, Oxford, Hart Publishing, 2004, p. 211. Kollonay Lehoczky explained the development of CEE labour law on the ground of lack of contractual relationship before the transitional period and its subsequent restoration in post-transitional terms.

explained by Kollonay-Lehoczky, the law was not based on contractual freedoms, but, rather, it was tied to the status subsumed under the concept 'worker taking part in building up socialism'.[229] Slovenia was a bit of an exception to this, at least in paradigmatic sense, given that its system was based on the self-management relationship amongst employees, and allowed some forms of collective accords.[230] Being such meagre sources of standard setting, communist collective agreements performed specific functions in comparison with the other European countries. As noted by Fahlbeck, these communist agreements nominally represented instruments for cooperation at the workplace level and, to some extent, instruments for protecting employees, but with the overall impression that 'their main thrust lies elsewhere'.[231] Thus, their focus, as explained by Fahlbeck, was not to regulate the obligations of employers, as might have been expected of collective agreements, but rather to lay down the commitments of employees and to set down rules aiming at improving efficiency at work.[232]

(c) Correlative to the underdevelopment of autonomous regulation was the peculiar regulatory style of the communist labour codes. The substantive provisions of statutory legal provisions were fairly detailed, bestowing a wide range of rights to employees in coercive and mandatory fashion.[233]

With the onset of the transitional period, the foundations of collective bargaining and collective agreements, changed profoundly, including the three vital features. But what was the guiding paradigm shaping their transformation? To answer this, this study claims that the creation of the legal and institutional framework for collective bargaining was set within a twofold narrative:

(i) *Regulation/Institutionalisation of industrial relations*. The lack of meaningful collective bargaining practices in the communist period meant that, with the onset of the 1990s' reformative processes, the CEE countries had to introduce basic provisions allowing free collective bargaining and free operation of trade unions and employers' associations. In other words, the

---

229. Kollonay Lehoczky 2004, p. 211.
230. Concise classification and explanation of the self-management bodies can be found in Warner, M., 'Yugoslav "Self-Management" and Industrial Relations in Transition' *Industrial Relations Journal*, 1990, vol. 21, no. 3, pp. 209–220.
231. Fahlbeck, R., 'Collective Agreements: A Crossroad between Public Law and Private Law', *Comparative Labour Law Journal*, 1987, vol. 3, no. 2, p. 283.
232. *Ibid.*, pp. 283–286.
233. For example, this was the case with the 1965 Czechoslovakian Labour Code, *see* Barancová, H., 'Labour Law in the Slovak Republic, Present Situation and Future Trends' in R. Blanpain and L. Nagy (eds), *Labour Law and Industrial Relations in Central and Eastern Europe (from Planned to Market Economy)*, Bulletin of Comparative Labour Relations, no. 31, The Hague, Kluwer Law International, 1996, p. 139. Similarly, the 1974 Polish Labour Code greatly restricted the possibility of concluding collective agreements, *see* Sewerynski, M., 'Development of the Collective Bargaining System in Poland after the Second World War', *Comparative Labour Law Journal*, 1993, vol. 14, pp. 444. There are, however, views that the legal thinking was to some extent similar to the one in civil law of the west countries, *see* Sajo 1990.

legal systems had to be 'enriched'[234] with the new institutions alien to the previous legal setting. The most important ILO provisions on freedom of association and free operation of trade unions were an inspiration to that end.[235] This seemingly simple task was formally accomplished at the earliest transition stage. However, the institutionalisation of collective bargaining cannot be understood as a simple step of inserting provisions guaranteeing free and voluntary collective bargaining. Institutionalisation entails a broader scrutiny of all legal provisions in labour law with a view to ensuring that the overall legal system is conducive to free and voluntary collective bargaining and to free organisation of social partners. It is therefore a long-term task that requires more than a declaratory adoption of leading legal principles. Whether the process of institutionalisation has been fully accomplished will be explored in the second part of this study (Chapters 5, 6, and 7).

(ii) *Insertion of free market rationale.* With the onset of economic transition, the market narrative entered the CEE legal sphere with the twofold objective – first, in contrast to the contract-devoid basis of communist labour relations, the post-transitional CEE countries were faced with the task of building labour law systems based on a contractual relationship between employers and employees. This process was explained by Kollonay-Lehoczky as a restoration of contractual freedoms.[236] Second, the CEE policy makers had to respond to the challenge of ensuring that legal provisions facilitated, rather than hindered, economic growth. The latter task seemingly played more prominent role in the countries that opted for non-gradual 'shock therapy', such as Poland and the Czech Republic. The wide support for what were essentially free market ideas was described by Kollonay-Lehoczky:

> allergic response to anything that resembled the institutions of the past appeared in almost all social fields, but it was particularly intense in economic, employment and labour law since these areas of the law had been at the core of the ideology and foundation of the fallen regime.[237]

The misconception of the post-transitional legal thinking was that the insertion of a free market narrative should go hand in hand with outright deregulation.[238] On one hand, the insertion of a market narrative entailed lessening state involvement in labour

---

234. Bronstein, A., 'Trends and Challenges of Labour Law in Central Europe' in J.D.R. Craig (ed.), *Globalisation and the Future of Labour Law*, Cambridge, Cambridge University Press, 2006, p. 195.
235. Particularly, ILO Freedom of Association and Protection of the Right to Organise Convention No 87, 1948 and Right to Organise and Collective Bargaining Convention, No 98, 1949.
236. Kollonay Lehoczky 2004, p. 212.
237. *Ibid.*, pp. 210–211.
238. As far as deregulation is concerned, Regini has criticised the fact that regulation in terms of policy debates has been too often confused with regulation in economic terms. The former relates to the functioning of the market as opposed to state regulation, while the latter denotes various ways in which economic resources are produced and distributed. In this sense, Regini considered deregulation to be an ambiguous concept; *see* Regini, M., 'The Dilemmas of Labour

relations in order to create faster economic growth. Inspired by belief that free market ideas should govern labour, this approach represented a counter-narrative to the previous communist setting. But on the other hand, the application of market narrative and commitment to free market ideas paved the way to unfettered freedom for entrepreneurs and managerial powers at local levels. Taken together, these aspects rendered the process of institutionalisation of collective bargaining difficult and also underpinned the creation of decentralised industrial relations in CEE.

The previous observations demonstrated that there were substantial ambiguities in the introduction of market rationale. However, the policy reasoning described could not be applied to all the CEE countries to the same degree. As argued in Chapter 2, the policy makers' degree of dedication to the neoliberal reforms varied across CEE. It can be concluded that, overall, CEE labour law transformation did not have clear normative and conceptual underpinnings, but that the guiding paradigm lay in a continuum between institutionalisation and free market narrative. Judging from the national processes presented in Chapter 2 (and particularly the support which trade unions enjoyed from policy makers), it can be assumed that the institutionalisation narrative played a more prominent role in Slovenia and, within a certain time frame, in Slovakia. Meanwhile, in Poland and the Czech Republic, one may imply the predominant role of the market narrative. The following sections will further deconstruct the national processes of the four countries, with a view to providing more detailed explanations of these narratives.

3 THE DEVELOPMENT OF LABOUR LAW IN THE FOUR COUNTRIES

3.1 Slovenia

The lynchpin of the labour law in the federal country of Yugoslavia was the so-called self-management system. In contrast with the other CEE countries, Slovenia's labour law paradigm was a 'socialist' conception of a labour relationship where the workers worked in socially owned enterprises.[239] Since the enterprises were socially owned, workers were enabled to engage in decision-making about their operation, and to establish various forms of workers' representatives' bodies at the level of the workplace.[240] Despite this 'socialist' construction of the system, collective bargaining practices were limited in Slovenia and linked to the otherwise economically less important private sector.[241]

The transformation of the economy began in 1989, with the law which instigated the process of privatisation by delineating between private, mixed and social ownership (the latter originating from the previous self-management system).[242] However,

---

Market Regulation' in G. Esping-Andersen and M. Regini (eds), *Why Deregulate Labour Markets*, Oxford, Oxford University Press, 2000b, pp. 21–24.
239. *See* fn 162 for sources explaining the self-management paradigm.
240. Crowley and Stanojević 2011; Grdesic 2008.
241. Skledar, S., *Collective Bargaining Legislation Examined*, Dublin, Eurofound, 2003.
242. Končar 1996, pp. 157–159.

Chapter 3: The Genesis and Positioning of Collective Agreement

social property was legally protected throughout the 1990s which rendered the process of institutionalising collective bargaining rather slow.[243]

Slovenia introduced the first modern collective bargaining rules and principles in the early 1990s. To start with, following the dissolution from the federal state of Yugoslavia, Slovenia's Constitution introduced provision on freedom of association.[244] This period also saw the adoption of two vital pieces of legislation facilitating trade union operations, which are still in force today – the Act on Trade Union Representativeness of 1993 and the Act on Trade Union Organisation of 1990. The first legal provisions facilitating collective bargaining were initially introduced in the Act on Basic Rights of Employment Relationship of 1989 and the Employment Relationship Act of 1990, which were eventually replaced with the 2003 Employment Relationship Act. The Slovenian legal system underwent its most comprehensive reform in 2006, when the Act on Collective Agreements was adopted. Until that time, certain traits specific to Slovenian labour law developed, which were pivotal to the shape of post-2006 developments:

(i) First, the Act on Basic Rights of Employment Relationship of 1989 and the Employment Relationship Act of 1990 did not introduce comprehensive regulation of collective agreements.[245] These legal acts contained general regulation only of all types of collective agreements, regardless of the type of property and companies (private, mixed or socially owned).[246]

(ii) Second, a specific trait of Slovenian industrial relations until 2006 was the mandatory membership of individual employers in the Chamber of Commerce and Industry.[247] Given the fact that individual employers were obliged to be members of the Chamber, which was at the same time the major bargaining party on the employers' side, the collective agreements concluded had wide coverage. In this way, the mandatory nature of membership of the Chamber has been linked to the comparatively higher coverage rates of collective agreements achieved in Slovenia than in the other CEE countries. However, criticised for contravening the free and voluntary nature of collective bargaining,[248] mandatory membership was lifted in 2006.

(iii) Thirdly, a peculiarity of the system was that the collective agreements were in a certain sense considered mandatory, particularly with regard to collective agreements at cross-sectoral (in Slovenia entitled as 'general collective agreements') and sectoral levels. The quasi-mandatory nature was inherited from the socialist period and comes from the peculiar regulatory style of

---

243. In 2004, Vodovnik demonstrated that due to legislation protecting social property, the autonomy of collective bargaining parties was limited, see Vodovnik, Z., 'Slovenia' in R. Blanpain (ed.), *The Actors of Collective Bargaining*, Bulletin of Comparative Labour Relations, no. 51, The Hague, Kluwer Law International, 2004, p. 233.
244. *See* Article 76.
245. Končar 1996, p. 158; Vodovnik 2004, p. 232.
246. *Ibid.*
247. Gospodarska Zbornica Slovenije (GSZ).
248. Vodovnik, Z. and Korpič-Horvat, E., 'Slovenia' in R. Blanpain and F. Hendrickx (eds), *International Encyclopaedia for Labour Law and Industrial Relations*, The Hague, Kluwer Law International, 2015, p. 267.

statutory law. Specifically, the law did not regulate certain areas with enough precision, making it practically necessary to conclude collective agreements.[249] This 'mandatory' nature of collective bargaining was honed until 2006, when it was abolished after criticisms about incompatibility with the voluntary nature of collective agreements as understood within the ILO framework.[250]

The major overhaul of the legal framework on collective bargaining took place in 2006 with the adoption of the Act on Collective Agreements. This Act represents a seminal piece of law in the current legislative framework and no new law regulating collective bargaining has been enacted since. Drafted with the aim of facilitating free and voluntary collective bargaining, this Act addressed the three above described peculiarities of the previous setting. Mandatory membership to the Chamber was lifted.[251] The 2006 Act also regulated the most salient aspects of collective agreements and collective bargaining, including who should be the parties to these agreements, their validity and the procedure for concluding the agreements.[252] It is crucial to add that, even though the 2006 Act was pivotal to implementing free and voluntary collective bargaining, as a matter of fact industrial relations had already developed at three major bargaining levels throughout the 1990s and 2000s. In this sense, the 2006 Act represented an endorsement of the already established collective bargaining practice.

On a final note, it is useful to add that, based on historical developments, Slovenian scholars Vodovnik and Korpič-Horvat distinguished three 'generations' of collective agreements that have been in existence over the past two decades.[253] This division roughly explicates the gradual process of the institutionalisation of collective agreements in Slovenia:

(a) The first generation of collective agreements was concluded shortly after the 1990 Slovenian Constitution was promulgated. These were two cross-sectoral agreements (in Slovenian terminology 'general agreements'), covering public and private sector. On their basis, collective agreements at sectoral and company levels were concluded. Yet, bargaining autonomy was limited under the law because privatisation has not yet begun.

(b) The second generation of collective agreements was concluded after privatisation of socialist ownership had started. However, collective agreements were deemed mandatory and hence were not fully autonomous: statutory

---

249. Skledar 2003; Končar 1996, p. 169.
250. *Ibid.*
251. Vodovnik and Korpič-Horvat 2015, p. 267.
252. Končar 2010, pp. 46–47.
253. The following explanations of the three generations has been provided by Vodovnik and Korpič-Horvat 2015, pp. 278–279.

law required that certain conditions of work and employment should be regulated by collective agreements.[254]

(c) The third generation of collective agreements, concluded in line with the 2006 Act on Collective Agreements, were based on the free and autonomous will of social partners.

3.2 Slovakia

Collective agreements were of marginal importance in the former country of Czechoslovakia. The major reason behind their limited regulatory space was the specific regulatory style of the 1965 Labour Code. The 1965 statutory legal provisions consisted of a fairly elaborated mandatory and comprehensive regulation of most aspects of work and employment which did not leave much space for autonomous regulation. In addition, there was a further major legal constraint: the 1965 Labour Code allowed collective bargaining only on designated matters.[255]

The legal reform of collective bargaining had already begun in the early 1990s within the federal country of Czechoslovakia. The organisation of trade unions and employers' associations was made possible by the 1990 Act on the Association of Citizens.[256] In 1992, the Constitution of the Slovak Republic inserted freedom of association into its provisions.[257] The 1965 Labour Code remained valid, although in an amended version, until recodification in 2001.[258] Collective bargaining was legally postulated with the 1991 Act on Collective Bargaining which was adopted in the former country of Czechoslovakia, and which is still in force in amended version.

Although the legal system was modified a number of times (particularly regarding collective agreements extensions and, more recently, on trade union representativeness), the building blocks of collective bargaining system were legally anchored with the 1991 Act on Collective Bargaining and the Labour Code provisions. These laws regulated the procedure of collective bargaining, validity of collective agreements and other pertinent matters. The building blocks have basically remained unchanged since the early 1990s. What has been subject to gradual transformation is the content of collective agreements, and it very much depended on the regulatory style of the Labour Code that was changing over the time. Likewise, whilst the 1965 version consisted of mainly mandatory and comprehensive provisions, the subsequent legal amendments managed to gradually introduce more space for autonomous regulation by social partners. The most radical overhaul of the labour law framework took place in 2001.

---

254. As explained by Skledar, laws contained 'instructions' on the content of collective agreements, see Skledar 2003.
255. Pichrt and Štefko 2015, p. 94.
256. Barancová, H. and Olšovská, A., 'Slovakia' in R. Blanpain and F. Hendrickx (eds), *International Encyclopaedia for Labour Law and Industrial Relations*, The Hague, Kluwer Law International, 2014, p. 187 and p. 179.
257. *See* Article 37.
258. Barancová and Olšovská 2014, p. 49.

After 2001, subsequent legal amendments were, in general, introducing gradual deregulation, and a move towards more flexible labour relations.[259]

A specific feature of Slovak labour law is its tendency to frequent amendments, validating the argument that the process of labour law transformation is still ongoing in this country. The recent economic and financial crisis has had particular impact on labour law, and has led to certain innovative changes.[260] As explained by respondents in the interviews, the frequent legal amendments of the past two decades have been unsystematic and ad hoc, and involved the political balancing of the interests of employees and employers. The most contentious collective bargaining issue has been extensions of collective agreements – the subject of a number of legal reforms (which will be further discussed in Chapter 6).

3.3 The Czech Republic

The Czech Republic shares its legal foundations with Slovakia. The 1965 Czechoslovakian Labour Code, which in a comprehensive and mandatory manner regulated labour relations, continued to be in force in the post-transitional period, and it was recodified only in 2006.[261]

As has been the case in the other CEE countries, in the Czech Republic the institutionalisation of collective bargaining began in the 1990s, with the Act on Collective Bargaining, which set out the building blocks of a collective bargaining system. This Act remains valid today. The 1990 Act on the Association of Citizens enabled free trade union organisation.[262] Moreover, freedom of association has been officially guaranteed by the Charter of Fundamental Rights of 1992, the provisions of which are of constitutional nature.[263]

Several phases pertinent to labour law development can be distinguished:

(a) The 1965 Labour Code has been used to enter the transitional period. In fact, this Code remained valid until 2006, even though it was amended more than

---

259. Bulla, M., Czíria, L. and Kahancová, M., 'Impact of Legislative Reforms on Industrial Relations and Working Conditions in Slovakia', ILO Background Study, 2013, p. 1 and p. 6. The authors note that these adjustments were mainly visible in a gradual institutionalisation of precarious employment, bargaining decentralisation and limiting the involvement of social partners in policymaking.
260. Likewise, in the area of collective bargaining, the 2011 amendments to the Labour Code allowed opening clauses in the sectoral collective agreements and introduced – for the first time in Slovakia – the quantitative conditions for trade union representativeness at company level. These matters will be in more detail addressed in Chapters 6 and 7. Otherwise, the overview of the legal changes introduced with this amendment of 2011 can be found in Bulla et al., 2013.
261. Pichrt and Štefko 2015, p. 94.
262. This Act remained valid until the recent promulgation of the new Civil Code in 2014; *ibid.*, p. 235.
263. Article 26 of the Charter, which was enacted in 1992. The provisions of the Charter have power of constitutional law in the Czech Republic, *see* Pichrt and Štefko 2015, p. 105. English version of the Charter of Fundamental Rights and Freedoms is available at: http://www.usoud.cz/en/charter-of-fundamental-rights-and-freedoms/ (accessed 1 December 2017).

fifty times.²⁶⁴ One scholar noted that the version of the 1965 Labour Code which was at force in the early 1990s was not radically different from its communist version.²⁶⁵ In fact, in the early 1990s, only those provisions of the Labour Code typical of the communist setting that were regarded as 'embarrassing to the new order' were deleted – for example, such was the principle upon which all people were entitled to a job.²⁶⁶

(b) The major recodification of the Labour Code took place in 2006. The 2006 Labour Code has introduced far-reaching changes to labour law, principally inserting the market rationale and founding labour relations and collective bargaining on the freedom of contract.²⁶⁷

(c) Since 2006, the Labour Code has been amended more than forty times, with a view to gradually introducing flexible working patterns to the Czech legal system.²⁶⁸ The recent economic and financial crisis also induced salient labour law modifications. In the first place, in 2012, a legal amendment was introduced with the objective of facilitating labour market flexibility, and in the area of collective bargaining it was significant in curbing the trade union position at company level.²⁶⁹

As the previous observations demonstrated, Czech and Slovak laws share common features, due to their common heritage anchored in the 1965 Labour Code and the 1991 Act on Collective Bargaining. While the legal foundations of collective bargaining were postulated in both countries early in transition, the actual function and scope of collective agreements depended on numerous Labour Code changes in the subsequent decades. As is the case in Slovakia, labour law in the Czech Republic has a tendency to frequent change. And, as the respondents explained in the interviews, the changes made to the legal framework were done so in an ad hoc and unsystematic fashion, involving frequent balancing of the interests of employers and employees.

3.4 Poland

In communist Poland, the practice of collective bargaining was not far reaching. Collective agreements had been concluded only in a limited number of enterprises, and they had limited scope, because most aspects of work and employment were regulated by statutory rules in a coercive and mandatory fashion.²⁷⁰ The nature of collective

---

264. According to Pichrt and Štefko 2015, *ibid.*, p. 94.
265. Hager, M.M., 'Constructing a New Liberal Capitalism: Czechoslovakian Labor Law in Transition', *American University International Law Review*, 1992, vol. 7, no. 3, p. 504.
266. *Ibid.*, pp. 504–505, citing the 1965 Labour Code.
267. According to Pichrt and Štefko 2015, pp. 94–95. This Labour Code entered into force in 2007.
268. Pichrt and Štefko 2015, p. 94; Myant, M., 'Trade Unions in the Czech Republic', Report 115, Brussels, ETUI, 2010, p. 17.
269. *See* Verveková, S., 'The Case of the Czech Republic' in I. Guardiancich (ed.), *Recovering from the Crisis through Social Dialogue in the new EU Member States: the Case of Bulgaria, the Czech Republic, Poland and Slovenia*, Budapest, ILO, 2012a, pp. 58–59.
270. Sewerynski, M., 'Development of the Collective Bargaining System in Poland after the Second World War', *Comparative Labour Law Journal*, 1993, vol. 14, pp. 442–462.

bargaining was not autonomous, as the content of collective accords had to conform to the economic policies and plans issued along with the government regulations.[271]

In comparison with the other three countries, the Polish example is specific in that certain legal developments that had occurred in the 1980s paved the way for the forthcoming events. In fact, labour law transformation began officially earlier than in the other CEE countries. In 1980, the trade union movement 'Solidarity' was formed, subsequently playing a central role in the process of transition.[272] The first trade union provisions were adopted under the Act on Trade Unions in 1982, almost a decade before the other three CEE countries.[273] Laws regulating the state-owned enterprises were adopted in the 1980s. These provisions were prominent for establishing foothold for the upcoming decentralisation of industrial relations in the post-transitional context, by emphasising the importance of plant level standard setting. Likewise, from 1982, state enterprises were allowed to fix wages, initially, unilaterally via decisions of the plant management, but after 1984 through negotiated agreements at the plant level.[274] These plant level agreements, however, were not fully autonomous, because they were subject to approval by the 'founding organs' of the state enterprise.[275] Another law was passed in 1986 introducing two-level collective bargaining at branch and plant level. However, the collective agreements concluded pursuant to these legal provisions were not considered fully autonomous either. They had to conform to a set of governmental resolutions, and their provisions could have been more advantageous to employees only if expressly allowed by the law.[276]

As in the other three CEE countries, the legal transformation began with laws enabling free and voluntary collective bargaining being promulgated in the 1990s. In addition to the 1982 Act on Trade Unions (replaced by the 1991 Act on Trade Unions), the establishment of employers' associations was enabled by the 1991 Act on Organisation of Employers. The 1974 Labour Code, even though it was amended a number of times, has remained the main source of labour law in the post-transitional context. Section XI of the Labour Code, postulating collective bargaining freedoms was laid down in 1994.[277] The 1974 Labour Code has not been recodified since. The collective

---

271. Ibid., pp. 450–451.
272. The role of Solidarity in transitional transformation has been particularly the focus of work of David Ost, see Ost, D., *Defeat of Solidarity: Anger and Politics in Postcommunist Europe*, Cornell, Cornell University Press, 2005; Ost, D., *Solidarity and the Politics of Anti-Politics: Opposition and Reform in Poland Since 1968*, Philadelphia, Temple University Press, 1990. Also, see Paczynska, A., *State, Labor, and the Transition to a Market Economy – Egypt, Poland, Mexico, and the Czech Republic*, Pennsylvania, The Pennsylvania State University Press, 2009, pp. 48–55; Paczynska, A., 'Confronting Change: Labor, State, and Privatisation' *Review of International Political Economy*, 2007, vol. 14, no. 2, pp. 333–356.
273. The rationale behind the 1982 Act was rather peculiar. The government actually aimed to banish the operation of trade union Solidarity because of its revolutionary aspirations. However, this law allowed the establishment of new trade unions at the workplace, in a belief their establishment would not be harmful for the communist regime; as explained by Sewerynski 1993, pp. 452–460.
274. Ibid., p. 458.
275. Ibid., p. 459.
276. Ibid., p. 460.
277. Sewerynski, M., 'Toward a New Codification of Polish Labour Law', *Comparative Labour Law and Policy Journal*, 2004a, vol. 26, p. 58.

Chapter 3: The Genesis and Positioning of Collective Agreement

bargaining framework anchored in Chapter XI of the Labour Code, however, has remained largely unchanged since 1994. As is the case with the other CEE countries, the function and scope of collective agreements developed in line with the numerous Labour Code amendments.

4 THE EMANCIPATION OF COLLECTIVE AGREEMENTS IN CEE

The previous section underlined that during the communist era the regulatory role of collective bargaining was marginal and the collective agreements were not fully autonomous, as their power and substance was predefined and limited by statutory labour law and administrative regulation. With the insertion of the principles of free and voluntary collective bargaining, the transformation of labour law involved the task of remodelling collective agreements. In order to become autonomous instruments of regulation, collective agreements had to widen their substantive scope, essential so that collective agreements could regulate far more substantive matters than in the communist period. At the same time, becoming autonomous instruments of regulation was vital for enabling collective agreements to perform far more functions than in the previous pre-1990s period. In turn, this was necessary to accommodate market requirements. It has already been explained in Chapter 1 that the tendency of modern collective agreements is to perform several functions; for example, to be instruments of adaptability or to allow employees to participate in policy making.[278] At the same time, a correlating tendency of statutory law in Europe, also mentioned in Chapter 1, is to become 'devoid of substantive provisions and to be supplemented by procedural rules designed to guarantee right to collective bargaining'.[279] Thus, this study understands the process of collective agreements becoming autonomous sources of regulation from the pre- to post-1990s as their 'emancipation'.

In order to assess to what extent such emancipation has actually occurred in the four CEE countries, it is essential to look at: (1) changes in the legal nature of collective agreements; and (2) changes in the relationship between collective agreements and statutory labour law.

4.1 Collective Agreements: Defining the Legal Nature

The aim of this section is to explore how the legal nature of collective agreements in CEE has changed in the past decades. Under the previous communist systems, the state was the primary regulator of working life and labour law had a pronounced public law character. It is therefore relevant to ask whether labour law and collective agreements lost their public law nature and if they became connected to the private law sphere.

---

278. Bruun, N., 'The Autonomy of Collective Agreement' in R. Blanpain (ed.), *Collective Bargaining, Discrimination, Social Security and the European Integration*, Bulletin of Comparative Labour Relations, no. 48, The Hague, Kluwer Law International, 2003, p. 9. *See* Chapter 1, section 4.3.
279. Supiot, A., *Beyond Employment: Changes in Work and the Future of Labour Law in Europe*, Oxford, Oxford University Press, 2001, p. 98.

Comparative labour law in Europe provides no single answer as to whether labour laws and collective agreements should have private or public law nature. In some countries, collective agreements have a prevailing private law character, such as in the UK, Scandinavian countries and Italy, while in France, Spain and Belgium these agreements belong to the realm of public law.[280] German law considers collective agreements to be mixed private and public instruments.[281]

The legal scholarship provides no single answer either to the question of the legal nature of labour law and collective agreements, although it is often underlined that collective agreements have at least some public law features. In a seminal explanation by Fahlbeck, collective agreements are accorded an essentially private contractual nature, but enriched with public law qualities.[282] The public law character of collective agreement is most pronounced when it comes to legally extending powers of collective agreement,[283] but, even without it, collective agreements have a certain public law quality by virtue of the fact they may cover large percentages of employees in the labour market.[284] At the same time, the legal scholarship emphasises the importance of the autonomy of labour law. Likewise, Freedland notes that to be functional, labour law should 'evolve and operate as an independent subsystem of the general legal system within which it is located'.[285] On the other hand, it is emphasised that the autonomy is not absolute, given that labour law intersects with the other legal disciplines (such as contract law).[286]

When examining the current CEE labour laws one can note the following. In contrast to the pronounced public law nature that had pertained previously under the communist system, the current frameworks of the four countries stipulate that private law applies to labour law matters when the latter contains no regulation on the subject. This provision can be found in labour laws of all four countries. What can be inferred, therefore, is that that labour law occupies a space distinct from private law, but at the same time, it intersects with it. Yet, the process of reconnecting labour law to private law roots has been contentious in some CEE countries. In the Czech Republic and Slovakia provision of this kind has been the result of the process taking place over the past two decades, involving a gradual disconnection of labour law from the public sphere and its reconnection to the sphere of private law. In *Slovakia*, this process was embodied in a separation between the provisions of Labour Code and Civil Code. Only

---

280. Bruun 2003, p. 3.
281. Ibid.
282. Fahlbeck 1987, p. 270.
283. The legal possibility of extending the powers of concluded collective agreements to the entire sector or economy, otherwise practised by most European countries, will be with respect to the four countries in more details assessed in Chapter 6.
284. Fahlbeck 1987, p. 270.
285. Freedland, M., 'Otto Kahn-Freund, the Contract of Employment and the Autonomy of Labour Law' in A. Bogg, C. Costello, A.C.L. Davies and J. Prassl (eds), *The Autonomy of Labour Law*, Oxford, Hart Publishing, 2015, p. 31. On autonomy, *see also* Lord Wedderburn, 'Labour Law: From Here to Autonomy?', *Industrial Law Journal*, 1987, vol. 16, no. 1, pp. 1–29.
286. Freedland, M. and Kountouris, N., *The Legal Construction of Personal Work Relations*, Oxford, Oxford Monographs on Labour Law, 2011, p. 62; Collins, H. 'Contractual Autonomy' in A. Bogg, C. Costello, A.C.L. Davies and J. Prassl (eds), *The Autonomy of Labour Law*, Oxford, Hart Publishing, 2015, pp. 45–71.

Chapter 3: The Genesis and Positioning of Collective Agreement

in 2001 was the Labour Code to some extent reconnected to the Civil Code, by establishing a relationship based on subsidiarity.[287] Under this principle, the Civil Code provisions are applied whenever matters are not regulated by the Labour Code. In the *Czech Republic*, the discussion about the relationship between private law and labour law has been the most contentious of the four countries. As in the other CEE countries, the two branches of laws were completely separate in the pre-1990s period, but the gradual process of their reconnection began only in 2006. Firstly, the relationship between the two sets of laws was based on the principle of delegation in 2006. Pursuant to this principle, the provisions of the Civil Code applied only when expressly stipulated in the Labour Code.[288] After 2008, following a Constitutional Court judgment, the relationship was redefined on the basis of principle of *subsidiarity*, according to which the Civil Code rules apply whenever matters are not regulated by the Labour Code.[289] This principle was eventually inserted into the Civil Code in 2014.[290] The Slovak and Czech cases demonstrate something striking: the beginning of the process of (re)connecting labour law to private law came more than a decade after the official start of the transition process. At the same time, these two countries demonstrate the gradual and contentious nature of this process which was clearly driven by legacies of the predominantly public nature of labour laws in the previous pre-1990s setting.

Furthermore, the definition and legal nature of collective agreement is conceived similarly in all four countries, and in a rather broad way. The statutory legal definitions in the four CEE countries present collective agreements through their parties by specifying that they can be concluded by trade unions and employers' associations or employers. As observed by Casale, such understanding of collective agreements is widespread in CEE. Casale also noted that such understanding largely corresponds to the ILO definition of collective agreement:

> The term collective agreement means all agreements in writing regarding working conditions and terms of employment concluded between an employer, a group of employers or one or more employers' organisations, on the one hand, and one or more representative workers' organisations, or, in the absence of such organisations, the representatives of the workers duly elected and authorized by them in accordance with national laws and regulations, on the other.[291]

At the same time, what can be noted is that the CEE collective agreements have a legal basis in the general provisions of private law. More precisely, the legal scholarship in the four countries provides a similar understanding of the legal nature of collective agreements, which, in the end, have lost their predominant public nature and transitioned into an instrument legally anchored in private law. It is also possible to claim that collective agreements have some public law elements. Likewise, the

---
287. Barancová and Olšovská 2014, pp. 28–29.
288. Pichrt and Štefko 2015, p. 37.
289. *Ibid.*, pp. 37–39.
290. *Ibid.*, pp. 37–39.
291. ILO Recommendation concerning Collective Agreements, No 91, 1951; *see* Casale, G., 'Evolution and Trends in Industrial Relations in Central and Eastern European Countries', *The International Journal of Comparative Labour Law and Industrial Relations*, 2003, vol. 19, no. 1, p. 21.

statutory legal rules afford the legally binding status of the normative parts of collective agreements (which stipulate rules and conditions for work) to its parties.[292] In some views, the normative parts of collective agreements are even elevated to the status of a source of law for the subjects to whom these agreements apply.[293]

4.2 The Scope of Collective Bargaining Freedom

This chapter has so far demonstrated that collective agreements were entrenched in the realm of public law in the previous communist setting, and that transition involved the reconnection of labour law to the sphere of private law. It will be the aim of this section to provide some thoughts on how this transition reshaped the relationship between collective agreement and statutory legal regulation as two distinct, yet interlinked sources of standard setting for work and employment, while taking into account that these topics will be more deeply explored in subsequent chapters. There are two elements that are relevant for the discussion: (a) determination of the extent to which the substantive scope of collective agreements has widened in the past two decades, allowing collective agreements to regulate matters that had been in the hands of the state in the pre-1990s period; (b) understanding how the principle of collective autonomy is inserted in CEE. These two elements will be respectively discussed in the following sections.

4.2.1 *Widening the Substantive Scope of Collective Agreement*

Being overwhelmingly detailed and mostly regulating terms and conditions of work in a mandatory manner, the communist laws did not provide much substantive scope for autonomous regulation by collective agreements. Widening the substantive scope of collective agreements so that they can regulate matters that had been the subject of state regulation during communist period was a hallmark process in post-transitional labour law transformation. At the same time, this process was essential to facilitate the institutionalisation narrative and the market narrative of labour law transformation.[294] Enabling social partners to regulate matters as they wish is obviously an emanation of a free and voluntary system of collective bargaining and is a step in facilitating the institutionalisation of industrial relations. At the same time, broadening the scope of collective bargaining is a necessary prerequisite for facilitating the market narrative, allowing collective agreements to go beyond the role which had been assigned to them in the communist setting and to develop new and wider market-friendly set of

---

292. Swiatkowski however called for clearer regulation of collective agreements within the Polish constitution, see Swiatkowski, A.M., 'Are the Post-Socialists' Current Collective Bargaining Procedures Effective as a Means to Implement European Labour Law in Poland?', *Tilburg Foreign Law Review*, 2002, vol. 10, p. 175. On the other countries, see Vodovnik and Korpič-Horvat 2015, p. 286; Pichrt and Štefko 2015, p. 41; Barancová and Olšovská 2014, p. 193.
293. Hajn, Z. and Mitrus, L., 'Poland' in R. Blanpain and F. Hendrickx (eds), *International Encyclopaedia for Labour Law and Industrial Relations*, The Hague, Kluwer Law International, 2016, p. 52; Pichrt and Štefko 2015, p. 41.
294. The two narratives were presented in section 2.2 of this chapter.

functions.²⁹⁵ In this respect, it should be underlined that the ILO system of rules contains no specific instructions on what the collective agreements should look like. The ILO in principle affords wide substantive scope to collective agreements, which may, in the first place regulate terms and conditions of work and employment, as well as provisions regulating the relationship between employers and trade unions.²⁹⁶ At the same time, the ILO framework excludes very few matters from the scope of collective agreements, such as those relating to the management of enterprises.²⁹⁷

As the following comparative analysis demonstrates, broadening the substantive scope of collective agreements has been a long and gradual process in CEE:

(a) *The Slovenian 2006 Act on Collective Agreements* does not contain legal restrictions about matters that can be covered by collective agreements. However, this bargaining freedom is a result of the gradual processes of the past two decades. The previous sections have already demonstrated that the Slovenian collective agreements that were concluded in the 1990s were not fully voluntary, given that for a long period of time they retained a mandatory nature.²⁹⁸ It is only the above mentioned 'third generation of collective agreements',²⁹⁹ concluded pursuant to the 2006 Act on Collective Agreements, that emanated from free and voluntary bargaining. However, the tendency of the law remains to suggest certain matters to be regulated by collective agreements (in this sense, the collective agreements have a role of implementing statutory legal rules).³⁰⁰

(b) In *Slovakia,* the scope of bargaining freedom was subject to gradual widening. The 1965 Labour Code had an overwhelming regulatory style that had consisted of predominantly coercive provisions, in this way restricting the regulatory scope of collective agreements.³⁰¹ The provisions introduced at the beginning of the 1990s amended the Labour Code's provisions and to some extent managed to soften its coercive and mandatory nature.³⁰² However, the 1965 Labour Code remained valid until the new recodification

---

295. *See* section 4.3 of Chapter 1 on the major elements of discussions regarding the functions of collective agreements in the context of the debates over the modernisation of labour law in Europe.
296. According to the following ILO Conventions: Right to Organise and Collective Bargaining Convention No 98, 1949; Labour Relations (Public Service) Convention No 151, 1978; Collective Bargaining Convention No 154, 1981; ILO Recommendation concerning Collective Agreements, No 91, 1951; as reported by Gernigon, B., Odero, A. and Guido, H., 'ILO Principles Concerning Collective Bargaining' *International Labour Review*, 2000b, vol. 139, no. 1, pp. 39-40.
297. *Ibid.*
298. As explained in section 3.1; *see* Končar 1996, p. 169 and pp. 157-159.
299. *See* section 3.1 of this chapter.
300. Vodovnik and Korpič-Horvat 2015, pp. 286-287.
301. Barancová 1996, p. 139.
302. *Ibid.*, p. 139.

in 2001, when social partners were enabled to negotiate on any matters they saw fit.[303] Subsequent legal amendments further liberalised labour market relations.[304]

(c) In the *Czech Republic*, the scope of collective agreements has been also shaped in distinctive phases. The 1965 Labour Code marginalised the role of collective agreements by setting mandatory and extensive statutory provisions on work and employment. Collective bargaining was possible only on matters explicitly allowed for in the statutory provisions.[305] The 1991 Act on Collective Bargaining formally introduced collective bargaining freedoms. Nevertheless, the practice of collective bargaining was at the time still overwhelmed by the mandatory provisions of the 1965 Labour Code,[306] containing extensive protection of labour and work. It was only the 2006 Labour Code that formally liberalised the scope of bargaining. The principle of 'anything that is not expressly forbidden by the law is permitted' had been introduced with the 2006 Code, allowing social partners to exercise collective bargaining to a much larger extent.[307] However, even though the formal insertion of this principle represented a major step forward, its practical implication was mitigated by still mandatory and extensive regulatory style of the 2006 Labour Code.[308] The interviews with Czech social partners revealed that the content of collective agreements is still majorly predetermined by the extensive regulatory style of the Labour Code provisions.

(d) In *Poland*, as the interviews revealed, the social partners still consider the Labour Code to be fairly extensive. As explained throughout interviews, this is a major reason for employers not to enter into collective bargaining. The comprehensive regulatory style of statutory provisions is to be considered something of a legal remnant from the communist period, since the 1974 Labour Code originally introduced fairly mandatory and coercive provisions.[309] In the communist era, freedom of bargaining was heavily restricted – the agreements could contain more favourable provisions than the Labour Code only when authorised by the law or justified by the specific circumstances of the given sector or profession.[310] Moreover, the concluded agreements needed a registration and authorisation from the ministry

---

303. Barancová and Olšovská 2014, p. 49; Czíria, L., *2002 Annual Review for Slovakia*, Dublin, Eurofound, 2003c.
304. Barancová and Olšovská 2014, pp. 49–51.
305. Pichrt and Štefko 2015, p. 94.
306. As Pichrt and Štefko note, *ibid.*, the Labour Code was amended around fifty times between 1965 and 2006, when it was finally replaced with the new Labour Code.
307. *Ibid.*, p. 95.
308. Pichrt and Štefko 2015, p. 95, note that the 2006 Code was drafted in a way to combine high level of protection for employees via mandatory norms with the enhanced collective bargaining freedoms.
309. Sewerynski 1993, p. 444, notes that in the communist period, following the 1986 amendment to the Labour Code, the collective bargaining was limited to regulating specific conditions of work for a given sector or profession.
310. *Ibid.*, p. 460.

responsible for labour affairs.[311] The legal framework emerging at the beginning of the 1990s retained the mandatory and coercive regulatory style of the 1974 Labour Code. The 1994 Labour Code liberalised the scope of collective bargaining, but it was only in 2000 that the law introduced provisions guaranteeing social partners' freedom to self-regulate on any matter they see fit.[312] However, the Polish social partners claimed during the interviews that the Labour Code provisions still comprehensively regulate areas of work and employment, and this limits the incentives of social partners to engage in collective bargaining.

As the comparative analysis demonstrates, the expansion of the scope of collective agreements took place in each country with a national-specific dynamic. However, there are two distinct, yet interlinked phases that must be carefully delineated and accounted for: (a) insertion of legal rules officially recognising the rights of social partners to conclude collective agreements on any matters they see fit; (b) the dynamic of de facto liberalisation of the substantive scope of collective bargaining. De facto liberalisation involves gradual transformation of statutory regulation style from the predominantly mandatory style to the one which postulates minimum rights and further encourages collective bargaining by virtue of auxiliary legislation (the latter explained in Chapter 1).

As the national data in this section demonstrated, (a) formal insertion of the legal rules took place in the four countries more than a decade after the onset of the transitional period. As the comparative data show, the provisions annulling bargaining restrictions of these kinds were introduced in Slovenia and the Czech Republic only in 2006 and in Poland and Slovakia at the beginning of the 2000s. Thus, throughout the 1990s, the social partners in the four countries could not freely determine the substance of collective agreements. To determine the exact extent of de facto liberalisation (b), it would be necessary to engage in all-encompassing comparative consideration of individual labour law provisions in the four countries with a view to determining the extent of the mandatory and coercive regulatory style of the legal provisions. Given that this task would go well beyond the current research limits, it is only possible to rely on the observations of the interviewees, as well as existing knowledge in the scholarship. Both underline the fairly comprehensive regulatory style of the legislation. As highlighted during the interviews in Poland, the Polish Labour Code from 1974 (as amended) seems to be particularly extensive, containing fairly elaborated regulations on many aspects of work (working time, telework, remuneration and many other items). A similar observation was reported by the Czech interviewees. The interviewees have explained that such regulatory style can be interpreted as a factor rendering collective bargaining difficult, since employers do not see any advantage in

---

311. Florek, L., 'Problems and Dilemmas of Labour Relations in Poland', *Comparative Labour Law Journal*, 1992, vol. 13, p. 118.
312. Hajn, Z., 'Collective Labour Agreements and Contracts of Employment in Polish Labour Law', in M. Sewerynski (ed.), *Collective Agreements and Individual Contracts of Employment*, The Hague, Kluwer Law International, 2003, pp. 192–202; Swiatkowski 2002, p. 179.

engaging in negotiations. Among the four countries, it is the Slovenian legal regulations that seem to be the least detailed. As explained in this section, Slovenian legal rules are also unique in the fact they often do not contain precise regulation of elements of work and employment, instead suggesting alternative regulation by collective agreements.

4.2.2 Collective Autonomy

Collective autonomy is an emanation of collective bargaining freedoms vital for rendering distinct regulatory space to collective agreements from statutory labour law. The notion of collective autonomy was seminally coined by Sinzeimher, who claimed that equal opportunities in the area of social and economic conditions can only be achieved through collective self-determination, that is, through collective bargaining between the organisations of employers and employees.[313] However, collective autonomy, even though vital for shaping national labour laws, has been differently understood in European law. Despite obvious differences in understanding and defining the concept,[314] the country variations essentially safeguard the autonomy of social partners to conclude collective agreements and to negotiate and execute agreements.[315] The notion of autonomy has also been inserted into ILO architecture, first and foremost in Convention No 87, under which the exercise of the right to collective bargaining is subject to independence of trade unions and lack of interference from the public authorities.[316]

From an analytical point of view, the introduction of collective autonomy in CEE can be understood as the process of opening and guarding the regulatory space of collective agreements as autonomous sources of regulation. The exercise of collective autonomy requires space for the production of negotiated norms. Thus, collective autonomy implies that collective agreements should be viewed as distinct sources of standard setting, enjoying a substantial level of autonomy from the statutory legal rules. Corollary to the process of introducing collective autonomy into CEE is the process of building the *auxiliary* role of the state, which was explained in Chapter 1 (section 4.3). This has been succinctly underlined by Sciarra:

> The autonomy of a collective bargaining system is measured comparatively in relation to the degree of incisiveness exhibited by statute law, whether as an instrument of support for voluntary negotiating systems or as a substitutive regulatory instrument, or one fulfilling a purely alternative and subsidiary role with respect to solutions freely adopted by the collective actors. It was a central concept in the development of European labour law during the immediate post-war period, around which the rules of democratic systems for the

---

313. As interpreted by Le Friant, M., 'Collective Autonomy: Hope or Danger?', *Comparative Labour Law and Policy Journal*, 2013, vol. 34, p. 631.
314. The overview of European practice has been provided by Le Friant, *ibid.*, pp. 627–654.
315. Bruun 2003, pp. 1–2.
316. ILO Freedom of Association and Protection of the Right to Organise Convention No 87, 1948, see Gernigon, B., Odero, A. and Guido, H., 'Collective Bargaining' in *Fundamental Rights at Work and International Labour Standards*, Geneva, ILO, 2000a, p. 23.

representation of interests were constructed and barriers against legislative intervention violating freedom of association were erected.[317]

But how can collective agreements relate to statutory law? According to Supiot, collective agreements typically replace, prolong, develop or implement legislation.[318] It is clear from the quoted statement by Sciarra that statutory law can play different roles in relation to collective agreements; to reiterate, it can be an instrument of support, a substitutive regulatory instruments, or an alternative and subsidiary instrument for collective bargaining.

The legal and constitutional provisions of the four selected countries have formally recognised rights to collective bargaining and freedom of association early in the transitional period. Collective agreements, in that sense, have been recognised as autonomous sources of standard setting since the very beginning of the transformative processes. This represented a first step towards the institutionalisation of collective bargaining. Yet, the brief analysis in this chapter can provide no further recourse as to how collective autonomy was implemented in the legal system. What the previous section (4.2.2) demonstrated is that statutory labour law still exhibits considerable level of what Sciarra labels as 'incisiveness' into the collective agreements in the sense of predefining their substantive scope. But further assessment of the relationship between collective agreements and statutory laws requires more detailed exploration of the legal framework for collective agreements, which will be performed in the second part of this study.

5 CONCLUSION

This chapter has demonstrated that the labour laws of the four CEE countries have not only been exposed to a similar sets of factors and trigger events in the past twenty-five years, but also that the process of development of the legal framework for collective bargaining has had certain common or, at least, similar traits across the countries. While the points discussed in this chapter will be further elaborated in the second part of the study, there are some common traits and some important remarks that can be highlighted in relation to the two research questions.

In the first place, the *institutionalisation* narrative has played a prominent role in facilitating the formal adoption of legal provisions that formed the building blocks of the collective bargaining systems in the early transition period. In the early 1990s, the four CEE countries adopted basic constitutional and legal provisions guaranteeing collective bargaining and freedom of association, alongside the first labour codes, as a first formal prerequisite for the institutionalisation of collective bargaining. However, the institutionalisation of collective bargaining is a longer and more detailed process going beyond the formal and declaratory acceptance of major collective bargaining freedoms, and this was a process which took place gradually over years. This process

---

317. Sciarra, S., 'The Evolution of Collective Bargaining: Observations on a Comparison in the Countries of the European Union', *Comparative Labour Law and Policy Journal*, 2007, vol. 29, p. 7.
318. Supiot 2001, p. 98.

of gradual institutionalisation was facilitated by *legacies and path-dependencies*. This chapter demonstrated that there were some common legacies that predetermined the path in all four countries, but also some legacies which were country-specific.

The common legacy, in the first place, has been the all-encompassing regulatory scope of communist statutory labour law, which affected the substantive scope of collective agreements in the post-transitional period. As argued in section 4.2 of this chapter, the collective agreements' substantive scope has been gradually liberalised in the four countries. This point has been the most blatantly demonstrated by the example of three generations of collective agreements in Slovenia. At the same time, it is striking that the gradual liberalisation has been a complex two-phase process – in the first place, involving the insertion of the statutory legal provision allowing bargaining on any matters social partners see fit, and in the second place, involving the relaxation of the mandatory and coercive style of statutory labour law. The first phase was accomplished in the four countries more than a decade after the onset of the transitional process, but the accomplishment of the second phase is still questionable, as the Polish case exemplifies best. Another legacy shared by two of the countries examined – Slovakia and the Czech Republic, was the slow reconnection of labour law from public to private law.

Next to common legacies, one may also observe *country-specific legacies* which were vital for facilitating the institutionalisation narrative. In Slovenia, the legacy of self-management was key factor shaping the post-transitional industrial relations.[319] In Poland, the 1980s legislation played vital role in predetermining the shape of trade union decentralisation in post-transitional terms.[320]

Another significant trait in the four countries, has been the momentum with which the legal reforms took place and it demonstrates slow institutionalisation and the strong role of legacies. As inferred from section 2, whilst the first 'modern' legal provisions were adopted in the early 1990s, no substantial legal reforms took place in any of the four countries before the mid-2000s. Moreover, except for Slovenia, which entered the transition period with new labour laws, the other three countries were notably 'recycling' their communist-based labour codes for more than a decade after the official start of legal transformation. The most blatant example is Poland, where the (re)codification has never taken place, and the Labour Code originates from 1974, even though it has been modified a number of times.

The comparative findings presented allow some preliminary insights on the two research questions of this study. The significance of these findings for the *first research question* is the following: the substantive scope of collective agreements is somewhat restricted because statutory legal provisions often contain extensive mandatory regulation of conditions of work and employment. This has been particularly exemplified in Poland and the Czech Republic, where the interviewees claimed that social partners are not motivated to engage in collective bargaining on matters which have been already covered in law. The importance for the *second research question* is clear: the

---

319. As underlined by Crowley and Stanojević 2011.
320. As underlined by Sewerynski 1993, pp. 457–462.

institutionalisation of collective bargaining was gradual, with the slow 'emancipation' of collective agreements, which can be attributed to the role of the pre-1990s legacies.

Whether the reason for slow institutionalisation and gradual emancipation of collective agreement can be found in the lack of adequate legal regulation is a different question. The answer to it is deeply embedded in a broader set of issues related to social partners' weaknesses at all bargaining levels and to the lack of a general social dialogue tradition in CEE. It seems that the problem of overwhelming statutory regulation cannot simply be solved by relaxing the statutory regulation and providing a broader scope for collective agreements. This conclusion is amply demonstrated by the statement of the Polish trade union representative during the interview in Warsaw:

> The argument that the Labour Code is extensive is often used by the employers. But, this as such is not an issue. We could agree on making the labour code more flexible, and give more competence to the social partners, but there is one danger. There are a lot of companies which are not unionized. Therefore, who will take the responsibility on the side of employees in these companies?

Another similar statement made by a trade union representative during the interviews in Warsaw depicts the complexity of the processes which give rise to overwhelming state regulation:

> The representatives of employers' associations say that we have such detailed and complicated labour law at national level that there is no space for negotiations. We have detailed regulations on working time, minimum wage and any other issues. They [employers' associations] also say, if trade unions were willing to make the labour law more flexible, they would be much more open to negotiations at the sectoral level. But then the response of trade unions is the following: 'you [employers' associations] want us to make labour law more flexible, so that you might or might not come to negotiate with us about the topics which are exactly the same as those written now in the labour law'. The problem is therefore that the social partners do not trust each other.

The above considerations succinctly confirm Bluhm's finding that CEE countries face a liberalisation dilemma, given that the retreat of the state in these countries can generate the effect of strengthening managerial unilateralism.[321] The two statements made during the interviews fully support these findings: given that the trade unions are too weak, the statutory labour regulation is the only way to guarantee the adequate enforcement of rights. Thus, in this sense, the extensive regulatory style can be also viewed as a way of protecting the position of employees and trade unions. With these arguments in mind, it can be concluded that relaxing the imperative and comprehensive regulatory style can only go hand in hand with ensuring the rights of trade unions and encouraging their activities, particularly at the company level.

---

321. Bluhm, K., 'Resolving Liberalisation Dilemma: Labour Relations in East-Central Europe and the Impact of European Union' in M.A. Moreau and M.E. Blas-López (eds), *Restructuring in the New EU Member States: Social Dialogue, Firms Relocation, and Social Treatment of Restructuring*, Brussels, Peter Lang, 2008, p. 60.

CHAPTER 4
From Accession to the Economic and Financial Crisis: What Role for the EU?

1 INTRODUCTION

The start of the accession process in the 2000s has given a new dimension to the ongoing process of labour law transformation in CEE. From the beginning of the accession process, the EU played an active role in shaping the landscape of social dialogue in the CEE countries, mainly because social dialogue forms part of the *acquis communautaire* which the candidate countries are asked to transpose and implement. Building meaningful industrial relations within a relatively short time span represented a challenge for the CEE countries. It has been argued that EU support was essential to improve social dialogue and the weak organisation of trade unions.[322] The EU's reasons for tackling industrial relations in CEE were manifold. In the first place, on the eve of the 2004 enlargement, the EU faced a question of whether the social and economic dimensions of the CEE countries are compatible with those of the existing EU Member States.[323] The CEE countries that were about to join the EU had a substantially different landscape from the Member States, with lower rates of wages, economic development and labour standards. There was therefore an apprehension that enlargement would bring a regime competition in the EU,[324] by emphasizing deregulatory

---

322. Mailand, M. and Due, J., 'Social Dialogue in Central and Eastern Europe: Present State and Future Development', *European Journal of Industrial Relations*, 2004, vol. 10, no. 2, p. 195; Meardi, G., 'The Trojan Horse for the Americanisation of Europe? Polish Industrial Relations towards the EU', *European Journal of Industrial Relations*, 2002, vol. 8, no. 1, pp. 77-99.
323. Weiss, M., 'Industrial Relations and EU Enlargement' in J.D.R. Craig (ed.), *Globalisation and the Future of Labour Law*, Cambridge, Cambridge University Press, 2006, pp. 169-190.
324. Bohle, D., 'Trade Unions and the Fiscal Crisis of the State', *Warsaw Forum of Economic Sociology*, 2011, vol. 2, no. 1, p. 93.

incentives and 'race to the bottom'. Furthermore, the compatibility with the Member States had been questioned in the area of industrial relations – despite great variations in industrial relations, strong and independent trade unions represent the backbone of the Member States' systems, a feature differentiating the EU from other regions of the world. At the other end of the spectrum, the trade unions in CEE had been suffering from weaknesses inherited from the previous system. Therefore, closing the social 'gap' between the two groups of countries represented an important challenge for the EU. The other reasons for social dialogue in the candidate countries being a concern for the EU, is the fact that the performance of many EU-based mechanisms and policies relies on the functionality of national social dialogue mechanisms.[325] For example, the success of the European social dialogue depends on the capacities of national social partners to be able to engage in the same activities as European social partners or to implement EU-level collective agreements.[326] Also, the successful implementation of a number of EU-led instruments, such as the open method of coordination, rests on the active involvement of national stakeholders, including social partners.[327]

It is questionable to what extent the EU was able to influence the institutionalisation of industrial relations in the candidate countries, given the complex nature of this task, as well as the need to accomplish it in a relatively short time span. More than ten years after the four CEE countries have become Member States, it is time to evaluate how the EU affected social dialogue developments in the candidate countries. An additional incentive to engage in this exercise is provided by the recent economic and financial crisis that has not only tested the collective bargaining mechanisms and labour laws across the EU, but has also led the EU to adopt policy responses that have had repercussions for Member States' industrial relations. Thus, it appears relevant to re-evaluate the EU role in CEE industrial relations, by comparing, contrasting and looking for any possible inconsistencies between its pre-accession and post-crisis approach and influence.

By aiming to deconstruct and evaluate the ways in which the EU affected the development of the legal and institutional framework for collective bargaining in the four countries over the past two decades, the analysis in this chapter contributes towards answering the second research question of this study. This chapter is organised in the following manner. The following section 2 will be devoted to the role of the EU during the accession process in the four CEE countries. Section 3 explores the role of the EU from the perspective of the recent economic and financial crisis, while section 4 compares and contrasts its pre-accession role with its role during the recent crisis period.

---

325. This argument has been particularly advocated by Perez-Solorzano Borragan, N. and Smismans, S., 'The EU and Institutional Change in Industrial Relations in the New Member States' in S. Smismans (ed.), *The European Union and Industrial Relations: New Procedures, New Context*, Manchester, Manchester University Press, 2012, pp. 116–138.
326. Ibid.
327. Ibid.

2 THE EU ACCESSION PROCESS

It has been already mentioned that throughout the accession process, the CEE countries were transposing and implementing the social *acquis,* and that social dialogue represents a part of the accession criteria which candidate countries must fulfil in order to join the EU. The statement that social dialogue represents part of the accession criteria does not fully explain the nature of the EU's role in improving the social dialogue infrastructure in CEE, as there are a few related matters that require further clarification. In the first place, given the limited competence of the EU in the area of social dialogue and, more generally, in social sphere (which will be further clarified in section 2.1), what exactly represents social dialogue as a constituent part of the EU *acquis* is open to question. Also, it remains unclear whether the EU has adequate mechanisms at its disposal to ensure the effective transfer of rules on social dialogue and collective bargaining to the candidate countries. Finally, bearing in mind the great variety in Member States' industrial relations and the variety of national legal arrangements in relation to collective bargaining and collective agreements, it is questionable whether the EU can actually identify a body of rules that can be imposed upon the candidate countries. These are the questions that the following subsections will strive to answer.

In the first place, subsection 2.1 will explore how matters of social dialogue were understood in the context of the accession process, or in other words, what was the *message* which the EU directed towards the candidate countries. To determine the substance of such a message, the analysis will first consider whether there is a unique European social model (ESM) and European model of industrial relations that can be promoted to the candidate countries. After that, closer assessment of how social dialogue is understood in the accession *acquis* will be undertaken. After considering the content of the EU message, it is worth asking how it was presented to the candidate countries. Thus, the analysis in subsection 2.2 explores the mechanisms for its transfer to the candidate countries during the accession process. This analysis will be performed by using the analytical framework of Europeanisation. Finally, the effects of the EU's efforts will be discussed in subsection 2.3.

2.1 The Message of the EU During the Accession Process

2.1.1 *The ESM and the EU Model of Industrial Relations*

To be able to encourage collective bargaining improvements, the EU might ideally be expected to identify a single industrial relations model that the candidate countries could copy or use as a source of inspiration. Yet, the ability of the EU to single out a comprehensive model is contested and should be understood against the background of the great variety of industrial relations, economic and social narratives within the EU Member States. As a matter of fact, discussions about the existence and content of the industrial relations model of the EU arise from more general concerns about the ESM.

The existence and the content of the so-called ESM have been heavily discussed in academic literature and policy debates during the past few decades. Even though this phrase gained increased popularity, these debates have so far been unable to generate a well-defined and clear conceptualisation of the ESM or to link the existing definitions to a set of empirically tested assumptions.[328] The earliest conceptualisations of the ESM originate in the efforts to substantiate the landmark feature distinguishing the EU from the other parts of the world – the specific mix of economic and social policy objectives on which the EU economies rest. Likewise, back in the 1980s, Jacques Delors emphasised the salience of combining economic and social progress in an effort to promote social democratic values in the EU, as a contrast to the other regions in the world.[329] One of the first definitions of the ESM was coined by the European Commission in the White Paper on social policy, which enumerated a set of values such as democracy, personal freedom, social dialogue, equal opportunities for all, adequate social security and solidarity towards the weaker individuals in society.[330] A subsequent contribution came from the European Council which has been emphasizing constituent elements of the ESM since the early 2000s. The first catalogues of such constituent elements were put forward by the Lisbon and the Nice European Council in 2000, as well as by the Barcelona European Council in 2002,[331] including, *inter alia*, elements such as an active and dynamic welfare state, a high level of social protection, the importance of social dialogue, education and good economic performance.[332] The European Council retained a habit in subsequent conclusions of referring to the ESM and to its constituent elements. Nevertheless, the policy efforts described did not generate a clear and undisputable definition of the ESM – there has been no consensus about which elements form the ESM and how to define them.

Nor did academic debates bring a clear-cut definition of the ESM. In the first place, some authors contest the mere existence of the ESM as a model. The ESM is sometimes downgraded to the level of an 'analytical tool'[333] or 'normative vision...of a political project'.[334] Similarly, there are views which underline that the economic and

---

328. This has been particularly underlined by Jepsen, M. and Serrano Pascual, A., 'Introduction' in M. Jepsen and A. Serrano Pascual (eds), *Unwrapping the European Social Model*, Bristol, The Policy Press, 2006a, p. 1.
329. See Jepsen, M., Serrano Pascual, A.S., 'The Concept of the ESM and Supranational Legitimacy-Building', in M. Jepsen and A. Serrano Pascual (eds), *Unwrapping the European Social Model*, Bristol, The Policy Press, 2006b, pp. 25–26.
330. As reported by Jepsen and Serrano Pascual 2006b, p. 26; see European Commission, *White Paper – European Social Policy: A Way Forward for the Union*, COM(1994)333, Luxembourg, Office for Official Publications of the European Commission, 1994.
331. European Council, Presidency Conclusions, Lisbon, 23–24 March 2000; European Council, Presidency Conclusions, Nice, 7–10 December 2000; European Council, Presidency Conclusions, Barcelona, 15–16 March 2002.
332. The detailed overview of elements enlisted by the European Council since the early 2000s can be found in Vaughan-Whitehead, D., 'The European Social Model in Times of Crisis: An Overview' in D. Vaughan-Whitehead (ed.), *The European Social Model in Crisis: Is Europe Losing its Soul?*, Cheltenham, Edward Elgar, 2015, pp. 4–6.
333. Goetschy, J., 'Taking Stock of Social Europe: Is There Such a Thing as a Community Social Model?' in M. Jepsen and A. Serrano Pascual (eds), *Unwrapping the European Social Model*, Bristol, The Policy Press, 2006, and A. Serrano Pascual (eds), l area of the EUts of the EU agenda is particularly visible in the effects of the EU, but in some p. 47.
334. Wincott, D., 'The Idea of the European Social Model: Limits and Paradoxes of Europeanisation', in K. Featherstone and C.M. Radaelli (eds), *The Politics of Europeanisation*, Oxford, Oxford University Press, 2003, p. 280.

social variations among the EU countries preclude formulation of a full-fledged model and that it is only possible to talk about some common elements shared by Member States. For example, according to Schiek, common elements include societal responsibility towards individuals and prevention of distortion of competition.[335] For Goetschy, common elements could be the social values and principles contained in the EU Charter of Fundamental Rights, the EU social law and EU-specific modes of regulation, including collective bargaining.[336] Going one step further, Vaughan-Whitehead attempted to enumerate a catalogue of constituent elements of the ESM, in a fashion which closely resembles the policy attempts of the European Council described above. Likewise, Vaughan-Whitehead defined the ESM as having six key pillars; including improving working conditions, universal and sustainable social protection, inclusive labour markets, strong and well-functioning social dialogue, public services and services of general interest, and finally, social inclusion and social cohesion.[337]

The recent crisis period has additionally challenged the efforts to establish a single definition of the ESM, as it brought deterioration of the social landscape in most of the EU countries, including increased levels of inequality and unemployment. A recent study has therefore marked the ESM as facing an existential crisis, and raised concerns over the legitimacy, rationale and ability of the EU's social policies.[338] With the deterioration of working conditions, wages and social expenditures, Vaughan-Whitehead noted that the ESM rapidly altered its six foundational pillars.[339]

This rather brief overview of otherwise lengthy policy and academic debates demonstrates the vagueness of the concept of the ESM, as well as the lack of its unequivocal understanding. It also demonstrates that it is not possible to talk about a full-fledged and all-encompassing EU social model which could subsume the traits of Member States and be presented as such to the candidate countries. However, given that this section demonstrated that social dialogue has been signified as one of the constituent elements in some of the ESM definitions, it is still valid to ask whether the EU can identify a common understanding of this term in a sufficiently precise manner and present it to the candidate countries. Further clarification on the existence of and the traits of a European model of industrial relations will be needed.

A general view in the literature is that the EU contains no full-fledged comprehensive EU model of industrial relations, and that, at best, only some common elements and features of Member States' industrial relations can be highlighted. Here the most relevant elements of the debate will be presented. In relation to the EU accession process, Meardi, as well as Perez-Solorzano Borragan and Smismans, claimed that the EU contains no coherent normative theory and single industrial

---

335. Schiek, D., 'The EU's Socio-Economic Model(s) and the Crisi(e)s – Any Perspectives?' in D. Schiek (ed.), *EU Economic and Social Model in the Global Crisis*, Farnham, Ashgate, 2013, pp. 3-6.
336. Goetschy 2006, pp. 70-72.
337. Vaughan-Whitehead 2015, pp. 3-11; similar catalogue can be also found in Vaughan-Whitehead, D., *EU Enlargement versus Social Europe? The Uncertain Future of the European Social Model*, Cheltenham, Edward Elgar, 2003.
338. Barnard, C., 'EU Employment Law and the European Social Model: The Past, the Present and the Future', *Current Legal Problems*, 2014, vol. 67, no. 1, pp. 1-39.
339. Vaughan-Whitehead 2015, pp. 15-16.

relations model that can be promoted to the candidate countries.[340] This statement has been underpinned by the evidently different industrial relations in the Member States that are deeply embedded in the country-specific historical context and traditions. It has been argued that, although the EU countries' democratic systems rest on the active role of trade unions and employers' associations in governing social and economic issues, the European systems have developed without a strong theoretical underpinning and without a common ground that can be promoted to the candidate countries.[341] Nonetheless, there are scholars who focused on identifying common features of the Member States' industrial relations. In the early 1990s, Streeck stated that five elements distinguish the EU order of industrial relations from the rest of the world: strong and independent trade unions; public policy support and participation in the tripartite policy arrangement; a high floor of universally defined and publicly secured social rights; the degree of solidaristic wage settings; information, consultation and codetermination at firm level.[342] Nevertheless, in a subsequent evaluation of the five traits, Visser, in a more pessimistic tone, concluded that the EU countries share poor common foundations because the EU policies on these matters largely depend on the interests of national policy makers.[343] Furthermore, despite recognising that Member States' models differ substantially, Marginson and Sisson claimed that it is possible to identify the main contours of European industrial relations model.[344] These contours consist of the three distinct features which delineate EU industrial relations from the other systems in the world – the high degree of interest organisation on both employer and employee side, the legally established rights of the weaker party in the employment relationship, and the multi-employer structure of collective bargaining (the latter, however, does not exist in the UK).[345] An effort to identify a model that can be promoted to the candidate countries has been made by Lafoucriere and Green. As Chapter 1 already explained, Lafoucriere and Green constructed the *concerted model of regulation*. Claiming that this model represents an intrinsic part of the ESM, the authors have developed it around the idea that the participation of social partners is the major driver of economic and social progress.[346] With this in mind, the authors claimed that the concerted model of regulation:

---

340. Perez-Solorzano Borragan and Smismans 2012; Meardi, G., 'More Voice after More Exit? Unstable Industrial Relations in Central Eastern Europe', *Industrial Relations Journal*, 2007, vol. 38, no. 6, p. 504.
341. Perez-Solorzano Borragan and Smismans 2012, p. 120.
342. Streeck W., 'National Diversity, Regime Competition, and Institutional Dead-Lock: Problems in Forming a European Industrial Relations System', *Journal of Public Policy*, 1992, vol. 12, pp. 301–330.
343. Visser, J., 'The Five Pillars of the European Social Model of Labor Relations' in J. Beckert, B. Ebbinghaus, A. Hassel and P. Manow (eds), *Transformationen des Kapitalismus: Schriftenreihe aus dem Max Planck Institut für Gesellschaftsforschung Köln*, Frankfurt a/M: Campus Verlag, Band 57, 2006, p. 332.
344. Marginson, P. and Sisson, K., *European Integration and Industrial Relations: Multi-Level Governance in the Making*, Basingstoke, Palgrave Macmillan, 2006, pp. 28–53.
345. *Ibid.*, pp. 40–42.
346. Lafoucriere, C. and Green, R., 'Social Dialogue as a Regulatory Mode of the ESM: Some Empirical Evidence from the New Member States' in M. Jepsen and A. Serrano Pascual (eds), *Unwrapping the European Social Model*, Bristol, The Policy Press, 2006, pp. 234–235.

focuses more on 'process' than on 'content' and represents a move away from heavy general government legislation, insofar as it provides only a lowest common denominator for all sectors of the economy, in order to achieve a more appropriate sector/plant-based concerted regulation.[347]

Yet, except for identifying the crucial role of social partners, Lafoucriere and Green have not proposed further description and have not provided elements of their proposed model. Also, the authors have not suggested how this model can be transferred to the candidate countries. These authors have merely directed attention to the fact that a lack of EU definition of the basic concepts, such as autonomous social dialogue and collective agreement, can be unhelpful for candidate countries that have no developed social dialogue culture and are expecting guidance from the EU.[348] As explained in Chapter 1, the concerted model of regulation is complementary to the normative model proposed in this study, particularly as both subsume the common traits of industrial relations among the Member States. *The* model of articulated multi-employer bargaining of this study, however, has departed from the concerted model of regulation by proposing further analytical traits in an effort to describe the legal framework underpinning multi-level collective bargaining system.

The brief overview of literature demonstrates that while it is not possible to claim the existence of a comprehensive model of industrial relations at the EU level, Member States do have certain common traits that could be eventually promoted to the candidate countries. To further deconstruct the 'message' that the EU delivers to the candidate countries during the accession process, one has to take first a closer look at the legal and institutional framework of the EU and the understanding of social dialogue afforded by the EU within the accession *acquis*. After that, one can look into the mechanisms employed by the EU to transfer these messages to the candidate countries.

2.1.2 *Social Acquis Related to the Accession Process*

The EU has limited competences in the social sphere, which shares with the Member States.[349] The EU may not fully legislate in this area, and there are some areas which have been explicitly excluded from its legislative competences; pay, freedom of association, strike and lockouts.[350] Nevertheless, in the areas where the EU may not legislate, it may promote coordination of social policies among the Member States.[351] During the accession process, the candidate countries are asked to transpose and implement the social *acquis*. Anchored in the Treaties, the EU social *acquis* consists of several components. In the first place, in those areas where the EU has competences to legislate, the social *acquis* refers to *hard law*. This includes an array of secondary legislation on matters such as health and safety, antidiscrimination, information and

---

347. *Ibid.*, p. 234.
348. *Ibid.*, pp. 250-251.
349. Article 4 TFEU.
350. Article 153(5) TFEU.
351. Article 156 TFEU.

consultation rights. Next to this, the EU social *acquis* has a *soft law* component that includes various instruments enabling coordination of national policies in the areas which otherwise belong to the national competences. Given that EU law has limited competence in the member' states social sphere (Article 156 TFEU), soft law coordination of national policies is encouraged by the EU.[352] At the same time, the EU encourages social dialogue at the EU level, which can, in principle, be classified as *soft law*: the Treaties allow social partners at the EU level to reach EU collective agreements, which would normally be implemented by social partners in Member States (Articles 154-155 TFEU). Nevertheless, European social dialogue may also have *hard law* characteristics, because the collective agreements negotiated at the EU level can become legally binding, if endorsed by the Council in the form of directives.[353]

In a nutshell, the EU cannot legislate in the areas of collective bargaining, where its powers of intervention are limited, but it may support and complement the activities of the Member States in matters related to collective bargaining.[354] The result is that social *acquis* contains no closer identification of concepts pertinent to collective bargaining at the national level – the definition of major concepts, such as collective bargaining and collective agreements, remains the province of the Member State traditions. EU law, equally, contains no closer specification or suggestion as to the levels at which collective bargaining should take place in the Member States, even though most of the European countries' industrial relations (with the notable exception of the UK) hone multi-employer bargaining infrastructure. However, the principles associated with collective bargaining and social dialogue, upon which the national industrial relations systems rest, are principally protected by EU law because they closely reflect democratic and pluralistic values.[355] Collective bargaining and autonomy of social partners are essential elements of freedom of association, as

---

352. For more insights on the debate about the role of 'soft law' in constructing EU social policies and on its application in the Member States, *see* Trubek, D.M. and Trubek, L.G., 'Hard and Soft Law in the Construction of Social Europe: The Role of the Open Method of Coordination', *European Law Journal*, 2005, vol. 11, no. 3, pp. 343-364; Bercusson, B., *European Labour Law*, 2nd edn, Cambridge, Cambridge University Press, 2009, p. 186; Trubek, D.M. and Mosher, J.S., 'New Governance, Employment Policy and the European Social Model' in J. Zeitlin and D.M. Trubek (eds), *Governing Work and Welfare in a New Economy: European and American Experiments*, Oxford, Oxford University Press, 2003, pp. 33-59; López-Santana, M., 'The Domestic Implications of European Soft Law: Framing and Transmitting Change in Employment Policy', *Journal of European Public Policy*, 2006, no. 4, pp. 481-499.
353. *See* Article 155(2) TFEU. For more insights on European social dialogue and the application of Article 155(2) TFEU, *see*, *inter alia*, the following publications: Keune, M. and Marginson, P., 'Transnational Industrial Relations as Multi-Level Governance: Interdependencies in European Social Dialogue', *British Journal of Industrial Relations*, 2013, vol. 51, no. 3, pp. 473-497; Keller, B. and Weber, S., 'Sectoral Social Dialogue at EU level: Problems and Prospects of Implementation', *European Journal of Industrial Relations*, 2011, vol. 17, no. 3, pp. 227-243; Welz, C., *The European Social Dialogue under Articles 138 and 139 of the EC Treaty: Actors, Processes, Outcomes*, Alphen aan den Rijn, Kluwer Law International, 2008.
354. Veneziani, B., 'Austerity Measures, Democracy and Social Policy in the EU' Austerity' in N. Bruun, K. Lörcher and I. Schömann (eds), *The Economic and Financial Crisis and Collective Labour Law in Europe*, Oxford, Hart Publishing, 2014, p. 120.
355. *See* Veneziani 2014.

underlined by Blanpain.[356] Likewise, the Treaty rules recognise and promote the role of social partners and take into account the diversity of the national systems.[357] The Charter of Fundamental Rights of the EU contains provisions guaranteeing freedom of association, rights to collective bargaining and collective action, as well as information and consultation rights.[358]

Bearing in mind the legal observations presented, one may conclude that social dialogue is part and parcel of the EU legal sphere, but that it is also an imperfectly defined concept. This concept is multidimensional and broad, covering more than one area and being a part of the legal and institutional *acquis*.[359] As a part of the legal *acquis*, social dialogue is an integral element of many secondary legislative acts which ask for the social partners to be consulted.[360] In an institutional sense, social dialogue has been progressively afforded more regulatory space in the past decades, primarily via European social dialogue which has institutionalised a regulatory role of social partners.[361]

The lack of an adequate legal basis for intervening in the national systems of collective bargaining of *Member States* also limits the grounds on which the EU may intervene in the legal sphere of *candidate countries*. Since the EU contains no adequate description of the major concepts pertinent to collective bargaining, the *message* that the EU can pass onto the candidate countries cannot be sufficiently precise. Despite these limits, the European Commission paid close attention to the social dialogue developments during the accession process of the four countries selected. On what legal basis did the Commission do so? Social dialogue has been interpreted to form part of the Copenhagen criteria which were defined by the European Council in 1993 and formulated as the accession criteria for future Member States. The criteria involve, *inter alia*, institutions guaranteeing democracy, the rule of law and human rights, as well as a functioning market economy.[362] It is important to underline that the Copenhagen criteria do not explicitly call for social dialogue improvements in the candidate countries. Nevertheless, social dialogue has been interpreted as arising from the third Copenhagen criterion of a functional market economy.[363] Therefore, thanks to these

---

356. Blanpain, R., *European Labour Law*, 11th edn, Alphen aan den Rijn, Kluwer Law International, 2008, p. 702.
357. Article 152 TFEU.
358. Respectively, Article 12, Article 53 and Article 27 of the Charter.
359. As observed by Vaughan-Whitehead 2003, p. 218, and Vaughan-Whitehead, D., 'Social Dialogue in EU Enlargement: Acquis and Responsibilities', *Transfer: European Review of Labour and Research*, 2000, vol. 3, pp. 387–398.
360. For example, Regarding the implementation of the Council Directive 89/391/EC on the introduction of measures to encourage improvements in the safety and health of workers at work, as noted by Vaughan-Whitehead 2000, p. 391.
361. *Ibid.*, p. 392.
362. European Council, Presidency Conclusions, Copenhagen, 21–22 June 1993. The criteria read as follows: 'Membership requires that the candidate country has achieved stability of institutions guaranteeing democracy, the rule of law, human rights and respect for and protection of minorities, the existence of a functioning market economy as well as the capacity to cope with competitive pressure and market forces within the Union. Membership presupposes the candidate's ability to take on the obligations of membership including adherence to the aims of political, economic and monetary union.'
363. Perez-Solorzano Borragan and Smismans 2012, p. 123.

criteria, by the end of the 1990s, labour rights and social dialogue had become an irreversible part of the accession process.[364]

2.2 Transferring the Message: The Mechanism

2.2.1 *The Role of the European Commission*

The previous observations have indicated that the candidate countries were asked to boost industrial relations practices on the basis of the Copenhagen criteria. However, because of the lack of clarity on definition and elements of collective bargaining and social dialogue, the European Commission was vested with the powers of translating and interpreting the Copenhagen criteria to the realm of the candidate countries. The main policy instruments used to this end were the Commission's yearly assessment reports, evaluating the progress of candidate countries in meeting the accession criteria.

To be able to monitor and opine on social dialogue developments, the European Commission had to engage in broad and proactive interpretation of the social *acquis*.[365] According to some observers, the imprecise wording of the Copenhagen criteria gave wide 'entrepreneurial' powers to the Commission.[366] However, this study mitigates the latter statement about the ambiguity of the EU's 'message'. It can be also said that the lack of precise definition of major concepts and principles upon which the industrial relations rest, and of guidance on what the CEE collective bargaining systems should look like, actually deprived the European Commission of powers to prescribe more than general and vague formulations. The annual assessment reports of the European Commission contained only broad formulations, the typical ones prescribing formulations alike 'autonomous social dialogue to be promoted and strengthened', 'the tripartite structures should operate in a more regular way'.[367] In other words, the European Commission did not prescribe precise obligations of how industrial relations should develop in CEE, and it did not provide clear guidance on what the legal framework for collective bargaining should look like. Instead, the Commission had a general intention of encouraging collective bargaining at all levels and fruitful cooperation between social partners. It does not seem to be the case that the Commission took any closer ideological and normative stance on how the collective bargaining systems should evolve in CEE. However, judging from its intention to boost collective

---

364. As observed by: Kahn-Nisser, S., 'Conditionality, Communication and Compliance: The Effect of Monitoring on Collective Labour Rights in Candidate Countries', *Journal of Common Market Studies*, 2013, vol. 51, no. 6, p. 2.
365. As underlined by Perez-Solorzano Borragan and Smismans 2012, pp. 122–123.
366. *Ibid.*, p. 125. Similar explanations over the role of the European Commission in Grabbe, H., *The EU's Transformative Power: Europeanisation Through Conditionality in Central and Eastern Europe*, Basingstoke, Palgrave Macmillan, 2006, p. 78.
367. The archives of yearly assessment reports can be accessed at the European Commission webpage: https://ec.europa.eu/neighbourhood-enlargement/countries/package_en (accessed 1 December 2017).

bargaining practices at all possible levels, one may note that the Commission was not particularly in favour of the existing decentralised systems in the CEE countries.

Additionally, the European Commission developed a 'capacity building approach', with the objective of addressing the weaknesses and boosting the organisational and financial capacities of trade unions and associations of employers in the CEE countries. The Commission aimed to advance the accession process beyond the pure transposition of legal norms into national laws and to support collective bargaining activities in a more structural and bottom-up manner. To this end, capacity building was facilitated mainly through the financial and technical support channelled by several EU funding sources.[368] It is not easy to evaluate the success of these capacity building efforts in exact figures. According to one view, the capacity building was 'too ad hoc and too bureaucratic' and leading to 'very partial adoption of industrial relations practices'.[369] Furthermore, from a general point of view, it is questionable whether programme support of this kind can speed up the national processes of learning and transfer of knowledge, which cannot be achieved in a short time frame.[370] The social partners with whom the interviews for this study were held in the selected countries, reflected mainly positively on these EU-led projects, even though they noted that the concrete results are hard to estimate.

2.2.2 *Europeanisation: Notion and Mechanism*

The approach of Europeanisation was originally developed as an explanatory framework for describing and assessing the impact of the EU on the institutions and norms of the Member States. Subsequently, it was extended to the external EU dimension, but the original meaning of Europeanisation had to be modified in order to account for the differences between the Member States and candidate countries. The key difference in the approach arises from the fact that the candidate countries, unlike the Member States, do not participate in decision-making at the EU level, and may only engage in the top-down process of 'downloading' the EU norms and values.[371] Thus, the growing literature on Europeanisation in the context of the enlargement process has mostly dealt with assessing the effectiveness of the adaptational pressures of the EU regarding the transposition and implementation of the *acquis*.[372] Rule transfer goes beyond the

---

368. The capacity-building programmes were mainly financed through assistance instruments such as PHARE or Twinning. PHARE was designed in 1989 with the aim of supporting the economic restructuring in the former communist countries by facilitating various assistance projects. Twinning aimed to match civil servants from the EU Member States with public administration of the candidate countries to help with the transfer of knowledge and exchange of practices. For more detailed explanations, *see* Grabbe 2006, particularly, pp. 7–8 and p. 84.
369. Perez-Solorzano Borragan and Smismans 2012, pp. 132–133.
370. Bailey, D. and de Propris, L., 'A Bridge Too Phare? EU Pre-Accession Aid and Capacity-Building in the Candidate Countries', *Journal of Common Market Studies*, 2004, vol. 42, no. 1, pp. 77–98.
371. Further explanations can be found in Lindstrom, N., *The Politics of Europeanisation and Post-Socialist Transformations*, Basingstoke, Palgrave Macmillan, 2015, p. 35.
372. The enlargement-related focus on Europeanisation emerged from the works of Grabbe 2006; as well as Schimmelfennig, F. and Sedelmeier, U. (eds), *Europeanisation and Central and Eastern Europe*, Ithaca, Cornell University Press, 2005.

pure formal transposition of EU legal provisions into the national legal system and is understood in a broader fashion, also involving its implementation. In this context, a definition of Europeanisation provided by Radaelli is noteworthy as it puts to the fore the processes of going beyond pure formal transposition of rules:

> [Europeanisation consists of] processes of (a) construction, (b) diffusion, and (c) institutionalisation of formal and informal rules, procedures, policy paradigms, styles, 'ways of doing things', and shared beliefs and norms which are first defined and consolidated in the making of EU public policy and politics and then incorporated in the logic of domestic discourse, identities, political structures and public policies.[373]

In a similar fashion, Schimmelfennig and Sedelmeier understood Europeanisation in the context of the accession process as follows:

> We define 'Europeanisation' as a process in which states adopt EU rules. ... The rules in question cover a broad range of issues and structures and are both formal and informal. ... By analysing rule adoption, we focus on *institutionalisation* of EU rules at the domestic level - for instance, the transposition of EU law into domestic law, the restructuring of domestic institutions according to EU rules, or the change of domestic political practices according to EU standards (emphasis original).[374]

There are two mechanisms that need to be taken into account as drivers of Europeanisation: *conditionality* and *social learning*. *Conditionality* represents a mechanism facilitating the download of norms and values on the basis of the prospect of reward to the candidate countries.[375] The reward may come in a form of the prospect of membership, but it may also come in various forms of financial and institutional assistance. In the context of the current study, it is vital to understand that conditionality has been the main instrument guiding the effective transposition and implementation of the social *acquis*. It was based on the monitoring prerogatives of the European Commission, which assessed the progress in negotiations, and when necessary, utilised powers to slow or deter these negotiations.[376] As explained by Schimmelfennig and Sedelmeier, the mechanism of conditionality belongs to 'the external incentives model', under which the rule transfer is facilitated on the basis of external rewards and sanctions. The external – EU – incentives induce Europeanisation by potentially disrupting the 'domestic equilibrium', which can be understood as the distribution of preferences and bargaining power in domestic society.[377] Conditionality is effective when several criteria are fulfilled. The conditions should be sufficiently clear

---

373. Radaelli, C.M., 'The Europeanisation of Public Policy' in K. Featherstone and C.M. Radaelli (eds), *The Politics of Europeanisation*, Oxford, Oxford University Press, 2003, p. 30.
374. Schimmelfennig and Sedelmeier 2005, p. 7.
375. Sissenich, B., *Building States Without Society: European Union Enlargement and the Transfer of EU Social Policy to Poland and Hungary*, Plymouth, Lexington Books, 2007, p. 31; also, Schimmelfennig and Sedelmeier 2005, pp. 10–11.
376. Sissenich, B., 'The Transfer of EU Social Policy to Poland and Hungary' in F. Schimmelfennig and U. Sedelmeier (eds), *The Europeanisation of Central and Eastern Europe*, New York, Cornell University Press, 2005, p. 158.
377. Schimmelfennig and Sedelmeier 2005, p. 11.

(containing definition of the implications of the rules) and formal (containing binding rules). [378] The size and speed of reward are also relevant, as well as the credibility of the EU – in the sense of its powers to withhold the reward in the case of non-compliance.[379] Moreover, conditionality depends on the 'adoption costs'– the candidate country will be more likely to adopt the rule if the benefits of the award exceed the costs.[380] The costs often exist in the form of domestic opposition by so-called veto players.[381] That is to say, the rule adoption can empower certain domestic actors (e.g., trade unions or associations of employers) who may facilitate the progress of Europeanisation.[382] The domestic actors may speed up the Europeanisation process, but may also slow down the process should the rules not conform to their interests.[383]

While conditionality represents the major mechanism that facilitates rule transfer, the mechanism of *social learning* is also pertinent for explaining the transposition and implementation of the social *acquis*. Social learning dictates Europeanisation on the basis of whether the CEE countries consider the rule transfer appropriate in light of their own values and identities – social learning therefore does not rest on the mechanism of reward or punishment, but on actors' values and norms.[384] In this context, non-state actors may particularly dictate the dynamic of social learning, as they may adapt or promote those EU rules which they perceive as legitimate, and when transferring the rules, they can transform them to reflect their interests closely.[385] Social learning puts non-state actors at the forefront of the process, and it also emphasises the importance of a willing transposition of rules – by willingly engaging into the rule transfer and adapting the process in accordance with their needs, non-state actors guarantee the implementation of the rule. It can be assumed that social learning is particularly pertinent for Europeanisation of soft *acquis*, by empowering social partners to willingly engage into transfer of non-binding legal rules. There is a list of criteria which social learning should fulfil in order to be effective. In the first place, its effectiveness depends on the legitimacy of the rules (the candidate countries will more easily accept rules which they perceive as legitimate), identity (shared domestic and EU values) and absence of conflicting rules in the internal environment.[386]

---

378. *Ibid.*, pp. 12–16.
379. *Ibid.*
380. Schimmelfennig, F., Engert, S. and Knobel, H., 'The Impact of EU Political Conditionality', in F. Schimmelfennig and U. Sedelmeier (eds), *The Europeanisation of Central and Eastern Europe*, New York, Cornell University Press, 2005, p. 31.
381. Schimmelfennig and Sedelmeier 2005, p. 16.
382. Sissenich 2005, p. 161.
383. Sissenich 2007, p. 10. In contrast, Woolfson argues that because of the nature of the accession process, which involves mandatory 'download' of norms, the role of veto players is limited; Woolfson, C., 'Working Environment and "Soft Law" in the Post-Communist New Member States', *Journal of Common Market Studies*, 2006, vol. 44, no. 1, pp. 195–215, p. 204.
384. Schimmelfennig and Sedelmeier 2005, p. 18; Schimmelfennig, F. and Sedelmeier, S., 'Governance by Conditionality: EU Rule Transfer to the Candidate Countries of Central and Eastern Europe', *Journal of European Public Policy*, 2004, vol. 11, no. 4, pp. 669–687.
385. Schimmelfennig and Sedelmeier 2005, pp. 18–20; Sissenich 2007, p. 10; it should be also underlined that Schimmelfennig and Sedelmeier devised the third alternative mechanism of Europeanisation, the lesson-drawing model, which emphasises that the national actors adopt the EU rules as a result of the dissatisfaction with the status quo.
386. Sissenich 2007, p. 32; Schimmelfennig and Sedelmeier 2005.

Furthermore, social learning can also benefit from the determinacy of the rules in the sense of their clear and unambiguous content.[387]

The mechanisms of conditionality and social learning are intertwined and connected. Thus, the ways in which these two mechanisms interacted and dictated the transposition and implementation of the EU social *acquis* is not self-evident in the CEE countries. Yet, it seems that both mechanisms played a role in transposing social *acquis* in the four CEE countries.

2.3 Assessing the Effects of Europeanisation

Although on the eve of the EU enlargement the hope was raised that the accession process would help in enhancing collective bargaining in the candidate countries, in all likelihood the EU effects were far less tangible. The existing literature mostly evaluates the effects of Europeanisation in the area of social sphere and social dialogue as weak. These academic observations, however, arise from a general lack of comprehensive cross-country empirical evidence and were mostly generated through fragmented pieces of evidence. Overall, scholars have reported that the negotiations of the social chapters were as a matter of fact brief, that social policy was not a priority in the accession process compared to the other *acquis* areas, and that the negotiating chapters were closed without sufficient evidence of progress in the area of labour law.[388] The candidate countries found the social *acquis* to be less problematic than the other areas of law, and also focused on the transposition of secondary social legislation, while the other tasks were not necessarily followed through, including implementation of the transposed rules and improvements in the area of social dialogue.[389] Because the accession efforts were limited to the formal transposition of rules, a growing discrepancy between written provisions and their application arose.[390]

Furthermore, it has been claimed that there is no consistent impact of the hard social *acquis* on social standards in CEE.[391] Of all the areas of social *acquis*, the hope that the EU would leave a visible imprint was highest with respect to information and consultation rights, where the candidate countries were expected to transpose and implement the Directive on Information and Consultation (2002/14/EC).[392] This Directive was expected to lead to the institutionalisation of works councils (a topic which will be further discussed in Chapter 7), but studies have shown that its implementation had marginal effect on the state of industrial relations in the CEE

---

387. Schimmelfennig and Sedelmeier 2005, pp. 18–20.
388. Meardi 2007; Kahn-Nisser, S., 'External Governance, Convention Ratification and Monitoring: The EU, the ILO and Labour Standards in EU Accession Countries', *European Journal of Industrial Relations*, 2014, vol. 20, no. 4, p. 387.
389. Sissenich 2005, pp. 162 and 164; Sissenich 2007, p. 45.
390. Weiss 2006, pp. 185–186.
391. Drahokoupil, J. and Myant, M., 'Labour's Legal Resources After 2004: The Role of the European Union', *Transfer: European Review of Labour and Research*, 2015, vol. 21, no. 3, pp. 327–341; also Keune, M., 'The European Social Model and Enlargement' in M. Jepsen and A. Serrano Pascual (eds), *Unwrapping the European Social Model*, Bristol, The Policy Press, 2006, p. 182.
392. Directive 2002/14/EC of the European Parliament and of the Council establishing a general framework for informing and consulting employees in the European Community.

countries.[393] It is more challenging to evaluate the effects of the EU in the other areas of social *acquis*, where the outcomes are less obvious. In a recent study, Meardi provided a breakdown of existing knowledge about the EU's effect on CEE in different spheres of social *acquis*.[394] In the area of health and safety and working conditions, Meardi noted a lack of credible cross-country comparison, while in the area of equal opportunities, the rule compliance seems to have been limited. However, in some segments, such as working time, there is evidence of a worsening rather than an improvement in workers' positions as the result of the EU accession.[395] Moreover, Meardi noted that in the area of the soft *acquis*, the EU generated only some limited influence through the promotion of social pacts as part of the efforts to prepare candidate countries for accession to the European Monetary Union (EMU). In the area of social dialogue, Meardi noted that the effects of the EU were also limited – the accession-related policy documents (particularly National Reform Programmes) contained repeated mention of the necessity of improving social dialogue, although no meaningful improvements were followed through. In the post-accession period, due to the limited Europeanisation on social dialogue, multi-employer bargaining remained 'the weakest link', with collective bargaining deteriorating at sectoral and company level across the CEE countries.[396]

In opposition to the prevailing views demonstrating slight or no tangible effects of the EU, a study performed by Cook showed that the EU has had beneficial effects on collective labour rights in CEE. The author based her findings on a comparison of the state of collective labour rights in two groups of post-communist countries – those which underwent the accession process and those which did not – claiming that the improvements had been the result of a combination of democratic changes and the effects of the EU.[397]

To summarise the previous arguments, the EU's effects on the industrial relations of the CEE countries were indeed limited, and the focus of the EU's adaptational pressures was not directly concerned with the legal framework. The weak results came, first and foremost, from the imperfect functioning of the conditionality mechanism, given that the social sphere and particularly industrial relations improvements were not the focus of the Member States and the EU during the accession negotiations. Thus, the shortfall of industrial relations improvements in CEE did not affect the dynamic of accession negotiations. The social policy issues overall enjoyed low political salience and were not considered a priority of the accession process.[398] At the same time, as demonstrated in the previous sections of this chapter, the candidate countries lacked a precise *message* on how the legal and institutional framework for collective bargaining should evolve. The lack of a precise message ensues from the described inability of the

---

393. Drahoukopil and Myant 2015, p. 332; also Meardi 2012a, p. 32.
394. Meardi 2012a, pp. 25–61.
395. *Ibid.*
396. *Ibid.*, pp. 58–59.
397. As argued by Cook, L.J., 'More Rights, Less Power: Labour Standards and Labour Markets in East European Post-Communist States', *Studies in Comparative International Development*, 2010, vol. 45, no. 2, pp. 170–197.
398. As argued by Sissenich 2007, p. 37.

EU to provide basic common understandings of the major industrial relations concepts, such as collective agreements. In the capacity-building assistance projects, directed towards structural changes in social partners' functioning, the conditionality mechanism was not prominent: social learning had played a greater role. Yet, as argued in the previous section, it is rather difficult to assess the extent to which social learning dictated Europeanisation of the social rules.

Furthermore, when assessing the effects of Europeanisation in the area of social dialogue, it should be taken into account that the candidate countries were already tasked with implementing the far more elaborated economic *acquis*. The economic *acquis* was deemed to have a pronounced neoliberal pretext, and in this sense, the general message coming from the EU to candidate countries seems to have been rather contradictory, enmeshed between the social and economic dimensions.[399] In other words, the accession *acquis* reflected the tensions between the economic and the social sphere of the EU policies, as the EU could not have provided more *social* steering to the candidate countries than it could afford to own Member States. As such, this tension goes beyond the topic of enlargement and it is particularly visible in the disputed ability of the EU to connect to Member States' labour laws and social sphere, despite the long-standing efforts and undoubted great achievements in the social area of the EU.[400]

At the same time, one should stress that the Europeanisation effects have been enmeshed with influences originating from other external resources. In particular, from the legal perspective, ILO architecture has been rather prominent in institutionalising industrial relations in CEE. This has been particularly the case in the early 1990s, when the CEE countries were ratifying and transposing the treaties guaranteeing basic collective bargaining rights and principles and setting the autonomy of social partners. In this sense, one may argue that ILO legal rules have had a more important role in institutionalising industrial relations in the CEE countries than the EU, as the former served as a far more elaborated source of inspiration for basic collective bargaining principles. When it comes to collective bargaining levels, unlike EU law, the ILO rules have explicitly stated that social partners should enjoy the discretionary right to bargain collectively at whatever level they see fit. The corollary to this is the obligation of the authorities to provide conditions that allow collective bargaining at any level, if necessary.[401]

In the end, the role of the EU during the accession process in building the legal and institutional framework for collective bargaining can be evaluated as limited and indirect. As this section has demonstrated, the major reason for this has been the lack of a clear *message* that the EU could direct to the candidate countries, and the lack of adequate mechanisms to ensure the transposition and implementation of rules.

---

399. Drahokoupil and Myant 2015, pp. 331–332.
400. Hendrickx, F. and Giubonni, S., 'European Union Labour Law and the European Social Model: A Critical Appraisal' in M.W. Finkin and G. Mundlak (eds), *Comparative Labor Law*, Cheltenham, Edward Elgar, 2015, p. 402.
401. Gernigon, B., Odero, A. and Guido, H., 'ILO Principles Concerning Collective Bargaining' *International Labour Review*, 2000b, vol. 139, no. 1, pp. 41–43.

3 THE ROLE OF THE EU DURING THE CRISIS

3.1 The Context of the Crisis: A Changed Legal and Industrial Relations Environment

Europeanisation has structurally changed in CEE in the post-accession period, as it was no longer driven by the necessity of transposing and implementing the accession *acquis*. One would thus expect a diminished impact of the EU on the legal and institutional framework for collective bargaining in CEE. This section will deconstruct this statement in more detail.

The recent economic and financial crisis affected the European economies in asymmetric fashion, challenging the labour markets and labour standard-setting methods. With respect to the four CEE economies examined in this study, the worst affected was Slovenia, with sharp falls in GDP and rising public debts since 2009.[402] The Czech Republic was also fully affected by the crisis, with the fall in GDP, mostly because of declining exports, further causing labour market imbalances and increased unemployment.[403] Slovakia experienced a sharp shrinking of GDP in 2009 and recovery in 2010.[404] Poland seems to be the least affected with the crisis, and has even been seen by some as having managed to avoid its consequences.[405] Industrial relations across Europe also seem to have been affected by the crisis – the available studies have so far demonstrated growing trends in the decentralisation of industrial relations and growing erosion of sectoral collective bargaining across the Member States.[406] With respect to the four CEE countries selected, as Table 3 demonstrates, the coverage rates of collective agreements have been in decline since the pre-crisis period, with the sharpest decline in the two countries with the most developed multi-level bargaining framework, Slovenia and Slovakia.

---

402. As noted by Stanojević and Klarič, the fall of GDP was 5.8% in 2009 with significant rises of public debt, *see* Stanojević, M. and Klarič, M., 'The Impact of Socio-Economic Shocks on Social Dialogue in Slovenia', *Transfer: European Review of Labour and Research*, 2013, vol. 19, no. 2, p. 223.
403. With fall of GDP of 4.7% in 2009, *see* Verveková, S., 'The Case of the Czech Republic' in I. Guardiancich (ed.), *Recovering from the Crisis through Social Dialogue in the New EU Member States: The Case of Bulgaria, the Czech Republic, Poland and Slovenia*, Budapest, ILO, 2012a, p. 50.
404. Bulla, Czíria, and Kahancová, noting that in the first place, real GDP growth fell to -4.8% in 2009 and recovered at 4.5% in 2010, *see* Bulla, M., Czíria, L. and Kahancová, M., 'Impact of Legislative Reforms on Industrial Relations and Working Conditions in Slovakia', ILO Background Study, 2013, p. 6.
405. According to available studies, the crisis hit Poland already in 2009, but improvements were visible already in 2010; *see* Guardiancich, I. and Pliszkiewicz, M., 'The Case of Poland' in I. Guardiancich (ed.), *Recovering from the Crisis Through Social Dialogue in the New EU Member States: The Case of Bulgaria, the Czech Republic, Poland and Slovenia*, Budapest, ILO, 2012, pp. 71-77.
406. Overview of Member States' industrial relations related developments in the crisis period can be found in European Commission, *Industrial Relations in Europe 2014*, Luxembourg, Publication Office of the European Union, 2015. More legal perspective to the crisis-induced changes can be found in Bruun, N., Lörcher, K. and Schömann, I. (eds), *The Economic and Financial Crisis and Collective Labour Law in Europe*, Oxford, Hart Publishing, 2014.

Table 3 Collective Bargaining Coverage Before and After the Economic and Financial Crisis

	2006	2007	2008	2009	2010	2011	2012	2013
Czech Republic	50.2	50.4	49.8	44.4	51.2	49.0	50.4	47.3
Poland	n/a	15.7	n/a	n/a	n/a	14.8	14.7	n/a
Slovakia	40.0	40.0	40.0	40.0	n/a	35.0	n/a	24.9
Slovenia	96.0	94.0	92.0	92.0	80.0	75.0	70.0	65.0

Source: ICTWSS database 5.1 (Visser 2016).
Notes: Coverage rate is defined as in ICTWSS database 5.1 (Visser 2016), as a proportion of all employees, wage earners, with the right to collective bargaining, calculated as percentage, adjusted for the possibility that some sectors or occupations are excluded from the right to bargain. Data available until 2013.

The crisis also represented a challenge for labour laws across the European continent, affecting the ways in which labour standards are set. From the four countries examined in this study, Slovakia's legal and institutional framework for collective bargaining seems to have been the most influenced by the crisis. Likewise, in 2011 Slovakia's Labour Code introduced salient innovations by somewhat diminishing the role of trade unions and collective bargaining, especially at the sectoral level, although some of these legislative changes were short-lived. These changes introduced employers' consent as a necessary prerequisite for ensuring the extension of the validity of collective agreements to third parties.[407] This provision had a strong effect on the multi-level bargaining framework, given that no sectoral collective agreement has been extended until the new legal amendment came into force in 2014. At the same time, the crisis-related legal amendments of 2011 imposed a rather restrictive threshold for trade union representativeness at company level in Slovakia, rendering their organisation difficult. In the same year, the Slovakian Labour Code amendments for the first time allowed the conclusion of less favourable conditions for employees in collective agreements, as derogations from statutory law *in peius*. The ways in which the 2011 legal amendments affected the multi-level bargaining framework will be further discussed in Chapters 6 and 7.

3.2 EU Responses to the Crisis

Under the general framework of the Strategy for Europe 2020, which set an objective of delivering 'smart, sustainable and inclusive growth', the EU presented a list of institutional responses to the detrimental effects of the crisis across the Member States.[408] These EU responses have been versatile. In the first place, from 2009, with

---

407. Act no 557/2010 Coll, which entered into force at the beginning of 2011.
408. European Commission, *Communication 'Europe 2020 – A Strategy for Smart, Sustainable and Inclusive Growth'* COM(2010)2020, Luxembourg, Office for Official Publications of the European Commission, 2010.

the aim of strengthening economic governance, prominent legal amendments on monetary policies were introduced. These included secondary legislation known as 'Six-pack' (involving macroeconomic and fiscal surveillance) and 'Two-pack' (allowing reviews of national budgets by the EU).[409] Particularly notable were the provisions from the Six-pack introducing macroeconomic imbalance procedure (MIP). This enabled the European Commission to take measures, including financial sanctions (up to 0.1% of GDP), against Member States facing macroeconomic difficulties. Other measures involved the European Stability Mechanism Treaty,[410] providing financial assistance to members of the Eurozone and the Treaty on Coordination, Stability and Governance,[411] setting national public debt threshold, and introducing an obligation for Member States to introduce an automatic self-correction mechanism in their laws. Moreover, the Euro Plus Pact called for increased coordination of financial, tax, employment and several other policies in the Eurozone countries, with policy objectives, amongst others, of reducing unit labour costs, abolishing wage indexation and supporting decentralised wage bargaining.[412] All of the enlisted economic governance measures were incorporated into the European Semester policy cycle, formally introduced in the EU in 2011. Under the European Semester, the Member States coordinate economic and fiscal policies and have become obliged to draft and report on national policy programmes on these areas (NRPs), while the European Council has been empowered to adopt legally non-binding country-specific recommendations in a yearly timetable.

The EU mechanisms presented rely on a mix of preventive and corrective economic and monetary measures, including surveillance of national policies by the EU institutions. Much of the described measures are not legally binding and their enforcement is ensured predominantly through the policy recommendations, but this does not apply to instruments which rest on financial sanctions (European Stability

---

409. Six-pack refers to: Regulation 1175/2011 of the European Parliament and of the Council amending Council Regulation 1466/97 on the strengthening of the surveillance of budgetary positions and the surveillance and coordination of economic policies; Council Regulation 1177/2011 amending Regulation 1467/97 on speeding up and clarifying the implementation of the excessive deficit procedure; Regulation 1173/2011 of the European Parliament and of the Council on the effective enforcement of budgetary surveillance in the euro area; Council Directive 2011/85/EU on requirements for budgetary frameworks of the Member States; Regulation 1176/2011 of the European Parliament and of the Council on the prevention and correction of macroeconomic imbalances; Regulation 1174/2011 of the European Parliament and of the Council on enforcement measures to correct excessive macroeconomic imbalances in the euro area. Two-pack refers to: Regulation 473/2013 of the European Parliament and of the Council on common provisions for monitoring and assessing draft budgetary plans and ensuring the correction of excessive deficit of the Member States in the euro area; Regulation 472/2013 of the European Parliament and of the Council on the strengthening of economic and budgetary surveillance of Member States in the euro area experiencing or threatened with serious difficulties with respect to their financial stability.
410. Treaty Establishing the European Stability Mechanism, T/ESM 2012/en, Brussels, 2 February 2012.
411. Treaty on Stability, Coordination and Governance in the Economic and Monetary Union, T/SCG/en, Brussels, 2 March 2012.
412. European Council, Conclusions, Annex I *Stronger Economic Policy Coordination for Competitiveness and Convergence*, 24–25 March 2011, EUCO 10/1/11 REV 1.

Mechanism Treaty, Six-pack, Two-pack).[413] It is however striking that the EU economic governance has become increasingly affected by hard law measures and that the employment and social policies have become deeply embedded into the macroeconomic policy structure of the EU.[414] These measures also tackle the areas closely linked to the functioning of industrial relations. This is particularly the case with the Euro Plus Pact and the European Semester. The Euro Plus Pact prescribes the Member States' obligation to review wage setting mechanisms, and, where necessary, to also review the degree of centralisation of collective bargaining and the indexation systems. Despite obvious interference with the ways in which national collective bargaining systems function, the Pact, somewhat contradictorily, proclaims the necessity of maintaining the autonomy of social partners. Moreover, by looking at the country-specific recommendations adopted pursuant to the European Semester policy coordination cycle, one may conclude that European economic governance measures have encroached upon the ways in which collective bargaining systems work, including minimum wages and wage setting mechanisms.[415] In this sense, these country-specific recommendations represent a credible pressure on the collective bargaining systems of Member States, because the Council may issue recommendations which can relate to wage setting arrangements.

Thus, the EU economic governance measures, even though not necessarily legally binding, in an overall sense supported an environment that is conducive to decentralisation pressures. For this reason, existing studies have criticised the new institutional and policy architecture of the EU. Likewise, concerns have been raised that the effect of these policies is to reduce employee protection and trade unions,[416] and also that they underpin the erosion of multi-employer bargaining across European countries.[417] Furthermore, EU policies have been criticised for decreasing national discretion over social policies and shifting the focus of collective bargaining from multi-employer to company level arrangements.[418] Certain efforts have been recently made by the EU to address these criticisms. In 2013, the Commission announced a

---

413. For the overview and assessment of enforcement mechanisms, *see* De la Porte, C. and Heins, E., 'A New Era of European Integration? Governance of Labour Market and Social Policy since the Sovereign Debt Crisis', *Comparative European Politics*, 2015, vol. 13, pp. 8–28.
414. Bekker, S. and Palinkaš, I., 'The Impact of the Financial Crisis on EU Economic Governance: A Struggle Between Hard and Soft Law and Expansion of the EU Competences?', *Tilburg Law Review*, 2012, vol. 17, pp. 360–366; Bekker, S. and Klosse, S., 'EU Governance of Economic and Social Policies', *European Journal of Social Law*, 2013, vol. 2, pp. 103–120.
415. The list of country-specific reports by year can be found at: http://ec.europa.eu/europe2020/making-it-happen/country-specific-recommendations/index_en.htm.
416. Drahokoupil and Myant 2015, p. 335; Keune, M., 'Less Governance Capacity and More Inequality: The Effects of the Assault on Collective Bargaining in the EU' in G. Van Gyes and T. Schulten (eds), *Wage Bargaining Under the New European Economic Governance*, Brussels, ETUI, 2015, pp. 285–293.
417. Marginson, P., 'Coordinated Bargaining in Europe: From Incremental Corrosion to Frontal Assault?' *European Journal of Industrial Relations*, 2015, vol. 21, no. 2, pp. 97–114.
418. Veneziani, B., 'Austerity Measures, Democracy and Social Policy in the EU' Austerity' in N. Bruun, K. Lörcher and I. Schömann (eds), *The Economic and Financial Crisis and Collective Labour Law in Europe*, Oxford, Hart Publishing, 2014, p. 132.

proposal to strengthen the social dimension of the EMU,[419] while in 2015, it called for the establishment of the European Pillar of Social Rights to complement the social *acquis* as a reference framework in employment and social areas.[420]

The criticism described in the previous paragraph can be safely extended to the CEE countries. From the four selected countries, Slovenia is the only one whose wage setting mechanisms was particularly scrutinised by the EU during the recent crisis period. Specifically, Slovenia has been consistently asked within the country-specific recommendations to ensure that wage setting mechanisms promote growth in wages, with a view to encouraging competitiveness and job creation; to review the minimum wage setting mechanisms; and to review the indexation mechanisms linking wages to inflation growth. What can be concluded is that the EU's economic governance measures may be said to support the trend of decentralisation of collective bargaining that already existed in the CEE, and to give no incentive to the CEE countries to invest in the institutionalisation of collective bargaining at central levels. However, it is questionable to what extent the CEE countries can accommodate these requests. Bearing in mind that industrial relations is already decentralised at company and local levels (particularly in the Czech Republic and Poland), further downward pressure could result in the disintegration of the collective bargaining structure in CEE by emasculating the trade unions. In other words, eliminating the role of trade unions in the workplace provides more regulatory space for unilateral standard-setting (employers' unilateral decision-making) and individual negotiations between an employer and employee. This not only drives the CEE countries away from the multi-employer bargaining model, but also weakens the position of employees by shifting the powers from collective to individual standard setting. This topic will be more discussed in Chapter 7.

4 CONCLUSIONS

The overarching conclusion of this chapter is that changes within the legal framework were not the EU's primary concern in relation to collective bargaining in CEE, and in this sense the EU was providing only *indirect* pressure and guidance. Moreover, this chapter has demonstrated that the EU adaptational pressures have changed structurally over time: when comparing and contrasting the pre-accession and post-crisis developments, it becomes clear that the content of the EU's *message* to CEE has changed, both its normative and ideological underpinning, as well as the mechanisms for its transfer.

First, during the accession process, the candidate countries were called upon to enhance collective bargaining structures at all possible bargaining levels. While this

---

419. Olli Rehn's speech to the European Parliament on 22 May 2013, European Commission 'Social pillar of the EMU – Commission statement in the European Parliament', SPEECH/13/443, available at: http://europa.eu/rapid/press-release_SPEECH-13-443_en.htm.
420. Jean-Claude Juncker's speech to the European Parliament on 9 September 2015; European Commission 'State of the Union 2015: Time for Honesty, Unity and Solidarity', available at: http://europa.eu/rapid/press-release_SPEECH-15-5614_en.htm.

chapter demonstrated that the EU's rationale in supporting the candidate countries' industrial relations developments has not been specifically driven by any clear ideological or normative framework, the EU formally *preached the establishment of multi-level bargaining structures* and called for enhancing the social partners' voice in social and economic life. The EU's support was overshadowed by several elements, as discussed in section 2, in the first place due to far more elaborated economic *acquis*, which arguably supported market narrative rather than institutionalisation narrative of industrial relations in CEE. Furthermore, the *message* on collective bargaining developments lacked clarity and the instruments for implementation. The EU was challenged in its efforts to transmit the *message* to CEE, as the result of which the overall role of the EU regarding social dialogue developments was limited. At the same time, as this chapter demonstrated, the role of the EU in influencing change in the legal framework for collective bargaining in these countries was both *limited* and *indirect*.

How have these developments fared in the recent crisis period? The role of the EU in building the legal and institutional framework for collective bargaining in CEE has seemingly not diminished in the post-crisis phase, but it changed in terms of its normative and ideological underpinning, and the mechanisms for rule transfer. This chapter has demonstrated that, as in the pre-accession period, the EU's adaptational pressures in the post-period did not directly, but rather *indirectly* affected the legal framework for collective bargaining in CEE. But as a contrast to the pre-accession period, the crisis-related developments had a more distinct normative underpinning, by either providing support to the process of decentralisation of collective bargaining in Member States or by creating an environment which is conducive to such decentralisation. Even though the EU's post-crisis adaptational pressures do not rely on the strength of the accession-related instruments of conditionality and social learning, which may more effectively facilitate the transfer of the EU message in the CEE countries, it is evident that these measures have the effect of underpinning the already decentralised climate of CEE industrial relations, rendering the institutionalisation of collective bargaining at central levels difficult.

PART II Levels

CHAPTER 5
National Level: The Role of Tripartism

1 INTRODUCTION

In the early transition period, CEE countries introduced the notion of 'tripartism' to denote the particular type of social dialogue at the national level between trade unions, associations of employers and governments. This form of social dialogue quickly spread to the post-communist countries and became a CEE variation of similar corporatist experiences in Western Europe. In a nutshell, tripartism represented:

> a new postcommunist species of state – society interaction and a new brand of capitalism that is distinct from the three major variants of contemporary capitalism, including Western European neocorporatism.[421]

By the mid-1990s, all CEE countries had established tripartite bodies, providing institutionalised forums for discussion between governments and social partners on the most important social and economic matters. In an effort to enhance the legitimacy of decision-making during the transition process, governments welcomed their formation. Their introduction was also encouraged by the EU,[422] even though tripartite social dialogue did not represent a formal requirement for EU accession, and it was not an official part of the *acquis*. Already by 1990, a tripartite body named *the Council for Economic and Social Agreement* had been established in Czechoslovakia. It brought together representatives of the state, employers and trade unions. After the dissolution of the federal state in 1993, this body continued functioning in its Czech and Slovak

---

421. Iankova, E.A., *Eastern European Capitalism in the Making*, Cambridge, Cambridge University Press, 2002, p. 8.
422. As underlined by Meardi, G., *Social Failures of EU Enlargement: A Case of Workers Voting with Their Feet*, New York, Routledge, 2012a, p. 43 and p. 39. Ghellab and Vaughan-Whitehead suggested that national tripartite consultations could serve as a framework for decentralised bargaining, as is the case in Ireland or Italy, see Ghellab, Y. and Vaughan-Whitehead, D., *Sectoral Social Dialogue in Future EU Member States: The Weakest Link*, Budapest, ILO, 2003, p. 28.

variations. Slovenia and Poland formed their tripartite bodies in 1994. Tripartism has probably been the most discussed aspect of CEE industrial relations in the existing literature, attracting a considerable volume of studies. A possible explanation for such academic interest lies in the fact that the tripartite *fora* were the first locus of social dialogue and negotiations between trade unions and employers' associations since the onset of the transitional process, given the lack of such practices in the communist period. Overall, the development of CEE tripartism has received meagre evaluation; the most frequent labelling of it in the literature being 'illusory corporatism', a catchphrase originally coined by Ost.[423]

Tripartite functioning has faced various difficulties, including social partners' weaknesses and the lack of a social dialogue tradition, as well as the challenging macroeconomic climate marked by persistent unemployment and high inflation rates. As this chapter will demonstrate using four countries as its example, CEE tripartism has generated low outcomes in terms of the number of tripartite agreements achieved (social pacts, concluded between the state, trade unions and associations of employers). From the four countries analysed in this study, it is only in Slovenia that social pacts have been more or less regularly concluded in the past two decades. As this chapter will explain, of the four countries included in the analysis, Poland has the poorest record in concluding social pacts, while the Czech Republic and Slovakia have had only concluded a few since the early 1990s.

Even though the primary objective of this study is collective bargaining, the role of tripartism in shaping industrial relations in CEE cannot be discounted.[424] In this context, the primary goal of this chapter will be to look into the role of tripartism as a standard-setting locus and the role it has played in shaping the collective bargaining system in the past two decades. To that end, it will scrutinise the legal and institutional underpinnings of the tripartite bodies and social pacts in the four countries. In addition, a smaller segment of the chapter will be dedicated to cross-sectoral collective bargaining – of the four countries, only Slovenia has had a tradition of concluding collective agreements at cross-sectoral level.

The chapter proceeds as follows. Section 2 presents the major features of tripartism in the four selected countries. To that end, in addition to data from the interviews, this section relies on data from existing studies and literature, given that CEE tripartism, particularly in Slovenia and Poland, is a widely studied topic. Section

---

423. Ost claimed that CEE tripartism did not do much for resolving issues which coporatism in the West managed to resolve, labelling it accordingly as 'illusory', see Ost, D., 'Illusory Corporatism in Eastern Europe: Neoliberal Tripartism and Postcommunist Class Identities', *Politics & Society*, 2000, vol. 28, no. 4, pp. 503-530.
424. As explained in Chapter 1, section 1, collective bargaining is understood as negotiations between trade unions or organisations of workers and employers or employer' associations, conducted with a view to determining terms and conditions of work and employment or relationships between them. Social dialogue is understood in a broader fashion, covering all types of negotiations and consultations between state authorities, representatives of employers and employees, and all possible issues of common interest. These definitions are based on the ILO understandings, *see* Olney, S. and Rueda, M., *Convention No 154: Promoting Collective Bargaining*, Geneva, ILO, 2005, pp. 5-6.

3 contains analytical discussion of the cross-country differences. Finally, section 4 provides concluding thoughts, relevant for answering the two research questions posed in Chapter 1.

2 LEGAL AND INSTITUTIONAL FRAMEWORK IN THE FOUR COUNTRIES

What follows is an overview of the major elements pertinent to the legal and institutional framework of tripartite social dialogue in the selected countries: the power and functioning of the tripartite bodies, representativeness, history of social pacts and crisis-related developments. In addition, this section will briefly elaborate on the cross-sectoral collective agreements in Slovenia, since this country had collective agreements concluded at this level until the mid-2000s. Also, this section will briefly reflect on the regional tripartite dialogue which takes place in the Czech Republic, Slovakia and Poland, but it does not exist in Slovenia.

2.1 Slovenia

2.1.1 The Tripartite Body: Power and Functioning

The Economic and Social Council (*Ekonomsko socialni svet*) is the major tripartite body in Slovenia, established on the basis of the 1994 tripartite social pact, which was signed between social partners and the government (in Slovenia social pacts are entitled 'social agreements'). According to the Slovenian scholar Stanojević, the formation of this body was a result of political exchange between trade unions and the government – trade unions were enabled to participate in a more institutionalised form of tripartite decision-making in exchange for supporting anti-inflation measures.[425] The aforementioned 1994 social pact remained the legal basis for the functioning of the tripartite Council until today, defining its powers and competences. The work of the Council has never been given a statutory legal basis, despite it being suggested by the social partners in the mid-1990s.[426] Initially, this body gathered five members per side of state, trade unions and organisations of employers, but the structure of the tripartite Council increased to eight members on each side in 2007.[427] It decides on the basis of unanimity, but the decisions are not legally binding, as the body has only a consulting and advisory role. Notwithstanding the fact that it may not issue legally-binding decisions, the substantive competences of the Council as defined in its Rules of

---

425. Stanojević, M., 'The Rise and Decline of Slovenian Corporatism: Local and European Factors', *Europe-Asia Studies*, 2012, vol. 64, no. 5, pp. 863–864.
426. Stanojević and Krašovec noted that social partners agreed to have the tripartite body institutionalised in law in 1996, but this was not executed because of the conflict which broke soon between the two sides, *see* Stanojević, M. and Krašovec, A., 'Slovenia: Social Pacts and Political Exchange', in S. Avdagic, M. Rhodes, and J. Visser (eds), *Social Pacts in Europe: Emergence, Evolution, and Institutionalisation*, Oxford, Oxford University Press, 2011, pp. 243–244.
427. According to the Article 4 of its Rules on Operation, available in English language at: http://www.gsv.gov.si/en/economic_and_social_council/rules_on_the_operation_of_the_economic_and_social_council/ (accessed 1 December 2017).

Operation are broad, involving any economic and social matter, such as social insurance, social assistance, employment, labour relations issues, and economic policies.[428] According to the interviewees in Slovenia, this body has indeed been systematically involved in discussing all legislation concerning the social and economic sphere in the past two decades.

2.1.2 Representativeness

To participate in the work of the tripartite Council, the trade unions should conform to certain representativeness criteria which are defined by the Act on Trade Union Representativeness from 1993. Pursuant to this Act, trade unions at any level, including national level, should first and foremost have democratic character and be independent from the state and employer's organisation. In addition to these general criteria, the trade unions at national level should fulfil a quantitative criterion of having a membership base of at least 10% of employees in a particular sector or industry which it represents. There are no representativeness criteria which the employers' associations have to fulfil in order to participate in tripartite social dialogue.

2.1.3 History of Social Pacts

Given that it has led to systematic conclusion of social pacts (social agreements) since 1994, the Slovenian tripartite system represents the most institutionalised example of tripartite social dialogue of the four CEE countries under analysis. The scope of the social agreements in economic and social matters is wide, with the most prominent item being the wages policy. With the first wave of post-transitional economic reforms in Slovenia, the first social agreements were concluded in the years 1994, 1995 and 1996, after which the practice of concluding social pacts discontinued and resumed in 2003.[429] The social agreements concluded in the early 1990s were predominantly concerned with income policies, as they were aiming to tackle the macroeconomic challenges of high inflation and unemployment. In addition, the 1994 social pact was something of a landmark for instituting the tripartite body. The 1995 social pact was particularly significant for stipulating collective agreements as key instruments of wage determination, but also for defining a minimum wage.[430] The 1996 pact did not introduce any particular innovation – it mostly repeated the provisions of the pacts from 1994 and 1995.

After 1996, social dialogue went through a turbulent period, and no new social pacts were concluded until 2003. Instead, restrictive income policies were unilaterally enacted by the government on the basis of the law which was in force in the period

---

428. *See* Article 2 of its Rules on Operation.
429. The following overview of social pacts in this section is predominantly based on data from Stanojević, M., 'Social Pacts in Slovenia: Accommodation to the EMU Regime and the Post-Euro Development', *Warsaw Forum of Economic Sociology*, 2011, vol. 2, no. 1, pp. 113-125.
430. *Ibid.*, p. 115.

1997–1998. Between 1999 and 2001, social partners only managed to agree on a narrower social pact solely dealing with income policies. Finally, an all-encompassing social pact was concluded in 2003 and it remained valid until 2007. This pact was a landmark for its wage setting role and for the fact that its provisions were preparing the economy to enter the EU.[431] Nevertheless, it was sidelined with the election of a new government in 2004, which introduced a package of neoliberal measures, stimulating labour market flexibility.[432]

Following accession to the EU, another social pact was signed for the period 2007–2009. This pact aimed to accommodate the entrance of the economy to the EMU *post-factum*, for which reason it was mainly concerned with restrictive income policies and improving competitiveness.[433] When the recent economic and financial crisis hit the Slovenian economy, the process of agreeing a social pact became difficult. It was only in 2012 that social partners managed to agree on principles for the conclusion of a new social pact, and after long negotiations, one was concluded to cover the period 2015–2016.[434]

It can be implied from the above paragraphs that the social pacts which were consistently concluded in Slovenia played a set of distinct roles. In the first place, according to Stanojević, the social pacts concluded in the early 1990s contributed towards institutionalising the centralisation of collective bargaining, given that collective bargaining system represented an implementing mechanism for the income policies set out in the social pacts.[435] Another distinct role of social pacts is the fact that they led to the establishment of the tripartite body in the early 1990s, as explained above. Thirdly, in contrast with the other CEE countries, in Slovenia social pacts were used to facilitate accession to the EU and EMU and the government received the unanimous support of social partners in pursuing this goal.[436]

2.1.4 Crisis

Slovenia experienced marked GDP growth following its accession to the EU, but the crisis left outstanding effects on the economy, and recovery commenced only in 2014.[437] Tripartite social dialogue was particularly challenged during the economic and financial crisis years. Following the expiry of the social pact in 2009, the parties to social dialogue could not immediately agree on a new pact. In 2012, social partners

---

431. Stanojević and Krašovec 2011, p. 247; also *see* Stanojević 2011, p. 120.
432. *See also* Stanojević and Krašovec 2011, p. 248.
433. Stanojević 2011, pp. 124–125.
434. *See also* Guardiancich, I., 'The Case of Slovenia' in I. Guardiancich (ed.), *Recovering from the Crisis Through Social Dialogue in the New EU Member States: The Case of Bulgaria, the Czech Republic, Poland and Slovenia*, Budapest, ILO, 2012, p. 123; Guardiancich, I., 'Slovenia: The End of a Success Story? When a Partial Reform Equilibrium Turns Bad', *Europe-Asia Studies*, 2016, vol. 68, no. 2, pp. 205–231.
435. Stanojević 2011, p. 108.
436. *See also* Stanojević and Krašovec 2011, p. 247; also *see* Stanojević 2011, p. 120.
437. Guardiancich notes that with the crisis which plummeted in 2009, the bankruptcies were widespread, unemployment and public deficit on the rise, and Slovenia became one of the worst performers among the EU Member States, *see* Guardiancich 2016, pp. 205–206.

reached consensus on the guidelines for concluding a new pact, which was, as already mentioned, eventually signed at the beginning of 2015, to cover the period 2015–2016.[438] A further challenge to social dialogue arose in 2011, after the anti-crisis laws (on pension reform and on mini-jobs for students) had been promulgated despite the lack of tripartite support, which resulted in trade unions initiating referendums and declaring these laws void.[439]

2.1.5 Cross-Sectoral Agreements

Slovenia is the only country in in this study which has had a tradition of concluding legally-binding cross-sectoral agreements in private and public sector (known as 'general collective agreements'). These cross-sectoral agreements had covered the entire private and public sectors, stipulating a broad range of rules which were further specified at sectoral and company levels. A general private sector collective agreement was first concluded in 1990. It was regularly renewed until 2005, after which the focus of the collective bargaining system shifted onto the sectoral level,[440] though a general (cross-sectoral) collective agreement remained valid in the public sector. A specific cross-sectoral collective agreement was concluded in 2006, applicable only to employees from private sector which were left uncovered by any collective agreement after the cross-sectoral one ceased to be valid.[441] However, this collective agreement ceased to exist in 2010, and after that collective bargaining shifted completely to sectoral and company level.

2.2 Slovakia

2.2.1 The Tripartite Body: Power and Functioning

The history of tripartism started in the federal country of Czechoslovakia in 1990, when the federal tripartite *Council of Economic and Social Agreement*, aimed in the first place at maintaining social peace,[442] was formed. In the following years, this federal tripartite body dissolved and continued functioning under the two different variations in both Slovakia and the Czech Republic. *The Slovak Economic and Social Council* (*Hospodársky a sociálny výbor Slovenskej republiky*) officially commenced its work in 1993.

---

438. Guardiancich 2016; see also Kanjuo Mrčela, A., *Slovenia: New Social Agreement 2015–2016*, Dublin, Eurofound, 2015.
439. As explained by Guardiancich 2012, pp. 113–118.
440. Kanjuo Mrčela, A., *Living and Working in Slovenia – Collective Bargaining*, Dublin, Eurofound, 2017.
441. Collective agreement on pay, holiday bonuses and the reimbursement of work-related expenses, see Ignjatović, M., *Slovenia: Wage Flexibility and Collective Bargaining*, Dublin, Eurofound, 2009.
442. As described by Myant, M., Slocock, B. and Smith, S., 'Tripartism in the Czech and Slovak Republic', *Europe-Asia Studies*, 2000, vol. 52, no. 4, pp. 725–726.

Chapter 5: National Level: The Role of Tripartism

Despite common legacies, there is an impression that the Slovak variety of tripartism developed differently from its Czech counterpart. In particular, during the 1990s, the major difference was a comparatively more developed and constructive tripartite dialogue in Slovakia than in the Czech Republic.[443] As is the case in the other CEE countries, the Slovak tripartite Council has a consultative role and it may not issue legally binding decisions. Today this body consists of seven representatives per member group (trade unions, employers' associations and the government), and it currently operates on the basis of the statutory legal provisions. However, the legal basis and competences of the tripartite body have gone through several phases in the past two decades – depending on the actual political environment at the time, this tripartite body was provided with narrower or broader sets of competences. In this sense, Slovakia has the most vivid history of tripartite institutionalisation of the four CEE countries. In brief, the tripartism developed in the following phases:

(i) Between 1993 and 1999, the Economic and Social Council functioned on the basis of its own statute in the form of a tripartite agreement concluded between the social partners and the government. Enjoying distinct support from the government, this body played a salient role in several areas, including pension and health reform, and even in extending the validity of concluded collective agreements to third parties.[444]

(ii) After some debate, in 1999 the Act on Economic and Social Partnership provided the Council with a statutory legal basis.[445] Nevertheless, this Act remained valid until 2001 only.

(iii) In 2004, a new tripartite Council was established (renamed as the *Economic and Social Partnership Council – Rada hospodárskeho a sociálneho partnerstva*). The legal basis of this body was the tripartite statute agreed among the government and social partners. Not only was the legal basis of this body downgraded from statutory legal act to tripartite statute, but its competences were also more narrowly defined – the tripartite consultations could only lead to recommendations to the government.[446]

(iv) In 2007, a new tripartite body, the *Economic and Social Council*, was constituted. The basis of its institutionalisation was the Act on Trilateral Consultations at the National Level of 2007. Pursuant to the 2007 Act, the Council is defined, *inter alia*, as a body aiming at negotiating and reaching agreement in the fields of economic, social development and employment.[447] This tripartite body is still active today.

---

443. As can be implied from Myant, Slocock and Smith, *see ibid.*, pp. 733–734.
444. *Ibid.*, p. 733.
445. *See* Barancová, H. and Olšovská, A., 'Slovakia' in R. Blanpain and F. Hendrickx (eds), *International Encyclopaedia for Labour Law and Industrial Relations*, The Hague, Kluwer Law International, 2014, p. 52.
446. Czíria, L., *New Rules Adopted for Tripartite Social Dialogue*, Dublin, Eurofound, 2005.
447. *See* Article 2 of the 2007 Act.

2.2.2 Representativeness

The rules on representativeness allowing trade unions and employers' associations to participate in the work of the Slovak tripartite body have changed several times in the past two decades:[448]

(i) Until 2004, the rule was that for national level 'peak' organisations of social partners to be representative, they needed to be influential in the economy, to be active in at least five regions of the country and to represent at least 10% of the active population. The representatives of trade unions, employers and the government each had seven members in the tripartite body.

(ii) As of 2004, according to the statute of the Economic and Social Partnership Council, the national social partners' organisations were considered representative provided they employed (employers' associations) or represented (trade unions) at least 100,000 workers. Both trade unions and employers' associations would gain one seat in the tripartite body for every 100,000 employees.

(iii) With the legislative changes which entered into force in 2007, the rule of seven members per group was reintroduced. Trade unions should represent at least 100,000 employees from different sectors in the economy. Employers' associations have to bring together employers whose businesses cover several sectors of the economy or have competences in at least five regions, and they should employ at least 100,000 employees.

2.2.3 History of Social Pacts

The history of social pacts started in the federal state of Czechoslovakia, as the two social pacts (entitled as 'general agreements') were concluded in 1991 and 1992, before the formal dissolution of the country. The first agreement, concluded in 1991, was heralded as a building block of tripartism. Nevertheless, implementing this agreement was challenging because of the general economic climate, especially the drop in real wages.[449] As a result, the salience of tripartism was somewhat sidelined – despite trade union efforts, the second general agreement, concluded in 1992, contained rather general provisions and no specific wage commitments.[450] After the dissolution of the federal country, there were several social pacts concluded in Slovakia:[451]

---

448. The following overview of rules based on: Czíria, L., 'Collective Bargaining and Balanced Recovery: The Case of the Slovak Republic', Bratislava, Institute for Labour and Family Research, 2013, p. 5; Czíria, L., *Capacity Building for Social Dialogue in Slovakia*, Dublin, Eurofound, 2006.
449. Myant, Slocock and Smith 2000, p. 727.
450. *Ibid.*, p. 728.
451. The following overview based on: Czíria 2013, p. 4; Czíria, L., 'Slovakia: An Example of "Emancipated" Sectoral Social Dialogue?' in Y. Ghellab and D. Vaughan-Whitehead (eds), *Sectoral Social Dialogue in Future EU Member States: The Weakest Link*, 2003, Budapest, ILO.

(i) During the 1990s, several social pacts (general agreements) were concluded, respectively in years 1993, 1994, 1995 and 1996. Slovak scholar Czíria noted that these early general agreements were important in setting the national minimum wage and for contributing towards social and economic reforms.[452] Yet their overall significance was mitigated by the implementation problems that ensued, and these problems created tensions between social partners.[453]

(ii) The social dialogue reached a deadlock and no social pact could have been concluded after 1996. Only in 2000 was a social pact eventually signed, but its implementation was deemed unsatisfactory by trade unions. Since then, no further social pacts have been concluded in Slovakia.

Given that Slovakia has been a member of the Eurozone since 2009, a specific form of tripartite accord was adopted in relation to monetary union. This was the *Declaration on consensus regarding the implementation of the euro* from 2008, signed between the Slovak government and national cross-sectoral employer organisations, AZZZ SR and RUZ SR, together with trade union KOZ SR.[454] Unlike the crisis-related social pact that was concluded in Slovenia, this declaration did not represent a full-fledged and all-encompassing social pact. Nevertheless, it depicted a set of commitments to be undertaken by social partners and the government in view of preparations for the country to enter EMU.[455]

2.2.4 Crisis

The national social dialogue was particularly challenged during the crisis period and the general impression is that the trade unions lost political support and influence.[456] A special, crisis-related tripartite body was formed in 2009, entitled the *Economic Crisis Council*. However, this body did not have any substantial impact on industrial relations and was abolished shortly after its establishment.[457] No social pact was negotiated during the recent crisis period, although some prominent bilateral activities took place at national level. The most important activity was the conclusion of a bilateral agreement between the confederal trade union KOZ SR and the Slovak government in 2009 – *Memorandum on cooperation in solving the impact of the financial and economic crises on Slovak society* – expressing a list of mutual commitments towards resolving the negative consequences of the crisis in various policy areas.[458]

---

452. Czíria 2013, p. 4.
453. *Ibid.*
454. Czíria, L., *Social Partners Reach Consensus on Euro Implementation*, Dublin, Eurofound, 2008.
455. *Ibid.*
456. According to Kahancová, M., 'The Demise of Social Partnership or a Balanced Recovery? The Crisis and Collective Bargaining in Slovakia', *Transfer: European Review of Labour and Research*, 2013, vol. 19, no. 2, p. 177.
457. *Ibid.*, p. 173.
458. Czíria, L., *Slovakia: Impact of the Crisis on Industrial Relations*, Dublin, Eurofound, 2013b.

2.2.5 Regional Tripartite Social Dialogue

Apart from the tripartite structures which exist at national level, it is relevant to add that there is some form of regional tripartite social dialogue in Slovakia. The regional dialogue started in 1998 with the formation of regional tripartite bodies in four out of eight existing regions in the country. These bodies are made up of members of the regional state administration and social partners, and the legal basis for their activities are statutes agreed between the participating parties.[459] The impact of the regional social dialogue on industrial relations in Slovakia is nevertheless considered limited.[460]

2.3 The Czech Republic

2.3.1 The Tripartite Body: Power and Functioning

The tripartite system in the Czech Republic emerged from the federal tripartite body of Czechoslovakia. After the dissolution of the federal state, the Czech Republic continued its tripartite activity under the *Council for Social and Economic Affairs* (*Rada hospodářské a sociální dohody*). Myant noted that Czech tripartism was mostly dedicated to consultations on legislation and policy, and that in fact the tripartite Council never emerged as an 'arena for collective bargaining'.[461] The Czech tripartite Council has never functioned on the basis of statutory legal act. It has always operated on the basis of the tripartite statute, jointly adopted by the social partners and the government. Today, the Council is empowered to conduct tripartite negotiations about fundamental economic and social issues.[462] Nevertheless, even though it covers a broad range of areas within its remit, its role is considered predominantly consultative.[463] The Council gathers eight representatives of government, while national peak organisations of trade unions and employers' associations each have seven representatives. Its competences, as defined under the statute, have been subject to a number of amendments in the last two decades, according to which the powers of the tripartite Council fluctuated from a broader to a more limited set of prerogatives. There are several phases that can be identified:

(i) During the initial wave of tripartism, the Council was endowed with a broad range of competences, including decision-making on important social and economic policies, labour relations, as well as negotiations of tripartite

---

459. On regional social dialogue in Slovakia, *see* Machaliková, A., 'Tripartism in Slovak Republic' in G. Casale (ed.), *Social Dialogue in Central and Eastern Europe*, Budapest, ILO, 1999, pp. 288–304; Czíria 2006.
460. Czíria, L., *Tripartism Examined*, Dublin, Eurofound, 2003b.
461. Myant, M., 'Trade Unions in the Czech Republic', Report 115, Brussels, ETUI, 2010, p. 21.
462. *See* the unofficial translation in English of the Statute of Tripartite Council available at: http://www.vlada.cz/cz/za-premierem-a-vladou/statutes-5680/.
463. Kyzlinkova, R., Lehmann, S., Pojer, P. and Veverková, S., *Living and Working in Czech Republic – Collective Bargaining*, Dublin, Eurofound, 2017.

agreements.[464] The tripartite body was conceived as a forum for reaching social compromise on salient matters, particularly wages and unemployment.[465] As with the Slovak example, the initial set of competences of the Council has been subject to subsequent change – the two most important amendments took place in 1995 and 1997.

(ii) The 1995 statute narrowed the competences of the tripartite body, somewhat diminishing its importance. This consequently led to deterioration in social dialogue. The Council's competences were reduced to providing consultation, and it was no longer seen as an agreement-reaching body.[466] After 1994, in fact, there were no social pacts concluded in the Czech Republic.

(iii) Following the push from the newly elected government, the Council's original (pre-1995) set of competences were eventually restored with a major reconfiguration of its powers which took place in 1997.[467] Observers have nevertheless noted that the Council never managed to reinstate the influence it had in the early 1990s.[468] Although important policies came before it for discussion, in summary, the tripartite body in the Czech Republic failed to establish itself as an institution before which all legislation would have to be submitted for consideration.[469]

2.3.2 Representativeness

The representativeness criteria were introduced only in 1996. Before then, the statute of the tripartite body listed organisations that could participate in tripartite social dialogue. The representativeness criteria underwent several changes:[470]

(i) The 1996 statute defined a high quantitative threshold which social partners needed to fulfil in order to participate in tripartite social dialogue: the trade unions needed to have membership of at least 300,000 employees, while for employers' associations this threshold was 500,000.
(ii) In 2000, the threshold for trade unions was set at 200,000 employees, while the quantitative threshold for employers' associations was lifted.

---

464. Hála, J., Kroupa, A., Mansfeldova, Z., Kux, J., Vaskova, R. and Pleskot, I., *Development of Social Dialogue in the Czech Republic*, RILSA, 2002, p. 9.
465. Pollert, A., 'The Transformation of Trade Unionism in the Capitalist and Democratic Restructuring of the Czech Republic', *European Journal of Industrial Relations*, 1997, vol. 3, no. 2, pp. 209–210; *see also* Kubinková, M., 'Tripartism and Industrial Relations in the Czech Republic' in G. Casale (ed.), *Social Dialogue in Central and Eastern Europe*, Budapest, ILO, 1999.
466. Kubinková, *ibid.*, 1999, p. 130; Myant, Slocock and Smith 2000, p. 731.
467. Casale, G., Kubinková, M. and Rychly L., 'Social Dialogue – The Czech Success Story', Working Paper no 4, Geneva, International Labour Office, 2001, pp. 12–13.
468. Myant, Slocock and Smith 2000, pp. 731–734; Kubinková 1999, p. 130.
469. Hála et al., 2002, pp. 9–10.
470. The overview based on data from: Hála, J. and Kroupa, A., *Council of Economic and Social Agreement Tightens Representativeness Criteria*, Dublin, Eurofound, 2005; Kroupa, A. and Hála, J., *Capacity Building for Social Dialogue in the Czech Republic*, Dublin, Eurofound, 2006, p. 5.

(iii) In 2002, the threshold remained at 200,000 for trade unions, but for employers' associations it was introduced at 150,000.
(iv) Finally, since 2004, the statute defines that the associations of employers must represent at least 400,000 employees as members. The threshold for trade unions is 150,000. In addition, the statute defined several qualitative criteria for trade unions including, among others, that they should be independent and active nationwide, while the employers' associations should cover small, large and medium businesses and operate on a nationwide basis.

2.3.3 History of Social Pacts

The Czech Republic does not have a significant record of concluding social pacts. Social pacts (called 'general agreements') were concluded on a yearly basis only until 1994, and they were predominantly concerned with general economic and social issues, particularly wages. Their regulatory importance was limited – these agreements were interpreted as vague and difficult to implement in practice,[471] and the government considered them merely as political intent rather than binding instrument.[472] On top of that, their negotiations were usually lengthy and problematic. Over time, the government lost interest in conducting tripartite social dialogue, for which reason no general agreement was concluded after 1994, as already described in this section of the chapter. There were only unsuccessful attempts to conclude social pacts. Likewise, in 1998, trade unions rejected an initiative of the government to conclude a social pact, believing that these types of agreements could too easily be ignored or overruled.[473]

2.3.4 Crisis

The recent financial crisis did not bring much legal or institutional change to the Czech tripartite system, and no social pact has been concluded since this period. Some efforts on the part of social partners to advance social dialogue were nevertheless visible. Likewise, in 2010 the tripartite Council reached the agreement on the document titled *Ways out of the crisis: 38 common measures of the government, trade unions and employers*.[474] This tripartite success is mitigated – the government elected shortly after the document was agreed did not endorse the proposed measures.[475]

---

471. Myant 2010, pp. 21–22; Pollert 1997, p. 210.
472. Myant, M., 'Czech and Slovak Trade Unions', *Journal of Communist Studies*, 1993, vol. 9, no. 4, p. 69.
473. Myant 2010, p. 22.
474. Verveková, S., 'The Case of the Czech Republic' in I. Guardiancich (ed.), *Recovering from the Crisis Through Social Dialogue in the New EU Member States: The Case of Bulgaria, the Czech Republic, Poland and Slovenia*, Budapest, ILO, 2012a, p. 55 and p. 61; see Verveková, S., *Tripartite Agreement on Short-Term Anti-Crisis Measures* Dublin, Eurofound, 2010.
475. Verveková, S., *Trade Unions Abandoned Tripartite Talks*, Dublin, Eurofound, 2012b.

Chapter 5: National Level: The Role of Tripartism

2.3.5 *Regional Tripartite Social Dialogue*

As is the case with Slovakia and Poland, a limited form of regional social dialogue has developed in the Czech Republic since 1991. It operates on the basis of tripartite statutes agreed between participating parties.[476] No agreements have been concluded at this regional level, and it can be noted that the impact of this type of social dialogue is limited.

2.4 Poland

2.4.1 *The Tripartite Body: Power and Functioning*

The Tripartite Commission for Social and Economic Affairs in Poland was formed in 1994, on the basis of the tripartite Pact on State-Owned Enterprises in the Restructuring Process (signed in 1993). This tripartite body was built on a considerable trade union legacy and their influential role in facilitating the transitional processes – the trade union Solidarity, which had been established officially in the 1980s, played a major role in anti-communist activities. The intention behind forming the tripartite body was to legitimise the restrictive economic reforms which were pursued at the time and to help accelerating the privatisation process.[477] At the same time, the major goal of the tripartite Commission was maintaining and guaranteeing social peace. This body has been in existence until a recent reconfiguration which took place in 2015 and it was composed of representatives of the government, trade unions and employers' associations.[478] Before the major reconfiguration of 2015, the legal basis of the tripartite Commission had undergone change in the following phases:

> (i) Until the early 2000s, the Polish tripartite Commission did not have any statutory legal basis, and its powers and competences were decided by the 1994 governmental decree. In general, the Commission had a consultative role and its decisions were non-binding. Only in a smaller segment of its remit, related to income policies, did the tripartite Commission function on the basis of law – this was a statutory legal act, passed in 1994, which empowered the Commission to set the criteria for wage increases at company level.[479] Nevertheless, the functioning of the Commission was substantially

---

476. For more information, particularly on trade union activities at regional level, *see* Hála et al., 2002, pp. 64–70.
477. The circumstances which led to the adoption of the 1993 Pact and forming the tripartite body have been succinctly described by Iankova 2002, pp. 105–113.
478. Guardiancich, I. and Pliszkiewicz, M., 'The Case of Poland' in I. Guardiancich (ed.), *Recovering from the Crisis Through Social Dialogue in the New EU Member States: The Case of Bulgaria, the Czech Republic, Poland and Slovenia*, Budapest, ILO, 2012, p. 75. The trade unions are: All-Poland Alliance of Trade Unions (OPZZ), Independent Self Governing Trade Union 'Solidarity' (NSZZ Solidarnosc), Trade Union Forum (FZZ). The employers' associations are: Polish Confederation of Private Employers Lewiatan (PKPP Lewiatan), Polish Crafts Union (ZRP), Business Centre Club (BCC), Confederation of Polish Employers (KPP).
479. Iankova 2002, p. 110.

hampered because decisions on wage increases had to be taken unanimously – in fact, it managed to reach an agreement on this matter only in year 1996.[480]

(ii) In 2001, the Act on the Tripartite Commission for Social and Economic Affairs and the Voivodeship Committees of Social Dialogue,[481] provided a statutory legal basis for the tripartite body. This Act remained valid until 2015. Under its provisions, the Commission played a consultative role and could not issue legally binding decisions. Yet, judging from the fact that no social pacts were concluded during this period, the tripartite system has not substantially benefited from this formal (statutory) institutionalisation – in comparison with the other three countries, Poland has the poorest record of agreements concluded at the tripartite level. The major reason behind the low output has been the tension and conflict between the social partners, particularly between the major trade unions, OPZZ and Solidarity.[482]

(iii) Finally, in July 2015, the Act on the Social Dialogue Council and Other Institutions of Social Dialogue was enacted, replacing the former tripartite body with the *Social Dialogue Council*. This body is designed to have substantially broadened competences compared with its predecessor.[483]

2.4.2 Representativeness

No representativeness criteria were anticipated when the tripartite body was initially formed, and all signatories to the 1993 Pact on State-Owned Enterprises in the Restructuring Process were automatically considered its members. In 2001, the Act on the Tripartite Commission introduced representativeness criteria, enabling several other organisations of social partners to join the tripartite system.[484] In fact, the 2001 representativeness rules listed the organisations of social partners that were considered representative and could automatically participate in tripartite social dialogue.[485] In addition, the provisions defined the conditions which other, non-listed organisations of trade unions and employers' associations should fulfil in order to be considered representative. This included a quantitative threshold of 300,000 employees that trade unions needed to count in their membership, as well as 300,000 employees working for

---

480. In other years, these decisions were made unilaterally by the government, as explained by Gardawski, J. and Meardi, G., 'Keep Trying? Polish Failures and Half- Successes in Social Pacting', *Warsaw Forum of Economic Sociology*, 2010, vol. 1, no. 2, pp. 74-75.
481. Voivodeship referring to 'regional' in the Polish context.
482. Trappman, V., *Fallen Heroes in Global Capitalism Workers and the Restructuring of the Polish Steel Industry*, New York, Palgrave Macmillan, 2013, pp. 88-89.
483. Hajn, Z. and Mitrus, L., 'Poland' in R. Blanpain and F. Hendrickx (eds), *International Encyclopaedia for Labour Law and Industrial Relations*, The Hague, Kluwer Law International, 2016, p. 39.
484. See Gardawski, J., *The Development of the National Tripartite Commission*, Dublin, Eurofound, 2002.
485. Thus, from the side of trade unions, Solidarity and OPZZ, as well as FZZ as of 2003; while on the side of employers, KPP, ZRP and PKPP Lewiatan.

the entities that are members of the employers' associations.[486] The provisions granting automatic membership to the tripartite Commission were subsequently lifted.

The 2015 Act on Social Dialogue Council and Other Institutions of Social Dialogue has once more modified these provisions, requiring trade unions to have a membership of at least 300,000 employees working in at least half of the sections of the economy. The same quantitative threshold applies to employers' associations.[487]

2.4.3 History of Social Pacts

Of the four CEE countries, Poland has the poorest track record of concluded social pacts, the main reason being the conflicting relationships among social partners. In fact, the entire history of social pacts consists of only two agreements signed before 1990, and one agreement signed after 1990. The two pre-1990 pacts assisted in the economic and political transition from communism to free market:[488]

(1) The 1980 *August agreement* or *Gdansk agreement* was famous for allowing the formation of trade unions, and this represented a landmark political and democratic step. In 1980, Solidarity became the first independent trade union in the CEE countries to come into existence pursuant to this agreement. With the imposition of martial law in the same year, its activities were soon banned, but even so Solidarity continued to operate as an underground organisation.
(2) The *Round table agreement*, concluded in 1989, facilitated the transformation of the social and economic system, allowing the first free elections in the country and reinstating Solidarity as a legal organisation.

After the onset of transition, only one social pact was concluded. This was the 1993 *Pact on State-Owned Enterprises in the Restructuring Process*, notable for establishing the tripartite Commission. This pact assisted market transformation by providing trade union acceptance for the privatisation of the state-owned enterprises.[489] At the same time, the Pact contributed towards the shape of the current collective bargaining system – by emphasising the role of employees in the privatisation of the state-owned companies, the company became the key level for deciding on social and economic transformation.[490] The 1993 pact did not constitute a typical social pact: it consisted of three separate agreements, which taken together represented a full-fledged social pact. In the process of its making, the government and the employers' organisation had held separate negotiations with trade unions and eventually concluded

---

486. Gardawski 2002, *ibid*.
487. Hajn and Mitrus 2016, p. 249 and p. 259.
488. As reported by Gardawski and Meardi 2010, pp. 71–72.
489. Iankova 2002, p. 107.
490. Sewerynski, M., 'Development of the Collective Bargaining System in Poland after the Second World War', *Comparative Labour Law Journal*, 1993, vol. 14, pp. 475–476.

three agreements, notably with OPZZ, Solidarity and the remaining seven trade unions which had participated in the social dialogue.[491]

Although no social pacts were concluded after 1993, some authors have nevertheless provided a more balanced assessment of the history of social pacts. Gardawski and Meardi noted that a more thorough assessment of the interaction among actors reveals 'that there have been very serious attempts at social pacts, and there have been some unintended effects of these attempts',[492] having in mind that social partners managed to achieve some important bilateral accords in the past years.

One of the most prominent attempts took place in 2003, when the government proposed a comprehensive social pact, but the trade union side (notably Solidarity) showed no interest in the package.[493] Eventually, in the same year, a bilateral agreement was signed between OPZZ and employer' confederations proposing labour law changes in several areas. These proposals were partially accepted by the government and turned into a legislative proposal.[494] Another initiative aiming for a comprehensive social pact was put forward by the government in 2007, but the two major trade unions did not agree on the proposed measures.[495]

Mention may also be made of other examples of bilateral agreements concluded between social partners. One example is the 2003 agreement concluded between one of the major trade union organisations, OPZZ, and the two major employers' organisations (PKPP Lewiatan and ZRP) on a range of issues which could not have been agreed at the tripartite level.[496] Furthermore, in 2004, trade unions and employers' associations reacted to the governments' proposal on the transposition of the Directive on Information and Consultation by reaching an agreement to minimise the role of works councils.[497]

2.4.4 Crisis

The recent economic and financial crisis temporarily increased social dialogue practices at the tripartite level.[498] In 2009, the social partners bilaterally agreed on thirteen anti-crisis common points, which were to some extent accepted by the government and turned into statutory legal provisions.[499] Nonetheless, as social dialogue deteriorated and in 2013 the three major trade unions decided to give up their membership of the

---

491. Iankova 2002, pp. 106–107.
492. Gardawski and Meardi 2010, p. 70.
493. *Ibid.*, pp. 79–81.
494. Gardawski, J., *OPZZ and Four Employers' Confederations Sign Bipartite Agreement*, Dublin, Eurofound, 2004.
495. Gardawski and Meardi 2010, p. 83; Towalski, R., *Social Partners Sign Social Pact Declaration*, Dublin, Eurofound, 2007.
496. Gardawski 2004.
497. *See* Meardi 2012a, pp. 48–49.
498. Bernaciak, M., 'Social Dialogue Revival or "PR Corporatism"? Negotiating Anti-Crisis Measures in Poland and Bulgaria', *Transfer: European Review of Labour and Research*, 2013, vol. 19, no. 2, pp. 239–251.
499. Meardi, G. and Trappman, V., 'Between Consolidation and Crisis: Divergent Pressures and Sectoral Trends in Poland', *Transfer: European Review of Labour and Research*, 2013, vol. 19, p. 199.

Chapter 5: National Level: The Role of Tripartism

tripartite body, this led to discussions over reforming tripartism in Poland.[500] These discussions led to the formation of a new tripartite body, the *Social Dialogue Council* (*Rada Dialogu Społecznego*), in March 2015[501] replacing the one which had been in operation for more than two decades.

2.4.5 Regional Tripartite Social Dialogue

Regional tripartite social dialogue is conducted between social partners and national and regional government. There are seventeen regional social dialogue teams, which have been established pursuant to the 2001 Act on Tripartite Commission.[502] However, as the interviewees from the Polish trade unions explained, the outcome of regional social dialogue has been limited, as these bodies do not have real decision-making powers, but may only voice opinions which are not legally binding. In addition, in several sectors of the economy it is possible to find tripartite sectoral committees which have only an advisory role.

3 COMPARATIVE OVERVIEW OF LEGAL AND INSTITUTIONAL TRAITS

3.1 Social Pacts: Weak Instruments of Standard Setting in CEE

The concept of social pact has been not unequivocally defined in the literature. *In broad terms*, social pacts can refer to any form of tripartite agreements concluded between organisations of trade unions, organisations of employers and the state, with a view to regulating a broad range of social and economic matters, including welfare and income policies. Such a broad conceptualisation of social pacts has also been proposed by Natali and Pochet:

> Social pacts can be defined as a set of formal or informal agreements between representatives of governments and organised interests, who negotiate and implement policy change across a number of interconnected policy areas.[503]

In a narrower sense, as proposed by Avdagic, social pacts are only publicly announced formal policy contracts between the government and social partners over income, labour market, or welfare policies that identify policy issues and targets, the means to achieve them, and the tasks and responsibilities of the signatories.[504] This

---

500. Czarzasty, J., *Poland: National-Level Tripartite Social Dialogue Back on Track*, Dublin, Eurofound, 2015.
501. *Ibid.*
502. Gardawski, Mrozowicki and Czarzasty 2010, p. 23. Full name is the Act on the Tripartite Commission for Social and Economic Affairs and the Voivodeship [regional] Committees of Social Dialogue.
503. Natali, D. and Pochet, P., 'The Evolution of Social Pacts in the EMU Era: What Type of Institutionalisation?', *European Journal of Industrial Relations*, 2009, vol. 15, no. 2, pp. 148-149.
504. As defined in: Avdagic, S., 'The Conditions for Pacts: A Fuzzy-Set Analysis of the Resurgence of Tripartite Concertation' in S. Avdagic, M. Rhodes, and J. Visser (eds), *Social Pacts in Europe: Emergence, Evolution, and Institutionalisation*, Oxford, Oxford University Press, 2011, pp.

narrower understanding of social pacts excludes other possible forms of agreements, such as declaratory agreements, general statements of intent or bilateral agreements between trade unions and employers.[505] When explaining social pacts, it is also crucial to add that their constituent ingredient is *state sponsorship*, as these agreements are concluded in the 'shadow of the state', even when the style of free collective bargaining is formally maintained.[506]

The history of social pacts in CEE as presented so far in this chapter consists of different forms of tripartite arrangements. Section 2 has attempted to distinguish between social pacts in the narrow sense and the other forms of accords that may be found in CEE. For example, this latter category would encompass the Slovak 2008 declaration about the implementation of the euro, or the Polish agreements concluded on a bilateral basis between social partners at the national level. The track record of concluded social pacts in the four countries is modest – with the exception of Slovenia, where social pacts have been systematically concluded over the past two decades, their conclusion has been more an exception than a rule in the other three countries. Slovakia concluded social pacts until 2001, while the Czech Republic did so only until 1994. Poland has the poorest track record, with a single pact concluded in 1993, and even this was concluded in a specific form, consisting of three separate agreements which cumulatively represented a full-fledged social pact.

The poor track record described above evidences the modest impact of the social pact as a source for setting standards in CEE. With the exception of Slovenia, the social pacts are underused instruments. On a more general level, one may note a genuine lack of negotiated outcomes at this level. Therefore, one may conclude that the national level in CEE is a weak element within a multi-level framework of standard setting. However, it is also true that the practice of concluding social pacts is rather inconsistent in the Member States of the EU, and for that reason there is no clear guidance to be offered or standard formula that can be promoted to CEE countries. Social pacts were concluded in several countries in the 1990s (among others, Italy, Spain, Portugal) – they represented comprehensive agreements regulating a broad range of matters, but particularly facilitating entry to the EMU and dealing with economic difficulties.[507] The format in which social pacts were concluded in the EU has also varied. In some cases, social pacts would cover a broad range of items at once (horizontal pacts) or they would sequentially cover different items in different accords at different times, generating similar effects as horizontal pacts (longitudinal pacts).[508] The practice of concluding social pacts, which was pervasive across several Member States of the EU

25–26. A similar definition can be found in Avdagic, S., 'When Are Concerted Reforms Feasible? Explaining the Emergence of Social Pacts in Western Europe', *Comparative Political Studies*, 2010b, vol. 43, no. 5, p. 637.

505. Avdagic 2011, pp. 25–26.

506. As underlined by Traxler, F., 'National Pacts and Wage Regulation in Europe: A Comparative Analysis' in G. Fajertag and P. Pochet (eds), *Social Pacts in Europe: New Dynamics*, Brussels, ETUI/OSE, 2000, p. 403.

507. *See* Visser, J., 'Beneath the Surface of Stability: New and Old Modes of Governance in European Industrial Relations', *European Journal of Industrial Relations*, 2005, vol. 11, no. 3, pp. 288–289; Meardi 2012a, p. 44.

508. The division presented by Natali and Pochet 2009, p. 149.

in the 1990s, did not run counter to the decentralisation trend, but, rather, ran alongside it. Where social pacts were concluded, they contributed towards a more efficient governability of the collective bargaining system, especially by facilitating wage moderation.[509] Likewise, in some countries, social pacts performed the role of 'procedural rationalisation' of the collective bargaining systems (as is the case in Italy or Spain) by introducing the provisions relevant for decentralisation and negotiating procedure at lower levels.[510] In line with the logic of Traxler's 'organised decentralisation' the social pacts did not constrain, but rather supported collective bargaining at sectoral and company levels.[511] An example is the Italian social pact of 1993, known for establishing a two-tier system of collective bargaining at sectoral and company levels. Or the two Dutch social pacts in 1982 and 1993, which facilitated collective bargaining reform and supported greater decentralisation.[512]

On the whole, the CEE social pacts do not perform similar functions. Nevertheless, some CEE pacts did have long lasting effect on industrial relations. Clearly, that is the case in Slovenia, where social pacts, together with the national level cross-sectoral collective agreements, have facilitated the collective bargaining system by setting provisions to be further specified at sectoral and company levels. In this sense the Slovenian national standard-setting level (tripartite or bipartite) has played a prominent role in facilitating the normative model of articulated multi-employer bargaining (proposed in Chapter 1), by setting the framework of standards at a higher level to be further specified or implemented at lower levels. Poland provides a contrasting case. The 1993 Polish social pact postulated the enterprise as the main locus of standard setting: the employees in the enterprises were given a key role in the privatisation process. This 1993 pact thus represented one of the key building blocks of the progressive decentralisation in industrial relations that is to be found in today's Poland. However, a different role was played by the two pre-1990s Polish social pacts which contributed towards the institutionalisation of industrial relations by facilitating free trade unionism. In the two remaining countries of Slovakia and the Czech Republic, it cannot be said that social pacts had tangible impact on the structure of collective bargaining (although, in the 1990s, as demonstrated in section 2, the Slovak tripartite body was involved in decision-making on the extensions of sectoral collective agreements to those employers not covered by these agreements).

Moreover, as well as having little influence on the collective bargaining system, the overall impact of social pacts (outside the framework of collective bargaining) was limited. Those that existed in CEE had a rather modest role, receiving lukewarm

---

509. Molina, O., 'Social Pacts, Collective Bargaining and Trade Union Articulation Strategies', *Transfer: European Review of Labour and Research*, 2008, vol. 14, no. 3, p. 400.
510. Marginson, P. and Sisson, K., *European Integration and Industrial Relations: Multi-Level Governance in the Making*, Basingstoke, Palgrave Macmillan, 2006, p. 126.
511. Regini, M., 'Between Deregulation and Social Pacts: The Responses of European Economies to Globalization', *Politics & Society*, 2000a, vol. 28, no. 1, p. 13; notion of 'organised decentralisation' coined by Traxler, F., 'Farewell to Labour Market Associations? Organised versus Disorganised Decentralisation as a Map for Industrial Relations' in F. Traxler and C. Crouch (eds), *Organised Industrial Relations in Europe: What Future?*, Aldershot, Avebury, 1995, pp. 3–19.
512. Molina 2008.

evaluation by the scholars. Avdagic and Crouch, likewise, noted that the CEE social pacts had little impact on overall macroeconomic management, and could hardly be described as negotiated policy adjustments tailored to improve coordination at different levels.[513] Instead, they were used to legitimise neoliberal policies and often represented a response to a specific problem.[514] Meardi noted that Slovakia, Poland and the Czech Republic opted for unilateral enforcement of macroeconomic convergence to deal with public debt rather than concluding social pacts.[515] Ost noted that social pacts were not used for genuine bargaining between two sides, but rather to urge labour complicity for neoliberal policies.[516]

Another problem in CEE was the fact that concluded social pacts were not necessarily fully implemented. As described in section 2 of this chapter, the problem of limited or inadequate implementation was common to the four countries at different times in the past decades. As Slovak interviewees explained, social pacts in their country were considered merely as 'gentlemen's agreements' which the contracting parties did not necessarily consider binding. As section 2 has demonstrated, this lack of full implementation was a feature of Czech and Slovak industrial relations in particular, that also had a far-reaching effect on the fate of the tripartite social dialogue. In Slovakia, the trade unions' discontent over the implementation of social pacts, and the resultant disagreements between social partners and the government led to the breakdown of social dialogue in 1997.[517] When another general agreement was concluded in Slovakia in 2000, it also was not fully implemented. In the Czech Republic, after the unsatisfactory implementation of a series of social pacts in the early 1990s, the general interest in tripartite social dialogue diminished and no other social pacts have been concluded since.[518] How to explain the lack of full implementation of the agreed deals? This can certainly be ascribed to the weaknesses of the social partners in CEE countries, in addition to the general weaknesses in the collective bargaining systems and low coverage rates of collective agreements at any level. The industrial relations scholar Crouch highlighted strong inter-union organisation and organised 'articulation' of social partners at different levels as particularly important for the successful implementation of agreed tripartite accords.[519] However, the capacities of social partners at sectoral and company level are weak in CEE, and the commitments

---

513. Avdagic, S. and Crouch, C., 'Organised Economic Interests: Diversity and Change in an Enlarged Europe' in P.M. Heywood, E. Jones, M. Rhodes and U. Sedelmeier (eds), *Developments in European Politics*, Basingstoke, Palgrave Macmillan, 2006, p. 211.
514. Ibid.
515. Meardi 2012a, p. 55.
516. As also underlined by Ost, D., '"Illusory Corporatism" Ten Years Later', *Warsaw Forum of Economic Sociology*, 2011, vol. 2, no. 1, pp. 19–20; also, Ost, D., 'Illusory Corporatism in Eastern Europe: Neoliberal Tripartism and Postcommunist Class Identities', *Politics & Society*, 2000, vol. 28, no. 4, pp. 503–530.
517. Czíria 2013, p. 4.
518. Myant, Slocock and Smith 2000, p. 731; the issue of implementation has been also described in Cox, T.M. and Mason, B., 'Interest Groups and the Development of Tripartism in East Central Europe', *European Journal of Industrial Relations*, 2000a, vol. 6, no. 3, p. 338.
519. Colin Crouch, who considered the articulation of social partners' structure to be one of the key determinants of industrial relations; see Crouch, C., *Industrial Relations and European State Traditions*, Oxford, Oxford University Press, 1993.

agreed at the tripartite level may not necessarily be implemented through collective agreements at sectoral and company levels.[520]

The low number of concluded social pacts, their limited scope and limited implementation are the reasons that CEE tripartism has received lukewarm reviews in the scholarship, the most famous and much referenced labels being 'illusory corporatism' and 'fragile shell'.[521] The interviewees, particularly in Slovakia, the Czech Republic and Poland, have also evaluated the role of tripartite social dialogue as weak. It is also rather difficult to find a more positive assessment of the CEE tripartism in the literature. In a minority opinion, Mailand and Due have explained that despite the lack of a solid track record, tripartite social dialogue has nevertheless achieved a number of tangible results, and has assisted in developing and maturing the social dialogue culture.[522] Iankova and Turner have argued that tripartism gave voice to the trade unions and represented a model of democratisation within the post-communist economic and political setting.[523] Furthermore, the recent economic and financial crisis period has shown some positive signs, evidencing that the role of tripartism cannot be fully dismissed in CEE. The best example is the Polish reform which took place in 2015 and which led to revival of tripartism in this country.

3.2 Institutionalisation of Tripartite Bodies

The four countries had their tripartite bodies established in the first half of the 1990s. The rationale behind their introduction was mostly related to the idea of maintaining social peace and providing greater legitimacy to decision-making in difficult economic situation which surrounded the process of privatisation. There are authors who underline that formation of tripartite institutions was also promoted by the external actors (ILO and EU).[524] In an effort to build meaningful and effective tripartite models, CEE countries were looking at the examples of the EU countries, particularly tripartite bodies in Germany and Austria.[525] The early 1990s period also coincided with the

---

520. The thesis that the weak social partners in CEE are not able to make credible commitments in social pacts has been particularly underlined by Keune, M. and Pochet, P., 'Conclusions: Trade Union Structures, the Virtual Absence of Social Pacts in the New Member States and the Relationship Between Sheltered and Exposed Sectors' in P. Pochet, M. Keune and D. Natalie (eds), *After the Euro and Enlargement: Social Pacts in the EU*, Brussels, ETUI, 2010, p. 402.
521. Ost 2000; Pollert, A., 'Ten Years of Post-Communist Central Eastern Europe: Labour's Tenuous Foothold in the Regulation of the Employment Relationship', *Economic and Industrial Democracy*, 2000, vol. 21, no. 2, p. 186.
522. Mailand, M. and Due, J., 'Social Dialogue in Central and Eastern Europe: Present State and Future Development', *European Journal of Industrial Relations*, 2004, vol. 10, no. 2, pp. 190–191.
523. Iankova, E. and Turner, L., 'Building the New Europe: Western and Eastern Roads to Social Partnership', *Industrial Relations Journal*, 2004, vol. 35, no. 1, p. 85.
524. Meardi 2012a, pp. 43–44; Mailand and Due 2004, pp. 183–184; Ghellab and Vaughan-Whitehead 2003, p. 28, mentioning the examples of Ireland and Italy.
525. This argument was mentioned in few instances in the literature; *see* e.g. Pollert 2000, p. 186; Bluhm, K., 'Resolving Liberalisation Dilemma: Labour Relations in East-Central Europe and the Impact of European Union' in M.A. Moreau and M.E. Blas-López (eds), *Restructuring in the New EU Member States: Social Dialogue, Firms Relocation, and Social Treatment of Restructuring*, Brussels, Peter Lang, 2008, p. 63; Casale, G., 'Experiences of Tripartite Relations in Central

transposition of the major ILO treaties which ensured the insertion into the legal systems of the basic principles of collective bargaining and social dialogue. In fact, the formation of the tripartite bodies in CEE was a significant moment because it was the first step towards the institutionalisation of industrial relations in the post-communist environment. Given the lack of experience in social dialogue, participation in the tripartite institutions seemed at the time the most convenient way to ensure a 'voice' for the trade unions.

The previous section demonstrated that the functioning of various tripartite bodies in CEE was sometimes difficult, and their powers and competences have changed a number of times in the selected countries. In Slovenia and the Czech Republic, the tripartite institution has never been given a statutory legal basis, and in Poland it was not until 2001 that tripartism was acknowledged in statutory law. As noted by an interviewee in Poland, the legitimacy of the tripartite body was disputed until 2001 because it operated on the basis of governmental decree. As section 2 of this chapter demonstrated, in the past two decades, in Slovakia, particularly, tripartism has gone through different phases while the legal basis has fluctuated between statute and tripartite agreement. Yet, judging from the examples of these four countries, whether a tripartite body functions on the basis of statutory legal act or tripartite agreement seems to have no relevance to the frequency and quality of the outcomes of tripartite negotiations. This conclusion is underpinned by the fact that regardless of the legal basis of the tripartite body, the track record in concluded social pacts is rather limited (with the exception of Slovenia). In Slovenia, where tripartite body functions on the basis of tripartite agreements, social pacts have been concluded consistently since the early transitional period – but it can be also argued that Slovenian tripartism enjoyed a wider legitimacy since it was underpinned by tripartite agreement rather than statutory act. A telling example is found in Poland, where affording a statutory legal basis to the tripartite institution in the early 2000s did not generate any social pacts. Regardless of the legal basis on which the tripartite bodies function, their competences have been broadly defined in all four countries and did not prevent social partners from entering into any tripartite negotiations and concluding any forms of negotiated agreements if they wished to do so.

A further issue is that the tripartite bodies have a predominantly advisory role, and that in none of the four countries can the tripartite body issue legally binding decisions. Despite this, the tripartite institutions have played, at different instances and in different forms, a significant role in relation to pressing social and economic matters. In Slovenia and in the Czech Republic the interviewees have confirmed that no law was enacted before consultation in the tripartite body had taken place. In Slovenia, during the recent crisis period, an interesting exception to such a consultative role is found in 2011, when the anti-crisis package of laws was enacted without prior consultation at the tripartite level. As explained in section 2.2, these laws were eventually withdrawn, following the referendum initiated by the trade unions. An example of a tripartite institution playing a significant role in relation to vital economic and social matters is

---

and Eastern European Countries', *The International Journal of Comparative Labour Law and Industrial Relations*, 2000, vol. 16, no. 2, p. 131.

in the area of wages policy in Poland. Here, tripartite social dialogue is a formal requirement in determining minimum wage levels and the tripartite body also traditionally provides its non-binding opinion to the government regarding wage increases.[526]

The weak outcomes of social dialogue in CEE can be mostly ascribed to the lack of social dialogue tradition and to conflicts among the participants in the tripartite dialogue. The social partners' proposals have been in various instances dismissed by the governments, or the governments did not at specific periods of time provide enough support for social dialogue. An example of the latter is the Czech Republic, where Myant mentions that governments considered tripartism a forum to find out the opinion of the social partners.[527] Generalisations on this point, however, should be made cautiously, because, as demonstrated in relation to Poland, government initiatives to conclude social pacts were not always met with enthusiasm on the social partners' side. One can also find instances where the modest outcomes of CEE tripartism were linked to the ways in which the competences and powers were defined within their founding acts. Examples of this have been evidenced in section 2, in relation to the Czech tripartite statute of 1995 and the Slovak configuration of tripartism between 2004 and 2007. In both cases, the competences of tripartite bodies were narrowly set and this prevented tripartite agreements being reached.

On a final note, it is worth mentioning that *the topic of representativeness* had particular relevance for the institutionalisation of CEE tripartism in the 1990s as it was necessary to identify social partner organisations that could participate in tripartite social dialogue. Because they set criteria for social partners' participation in social dialogue, the gradual enactment of rules on representativeness was an important step for improving the legitimacy of decision-making at this level. Section 2 demonstrated that the representativeness rules were shaped gradually in these countries. The Czech and Slovak examples are particularly telling, with their rules changing several times in the past two decades. Nevertheless, as evident from section 2, the introduction of rules in 1990s and their further reshaping in subsequent years did not generate any impact on the track record of concluding social pacts.

4 CONCLUDING REMARKS

4.1 Explaining the Development of the Legal and Institutional Framework for Tripartite Social Dialogue

This chapter has demonstrated that only in Slovenia did tripartism emerge as an important locus for standard setting, although its salience has fluctuated over time. In the other CEE countries, the experiences with tripartism were far more modest.

---

526. For more detailed description of wage-setting mechanisms in Poland, *see* Towalski, R., *Wage Formation: Poland*, Dublin, Eurofound, 2009, available at: http://www.eurofound.europa.eu/observatories/eurwork/comparative-information/national-contributions/poland/wage-formation-poland (accessed 1 December 2017).
527. Myant 2010, p. 22.

Moreover, in all CEE countries the significance of tripartism was more pronounced in the early 1990s, and it has lost significance over time. Nevertheless, as section 2 demonstrated, there were some reassuring signs of its revival during the recent crisis period.[528] Tripartism in CEE has attracted considerable academic attention, and the following remarks will draw on sources of rich scholarship. As the following lines will demonstrate, the overall impression stemming from the academic literature is that the lack of policy support has been the most decisive factor determining the fate of tripartism in CEE. In addition, the interviewees, particularly in Slovakia, the Czech Republic and Poland, have underlined that the tripartite dynamic and outcome suffered from the conflicts between the parties participating in the tripartite social dialogue.

The previous sections underlined that *the Polish variation of tripartism* has been weakest in the past two decades compared with the other countries. Nevertheless, the Polish tripartite institution was endowed with some pertinent competences, such as setting minimum wages and maximum wage increases.[529] There are two major factors which have shaped Polish tripartism. Although the tripartite bodies were originally constituted with a view to maintaining social peace, the lack of consistent support from the policy makers was the main reason that they did not develop into institutions able to have a major say in reformative processes.[530] Other influential factors were the lack of unity on the trade union side and conflicts among the two major trade unions (Solidarity and OPZZ), alongside their ideological and political divisions.[531]

The Czech variation of tripartism did not generate substantial outcomes in terms of social pacts either: it emerged as a consultative body and social partners regarded it merely as a lobbying venue.[532] Lack of policy support seems to have been the major determinant of Czech tripartism – policy makers and trade unions lost interest in it since the mid-1990s.[533] At the same time, Czech tripartism was further challenged by trade union weaknesses and their inability to win concession from the government.[534]

Initially, the major determinant of *Slovak tripartism* was the support which it received from the government.[535] Gradually, this support faded, leading to the

---

528. A trend of reviving tripartism in CEE during the recent crisis period has been otherwise underlined in a recent study by Kahancová, M., 'Central and Eastern European Trade Unions after the EU Enlargement: Successes and Failures for Capacity Building', *Transfer: European Review of Labour and Research*, 2015, vol. 21, no. 3, p. 348.
529. As noted by Avdagic, S., 'Tripartism and Economic Reforms in Slovenia and Poland' in L. Fraile (ed.), *Blunting Neoliberalism: Tripartism and Economic Reforms in the Developing World*, Basingstoke, Palgrave Macmillan, 2010a, pp. 43–45.
530. Cox, T.M. and Mason, B., 'Interest Groups and the Development of Tripartism in East Central Europe', *European Journal of Industrial Relations*, 2000a, vol. 6, no. 3, pp. 342–343. Avdagic, likewise, notes that governments in Poland tended to bypass tripartite negotiations, *see* Avdagic, S., 'State-Labour Relations in East Central Europe: Explaining Variations in Union Effectiveness', *Socio-Economic Review*, 2005, vol. 3, p. 32.
531. Avdagic 2010a, pp. 44–45; *see* Trappman 2013, pp. 88–89.
532. Myant, Slocock and Smith 2000, p. 731.
533. Myant, Slocock and Smith 2000, pp. 729–733; Pollert 1997, p. 210.
534. *See* Myant, Slocock and Smith 2000, pp. 725–733.
535. Myant, Slocock and Smith 2000, pp. 733–734.

marginalisation of tripartism from the mid-1990s onwards.[536] An important explanatory factor in distinguishing the Czech and Slovak experiences is the centralised representation of the Slovak trade unions which remained a blueprint of Slovak industrial relations.[537] However, Slovak variation of tripartism, as its Czech counterpart, has never emerged as an institution with significant say in reform processes.[538]

Since it is the only CEE country that could be described as having a coordinated market economy (as explained in Chapter 2, section 3.1), and having the most elaborated history of social pacts, *Slovenia* has attracted much attention from CEE scholars. Describing the Slovenian 'exceptionalism', Crowley and Stanojević offered several explanatory factors – relatively favourable economic circumstances during the reform period compared to the other CEE countries, the helpful role of the legacies which favoured an active role for social partners, the gradual approach in conducting market reforms, and the fact of basic compromise on major social and economic items between the social partners and the state.[539] Slovenian trade unions were exceptional in gradually developing into 'neocoporatist, intermediary organisations'.[540] As the previous section demonstrated, the Slovenian model of tripartism has therefore had substantial impact on standard setting and collective bargaining, particularly at the beginning of the 1990s.

4.2 Standard Setting at National Level

To what extent does the current legal and institutional framework support and promote social dialogue at national level? To summarise the findings of this chapter, only in Slovenia can social pacts be considered an important locus for standard setting (together with bilateral cross-sectoral collective agreements which, for almost two decades, have represented an additional source of standards for all employees in the economy). The experiences of the other three countries, regarding tripartite and/or bipartite social dialogue and collective bargaining at national level, may not fit the logic of the normative articulated multi-employer bargaining model proposed in Chapter 1. In these countries, national tripartite rules form a weak link in the normative articulated multi-employer model. As this chapter has demonstrated, the negotiation of standards at national level is weak and when tripartite agreements exist, their impact

---

536. Pollert 2000, pp. 189–190; Bohle, D. and Greskovits, B., 'Slovakia and Hungary: Successful and Failed Euro Entry Without Social Pacts' in P. Pochet, M. Keune and D. Natalie (eds), *After the Euro and Enlargement: Social Pacts in the EU*, Brussels, ETUI, 2010, pp. 345–369.
537. At least, when compared to the other CEE countries, *see* Duman, A. and Kureková, L., 'The Role of State in Development of Socio-Economic Models in Hungary and Slovakia: The Case of Industrial Policy', *Journal of European Public Policy*, 2012, vol. 19, no. 8, p. 1217 and Kahancová, M., 'From Bargaining to Advocacy: A Trade-off Between Improved Working Conditions and Trade Union Fragmentation in Slovakia' in M. Bernaciak and M. Kahancová (eds), *Innovative Union Practices in Central-Eastern Europe*, Brussels, ETUI, 2017, p. 180.
538. Bulla, M., Czíria, L. and Kahancová, M., 'Impact of Legislative Reforms on Industrial Relations and Working Conditions in Slovakia', ILO Background Study, 2013, p. 9.
539. Crowley, S. and Stanojević, M., 'Varieties of Capitalism, Power Resources, and Historical Legacies: Explaining the Slovenian Exception', *Politics & Society*, 2011, vol. 39, no. 2, pp. 268–295.
540. Stanojević 2012, p. 863.

on the collective bargaining structure is modest. In fact, the Polish social pact experience goes against the logic of Chapter 1s proposed normative model – the 1993 Pact did not contribute towards shaping a multi-employer bargaining system, instead it generated a resolute support for standard setting at decentralised, local levels. The idea that tripartism is a weak element was put forward in a report by the European Commission in 2002 which noted a lack of linkage between what is discussed at the national and decentralised levels of collective bargaining in CEE.[541] This thesis still appears relevant today.

Did the legal framework in any way cause such limited tripartite outcomes in the three countries? This chapter did not find any conclusive evidence of that – with a few exceptions (the restrictively-defined competences of tripartite bodies in Slovakia and the Czech Republic during a certain limited period of time), CEE tripartism has not been found to be constrained by restrictively-defined powers and competences. On the contrary, a telling example of the law not being able to boost tripartite social dialogue is the Polish tripartite Commission. Despite being given a statutory legal basis in 2001, the outcomes of the Polish tripartite Commission have remained poor.

---

541. European Commission, *Industrial Relations in Europe 2002*, Luxembourg, Office for Official Publications of the European Communities, 2002, p. 106.

CHAPTER 6
Evolution of Sectoral Collective Agreement

1 INTRODUCTION

This chapter scrutinises the legal and institutional framework for collective bargaining at sectoral level in the four CEE countries. In Chapter 1 this study underlined weak multi-employer bargaining practices in the CEE, resulting in a low number of concluded collective agreements at sectoral level. Yet, as Table 4[542] demonstrates, the country figures vary. As data in this table demonstrate, of the four countries examined in the study, Slovenia has the most developed sectoral activity, with almost all sectors covered by collective agreements. Sectoral activity is fairly developed in Slovakia, with many sectors having a collective agreement. The Czech Republic has considerably less sectoral activity than Slovakia, and in Poland, sectoral collective bargaining is almost of marginal importance – the agreements at this level cover not more than 3% of the workforce.

On the basis of the industrial relations features of the four countries presented in Chapter 2, it can be assumed that the legal framework in Slovenia is by far the most supportive of the normative model of articulated multi-employer bargaining which was proposed in Chapter 1. It can be assumed that Slovak legal framework to some extent resembles the proposed model, too. It can be equally assumed that the legal framework in the Czech Republic and Poland is less likely to resemble that model, with Poland having the least favourable framework for multi-employer bargaining.

What this study has so far revealed is that the differences between industrial relations in the CEE countries and the other EU Member States particularly impinge upon the notion and role of sectoral collective agreements. In other words, it is sectoral

---

542. In Table 4, the differences in total and sectoral coverage rates with respect to Slovenia can be explained by the use of extension mechanisms. Moreover, the total coverage rates in the Czech Republic, Slovakia and Poland are comparatively lower than in Slovenia, due to the less pronounced use of extension mechanisms and prevailing regulatory role of collective agreements at company level.

collective bargaining which represents the major discrepancy between industrial relations in the old and new Member States of the EU. While sectoral collective agreement represents, to a varying extent, a lynchpin of the industrial relations models in the 'old' EU, that is not the case in the CEE countries.

Table 4   Industrial Relations at Sectoral Level

Country	No. of Sectoral Collective Agreements	Coverage of Sectoral Collective Agreements	Total Coverage*
Slovenia	Forty-six public and private sector collective agreements registered since 2013	n.a.**	Rates falling from 96% in 2006 to an estimated 65% in 2013
Slovakia	Falling from thirty-seven in 2007 to twenty in 2013	<40% between 2008 and 2011	Rates falling from 40% in 2006 and 35% in 2011 to 24.9% in 2013
The Czech Republic	Twenty-four in 2012, 2013 and 2014	15% in 2013; according to some estimations, falling down to 13% in 2014	About 50.2% in 2006; 50.4% in 2012 and 47.3% in 2013 (ICTWSS data) ***; or around 30% since 2006 (Eurofound)
Poland	Eighty-six in 2014	around 3% in the past two decades	15.7% in 2007, 14.8% in 2011 and 14.7% in 2012

Sources: Combined data from Eurofound, Worker-Participation (ETUI); also, Bulla, Czíria and Kahancová (2013), ICTWSS database 5.1, Visser (2016), data from the interviews.
Notes: *This column refers to the coverage rates regarding collective agreements concluded at all existing collective bargaining levels in the country. It contains data on selected years only in view of comparing and contrasting pre- and post-crisis coverage rates (for detailed overview of coverage rates trends *see* Table 3 in Chapter 4 and Figure 1 in Chapter 1).
** No official data on the percentage of sectoral coverage, although the interviewees explained that the high level of total coverage is predominantly based on sectoral collective bargaining.
*** The data includes only the collective agreements concluded by the largest trade union confederation ČMKOS.

It could be claimed that sectoral collective agreements were at the forefront of the reform of industrial relations in both groups of countries in the past decades, but for different reasons. In West European countries, the regulatory role of sectoral collective agreement has undergone significant reform because of the downward pressures of organised decentralisation. These agreements have, as a rule of thumb, become preoccupied with defining the rules and conditions for setting standard setting at lower

Chapter 6: Evolution of Sectoral Collective Agreement

levels, rather than establishing the substantive rules.[543] However, these substantial industrial relations reforms did not necessarily entail drastic changes to the statutory legal framework.[544]

On the other hand, the instigation of sectoral collective bargaining in CEE countries represented a bottom-up process which did not involve the downward pressures that existed in the 'old' Member States. The instigation of legal rules about sectoral collective bargaining was embedded in the wider framework of profound legal transformation which was presented in Chapter 3. Establishing a functional legal framework for sectoral bargaining was subject to successful resolution of several challenges. In the first place, defining and identifying the parties to sectoral agreements has been a rather challenging task in most of the CEE countries because sectoral social partners were being created from scratch from the early 1990s. The sudden responsibility given to social partners to autonomously regulate matters that had been for decades covered by statutory legal regulation has tied the resurgence of sectoral collective agreements to a set of vital questions. Will collective agreement at sectoral level manage to become the hallmark of the legal and institutional system, as has been the case in the majority of the countries in the EU? In which direction will labour law transformation evolve and how will it affect sectoral collective agreements? Will the emphasis on decentralisation and local standard setting, aiming to support flexible labour relations and economic efficiency, preclude collective bargaining at sectoral level?

With a view to performing the analysis, this chapter dissects the concept of sectoral collective agreement into several thematic elements. Section 2, therefore, presents the legal and institutional framework for sectoral collective bargaining in the four countries as follows. Section 2.1 explores the definition and origin of sectoral collective agreement while section 2.2 examines its content. Section 2.3 explores the

---

543. The ways in which downward decentralisation affected sectoral collective agreements in the EU (with focus on 'older' Member States) has been widely addressed from various angles in a number of studies; for industrial relations aspects, see e.g. Visser, J., 'Beneath the Surface of Stability: New and Old Modes of Governance in European Industrial Relations', *European Journal of Industrial Relations*, 2005, vol. 11, no. 3, pp. 287–306; Marginson, P. and Sisson, K., *European Integration and Industrial Relations: Multi-Level Governance in the Making*, Basingstoke, Palgrave Macmillan, 2006. More recent crisis-related approach has been provided in Marginson, P., 'Coordinated Bargaining in Europe: From Incremental Corrosion to Frontal Assault?' *European Journal of Industrial Relations*, 2015, vol. 21, no. 2, pp. 97–114. For legal aspects, see e.g. Sciarra, S., 'The Evolution of Collective Bargaining: Observations on a Comparison in the Countries of the European Union', *Comparative Labour Law and Policy Journal*, 2007, vol. 29, pp. 1–28; for comparative legal analysis in historical context see Hepple, B. and Veneziani, B. (eds), *The Transformation of Labour Law in Europe: A Comparative Study of 15 Countries 1945-2004*, Oxford, Hart Publishing, 2009. For legal aspects of decentralisation in the context of the recent economic and financial crisis, see the following collection of essays: Bruun, N., Lörcher, K. and Schömann, I. (eds), *The Economic and Financial Crisis and Collective Labour Law in Europe*, Oxford, Hart Publishing, 2014.
544. Bruun noticed that labour law legislation has been quite stable in the majority of the European countries since the 1980s and that the collective agreements changed their nature and function without major legal transformation, see Bruun, N. 'The Autonomy of Collective Agreement' in R. Blanpain (ed.), *Collective Bargaining, Discrimination, Social Security and the European Integration*, Bulletin of Comparative Labour Relations, no. 48, The Hague, Kluwer Law International, 2003, pp. 8–9.

articulation of sectoral collective agreements with the other standard-setting sources. The analysis in this section specifically focuses on how sectoral collective agreements – and collective agreements in general – are connected to the statutory legal rules: in a top-down hierarchical multi-level framework, sectoral collective agreement is a link connecting statutory legal regulation with the local collective agreements, the latter being the main source of substantive regulation of work and employment.[545] The question of articulation between the rules at sectoral and company level will be dealt with in the following Chapter 7. Section 2.4 addresses the question of who can sign sectoral collective agreements. Section 2.5 explores the legal rules on the extension of collective agreements, bearing in mind the importance of this legal instrument for industrial relations and particularly for sectoral collective bargaining. Section 2.6 addresses several matters otherwise not covered in the previous sections (personal scope, duration, registration and collective bargaining procedure). Section 3 contains comparative analysis of the traits presented, and section 4 provides concluding notes on the chapter.

2 FOUR COUNTRIES: OVERVIEW OF THEIR LEGAL AND INSTITUTIONAL FRAMEWORK

2.1 The Sectoral Collective Agreement: Definition and Origin

2.1.1 *Slovenia*

The Slovenian Collective Agreement Act, adopted in 2006, which regulates the most important aspects of collective bargaining and collective agreements, does not contain a specific definition of sectoral collective agreement. In fact, the 2006 Act does not define the levels at which collective bargaining may take place, in this sense giving the social partners freedom to negotiate at whatever collective bargaining levels they decide. Sectoral collective agreements are regularly concluded in Slovenia.[546] Sector is the predominant level of collective bargaining in Slovenia, despite the decentralisation trend that has occurred during the past decade.[547] The available data have demonstrated that sectoral collective agreement has remained an important venue for defining wages and working time even during the recent economic and financial crisis period.[548] A recent study demonstrated that the legal and institutional framework for

---

545. As explained in section 4.3 of Chapter 1, having in mind the weak role of cross-sectoral standard-setting level.
546. According to data from Eurofound by Kanjuo Mrčela, in total forty-six public and private sector agreements had been registered since 2006, although not all collective agreements had been updated recently, *see* Kanjuo Mrčela, A. *Living and Working in Slovenia – Collective Bargaining*, Dublin, Eurofound, 2017.
547. *See* Chapter 1, Figure 1.
548. *See* Kanjuo Mrčela 2017.

sectoral bargaining did not significantly alter with the recent crisis, although with the decentralisation trend, certain increase of social partners' autonomy at the sectoral level is detected.[549]

The legacy of collective bargaining to some extent dates back to the beginning of the twentieth century.[550] Although the prominence of collective bargaining significantly decreased after the Second World War, a partial revival took place with the first collective agreements concluded pursuant to the 1971 Federal Act on Basic Rights from Employment Relationship.[551] However, the regulatory role of collective agreements concluded before the 1990s was limited – they existed in a minor part of the private economy (craftsmen), and they were not fully autonomous, because their scope was limited by statute.[552] The economy was otherwise based on the paradigm of self-management, by which employees could organise themselves into various types of bodies, and could also conclude different forms of agreements and accords. As explained in Chapter 2, the peculiarity of the Slovenian pre-1990s system was exactly this 'socialist' conception of labour relations, honed under the paradigm of self-management by which the workers were deemed to be the 'social owners' of the means of production and could set conditions of work for themselves.[553] Even though the legacy of self-management should be linked to company-level processes in the first place, it should be nevertheless considered as one of the reasons behind post-transitional industrial relations developments in Slovenia. Self-management, as a way of organising employment relations, overall, allowed for mobilisation of labour resources and consequently led to important institutional arrangements in industrial relations.[554]

The instigation of the market economy brought gradual changes to collective agreements in Slovenia. As Chapter 3 demonstrated, collective agreements in Slovenia have gone through different phases of development in the past two decades. These phases describe the development of sectoral collective agreement, and its importance for industrial relations in that country. In the early 1990s, as argued by Slovenian

---

549. Stanojević, M. and Kanjuo Mrčela, A., 'Social Dialogue during the Economic Crisis: The Impact of Industrial Relations Reforms on Collective Bargaining in the Manufacturing Sector: Slovenia', Project: *The Impact of Industrial Relations Reforms on Collective Bargaining in the Manufacturing Sector*, Brussels, European Commission, 2014, p. 23 and p. 42; Stanojević, M. and Kanjuo Mrčela, A., 'Slovenia at the Crossroads: Increasing Dependence on Supranational Institutions and the Weakening of Social Dialogue', *European Journal of Industrial Relations*, 2016, vol. 1, no. 14, pp. 1–14.
550. *See* the historical overview in Skledar, S., *Collective Bargaining Legislation Examined*, Dublin, Eurofound, 2003.
551. *Ibid.*
552. *Ibid*; also, Vodovnik, Z. and Korpič-Horvat, E. 'Slovenia', in R. Blanpain and F. Hendrickx (eds), *International Encyclopaedia for Labour Law and Industrial Relations*, The Hague, Kluwer Law International, 2015, p. 278.
553. As explained earlier (*see* Chapter 2, section 3.1. and Chapter 3, section 3.1), under the self-management paradigm workers were considered owners of the company production and were enabled to engage in decision-making about the enterprise's operation, and establish various forms of workers' representatives' bodies at the level of the workplace. For the list of sources explaining the self-management paradigm, *see* fn 162.
554. This argument has been particularly underlined by Crowley and Stanojević; *see* Crowley, S. and Stanojević, M., 'Varieties of Capitalism, Power Resources, and Historical Legacies: Explaining the Slovenian Exception', *Politics & Society*, 2011, vol. 39, no. 2, pp. 268–295.

scholars Vodovnik and Korpič-Horvat, the 'first generation' of collective agreements was not delivered autonomously, because the process of privatisation had not yet started: the freedom of social partners to negotiate collective agreements in not yet privatised sectors was limited by legislation protecting 'social property'.[555] At the same time, the early 1990s' legislation did not contain clear rules about collective agreements: Slovenian scholar Končar noted that the law 'insufficiently and inadequately' defined collective agreements and that it did not distinguish between collective agreements concluded for different types of ownership (private, public or social, and mixed).[556] The 'second generation' of collective agreements was concluded with the process of privatisation, and the 'third generation' after the 2006 Collective Agreements Act, which brought a comprehensive and systematic legal reform in Slovenia.[557] The early 1990s' legislation stipulated the levels at which collective bargaining could take place (national or cross-sectoral, sectoral and company levels). Although the 2006 Act on Collective Agreements deleted such provision, by the time it was promulgated, Slovenian industrial relations were firmly developed at three major levels (cross-sectoral, sectoral and company).

2.1.2 Slovakia

Slovak labour law does not recognise the concept of sectoral collective agreements as such, but a rather different concept of 'higher-level collective agreements'. In fact, the delineation between enterprise-level collective agreements and higher-level collective agreements in the legal framework – the Labour Code and the Act on Collective Bargaining – represents one of the building blocks of the Slovak legal and institutional framework. These two vital concepts of Slovak labour law were introduced at the very onset of the transitional period, with the 1991 Act on Collective Bargaining. Although the two concepts have never been changed, the legal framework provides no sufficiently precise definition or explanation of the higher-level collective agreements. According to the Act on Collective Bargaining,[558] higher-level collective agreements are to be understood in relation to the parties involved – these collective agreements are concluded between the trade union and the organisation of employers operating at 'the higher level'. It remains unclear to what extent these collective agreements can be considered sectoral – the concept of 'higher-level' only specifies that these agreements be concluded at a higher level than company. It is not clear if these agreements can be concluded for an entire sector or for part of it. Neither is it clear whether this concept also includes the notion of cross-sectoral agreements.

---

555. Vodovnik and Korpič-Horvat 2015, pp. 278–279.
556. The Act on Basic Rights of Employment Relationship of 1989, *see* Končar, P., 'Changes and Adaptations of Labour Law and Industrial Relations in Slovenia' in R. Blanpain and L. Nagy (eds), *Labour Law and Industrial Relations in Central and Eastern Europe (from Planned to Market Economy)*, Bulletin of Comparative Labour Relations, no. 31, The Hague, Kluwer Law International, 1996, p. 158.
557. Vodovnik and Korpič-Horvat 2015, pp. 278–279.
558. Act on Collective Bargaining (No 2/1991), as amended, *see* Article 2.

As demonstrated in Chapter 1, as well as in Table 4, sectoral collective bargaining is relatively more developed in Slovakia in comparison with Poland and the Czech Republic. It should be added that in the recent crisis period, the incidence of sectoral collective bargaining has decreased.[559] In Slovakia, the social partners could not rely on a legacy that was favourable to collective bargaining. The practice of sectoral collective bargaining and its legal framework had to develop from scratch from the early 1990s, having in mind that in the communist period, collective bargaining was marginal and the provisions of the 1965 Labour Code did not leave much regulatory space for collective agreements.[560]

2.1.3 *The Czech Republic*

Much of what has been said about Slovakia can be extended to the Czech Republic. As in Slovakia, Czech law does not recognise the notion of sectoral collective agreement but rather it relies on the concept of 'higher-level collective agreement'. The division between higher-level and enterprise-level agreements dates back to the Act on Collective Bargaining adopted originally in the federal country of Czechoslovakia in 1991. As in Slovakia, this division has remained basically unchanged in the Czech Republic. Here, too, this division represents one of the building blocks of the legal framework for collective bargaining. Slovakia and the Czech Republic define higher-level collective agreements in exactly the same manner, by stipulating that these agreements are entered into force between the trade union and an employer association organised at the 'higher level'. The two countries share the same legacies – the legal framework anchored in the 1965 Labour Code which regulated collective bargaining in a restrictive fashion, was adopted in the federal country of Czechoslovakia. It was with this legal act that both the Czech Republic and Slovakia entered the transitional period. The practice of concluding sectoral (higher) level collective agreements began only with the onset of transition in both countries and their role and substance have been shaped during the past two decades in line with subsequent Labour Code changes. A key difference between the two countries is that sectoral (higher) level collective agreements were not the focus of post-transitional transformation processes in the Czech Republic – instead, the focus was on enterprise-level developments. The sectoral agreements were not actively supported by the government, and because the trade unions were decentralised, the enterprise was the main focus of collective bargaining systems.[561] As a result, sectoral (higher) level collective bargaining has been in continuous decline in the

---

559. According to Czíria, from sixty agreements in 1999; forty-two in 2005; to fewer than forty in the crisis period, *see* Czíria, L., 'Collective Bargaining and Balanced Recovery: The Case of the Slovak Republic', Bratislava: Institute for Labour and Family Research, 2013a, p. 7.
560. Pichrt, J. and Štefko, M., 'Czech Republic' in R. Blanpain and F. Hendrickx (eds), *International Encyclopaedia for Labour Law and Industrial Relations*, The Hague, Kluwer Law International, 2015, p. 94.
561. As explained by Myant and Smith, *see* Myant, M. and Smith, S., 'Czech Trade Unions in Comparative Perspective', *European Journal of Industrial Relations*, 1999, vol. 5, no. 3, pp. 265–285. *See also* Pollert, A., 'The Transformation of Trade Unionism in the Capitalist and Democratic Restructuring of the Czech Republic', *European Journal of Industrial Relations*, 1997, vol. 3, no. 2, pp. 203–228.

Czech Republic since the 1990s, reaching its lowest point in 1998 with only around 11% coverage.[562] Today, the incidence of higher-level bargaining is less pronounced than at company level. This includes the recent crisis period, when according to the available data, the coverage was around 13% in 2014.[563]

2.1.4 Poland

Section XI of the Labour Code postulates collective bargaining freedoms and basic institutes of collective labour law. As is the case in Slovakia and in the Czech Republic, the law does not contain a definition of 'sector' or 'sectoral collective agreement'. Instead, since 1986, the Labour Code has made a distinction between 'single-enterprise' and 'multi-enterprise agreements'.[564] This distinction represents one of the cornerstones of the legal framework for collective bargaining in Poland. The Labour Code defines multi-enterprise collective agreements by their signatories, which are the multi-enterprise trade union body and the appropriate statutory body of an employers' association.[565] However, no further specification of these agreements is provided in law – it is not clear whether the legal concept of multi-enterprise collective agreements refers to collective agreements concluded for several companies only (which is mostly the case in practice),[566] or for the entire sector or profession. In fact, as became evident during the interviews in Poland, 'sector' is not a legal term at all in labour law and is used only in common parlance with a common sense understanding.

In reality, multi-enterprise collective agreements have marginal relevance, covering not more than 3% of the entire economy.[567] A closer look into the context in which these agreements have been concluded reveals their specific legal nature. Because they are mostly concluded by one or more enterprises that dominate a given sector, Trappman refers to them as 'quasi single-employer agreements'.[568] Only a limited number of these agreements have a genuine sectoral scope – in fact, Trappman noted that there are only six collective agreements covering an entire sector (collective agreement in the steel industry being one of them).[569] The interviews highlighted that,

---

562. Myant, citing ČMKOS data; see Myant, M., 'Trade Unions in the Czech Republic', Report 115, Brussels, ETUI, 2010, p. 18.
563. According to estimation by Eurofound, the coverage rates of higher-level collective agreements have varied in the past period, but they normally amount to around 15%, with the figure falling down to around 13% in 2014; see Kyzlinkova, R., Lehmann, S., Pojer, P. and Veverková, S. *Living and Working in Czech Republic – Collective Bargaining*, Dublin, Eurofound, 2017.
564. This was law promulgated in November 1986, revising section XI of the Labour Code; see Sewerynski, M., 'Development of the Collective Bargaining System in Poland after the Second World War', *Comparative Labour Law Journal*, 1993, vol. 14, p. 460.
565. Article 241 (14) of the Labour Code.
566. As noted by Trappman, V., *Fallen Heroes in Global Capitalism Workers and the Restructuring of the Polish Steel Industry*, New York, Palgrave Macmillan, 2013, p. 105, citing Ghellab and Vaughan-Whitehead 2003.
567. Data from the interviews conducted in Warsaw. The number of these collective agreements varies from one year to another, but approximately there is between 170–175 multi-enterprise collective agreements registered in Poland.
568. Trappman 2013, p. 105.
569. Ibid.

Chapter 6: Evolution of Sectoral Collective Agreement

in fact, the sectors for which collective agreements were concluded were those labelled as 'problematic' for restructuring during the early stages of the privatisation process. Thus, concluding a collective agreement was deemed critical for dealing with the social aspects of their transition to market economy. At the same time, a peculiar feature of Polish industrial relations in the sectors which were labelled as problematic is the existence of tripartite sectoral committees, formed with the aim of ensuring smoother facilitation of the social aspects of transition.[570] As explained by interviewees, a total of fifteen tripartite sectoral committees were formed – the first was in the coal mining sector in 1992. However, their importance has been assessed as limited and diminishing over time; after accession to the EU, only two new sectoral committees were established. Moreover, they did not bring any additional boost to sectoral collective bargaining structures – these committees had the limited function of facilitating the social aspects of sector restructuring.

Sectoral collective bargaining in the post-1990s Poland is underdeveloped despite the existence of modest but relatively favourable legacies from the communist period. The collective bargaining which existed in Poland during the communist era was sectoral in nature; the economy followed a centralised logic and collective bargaining at enterprise level was deemed impossible.[571] These communist sectoral collective agreements were concluded in the enterprise sector (both public and private), and covered the entire sector or profession.[572] As a matter of fact, the conclusion of enterprise-level agreements was legally enabled only in 1986.[573] Nevertheless, it should also be recalled that these communist collective agreements were not free and voluntary, given that their content was largely restricted and predetermined by the coercive provisions of the statutory legal provisions. As noted by Polish scholar Sewerynski, the collective agreements at that time were in fact instruments for implementing the goals of the socialist system.[574]

Despite these legacies, sectoral collective bargaining did not achieve greater prominence in the post-transitional period, the major reason being the policy choices of governments, supported by social partners.[575] Also, the focus of post-transitional reforms was the enterprise – collective bargaining at higher (central) levels was not a policy priority.[576] This proposition was also confirmed during the interviews, with

---

570. *Ibid.*, p. 94.
571. Sewerynski 1993, pp. 445–446.
572. *Ibid.*
573. *Ibid.*, p. 460, with the legal amendment which introduced two-level bargaining structure.
574. *Ibid.*, p. 452.
575. The post-transitional trade union movement particularly backed the model of economic reforms in Poland. The ways in which trade union movement developed and shaped the post-transitional Poland has been particularly the focus of work of David Ost, as well as Agnieszka Paczynska; *see* e.g. Ost, D., 'Illusory Corporatism in Eastern Europe: Neoliberal Tripartism and Postcommunist Class Identities', *Politics & Society*, 2000, vol. 28, no. 4, pp. 503–530; Paczynska, A., *State, Labor, and the Transition to a Market Economy – Egypt, Poland, Mexico, and the Czech Republic*, Pennsylvania, The Pennsylvania State University Press, 2009.
576. As noted by Sewerynski, at the beginning of the 1990s, the enterprise was the main focus of policy transformation, and one of the reasons was the lack of adequate employers' organisation structures; *see* Sewerynski 1993, p. 468.

respondents stating that there have not been any serious efforts to build bargaining structures above company level since the beginning of the 1990s.

2.2 Content of Sectoral Collective Agreements

2.2.1 Slovenia

The 2006 Slovenian Act on Collective Agreements does not define matters that should be regulated by collective agreements, instead leaving the collective bargaining parties free to decide. This Act only stipulates that collective agreement consists of the contractual (obligatory) and normative parts.[577] In the contractual part of collective agreements, the parties may set out mutual rights and commitments, including provisions for dispute settlement. The normative part sets rights and conditions pertinent to the employment relationship, for example, conclusion of a contract of employment and its termination, pay for work, or health and safety conditions.

A general lack of comprehensive empirical data on these agreements in Slovenia prevents comprehensive analysis of their content and function. An earlier study has demonstrated that, in principle, collective agreements at different levels in Slovenia regulate identical or similar matters, but with different degree of rights and benefits afforded to the employees.[578] In any case, the items that have been traditionally covered by Slovenian sectoral collective agreements are wages and various elements of pay. Sectoral collective agreements are vital for defining nine wage tariffs, as explained by respondents during the interviews. Also, the interviewees confirmed that sectoral collective agreements represent the most salient standard-setting method – as one of the interviewees noted, it is also 'the easiest way of negotiations'.

The 2006 Slovenian Act on Collective Agreements contains no restriction on the matters that can be regulated within collective agreements. However, this bargaining freedom is a result of the gradual process of liberalisation of the scope of collective agreements that has taken place during the past two decades. Chapter 3, and the previous section of this Chapter (2.1), have already outlined the three generations of collective agreements which had evolved in Slovenia, as explained by Slovene scholars Vodovnik and Korpič-Horvat.[579] The first generation of collective agreements was not autonomous, primarily because statutory regulation, aiming at protection of 'social' property, restricted the scope of agreements.[580] The second generation was concluded after privatisation and it was no longer restricted by the need to protect 'social' property. However, the second generation of collective agreements was still not fully autonomous – the provisions of statutory labour laws, which did not provide precise regulation, required that these collective agreements *should* regulate certain matters

---

577. Article 3 of The 2006 Slovenian Act on Collective Agreements.
578. Natlacen, M.P., 'The Evolving Structure of Collective Bargaining in Europe: National Report of Slovenia', Project VS/2003/0219 – SI2.359910, European Commission and University of Florence, 2004b, p. 20.
579. Based on Vodovnik and Korpič-Horvat 2015, pp. 278–279.
580. Ibid.

and issues.[581] The collective agreements therefore had practically a *mandatory* character. At the same time, their character was *executive*: the task of these agreements was to implement the broad and imprecise statutory regulation.[582] The third generation of collective agreements concluded pursuant to 2006 Act on Collective Agreements is fully autonomous, and it does not restrict the right of social partners to negotiate on any matter they decide. Yet, the executive style of these legal provisions seems to have been retained to a certain extent – the statutory legal provisions often provide that some items *may* be regulated by collective agreements, particularly at sectoral level.[583] Slovenian scholars Vodovnik and Korpič-Horvat explain that the reason for statutory laws calling for the regulation of certain items in sectoral collective agreements is so that they are not regulated at lower, company level, where employee strength is weaker.[584] In this way, the law promotes sectoral collective bargaining and at the same time represents a barrier against uncontrolled decentralisation.

2.2.2 Slovakia

The content of collective agreements is not closely prescribed in law, and social partners can freely decide their topics. There is a distinction between the normative and contractual part of collective agreements, as is the case in Slovenia.[585] This freedom to bargain on any matter which social partners consider appropriate has been the result of the process of gradual liberalisation, as described in Chapter 3. With the beginning of economic transition, the 1965 Labour Code continued to be applied in a modified version in Slovakia, but it continued to restrict collective bargaining freedoms by honing a mandatory and coercive style of regulation.[586] It was only the 2001 amendment to the Labour Code that formally enabled social partners to negotiate on any matter which they deemed fit.[587] Unfortunately, as in the case of the other CEE countries examined in this study, there is no reliable and comprehensive empirical data which could provide a list of the items regulated by higher-level collective agreements. There is also no data demonstrating how the content of collective agreements changed in the past two decades in line with the process of gradual liberalisation of the legislative framework. On these points the existing studies made general remarks only.

---

581. Skledar 2003. The legal framework prior to the 2006 Act on Collective Agreements consisted of the federal (Yugoslav) the Act on Basic Rights of Employment Relationship of 1989 and the Slovenian Employment Relationship Act of 1990. These two acts regulated conclusion of collective agreements until 2006 (the provisions of these two acts relevant for collective agreements remained valid even after the new Employment Relationship Act was passed in 2003, but only until 2006).
582. *Ibid.*
583. As already mentioned in Chapter 3, section 4.2.1.
584. Vodovnik and Korpič-Horvat 2015, p. 281.
585. Barancová, H. and Olšovská, A., 'Slovakia' in R. Blanpain and F. Hendrickx (eds), *International Encyclopaedia for Labour Law and Industrial Relations*, The Hague, Kluwer Law International, 2014, pp. 197–198.
586. Barancová, H., 'Labour Law in the Slovak Republic, Present Situation and Future Trends', in R. Blanpain and L. Nagy (eds), *Labour Law and Industrial Relations in Central and Eastern Europe (from Planned to Market Economy)*, Bulletin of Comparative Labour Relations, no. 31, The Hague, Kluwer Law International, 1996, p. 139; Barancová and Olšovská 2014, p. 49.
587. *See* Chapter 3, section 4.2.

A recent study has claimed that the changes to the Slovakian legal framework in the past two decades have ensured its gradual adjustment to labour market flexibility, and has also impacted on the decentralisation of collective bargaining in that country.[588] An earlier study has demonstrated that higher-level collective agreements in Slovakia usually cover matters of employment, working conditions, health and safety, wages, cooperation and communication between trade unions and management, and conflict resolution.[589] That study did not, however, offer sufficiently detailed specification of these elements as to allow closer identification of the nature and function of these agreements. It has also been claimed that collective agreements often closely replicate the provisions of the Labour Code.[590]

2.2.3 The Czech Republic

Czech law does not predetermine the content of collective agreements, even though, as in the other three CEE countries, there is a distinction between the normative and contractual parts of collective agreements.[591] In the past two decades, this freedom of social partners to regulate matters they wish has undergone a gradual transformation. As already stated in Chapter 3, the provisions formally guaranteeing basic collective bargaining freedoms had been inserted into the legal framework in the early 1990s.[592] In practice, social partners could not freely decide on the content of collective agreements until 2006 since the legal framework allowed bargaining only on listed matters. In 2006, the legal framework fully liberalised bargaining scope by introducing a principle stating that 'anything that is not expressly forbidden by the law is permitted'.[593]

As with the other three CEE countries, there are no comprehensive empirical data assessing the contents of the existing higher-level agreements. Yet, existing studies have suggested that higher-level collective agreements do not regulate more than a few rights, due to the detailed and rigid regulation in the Labour Code, with the most important elements being wages and the different elements of pay.[594] The interviewees noted that, in general, these collective agreements have 'poor content' – the rights prescribed by these agreements represent only a slight upgrading of the rights already regulated by statutory labour laws.

---

588. Bulla, M., Czíria, L., Kahancová, M., 'Impact of Legislative Reforms on Industrial Relations and Working Conditions in Slovakia', ILO Background Study, 2013, p. 1 and p. 6.
589. The result of the survey of fifty-six higher-level collective agreements conducted by the Slovak Research Institute of Labour, Social Affairs and Family conducted for the period between 1999 and 2003; as cited in Czíria, L., *Collective Bargaining Procedures, Structures and Scope*, Dublin, Eurofound, 2002.
590. Czíria, L., 'Slovakia: An Example of 'Emancipated' Sectoral Social Dialogue?' in Y. Ghellab and D. Vaughan-Whitehead (eds), *Sectoral Social Dialogue in Future EU Member States: The Weakest Link*, 2003a, Budapest, ILO, pp. 392–393.
591. Pichrt and Stefko 2015, p. 260.
592. *See* Chapter 3, section 4.2.
593. As noted by Pichrt and Štefko 2015, p. 95.
594. Pichrt and Štefko 2015, p. 258; *see also*, Tomes, I., 'The Evolving Structure of Collective Bargaining in Europe: National Report of the Czech Republic', Project VS/2003/0219-SI2.359910, European Commission and University of Florence, 2004, pp. 12–13.

2.2.4 Poland

The previous section has demonstrated the marginal relevance of multi-enterprise collective agreements in Poland. Thus, it seems almost redundant to discuss Poland in this section. Yet, it is worth commenting that, as in the other CEE countries, the Polish Labour Code does not formally predetermine the content of these collective agreements. The Labour Code only stipulates that the collective agreements consist of normative and obligational parts and provide that social partners should respect the rights of third parties and may not derogate from unconditionally binding provisions of labour law.[595] As explained during the interviews, collective agreements at any level typically include matters such as wages, working time and bonuses. Moreover, as already pointed out in Chapter 3,[596] the Labour Code in a formal sense fully liberalised collective bargaining freedoms only in 2000, allowing social partners to negotiate on any matters they see fit.[597] Yet, as explained during the interviews, social partners still consider the Labour Code to be fairly extensive. This argument is used by employers as a reason not to engage in collective bargaining, claiming that matters pertinent to conditions of work are already covered in statutory law in a fairly elaborate manner. The comprehensive regulatory style of statutory provisions is a legal remnant from the communist period. The 1974 Labour Code contained fairly mandatory and coercive provisions, and the collective agreements could have contained more favourable provisions for employees only when authorised as such by law, or when justified by the circumstances of the sector or profession.[598]

2.3 The Articulation of Sectoral Collective Agreements

2.3.1 Slovenia

As in the other CEE countries examined in this study, in Slovenia the relationship between statutory legal rules and collective agreements is based on hierarchical top-down logic, combined with the principle of favourability. Under the logic of top-down hierarchy, collective agreements at higher levels prevail over collective agreements at lower levels, and statutory legal regulation prevails over collective agreements. At the same time, because of the principle of favourability, the lower level agreements may only contain more favourable conditions for employees than the

---

595. Article 240.
596. Chapter 3, section 4.2.
597. Swiatkowski, A.M., 'Are the Post-Socialists' Current Collective Bargaining Procedures Effective as a Means to Implement European Labour Law in Poland?', *Tilburg Foreign Law Review*, 2002, vol. 10, p. 179; also, Hajn, Z., 'Collective Labour Agreements and Contracts of Employment in Polish Labour Law' in M. Sewerynski (ed.), *Collective Agreements and Individual Contracts of Employment*, The Hague, Kluwer Law International, 2003, p. 192.
598. Sewerynski notes that in the communist period, the collective bargaining was limited to regulating specific conditions of work for a given sector or profession, *see* Sewerynski 1993, p. 444 and p. 460.

collective agreements at the higher level.[599] Thus, sectoral and company level collective agreements may only improve upon statutory legal rules to the benefit of the employees. Any provisions in collective agreements setting lower conditions of employment than those provided under the law would be considered invalid. Until 2005, cross-sectoral collective agreements, which covered terms and conditions of work and employment for the entire economy, were the main link connecting statutory labour regulation with collective agreements in Slovenia. When these cross-sectoral agreements ceased to exist, the sectoral collective agreements remained the main connector between collective agreements at company level and statutory labour law.[600]

While, as a rule of thumb, collective agreements may not stipulate less favourable conditions for employees than the statutory legal provisions, there are certain exceptions. The provisions of the 2006 Act on Collective Agreements allow collective agreements to provide less favourable rights and working conditions, under the conditions stipulated in collective agreement of higher level.[601] Moreover, the Employment Relationship Act specifies the cases in which collective agreements can lay down less favourable rights to employees than the standards of the legislation.[602] These cases, for example, include overtime and working time regulations, as well as fixed-term employment contracts. In practice, as reported by interviewees, so-called opening clauses are inserted in the sectoral collective agreements based on these provisions, allowing derogations to the detriment of employees (*in peuis*). To protect the employees' side, the Employment Relationship Act sets out detailed conditions for these derogations which, consequently, may not stipulate rights below the lowest possible statutory limit. There is no reliable empirical data on the use of the derogatory statutory provisions, but a recent study has demonstrated their growing use in the recent period with a view to alleviating the detrimental effects of crisis at the company level.[603]

2.3.2 Slovakia

As in the other CEE countries examined in this study, in Slovakia the relationship between statutory legal rules and collective agreements is based on hierarchical top-down logic, combined with the principle of favourability. As in the other three countries, collective agreements may not contain less favourable provisions for employees than those stipulated in statutory law. The fact that the higher-level collective agreements may only improve the rights anchored in the law demotivates the employers to conclude collective agreements, or these agreements simply reiterate what has been already stipulated by the statutory regulation.[604]

---

599. As explained by Končar 1996, p. 168.
600. As explained in Chapter 5, section 2.1.
601. *See* Article 4 and Article 5 of the Act on Collective Agreements.
602. *See* Article 9. The unofficial translation in English of the Employment Relationship Act of 2013, which can be downloaded at: http://www.mddsz.gov.si/en/legislation/.
603. With respect to working time, *see* Stanojević and Kanjuo Mrčela 2014, p. 33.
604. As underlined during interviews in Slovakia. *See also* Czíria, L., *Collective Bargaining Procedures, Structures and Scope*, Dublin, Eurofound, 2002; Czíria 2003a, pp. 392-393.

With the labour market reforms instigated by the recent economic crisis, Slovak labour law introduced an important and – for the CEE – quite innovative exception to the favourability rule. The exceptions turned out to be only temporary: the provisions of the Labour Code promulgated in 2011[605] allowed for some form of opening clauses, but they were overturned by another set of amendments only a year later.[606] These legal innovations allowed collective agreements at any level to stipulate less favourable conditions for employees than the statutory legislation provided for, in several thematic areas. The statutory legal provisions aimed however at 'controlling' the extent of derogation, by not allowing rights to be lowered below certain limits, thus protecting employees against the uncontrolled downward spiral of their rights at company level. The Labour Code allowed the following derogations:

- Collective agreements were allowed to set a longer probationary period than in the statutory legal rules, but no more than six months (Article 45).
- Collective agreements were allowed to set a longer period of notice for workers' dismissal but only under certain circumstances defined by Article 62(9).
- Collective agreements were allowed to set different reasons for dismissal from those defined in labour law (Article 63(3)).
- Collective agreements were allowed to extend the limits of overtime, by permitting extra working hours in addition to those already stipulated in labour law (Article 97(12)).
- Collective agreements allowed employers to suspend an employee from work for breaching labour discipline for a different (longer) period of time than stipulated in labour law (Article 141).

2.3.3 *The Czech Republic*

As in the previous cases, the top-down logic of hierarchy of rules, combined with the favourability principle, dominates the relationship between statutory law and collective agreements in the Czech Republic. Thus, the rule of thumb is that collective agreements may only improve standards from the statutory regulation. However, certain exceptions to this rule have been introduced into Czech labour law since 2006. The Czech Labour Code contains a complex web of rules – there is a general provision which allows stipulating less favourable provisions in collective agreements 'when not specifically prohibited or when the nature of derogation is not impermissible'. This provision also defines limits to these derogations – the highest or lowest admissible levels of Labour Code standards should be respected. Thus, the Labour Code aims at

---

605. Act no 257/2011 Coll.
606. Act no 361/2012 Coll., in effect since 2013. These legal innovations were particularly welcomed by the employers, *see* Bulla et al. 2013, p. 27.

'controlling' the extent to which it is possible to stipulate less favourable provisions. As highlighted during the interviews, there are, however, only two areas where the Labour Code actually further specifies these derogations, and where it is, consequently, possible to stipulate opening clauses: extra work and extra payments. As explained during the interviews, the practical reach of these provisions is marginal – opening clauses, or clauses with similar function are rarely used in practice. As one of the interviewees from the trade union side explained:

> If you want to avoid collective bargaining, you can always prepare internal regulation and therefore you don't need to count on derogation possibilities.

2.3.4 Poland

As is the case in the other countries examined in this study, the Polish Labour Code sets the logic of top-down hierarchy, combined with the favourability principle, as the guiding principles regulating the relationship between collective agreements and statutory labour law. Therefore, as in the other three CEE countries, collective agreements may only improve the conditions of work and employment as defined under the statutory law. The multi-enterprise agreements, or any collective agreements, may consequently not set lower standards than those stipulated in statutory law. Even if such a legal possibility were to exist, its practical reach would be limited, due to the rather marginal importance of multi-enterprise collective bargaining in Poland. However, a unique aspect of the Polish Labour Code in comparison with the other three countries is the possibility of suspending either a part or the entire collective agreement at any level. That is, the Labour Code provisions allow the suspension of a collective agreement if justified by the employer's financial situation, but only for up to three years. With respect to multi-enterprise agreements, there are no data showing how the suspension affects sectoral coverage of collective agreements.[607]

2.4 The Parties and Rules on Representativeness

2.4.1 Slovenia

A specific feature of Slovenian social partners in comparison with the other three CEE countries is the comparatively more developed sectoral organisation.[608] This feature is important in contributing towards more developed sectoral collective bargaining than in the other CEE countries. Sectoral trade unions are mostly members of the national confederal associations of trade unions (there are currently seven such confederations

---

607. As noted by Eurofound sources, *see* Czarzasty, J. and Mrozowicki, A., *Living and Working in Poland – Collective Bargaining*, Dublin, Eurofound, 2017.
608. Parissaki, M. and Vega Vega, S., *Capacity Building for Social Dialogue at Sectoral and Company Level in the New Member States, Croatia and Turkey*, Dublin, Eurofound, 2008; Kahancová 2017.

Chapter 6: Evolution of Sectoral Collective Agreement

in Slovenia).[609] There are also sectoral (more specifically, branch and professional) trade unions, which are not affiliated to confederations.

When it comes to the employers' side, a hallmark of Slovenian industrial relations is the substantially more pronounced involvement of employers' associations in collective bargaining than in the other CEE countries, contributing to relatively more developed sectoral collective bargaining. In this respect, a peculiar feature of Slovenian sectoral collective bargaining has been the traditionally prominent role of the Chamber of Industry and Commerce in industrial relations.[610] The Chamber, which was established during the pre-1990s socialist era, apart from representing the interests of businesses, also engages in collective bargaining. This model of chamber organisation had been developed under the German and Austrian influences of the beginning of the twentieth century.[611] At the outset of the transitional period, since no other employers' association existed in Slovenia, the Chamber of Industry and Commerce was the only available party to conclude sectoral and cross-sectoral collective agreements. The statutory legal rules even contained a reference to the Chamber as the main bargaining party at the employers' side.[612] All individual employers were obliged to be its members. The mandatory model of membership of the Chamber had two distinct benefits. The first benefit was an almost absolute coverage rate for collective agreements (as explained in Chapter 2), although some doubts have been raised as to whether this mandatory model complied with the principle of voluntary collective bargaining as understood by the ILO conventions.[613] The second benefit was that the Chamber, by actively engaging in collective bargaining from the early 1990s, compensated for lack of organisation and capacity in the other employers' associations which were slowly emerging.[614] However, after the promulgation of the 2006 Act on Collective Agreements, mandatory membership of the Chamber of Industry and Commerce was lifted.

Trade union freedoms were inserted into constitutional provisions in the early 1990s, enabling the unions to establish themselves and operate at various levels.[615] However, there are no specific legal rules on the set up of organisations of employers. When it comes to representativeness, the legal framework contains provisions for trade unions only and no such rules for employers' associations. The legal rules on trade union representativeness were postulated early in the transition period, pursuant to the Act on Trade Union Representativeness from 1993. These rules have remained

---

609. These are: Association of Free Trade Unions of Slovenia (SSS), Confederation of Trade Unions Slovenia (Pergam), New Trade Union Confederation of Slovenia (KNSS), Confederation of Trade Unions (K-90), Slovenian Association of Trade Unions (Alternativa), Association of Workers' Trade Unions of Slovenia (Solidarnost), Confederation of Public Sector Trade Unions.
610. As already noted in Chapter 2, section 3.1.
611. Skledar, S., *Government Wants Voluntary Membership of Chamber of Commerce and Industry*, Dublin, Eurofound, 2005.
612. The 1989 Act on Basic Rights of Employment Relationship.
613. Vodovnik and Korpič-Horvat 2015, p. 267.
614. Thus, today, apart from the Chamber of Commerce and Industry (GSZ), and Chamber of Crafts (OZS), there are also Slovenian Employers' Association (ZDS) and Small Companies and Crafts Association (ZDODS). These organisations were formed in the 1990s.
615. Freedom of association, as inserted in the Constitution of Slovenia of 1991 in the Article 76.

unchanged ever since.[616] Trade unions will be deemed representative on the decision of the minister responsible for labour affairs, once several criteria are fulfilled. These criteria prescribe that trade unions should be democratic in character, be independent from the state and employers, have been in existence for at least six months and have their own funding. In addition, there are quantitative criteria which trade unions need to fulfil – the association or confederation of trade unions at the national level needs to have in its membership at least 10% of workers from an individual branch, activity or profession. For employers' organisations, the criteria for representativeness have been brought in 'through the back door' in setting the conditions for extending the validity of a sectoral collective agreement to the entire sector. In these cases, an employer association must employ at least half of all the workers in the companies covered by the proposed extension.[617]

2.4.2 Slovakia

Collective bargaining at sectoral level usually takes place between trade unions and organisations of employers organised at sectoral level. In contrast with Poland and the Czech Republic, the sectoral dimension of trade unions and employers' associations is fairly well developed in Slovakia.[618] The most powerful trade union confederation, bringing together the largest percentage of trade unionists in the country and 28 sectoral trade union organisations which enter into the sectoral ('higher') level collective agreements, is KOZ SR.[619] As is the case in the other CEE countries, but with notable exception of Slovenia, the capacities of employers' associations are less developed than those of trade unions. The associations of employers had to form from scratch in the early 1990s. Currently, there are two major employers' organisations at confederal level which bring together sectoral organisations of employers.[620] Moreover, an issue that interviewees described as relevant is that individual employers often give up membership of the employers' associations in order not to be bound by higher-level collective agreements.

The legal framework for the organisation of social partners in Slovakia was postulated early in the transitional period by inserting freedom of association in the

---

616. Official Gazette no 13/93. List of representative trade unions can be found at the following website (in Slovenian): http://www.mddsz.gov.si/si/delovna_podrocja/delovna_razmerja_in_pravice_iz_dela/socialno_partnerstvo/seznam_reprezentativnih_sindikatov/ (accessed 1 December 2017).
617. Article 12 of the 2006 Act on Collective Agreements.
618. See Kahancová, M., 'From Bargaining to Advocacy: A Trade-off Between Improved Working Conditions and Trade Union Fragmentation in Slovakia' in M. Bernaciak and M. Kahancová (eds), *Innovative Union Practices in Central-Eastern Europe*, Brussels, ETUI, 2017, p. 180; Parissaki and Vega Vega (2008).
619. The other trade union confederations are: Independent Christian Trade Unions of Slovakia (NKOS), General Free Trade Union Association (VSOZ), Confederation of Art and Culture (KUK); for more information, see Czíria, L., *Living and Working in Slovakia*, Dublin, Eurofound, 2017.
620. Federation of Employers' Association of the Slovak Republic (AZZZ SR) and National Union of Employers of the Slovak Republic (RUZ SR) as the two major confederations; but there is also the Association of Cities and Municipalities (ZMOS), according to Czíria, *ibid*.

Slovak Constitution in 1992.[621] The Act on the Association of Citizens was promulgated in 1990 and represented a legal basis for both trade unions and associations of employers to be set up. Slovak labour law contains no rules about representativeness at 'higher' bargaining levels, neither for trade unions nor for associations of employers. There are only 'quasi-representativeness' rules which come into play regarding the extension of the validity of collective agreements, and these rules have been subject to certain modification over the last several years. Until 2009, collective agreements could have been extended if the parties which concluded the agreement were the largest in the sector (the employers' associations employing the largest number of employees and the trade unions representing the largest number of employees). Since 2009, the condition on the trade union representativeness has been lifted, but the condition regarding employers' organisations has remained valid.

2.4.3 The Czech Republic

With the demise of communism, the Czech trade unions had to go through difficult restructuring. Given that their role was insignificant in the communist system, in the 1990s, trade unions were struggling to be accepted as social partners and at the same time they were facing the challenges of breaking with the ideology and thinking of the past.[622] The post-1990s trade union movement was additionally challenged by declining trade union rates and by the continuous decline of bargaining coverage.[623] The estimate is that the trade union density rates in 2009 were as high as 10%.[624] Today, the trade union picture is dominated by one confederation, ČMKOS, which brings together sectoral level trade unions. It is worth noting that ČMKOS is a successor of the former Czech and Slovak confederation which was formed in 1990. Today, ČMKOS represents an association of 29 sectoral trade unions that are involved in collective bargaining at higher level in the Czech Republic.[625] There are also two other trade union confederations.[626] At the beginning of the 1990s, the employers' associations were formed from scratch and, as in other CEE countries, they struggled with building collective bargaining capacities.[627] A peculiar characteristic of Czech industrial relations is that in the past two decades, employers have not always been motivated to engage in higher-level collective bargaining. As reported by the interviewees, the employers'

---

621. *See* Article 37.
622. Myant and Smith 1999, p. 266.
623. According to data from the largest trade union confederation ČMKOS, fall-off from union membership was from 67% in 1993 to 33% in 1997, *ibid.*, pp. 268–269.
624. Myant, M., 'The Impact of the Economic Crisis on Collective Bargaining in the Czech Republic', *Transfer: European Review of Labour and Research*, 2013, vol. 19, no. 2, p. 188.
625. As reported in Kyzlinkova et al. 2017. The largest sectoral trade union is the Czech Metalworkers' Federation KOVO (OS KOVO).
626. Apart from Czech-Moravian Confederation of Trade Unions (ČMKOS), there is Association of Autonomous Trade Unions of the Czech Republic (ASO ČR) and Confederation of Art and Culture (KUK).
627. Currently there are two major confederations, affiliating sectoral associations which engage in higher-level collective bargaining, Confederation of Employers' and Entrepreneurs' Associations of the Czech Republic (KZPS ČR) and Confederation of Industry of the Czech Republic (SP ČR).

organisations tended to use the Civil Code as a legal basis for their establishment – the reason was that organising under the Act on the Association of Citizens would oblige them to participate in collective bargaining. An example is the metals sector – as explained during the interviews, there is no collective agreement concluded in the automotive industry, which represents a prominent part of the Czech economy. The reason is that the association of employers, which represents almost all employers in this industry, does not engage in collective bargaining because it was not established pursuant to the Act on the Association of Citizens. The described legal peculiarity was resolved after the interviews had taken place – as of 2014, the Civil Code represents the only legal basis for the establishment of social partners.[628] Another, distinct problem is that in some cases individual employers give up membership of employers' associations in order to avoid being bound by collective agreements. This matter inspired a provision which was introduced in 2007, stipulating that individual employers are obliged to remain bound by collective agreements even after giving up their membership of the association.[629]

As in other CEE countries, the provision allowing the free organisation of trade unions and employers' associations was inserted into the legal framework early in the 1990s. Freedom of association is guaranteed in the Charter of Fundamental Rights and Freedoms, which is itself an integral part of constitutional order.[630] In 1990, the Act on the Association of Citizens allowed free organisation of trade unions and employers' associations. As already mentioned, since 2014, it has been the Civil Code which forms the sole legal basis for the organisation of social partners.[631] Czech laws do not contain rules on representativeness at sectoral or company level. As is the case in Slovakia, rules concerning representativeness exist only indirectly – the extensions of collective agreements' validity may take effect only if the employer association represents the largest number of companies, or the trade union represents the largest number of employees in the sector.

2.4.4 Poland

As in the other countries under examination, basic provisions allowing free and voluntary organisation of social partners were introduced at the very outset of the transitional period. For employers the legal basis was the Act on Organisation of Employers of 1991 and for trade unions, the Act on Trade Unions of 1982, which was subsequently replaced by the Act on Trade Unions of 1991. However, compared with the other three CEE countries, social partners in Poland have the least developed sectoral structure. As interviewees explained, the less pronounced sectoral dimension

---

628. Pichrt and Stefko 2015, pp. 234–235.
629. Hála, J., *Czech Republic – Developments in Social Partner Organisations: Employer Organisations*, Dublin, Eurofound, 2010.
630. The Charter of Fundamental Rights and Freedoms dates from 1993. The English version can be accessed at: http://www.usoud.cz/fileadmin/user_upload/ustavni_soud_www/prilohy/Listina_English_version.pdf.
631. In the version which came into effect on 1 January 2014, Act no 89/2012 Coll., which labels all the organisations as 'associations'; see Pichrt and Štefko 2015, p. 235.

of social partnerships is a result of fragmentation of industrial relations and the fairly broad independence of company level trade unions. Sectoral trade unions and sectoral employers' organisations have very limited influence on what is going on in the companies. The sectoral representation of employers' associations is particularly weak,[632] and, as is the case with the other CEE countries, these organisations were being formed in the early 1990s from no pre-existing base. Another problem, as the interviews demonstrated, is that employers' associations tend to avoid using the Act on Organisation of Employers of 1991 as the legal basis of their establishment, since it would oblige them to participate in collective bargaining. Some interviewees (on trade union side) therefore see the employers' associations as lobbying, rather than bargaining organisations.[633] For example, there is no multi-enterprise collective agreement in the metals sector, which, according to the interview data, employs around two million workers, because the trade unions lack a counterpart to negotiate with.

The Polish Labour Code introduces a complex web of rules defining the parties to multi-enterprise collective agreements. According to the Labour Code, such collective agreements may be concluded between a multi-enterprise trade union and an employers' association.[634] A federation can also conclude such an agreement on behalf of a multi-enterprise trade union as its member. Moreover, the Labour Code specifies that if more than one trade union represents employees, then a joint representation will be formed, or trade unions will act together. On behalf of employers' organisations, a federation or confederation organisation can have the right to conclude multi-enterprise collective agreement. The Polish Labour Code contains rules about the representativeness of trade unions concluding a multi-enterprise collective agreement,[635] according to which, they should be either: (a) representative under the Tripartite Act; or (b) have in association at least 10% of employees covered by its statues, but not less than 10,000 employees; or (c) represent the largest number of employees for whom the multi-establishment agreement is being concluded. A trade union will automatically be considered representative if it is a member of a representative national confederation. There are no rules about representative employers' associations that would govern the conclusion of multi-enterprise collective agreements. One interviewee from the trade union side touched upon this matter, at the same time explicating the issue of the underdeveloped capacity of employers' associations:

---

632. Towalski notes that, having in mind their weak organisation, employers' associations rarely engage in bilateral dialogue with trade unions, *see* Towalski, R., *Employers' Organisations Examined*, Dublin, Eurofound, 2002.
633. Otherwise, the main employers' associations are: Confederation Lewiatan (Konferacja Lewiatan), Employers of Poland (Pracodawcy RP), Polish Crafts Union (ZRP), Business Centre Club (BCC).
634. *See* Article 241 (14) of the Labour Code, Solidarity trade union is the only national 'peak' level trade union directly engaging in sectoral level collective bargaining, according to Czarzasty, J., *Capacity Building for Social Dialogue in Poland*, Dublin, Eurofound, 2006, p. 15. There are also two trade union confederations, which members engage in collective bargaining at this level; these are: All-Poland Alliance of Trade Unions (OPZZ), Trade Unions Forum (FZZ).
635. Article 241 (17) of the Labour Code.

One can observe rapid development of different kinds of employer organisations at the sectoral level. They are established in accordance with the law on employers' organisations. But, no private employer organisation is a member of any sectoral collective agreement. Thus, I would like employer organisations to change, and we also want to start talking about the representative nature of employers' organisations.

2.5 Mechanism of Erga Omnes Extension (General Applicability of Collective Agreements)

2.5.1 Slovenia

The practice of extending sectoral collective agreements' validity to third parties is common in Slovenia.[636] The rules and conditions for extensions are stipulated in the 2006 Act on Collective Agreements. Accordingly, the extensions can take place upon a decision delivered by the minister responsible for labour affairs, based on the application of one of the parties to the collective agreement. The extended validity will cease to exist only upon the termination of the collective agreement. The agreement can be extended to an entire sector or to part of it. As this chapter has already demonstrated, for collective agreements to be extended certain rules of quasi-representativeness apply regarding the associations of employers – their members should employ more than half of all the workers working for those employers for whom an extension of the collective agreement has been proposed.[637]

The legal rules on collective agreements' extensions were initially introduced with the 2006 Act on Collective Agreements, and before that time the Slovenian legislation did not recognise this legal instrument.[638] However, extensions of collective agreements were, in practice, delivered through the back door, because of the mandatory membership to the Chamber of Commerce and Industry, which ensured wide coverage of concluded sectoral agreements. At the same time, the relatively greater coverage of collective agreements in Slovenia also originated in the practice of concluding cross-sectoral collective agreements (called 'general agreements'), a practice which had existed in both private and public sectors until 2005.[639]

---

636. According to the available data from the recent economic and financial crisis period, eight out twenty-five sectoral collective agreements in private sectors have been extended since 2008, see Kovačič, H., *Slovenia: Changes to Wage-Setting Mechanisms in the Context of the Crisis and the EU's New Economic Governance Regime*, Dublin, Eurofound, 2014.
637. See Article 12 of the 2006 Act on Collective Agreements. The unofficial translation in English available at the webpage of the Slovenian Ministry of Labour, Family, Social Affairs and Equal Opportunities, see: http://www.mddsz.gov.si/en/legislation.
638. Končar, P., '*EU v. National Industrial Relations Perspective*: The Slovenian Perspective' in M. Ronnmar (ed.), *EU v. National Industrial Relations Perspective: Comparative and Interdisciplinary Perspectives*, Alphen aan den Rijn, Kluwer Law International, pp. 46–47.
639. As explained in Chapter 5, section 2.1.

Chapter 6: Evolution of Sectoral Collective Agreement

2.5.2 Slovakia

The extension of collective agreements has been one of the most contentious issues in Slovakian labour law in the past two decades. The individual employer's consent to the extension has been the most controversial component of this issue. In practice, an attempt to gain employers' consent was usually met with opposition, particularly from those companies without trade union organisation. For many years, therefore, the extensions were applied only to a list of certain employers, while extensions which would enable collective agreement to cover an entire sector, were not existing in practice. For example, as the interviews in Slovakia revealed, in the metals sector, in 2002, out of 126 companies whom the metals trade union OZ KOVO asked to apply extensions, only 26 gave permission. This issue was partially resolved by linking the extensions to the General Industrial Classification of Economic Activities (NACE) code since 2007 – a rule which was inserted was that each employer whose business activity belonged to the respective NACE code would be bound by the extended agreement. [640] However, the frequent legal changes in the past two decades have made the number of extensions variable from one year to another. As the data in Table 5 show, the extensions were practised basically only between 2008 and 2010, when the legal framework did not contain overly restrictive provisions.

Table 5   Slovakia – Number of Extended Agreements

	2007	2008	2009	2010	2011	2012	2013
No. of extensions	0	2	5	0	0	0	0

Source: Bulla et al. (2013), p. 32, based on data from the Slovak Ministry of Labour, Social Affairs and Family of Slovakia.

The legal framework was developing in the following manner:[641]

(i) The 1991 Act on Collective Bargaining originally allowed extensions upon the request of one of the signatories of the higher-level collective agreement or the ministry responsible for labour and social affairs. The decision on the extension was taken by a tripartite committee formed within the ministry

---

640. As explained by Berdnarik, R. *Slovakia: Extension of Multi-Employer Collective Agreements Marks a Turning Point* Dublin, Eurofound, 2015. The statistical classification of economic activities in the European Community (General Industrial Classification of Economic Activities – NACE) is the basic reference aiming to classify the economic activities in the EU. NACE has been transposed and implemented by the CEE countries after they became the members of the EU.
641. This breakdown of legal amendments is based on data from interviews and from Eurofound; particularly: Czíria 2002; Czíria, L., *Legislation Amended to Extend Collective Agreements*, Dublin, Eurofound, 2007; Czíria, L., *Employers Oppose New Collective Agreement Extension Rules*, Dublin, Eurofound, 2008; Czíria, L., *Government Plans Changes to Collective Bargaining Laws*, Dublin, Eurofound, 2010. See also, Bulla et al. 2013 and Barancová and Olšovská 2014, p. 199.

responsible for social affairs. The agreement could have been extended to employers pursuing similar business activities.

(ii) In 2004, the rules on extensions were amended for the first time. The major change was the insertion of a condition that *the employers' consent* be requested and, once given, the extension would take place. The provision resulted in a drastic reduction of extensions – in 2005 and 2006, only four agreements were extended.

(iii) In 2007, the legal rules were modified again and the employers' *consent was no longer required*. The modified provisions asked for each signed high-level collective agreement to be categorized under the respective NACE code, which made the extensions automatic against the employers whose prevailing business activity fell within the code. The decision on the extension was made by the Ministry of Labour and Social Affairs upon the recommendation of a tripartite committee formed for this purpose. The 2007 rules contained a list of conditions under which the extensions could not take place, for example, if the employer were already bound by another high-level collective agreement, or if the enterprise was small.

(iv) After the ILO experts were consulted, the legal rules on extensions were modified with effect from the beginning of 2010. The new provisions did not reintroduce the consent of the employers, but extensions were made conditional upon the request of one or both contracting parties. Furthermore, extensions could have been applied to some or all employers in the sector corresponding to the respective NACE code. The extended agreement had to have been concluded by a higher-level trade union organisation representing the largest number of employees in the sector. A list of circumstances setting out reasons for not imposing extensions against certain types of employers was added, for example regarding those declared bankrupt, small employers or those employing people with disabilities.

(v) In 2010, the law *reintroduced the condition of employers' consent* to the extensions. This rendered extensions to a whole sector virtually impossible. Consequently, between years 2010 and 2013 no higher-level collective agreement was extended.

(vi) As of the beginning of 2014, extensions can again be practised *without the consent* of the respective employer. The procedure may be initiated by one or both parties to the collective agreement and the decision on the extension is delivered by the ministry responsible for labour and social affairs. There is a list of exceptions under which the extensions may not be imposed, such as against the employers already bound by other higher-level collective agreements or those who are employing more workers than the association which concluded the agreement in the first place. A case has been filed before the Constitutional Court challenging these provisions but it has not been resolved within the time frame covered in this study.

2.5.3 *The Czech Republic*

Despite the fact that there are legal provisions in place which allow the binding effect of collective agreements to be extended to non-signatory organisations, these provisions have not been regularly exercised.[642] The interviewees explained that employers are generally opposed to the extensions. Specifically, employers do not see added value in the extensions because they do not generally consider sectoral (higher-level) collective agreements useful, claiming that these agreements anyways have a 'poor content'. The legal framework allowing the extensions has gone through several revisions in past decades:[643]

(i) The 1991 Act on Collective Bargaining allowed extensions on the basis of the decision of the ministry responsible for labour and social affairs, provided that the employer had been engaged in comparable business activity or operated a similar business.
(ii) While the provision remained in force for more than a decade, following a Constitutional Court ruling it was eventually rescinded in 2005. The claimants argued before the Court that collective agreements are of a private law nature and cannot be imposed on third parties against their will.[644] The Court did not opine on the legal nature of collective agreements. However, it rescinded the said provision, stating that the extensions can be practised only if the condition of legitimacy in the sense of certain level of representativeness of social partners is fulfilled. Moreover, the Court held that the extensions should be exceptionally, rather than regularly, applied.

Therefore, following the aforementioned ruling of the Constitutional Court, in 2005, extensions were made conditional upon additional elements: both the signatory trade union and the signatory employers' association had to be the largest in the sector in terms of membership. The extensions could have been applied on the basis of a joint proposal by the signatory parties, and would have been imposed upon all employers whose prevailing business activity belongs to the respective NACE sector. Extensions would not be applied to small companies with less than twenty workers. However, the extension mechanism described eventually proved rather restrictive in practice, as only three collective agreements were extended under these rules (in construction, ceramics and textile industry).

---

642. According to the data from interviews, only several sectors have had collective agreements extended; construction, textile and transportation. The construction sector was the first to have the extended collective agreement.
643. The overview of the legal provisions is based on information from Eurofound; *see* Kroupa, A., *Extension of Collective Agreements to Increase Sectoral Coverage*, Dublin, Eurofound, 2006 and Kroupa, A. and Hála, J., *Capacity Building for Social Dialogue in the Czech Republic*, Dublin, Eurofound, 2006.
644. *See* the text of the ruling, issued in 2003, available in English on the webpage of the Czech Constitutional Court: http://www.usoud.cz/en/decisions/?tx_ttnews[tt_news]=560&cHash=9e1df2c3fda76cdfcf34e6843bca6e56S (accessed 1 December 2017).

(iii) With the major labour law reform in the Czech Republic taking place in 2007, extensions were linked to employers pursuing business activity under the prevailing NACE code. Furthermore, the new rules prescribed that the extension proposal should be submitted by both parties, while at least one of them must fulfil specific condition in terms of membership: (i) the employers' association should employ the highest number of employees in the sector; or (ii) the trade union association should represent the highest number of employees in the sector. Yet, from the trade union point of view, the legal rules could be interpreted as restrictive – the interviewees explained that in the metals sector no higher-level collective agreement was extended because there had been no consent between the sectoral social partners on this matter.

2.5.4 Poland

It has already been stated that collective agreements concluded at this level are of marginal relevance in Polish industrial relations; therefore, extension practices have virtually no relevance and they have never been invoked. Nevertheless, the legal framework allows the extensions on the basis of the decision of the ministry responsible for labour and social affairs. Extensions can be exercised against those employers who are not covered by any multi-enterprise agreement and are operating in the same or similar business activity. The condition is that the extension is justified by social interests. The legal provisions can be interpreted as restrictive – the extensions may take place upon joint request of social partners which concluded the agreement.[645]

2.6 Other Issues

2.6.1 Personal Scope of Collective Agreements: To Whom Do the Collective Agreements Apply?

2.6.1.1 Slovenia

The 2006 Act on Collective Agreements[646] stipulates that if a collective agreement was concluded by a representative trade union, it will cover all employees, irrespective of their trade union membership. At the same time, the 2006 Act provides that individual employers who have given up their membership of the employers' association will remain bound by the sectoral collective agreement for a maximum of one year.

---

645. Hajn, Z. and Mitrus, L., 'Poland' in R. Blanpain and F. Hendrickx (eds), *International Encyclopaedia for Labour Law and Industrial Relations*, The Hague, Kluwer Law International, 2016, p. 269.
646. *See* Article 11.

2.6.1.2 *Slovakia*

Higher-level collective agreement binds the parties that concluded the agreement. The collective agreement applies to all employees working for the employers who are bound by the agreements, irrespective of their trade union membership. Upon conclusion, the collective agreement is accompanied by a list of the employers' associations who are signatories, and it is also marked with the relevant NACE classification code so that it can be subsequently extended to employers whose prevailing business activity belongs to this code.[647]

2.6.1.3 *The Czech Republic*

The Czech Act on Collective Bargaining stipulates that the collective agreement is binding for signatory employers' associations and their members. It is a legal rule that the individual employers will remain bound by the collective agreement even after giving up membership of the association. The collective agreement applies to all employees working for the employers who are bound by the agreements, irrespective of their trade union membership.

2.6.1.4 *Poland*

The Labour Code stipulates that the provisions of collective agreements cover all workers working for employers bound by the agreement, irrespective of their trade union affiliation. The legal rules contain no further specification on this topic.

2.6.2 Registration and Duration

The collective agreements concluded at sectoral level in the four CEE countries are registered under the respective ministries responsible for social and labour affairs.

The rules on the duration of sectoral collective agreements vary in the four countries. *The Slovenian 2006 Act on Collective Agreements* sets out that the parties to the collective agreement should determine its duration. If the parties have not determined a notice period, then the collective agreement can be rescinded by each party with at least six months advance notice. Similarly, *Slovakian* law prescribes that the parties should determine the duration of higher-level collective agreements, and, unless differently specified, the agreement will last for one year. In *Poland*, according to the Labour Code, multi-enterprise collective agreements can be concluded for an indefinite period of time, but they may also be concluded for a fixed period. Prior to the expiry of the agreement, the parties may extend its validity for a definite period or recognise the agreement as having indefinite validity. In the *Czech Republic*, the Labour

---

647. *See* Bulla et al., 2013, p. 31.

Code prescribes that a collective agreement can be entered for a fixed or indefinite period of time, with a notice period of six months.

2.6.3 Procedure for Collective Bargaining

The collective bargaining procedure is stipulated in law in the four countries. In *Slovenia, Slovakia* and *the Czech Republic*, the law stipulates that the bargaining procedure starts with a written proposal from a trade union or employers' association. In these countries, the legal rule is that the other side has an obligation to reply to the proposal within a time limit which is set differently. By imposing a duty on the social partners to respond to the initiative to conclude a collective agreement, the laws of these countries impose the duty to bargain in good faith. Nevertheless, this does not translate into an obligation to sign a collective agreement. However, in *Slovakia*, the other side has no obligation to reply to the proposal if it is contrary to its legitimate interests. In *Poland*, the collective bargaining procedure is specific in comparison to the other three countries. According to the Labour Code, there is no general obligation on the other party to respond to the bargaining proposal. The Polish Labour Code only specifies several circumstances under which the other party may not refuse the request for collective bargaining. This could be when negotiations concern employees not already covered by any agreement, when the agreement should address the difficult economic situation of employer or material situation of employees, or the bargaining proposal was issued within prescribed time limit prior to expiry of current agreement.[648] According to the Polish Labour Code, there is an obligation of the parties to bargain in a good faith. The Labour Code specifies that good faith means making allowances to trade unions as far as possible regarding the economic situation, refraining from demands that exceed the financial capability of the employer, and respecting the interests of employees not covered by the agreement.[649] Moreover, the Labour Code also explicitly states that employers are obliged to provide information to trade unions on their economic situation.

3 COMPARATIVE OVERVIEW: SECTORAL COLLECTIVE AGREEMENTS IN CEE

Section 2 has presented an overview of the development of the current legal and institutional framework for sectoral collective bargaining in the four countries. The current section will analyse the presented elements with a view to providing insights relevant for answering the two research questions of this study.

---

648. Article 241 (2) of the Labour Code.
649. Article 241 (3) of the Labour Code.

3.1 The Concept of Sectoral Collective Agreement in CEE

3.1.1 Definition of Sectoral Collective Agreement in the Legal Framework

The legal overview in section 2 has clearly demonstrated that the legal regulation of sectoral collective agreements differs in the four CEE countries and that the legal notion of sectoral collective agreement has been shaped through specific national circumstances. It is only Slovenia's law which did not explicitly delineate the levels at which collective bargaining may take place, and it did not accordingly delineate different types of collective agreements. Even before the 2006 Act on Collective Agreements was adopted in Slovenia, the collective bargaining was well developed at sectoral level. Unlike in Slovenia, in the other three countries the legal framework *preceded* the building of the industrial relations practices. Thus, from the beginning of the transitional period, the legal frameworks in Poland, the Czech Republic and Slovakia postulated the notions of 'higher-level' and 'multi-enterprise' agreements, which subsequently emerged as the building blocks of industrial relations in these countries. As the legal overview in the previous section has demonstrated, these notions of collective agreements do not necessarily coincide with sectoral collective agreements. In fact, the three legal systems do not provide a precise definition of multi-employer and higher-level agreements and how they correlate with the notion of sector. It is most likely that these terms were designed in order to distinguish enterprise-level agreements from all the other collective agreements. Possible explanations for such an enterprise-focused regulatory style arise from the nature of the transitional processes, since at the beginning of the 1990s, enterprise-level agreements were the predominant – and in many sectors often the only – method of autonomous standard setting between social partners. At that time, trade unions were facing difficulties in post-communist restructuring, while employers' organisations were only slowly emerging. This rendered centralised collective bargaining difficult at sectoral level. A particular exception to this scenario was Slovenia, where the lack of employers' capacities was compensated for by the bargaining role of the Chamber of Commerce and Industry. In the other three countries, in some sectors, the employers' side still faces difficulties organising and engaging in collective bargaining at sectoral level.

However, it should be made clear that there are no definite criteria against which the legal concept of sectoral collective agreements in CEE can be scrutinised. The ILO architecture contains broad rules regarding collective agreements and their content, but it does not provide precision on sectoral collective agreements. What undoubtedly stems from the ILO framework, specifically, the ILO Recommendation No 91 from 1951, is the binding nature of collective agreements and their precedence over individual labour contracts.[650] The ILO Recommendation No 163 from 1981 explicitly allows the bargaining parties to freely choose the level at which collective bargaining will take place.[651] However, the notion of sector and sectoral collective agreements does not follow from the ILO rules; nor does the ILO architecture imply that countries

---

650. ILO Recommendation concerning Collective Agreements, No 91, 1951.
651. ILO Recommendation concerning the Promotion of Collective Bargaining, No 163, 1981.

are obliged to define sectoral collective agreements. The Member States' legal frameworks vary and provide no further guidance on how to define sectoral collective agreements. What is certainly common to all the continental European countries is that increasingly, over several decades, the understanding of sectoral collective agreements has been subject to change, due to pressures arising from the trend towards 'organised decentralisation'.[652] This trend has particularly influenced the scope and understanding of sectoral collective agreements by reshaping their relationship with enterprise-level collective agreements. Accordingly, the general trend across European countries has been that sectoral collective agreements no longer contain detailed substantive provisions. Instead, the trend is that these agreements focus on setting the framework for further collective bargaining arrangements at lower, company level.[653] The economic and financial crisis has further reinforced this trend across the European countries, inspiring labour law reforms across the continent, mostly with the aim of facilitating the expansion of company-level standard setting.[654]

For further understanding of sectoral collective agreement in the four CEE countries, it is also necessary to take into account its scope (content) and the legal possibilities of extending its validity to the third parties in the sector.

3.1.2 The Content of Sectoral Collective Agreement

The ILO architecture provides no closer identification of the matters which should be covered by collective agreements. In principle, it follows from the ILO rules that collective agreements should cover terms and conditions of work and employment, as well as relations between workers and employers (respectively, the normative and contractual parts of collective agreements).[655] The ILO rules specify that some elements can be excluded from the agreements, for example, discriminatory clauses or clauses contravening minimum statutory legal standards.[656]

Chapter 3 of this study has already explained that the expansion of the substantive scope of collective agreements was taking place in a country-specific dynamic.[657] At the same time, that chapter explained that such expansion entailed two interlinked processes: (a) formal legal insertion of rules guaranteeing the legal freedoms of social

---

652. Notion of 'organised decentralisation' coined by Traxler, F., 'Farewell to Labour Market Associations? Organised versus Disorganised Decentralisation as a Map for Industrial Relations' in F. Traxler and C. Crouch (eds), *Organised Industrial Relations in Europe: What Future?*, Aldershot, Avebury, 1995, pp. 3–19.
653. Marginson and Sisson 2006, pp. 163–164.
654. As discussed by Jacobs, A., 'Decentralisation of Labour Law Standard Setting and the Financial Crisis' in N. Bruun, K. Lörcher and I. Schömann (eds), *The Economic and Financial Crisis and Collective Labour Law in Europe*, Oxford, Hart Publishing, 2014, pp. 171–192.
655. As explained by Gernigon, Odero and Guido, based on the following ILO sources: ILO Right to Organise and Collective Bargaining Convention, No 98, 1949; Labour Relations (Public Service) Convention No 151, 1978; Collective Bargaining Convention No 154, 1981; ILO Recommendation concerning Collective Agreements, No 91, 1951; *see* Gernigon, B., Odero, A. and Guido, H., 'ILO Principles Concerning Collective Bargaining' *International Labour Review*, 2000b, vol. 139, no. 1, p. 39.
656. *Ibid.*, p. 40.
657. *See* Chapter 3, section 4.2.

Chapter 6: Evolution of Sectoral Collective Agreement

partners to negotiate on any matters they see fit; and (b) de facto liberalisation, which included gradual transformation of statutory regulation style from being predominantly mandatory to one which postulates minimum substantive rights and encourages autonomous standard setting by means of collective bargaining. Chapter 3 demonstrated that the first task (a) was accomplished in the four CEE countries relatively late – more than a decade after the onset of the transitional processes. With respect to the second task (b), Chapter 3 demonstrated that it was accomplished to varying degrees, having in mind that there is still a rather comprehensive regulatory style of legislation in CEE, particularly in Poland and the Czech Republic. Slovenia is somewhat exceptional, as the current chapter noted – the legal framework to some extent hones an executive style of legal regulation, whereby legal provisions often provide recourse to regulation of certain matters by collective agreements. In this sense, one may also note that the Slovenian legal framework performs a salient promotional role, by explicitly suggesting that collective agreements may provide closer regulation on some matters.

CEE studies suffer from a lack of comparative and comprehensive data on collective agreements, which would otherwise enable this study to fully grasp the standard-setting weight of sectoral collective agreements. It would be particularly useful to monitor how the substance of the concluded sectoral collective agreements changed alongside the developments of the legal framework over the past two decades. What can be summarised from the available studies and comments from the interviewees is the following. As far as Slovenia and to some extent Slovakia are concerned, sectoral collective agreements play a prominent role in industrial relations. This is particularly the case in Slovenia, where the interviewees underlined the salience of sectoral collective bargaining in setting wages (even though recent data suggest certain decentralisation trend).[658] As far as the available data allow a conclusion, Slovak sectoral collective agreements have been gradually moving in the direction of accommodating the decentralisation of bargaining and of providing gradual adjustment of the legal framework towards labour market flexibility.[659] It seems that the picture is somewhat different in the Czech Republic and Poland. The existing data suggest that higher-level agreements in the Czech Republic usually regulate few items and provide a light upgrade of standards for employees' from those standards laid down by statutory regulation.[660] The country where sectoral agreements have the least regulatory importance is Poland, where the interviewees emphasised that employers often argue that the provisions of Labour Code are already so extensive that they see no purpose in engaging in collective bargaining. It has been also pointed out during the interviews in Poland that collective agreements often simply reiterate what the law has already stated.

---

658. Stanojević and Kanjuo Mrčela 2014, Stanojević and Kanjuo Mrčela 2016.
659. Particularly underlined in a recent study by Bulla et al. 2013, p. 6.
660. Pichrt and Štefko 2015, pp. 258–259; data from interviews.

3.1.3 Mechanism of Erga Omnes Extension (General Applicability of Collective Agreements)

Almost all EU countries recognise the legal possibility of extending the validity of collective agreement to employers who were not signatory parties to it, but belong to the same sector or perform similar business activities.[661] The extensions may not necessarily reflect the interest of individual employers, who might consider them to be depriving from the opportunities to offer more competitive conditions in the sector. Yet, there are many advantages to this instrument. In the first place, extensions can substantially increase coverage of collective agreements, and as such, can be regarded as instruments for promoting collective bargaining.[662] In a legal sense, extensions can ensure the application of minimum sectoral standards, defined by a sectoral collective agreement, including the sectoral minimum wage.[663] Nevertheless, the extensions may at the same time be criticised for running against the logic of voluntary organisation – employers may, by virtue of this mechanism, become involuntarily bound by collective agreement.[664] The topic of extensions has not been thoroughly regulated within the ILO system. The ILO has declared this instrument compatible with freedom of association, but it also held that the state can prescribe limits to the extensions.[665] In this context, the ILO Collective Agreements Recommendation No 91 of 1951 stipulates that extensions can be made subject to several conditions:

> (a) that the collective agreement already covers a number of the employers and workers concerned which is, in the opinion of the competent authority, sufficiently representative; (b) that, as a general rule, the request for extension of the agreement shall be made by one or more organisations of workers or employers who are parties to the agreement; (c) that, prior to the extension of the agreement, the employers and workers to whom the agreement would be made applicable by its extension should be given an opportunity to submit their observations.[666]

The previous section has demonstrated that extensions are underused instruments in the four CEE countries. This is also evidenced in Table 6. If the use of the instrument of extensions is a criterion for assessing the promotional role of the state in industrial relations, then in the four countries such state role has been weak. Yet, this statement may not be fully applicable to Slovenia, where the extensions have been more regularly practised than in the other three CEE countries.

---

661. Here the discussion does not refer to the extensions of collective agreement to the non-unionised employees; as in all the CEE countries, the concluded collective agreement binds all the employees who work for the employer covered by the agreement, irrespective of the trade union affiliation.
662. Bruun, N., 'Legal and Judicial Avenues: The ILO' in N. Bruun, K. Lörcher, and I. Schömann (eds), *The Economic and Financial Crisis and Collective Labour Law in Europe*, Oxford, Hart Publishing, 2014, pp. 254–255.
663. Ibid.
664. Ibid.
665. As reminded by Bruun, *ibid*.
666. ILO Recommendation concerning Collective Agreements, No 91, 1951.

Chapter 6: Evolution of Sectoral Collective Agreement

Table 6   Use of Extension Mechanisms

Country	2009	2010	2011	2012	2013	2014
Slovenia	3	3	3	3	3	3
Slovakia	2	2	1	1	1	2
Poland	1	1	1	1	1	1
Czech Republic	1	1	1	1	1	1

Source: ICTWSS database 5.1 (Visser 2016).
Notes: 1 – Extension is exceptional, used in some industries only, because of absence of sector agreements, very high thresholds; 2 – Extension is used in many industries, but with thresholds and Ministers can decide not to extend agreements; 3 – Extension is virtually automatic and more or less general.

Slovenia allowed extensions only in 2006, but even before that time, almost complete coverage by sectoral collective agreements had existed mainly because of the mandatory membership of the Chamber of Commerce and Industry.[667] In Poland, extensions have never been applied because of the overall marginal role of multi-enterprise collective agreements. At the same time, Polish law sets somewhat restrictive conditions for extensions. In the Czech Republic, and also particularly in Slovakia, the changing legal framework has directly impinged on the frequency of collective agreement extensions during the past two decades. Likewise, depending on the actual wording of the law, the number of extensions varied from one year to another. In some years, the extensions were not applied because of the restrictive legal framework, asking for the approval of individual employers. When looking at the developments in Slovakia in the past two decades – particularly the fact that the consent of individual employers has been the most discussed item on the agenda and that, for a long time, the Slovak system has lacked a genuine concept of 'real' extensions to the whole sector – one may conclude that the Slovak legal system still struggles to recognise and incorporate the mechanism of extension. The latter argument can be also extended to the Czech Republic, where, during the past two decades, the topic of extension has provoked frequent legal amendments.

3.2   Sectoral Collective Agreement as an Instrument for Articulation

The described notion and function of sectoral collective agreements prompts further investigation of the relationship between collective agreements and statutory legal norms as the two distinct sources of labour regulation in CEE. Chapters 1 and 3 have already given some insights into the topic of articulation, which is in this study understood as a mechanism ensuring complementarity between decision-making at different levels. For this chapter it is vital to underline that sectoral collective agreements are the key articulating device within the multi-employer bargaining

---

667. As explained in Chapter 2, section 3.1.

system. It should be underlined that these agreements represent the main link between the system of collective agreements and the system of statutory legal rules (insofar as there are no concluded cross-sectoral collective agreements, which is the case in the four CEE countries – *see* Chapter 5).

In the majority of the European countries, a rule is that collective agreements at higher level prevail over agreements at lower levels and that statutory legal rules prevail over collective agreements. Additionally, the logic of favourability applies to these systems, as explained in Chapter 1. However, in recent decades the legal systems have started to introduce certain exceptions to the principle of firm vertical hierarchy of rules. An example of these exceptions includes the French *Loi Fillon* which provides that company level collective agreements have priority over agreements at a higher level. Another example is the different types of clauses that may be inserted in sectoral collective agreements, such as opening or hardship clauses in Germany, allowing stipulation of less favourable rules for employees at company level (derogation *in peius*).[668]

As the overview of the four CEE legal and institutional frameworks in this chapter has demonstrated, these countries' systems mostly rest on a one-way and top-down vertical hierarchy of rules, further strengthened by the mostly uncompromised nature of the favourability principle in the four countries. Deviations from the vertical hierarchy *in peius* (setting less favourable conditions than those prescribed in law or collective agreements at higher levels) are principally discouraged and not widespread in practice in CEE, as the overview of the four legal frameworks in Table 7 shows.

Table 7   *Overview of Legal Possibilities for Derogations* in peius *from Statutory Law*

Slovenia	Slovakia	The Czech Republic	Poland
Opening clauses in sectoral collective agreements	No derogation possible at the moment	Derogation under restrictive conditions and for few items only	Suspension of collective agreement, temporary and under certain conditions

Table 7 provides an overview of the legal methods chosen by the selected countries in view of allowing derogations *in peius* from statutory law. Slovenia's legal framework is seemingly the most flexible, as it allows deviation *in peuis* from the sectoral level arrangements. In this sense, opening clauses can be used to control the degree and substance of derogations within company level collective agreements. Slovak and Czech systems rest on a rigid top-down hierarchy of rules, with no legal possibility of deviation *in peius* (in Slovakia) or derogations under restrictive conditions and marginal practical importance (the Czech Republic). The Polish example runs contrary to the logic of organised decentralisation – by allowing suspension of collective

---

668. As explained by Jacobs 2014, p. 177; these clauses have been introduced in the 1980s and 1990s allowing different forms of deviations from sectoral norms, particularly in relation to wages and working time.

agreements at multi-enterprise level, the function of collective bargaining is frustrated. In these cases, if there is a single-enterprise agreement concluded, it will remain the only negotiated source of rights and conditions for employees and there will be no central level negotiation to play the role of 'checks and balances'.

The above arguments have assessed the systems of standard setting in CEE from a *formal and instrumental* point of view, but there has been no scrutiny of how the *substance (content)* of collective agreements relates to statutory legal rules. Previous chapters of this study have explained that, in most of the European countries, collective agreements are the major standard-setting instruments and sources of work standards and employment conditions. With the trend towards decentralisation which has dominated the landscape of most of the European countries in the past decades, and particularly during the recent economic and financial crisis, the substance of sectoral collective agreement has been subject to change. Regardless of the general tendency towards decentralisation, the degree to which the sectoral agreements have been modified differs in the European countries. As a general trend, the universal standard-setting feature of the sectoral collective agreement has been compromised, and the role of sectoral collective agreements has become one of providing more regulatory space for company-level collective agreements.[669] The sectoral agreements have started prescribing parameters to subsequent company collective agreements to a greater or lesser extent. It is notable to mention several possible scenarios which Marginson and Sisson underlined in explaining the role of sectoral collective agreement in this respect.[670]

First, the sectoral collective agreement may prescribe universal substantive standards, but leave the implementation to company level. *Second*, different clauses can be inserted in sectoral collective agreements, providing variation in implementation of the collective agreements. In this case, the universal standard remains in place. *Third*, certain instruments can be used to distribute the competences between different bargaining levels. In countries like Italy, the social pact serves as an instrument for defining the substantive competences of different bargaining levels, and deciding which matters would be respectively regulated at sectoral level or company level. Because the substantive competences of the two levels are strictly separated, company collective bargaining does not take place within the procedural framework defined in sectoral collective agreements. *Fourth*, the sectoral collective agreement may prescribe deviations from the universal standard by inserting different types of opt-out clauses.[671] Marginson commented that their use across the European continent has increasingly perforated sectoral collective agreements.[672] *Fifth*, sectoral collective agreements may play the role of incomplete framework agreements, by not setting the

---

669. Marginson 2015, pp. 100–101.
670. The delineation based on Marginson 2015 and Marginson and Sisson 2006, pp. 163–165.
671. Here the term 'opt-out' is used in a generic way to denote the variety of clauses used in many European countries, aimed at introducing enterprise-level deviations from the conditions set out at sectoral or cross-sectoral collective agreements. The deviations at the enterprise level are usually controlled by the framework and conditions stipulated in these sectoral or cross-sectoral agreements.
672. Marginson 2015, p. 101.

main substantive parameters, but rather encouraging substantive variation at company level. Within this scenario, the sectoral agreements neither decide the universal sectoral parameters nor the scope of company level negotiations.

How do the four CEE countries fit these scenarios? In CEE, the universal standard-setting function of sectoral collective agreements is, in general, compromised. This conclusion can be reached after observing the limited coverage rates of sectoral collective agreements, as presented in Table 4. The universal standard-setting function of sectoral collective agreement can be claimed to exist in Slovenia, and in the other three CEE countries' sectors where sectoral collective agreements have been concluded and have been extended to cover the entire sector. This reasoning is not only based on the fact of not so widespread sectoral collective bargaining. It should also be taken into account that sectoral collective agreements in the four CEE countries have often achieved only low levels of standards and merely a marginal upgrade from the standards set out in law. At the same time, statutory labour law often predetermines the substantive content of collective agreements by containing fairly detailed regulation of work and employment. Thus, where they exist, sectoral collective agreements have a modest regulatory role – their function is to set minimum levels in a sector, and to encourage further substantive variation at company level. But this sectoral minimum is rather low and does not provide much more of an upgrade to the benefit of employees than does statutory legal regulation. A clear example of sectoral collective agreements having modest regulatory importance was provided during the interviews in Slovenia. There, sectoral collective agreements normally include several tariff classes on wage. However, the lowest wage tariffs which are negotiated in these agreements have no practical importance: the wage levels set in these tariffs go even below the statutory minimum wage, which set mandatory provisions for the entire economy. Thus, the lowest wage tariffs do not apply in practice. In general, the interviewees in all four countries commented that the company is the main locus of decision-making.

It is implied from the previous lines, as well as from the data presented in Table 4, that sectoral collective agreements do not set firm parameters and conditions for company-level bargaining. Judging from the arguments presented, sectoral collective agreements mostly resemble the fifth scenario of the proposed classifications by Marginson and Sisson: incomplete framework agreements which set weak universal standards in the sector and encourage substantive variations between companies.

3.3 Parties and Representativeness

The first major challenge for CEE law at the outset of transition was to define legal rules allowing the free organisation of social partners and rules on representativeness. This is why most of the CEE countries ratified and implemented the relevant ILO provisions guaranteeing the independence of trade unions from the state and from the employers' side, as well as provisions allowing free organisation of trade unions and employers' associations in the early 1990s.[673] Defining these legal rules early on was an important formal step towards addressing the weak capacity of social partners, a problem stemming from the trade unions needing to face difficult restructuring, while, at the same time, the employers' associations had to form mainly from scratch. Regardless of the fact that the current legal systems stipulate clear and unambiguous legal rules on the organisation of social partners, the weakness of social partners is still present to some extent and has been highlighted as problematic.[674] Nevertheless, the role of law in addressing this weakness is not completely irrelevant, as in many instances law helped boost sectoral capacity – particularly on the employers' side. Slovenian country example illustrates this point. The legal rules in Slovenia required individual employers to be members of the Chamber of Commerce and Industry. Although this legal solution was criticised as being contrary to the ILO principles of the voluntary organisation of social partners,[675] it helped in consolidating the sectoral capacity of employers' associations in Slovenia. The Chamber was the main negotiating partner on employers' side and because all the individual employers were its members, this particular legal solution ensured wider coverage for concluded sectoral collective agreements. At the same time, this legal solution did not prevent other employers' associations from emerging and gradually building capacity for sectoral collective bargaining. There are other examples showing how the law can enhance the sectoral capacity of employers. As section 2 of this chapter demonstrated, the law in some countries (in Slovenia and the Czech Republic) has tackled the issue of individual employers giving up membership of the employers' associations by obliging them to respect the sectoral collective agreement, even after renouncing membership. A further problem in some countries, as presented in section 2, is that the employers' associations also may tend to establish themselves on a legal basis which would allow them not to engage in collective bargaining. This matter has been succinctly explained by the Czech trade union interviewee:

> In reality, the problem is whether there is a will for collective bargaining, not the form of organisation. In our country, it is possible to set up regular associations of employers, but then it is common that it is written in their statute that they do not deal with collective bargaining, that they are not competent for that. Then they say 'we are something like lobbying group, we do not bargain'.

In fact, the issue described has been resolved in the Czech Republic recently – as section 2 of this chapter explained, the Civil Code became the only possible legal basis on which both trade unions and employers' associations to be set up in 2014.

Another task which the CEE countries faced was drawing up the rules on representativeness. Section 2 of this chapter demonstrated that no such rules exist in

---
673. ILO Convention No 87 on Freedom of Association and Protection of the Right to Organise of 1948 and ILO Convention No 98 on Right to Organise and Collective Bargaining of 1949. As already noted in this study, Slovakia ratified these two conventions in 1993, Slovenia in 1992, the Czech Republic in 1993. Poland has been considered a party to these two conventions since 1957.
674. See e.g.: Ghellab, Y. and Vaughan-Whitehead, D., *Sectoral Social Dialogue in Future EU Member States: The Weakest Link*, Budapest, ILO, 2003; Parissaki and Vega Vega 2008.
675. Vodovnik and Korpič-Horvat 2015, p. 267.

the Czech Republic and Slovakia. In these two countries, there are only indirect rules, which apply with respect to the mechanism extending collective agreements. In Slovenia and Poland, rules on representativeness are formulated for trade unions only. Scrutinising these rules is difficult, as there are no well-defined criteria for what representativeness rules should look like. The experiences of European countries vary and it is not possible to draw any clear guidance. Most of the countries are based on one of the two models of representativeness: (a) a *proven or actual model*, whereby the organisation becomes representative based on the actual size of its membership; and (b) *assumed or implied*, in which the representative status is derived from membership of a confederation or higher-level organisation which is already recognised as representative.[676] Slovenia, as can be implied from data presented in section 2, adopted a *proven or actual model*, while Poland opted for a mixed model spanning the two options. The ILO framework requires from national laws that they base representativeness rules on objective, unbiased and pre-established criteria, set out in a procedure which ensures their impartiality and the absence of political interference,[677] but it contains no closer guidance on this matter. In general, representativeness criteria can help identifying legitimate partners for collective bargaining, but what can be concluded from section 2 is that the four CEE countries still struggle to define clear criteria for representativeness on the employers' side. Yet this problem may not originate in law and may not necessarily be fixed by law: the collective bargaining capacity of employers needs to be boosted in the first place. There are sectors in CEE that do not have an employers' organisation at all, so further discussion on representativeness is precluded. The problem which trade unions often face, as underlined by several interviewees in the four countries, is that they have no counterpart on the employers' side to negotiate with.

4 CONCLUSIONS

4.1 Development of Sectoral Collective Agreement

How can the development of the legal and institutional framework for sectoral collective agreements in the four countries be explained? In all four countries, the development of sectoral collective agreement has been enmeshed in a conundrum of policy choices and legacies. This chapter has demonstrated the following. In *Slovenia*, post-transitional industrial relations have been shaped under the favourable influence of self-management legacies, and the active role of the Chamber of Commerce and Industry which immediately participated in sectoral collective bargaining in the early 1990s. Inasmuch as industrial relations did not develop immediately but only

---

676. The division explained by Veneziani, B., 'The Intervention of the Law to Regulate Collective Bargaining and Trade Union Representation Rights in European Countries: Recent Trends and Problems', *Transfer: European Review of Labour and Research*, 1999, vol. 5, nos 1–2, pp. 126–127.
677. As reported by Jacobs, A., 'Article 11 ECHR: The Right to Bargain Collectively' in F. Dorssemont, K. Lörcher and I. Schömann (eds), *The European Convention on Human Rights and the Employment Relation*, Oxford, Hart Publishing, 2013, p. 320.

Chapter 6: Evolution of Sectoral Collective Agreement

gradually,[678] the same can be said of the legal framework – the major legal reform which took place in 2006 aimed at endorsing the industrial relations practices which had developed by that time, including well-developed sectoral collective bargaining. The *Czech Republic and Slovakia* could not benefit from the legacies of the communist era, as their sectoral practices were developing from scratch in the early 1990s. In 1991, their legal framework had postulated the two levels at which collective bargaining could take place (enterprise, and the somewhat more ambiguous concept of 'higher level'). After the dissolution of the two countries in 1993, their paths diverged somewhat – while the initial focus of the reforms in both Slovakia and the Czech Republic was on company-related processes, Slovakia's industrial relations have subsequently focused on sector level. Yet, both countries seem to have been modifying their legal rules in an ad hoc fashion – amendments at times reflected a different balance of interests between labour and employers, especially with respect to the extensions of sectoral collective agreements. Similarly, in Poland, the notion 'multi-enterprise' agreement had already been created by 1986. As section 2 explained, the model of reforms pursued in Poland was focused on the company. The sectoral level was not a priority of policy reform, as was underlined by the interviewee on the trade union side:

> In my personal opinion this was planned since the very beginning of the economic transformation. There was no political will on the side of the actors who were responsible for the economic transformation to give powers to trade unions. Due to this reason, although social dialogue was of course promoted, it was mostly promoted at the company level. And not at the sectoral level.
> This idea of the decentralisation was politically supported. What is the problem with Poland? When compared to Slovakia, which is trying to do something with sectoral bargaining, the approach of the Polish government is that the sector was privatised, therefore we don't have anything to do with sectoral level. This idea of improving competitive position and building industrial policy while not having any influence in the sectors which have been privatised is crazy for me.

4.2 Sectoral Collective Agreements: The Legal and Institutional Framework in CEE

The comparative assessment of the four countries' legal and institutional framework for sectoral collective bargaining, performed in this chapter, to a large extent corresponds to Bohle and Greskovits' classifications of CEE capitalism, and to the explanations of the type of economy and welfare given in Chapter 2. The country whose legal framework shows fewest features of the liberal market economy (LMEs)[679] is *Slovenia*, where the legislation does not, in principle, restrict in any way the possibility of convening sectoral collective bargaining, and also promotes the sector as a venue of standard setting. This was demonstrated in section 2 of this chapter. The Slovenian

---

678. The 'gradualist' approach to market transformation in Slovenia was particularly described by Crowley and Stanojević 2011.
679. Following the Varieties of capitalism dichotomy, as explained in Chapter 2 (sections 2.1.1 and 3.1).

case also provides a specific example of the limited role of the law in shaping industrial relations – by 2006, when the major legal reform took place, sectoral collective bargaining was already well developed. Slovenia's legal system, unlike in the other three countries, does not aim to define the notion of 'sectoral collective agreement.' The recognition of sectoral collective agreements exists only indirectly – legal provisions often call for the conclusion of the sectoral collective agreements.

On the other hand, the *Polish legal system* has not been shaped with sectoral collective bargaining in mind. In fact, there are several legal traits of Polish labour law which essentially restrict the ability to build fruitful sectoral collective bargaining. To mention the most blatant traits, the notion of multi-enterprise collective agreement is not clearly defined, there is no labour law reference to 'sector', the collective bargaining procedure is not clearly stipulated and the laws rendered extension of collective agreements rather difficult. By comparison, *the Slovak and Czech labour laws* are more supportive of sectoral collective bargaining. These two countries in fact have rather similar legal frameworks. In these two countries, what can be observed is the unclear designation of higher-level agreements with respect to 'sector' and the overly restrictive conditions for collective agreements' extensions (the latter particularly in Slovakia). Also, both Slovakia and the Czech Republic struggle to define the legal rules on the representativeness of both trade unions and employers' associations.

The four legal systems base the relationship between statutory labour law and collective agreements on a strict vertical and top-down hierarchy of rules. From the legal point of view, in Slovenia the pyramid of standard-setting sources at different levels seems to be the closest to the articulated multi-employer bargaining model presented in Chapter 1 and the notion of 'organised decentralisation'. The latter argument is particularly evident when taking into account the type of articulation between the laws and collective agreements, which is based on a flexible relationship between sectoral and company level sources and the legal possibility of derogating *in peius* from sectoral standards. The vertical articulation of legal rules at different bargaining levels is set differently in Poland and it least resembles the normative articulated multi-employer bargaining model postulated in Chapter 1. The reason for the latter is the poorly defined concept of 'multi-enterprise' level and the fact that, under certain legal conditions, the collective agreements at this level can be suspended. Thus, the legal articulation mainly takes place between statutory legal rules and collective agreements at company level, while the sector represents a weak focal point in the Polish system. In Slovakia and the Czech Republic, the laws are comparatively more supportive of sectoral and 'multi-employer' bargaining in comparison to Polish law. However, Slovak law seems to be more rigid than Czech law, because of: (i) fairly restrictive rules on the extension of collective agreements, which made the application of this instrument almost impossible in the past decade, except for a short period of time between 2007 and 2010; (ii) the lack of flexibility, in the sense that the law does not provide the possibility of collective agreements stipulating less favourable rules for employees (derogation *in peuis*). In the Czech Republic, there is possibility legal possibility to introduce derogations *in peius*, but it is not widespread in practice.

Overall, this chapter has demonstrated that certain legal traits of the four countries underpin decentralised industrial relations and underdeveloped sectoral collective bargaining – with the exception of Slovenia. With a view to protecting the rights and working conditions of employees, the legislators in the four countries aimed to set a minimum ('floor') of statutory rights which could eventually be upgraded in collective agreements. But, in reality, such a legally defined floor is usually low. At the same time the legal framework shows ambiguous support for centralised forms of collective bargaining and the employers' side has no clear incentive to engage in sectoral collective bargaining. If any sectoral collective agreements exist, they only slightly improve the rights and conditions stipulated in law. The regulatory power of the sectoral collective agreements is therefore weak and the real standard-setting power has been shifted to the local level, but there are distinct country variations which cannot be discounted and which this chapter has described.

CHAPTER 7
Company Level: Collective Bargaining and Other Forms of Standard Setting

1 INTRODUCTION

This chapter scrutinises the legal and institutional framework for collective bargaining at company level in the four CEE countries. In addition to collective bargaining, this chapter will also briefly reflect on the other possible forms of standard setting in companies. Some terminological explanations should be highlighted at this point. As explained in Chapter 1, the term 'company' is used when describing collective bargaining practices between an individual employer and local trade unions, without further specifying whether it takes place at plant level, within the unit of the company or for the entire company. In this sense, in this study the term 'company-level collective bargaining' is understood as equal to single-employer collective bargaining, and contrasts with collective bargaining which is practised by associations of employers. Similarly, the chapter uses the terms 'local' and 'basic' trade union organisations to denote the form of trade union organisation existing at company level, regardless of whether it is formed at plant level or at the level of the entire company.

This study has demonstrated already that company level is the main level for collective bargaining in the four CEE countries (with the exception of Slovenia where, in principle, the sector represents the cornerstone of industrial relations). As Chapter 2 highlighted, the prominence of local or company standard setting emerged as the result of specific post-transitional reforms, combined with the inability of trade unions at central levels to exert greater influence in the post-transitional context. Given the emphasis of industrial relations on decentralised decision-making, one could expect greater legal encouragement of company-level collective bargaining over bargaining at the other levels. The purpose of this chapter, however, is to test this presumption in the four CEE countries. It should be emphasised that because there is no practice of registering these collective agreements in any of the four countries, there is a lack of reliable and comprehensive statistical data which would allow more objective assessment of their content and nature, as well as of their linkages with collective agreements at the other bargaining levels. As explained during the interviews, the available data should in fact be treated as a mere estimation. Table 8 provides an overview of the existing data on the number of company collective agreements and their coverage. In Poland, company level is the most predominant form of collective bargaining. According to the available data, the number of single-establishment collective agreements in Poland was 8.142 in 2013, but these rates were slightly higher in pre-crisis years. Czech industrial relations are also predominantly developed at company level and the coverage rates of company collective agreements are considerably higher than 'higher-level' collective agreements. Around 31.3% of employees are covered by company collective agreements (data from 2014) in contrast to around 15% of employees covered by 'higher-level' collective agreements (as highlighted in Chapter 6). In Slovakia, around 30% of employees are covered by company collective agreements. Slovenia is an exception to the industrial relations trends described in the other three countries. As already noted in the previous chapter, sectoral collective agreements has been the cornerstone of the Slovenian industrial relations system since the 1990s, although there has been a persistent and gradual trend towards the decentralisation of industrial relations especially with the recent financial and economic crisis.

Furthermore, although the CEE countries are traditionally regarded as having decentralised collective bargaining, a closer look into the coverage rates in Table 8 shows that, in reality, a significant proportion of employees in the four countries is not covered by any collective agreement. In fact, collectively agreed norms and provisions do not apply to the majority of the employees in the labour market. Statutory legal regulation and, where existing, internal employers' regulation often remain the only applicable rules. The exception to this is Slovenia, but here the relatively higher coverage rates of collective agreements at any level can be in the first place attributed to the regulatory prominence of sectoral collective agreements.

Table 8 Industrial Relations at Company/Single-Enterprise Level

Country	No. of Company Level Collective Agreements	Coverage of Company Level Agreements	Total Coverage*
Slovenia	No data	No data	Rates falling from 96% in 2006 to an estimated 65% in 2013
Slovakia	No data	Around 30% in 2013	Rates falling from 40% in 2006 and 35% in 2011 to 24.9% in 2013

Country	No. of Company Level Collective Agreements	Coverage of Company Level Agreements	Total Coverage*
The Czech Republic	3,966 in 2014 (covering around 1.28 million employees), which is slightly below than 4.680 agreements in 2012, covering around 1.35 million employees	About 31.3% in 2014, as compared with 33.9% in 2012	About 50.2% in 2006; 50.4% in 2012 and 47.3% in 2013 (ICTWSS data);** or around 30% since 2006 (Eurofound)
Poland	In 2013 about 8,142 (slightly lower than 8,369 in 2008) covering about 1.68 million people	No estimated data on the coverage rate	15.7% in 2006, 14.8% in 2011 and 14.7% in 2012

Sources: Combined data from Worker-participation, Eurofound, ICTWSS database 5.1, Visser 2016, and data obtained at the interviews with the social partners in the four countries.

Notes: * This column refers to the coverage rates regarding collective agreements concluded at all existing collective bargaining levels in the country. It contains data on selected years only, in view of comparing and contrasting pre- and post-crisis coverage rates. The detailed overview of trends regarding coverage rates has been provided in Table 3 (Chapter 4) and Figure 1 (Chapter 1).
**The data includes only collective agreements concluded by the largest trade union confederation ČMKOS.

Although collective bargaining at company level is the most predominant form of bargaining in CEE industrial relations, it is struggling with its own challenges. In the first place, one should account for the fact that the CEE countries have been faced with a drastic trade union decline since the early 1990s, as evidenced in Table 9. Density rates have been particularly low in Poland in the past two decades. While the decline of membership rates have, on the whole, affected the entire industrial relations systems, the detrimental effects are the most tangible at company level, where trade unions may not attract a sufficient number of employees in membership. Moreover, the interviews in the four countries revealed that company collective bargaining in CEE is particularly challenged because of the predominance of small and medium enterprises (SMEs) in many sectors, where the setting up of trade unions is by nature difficult. Setting up a trade union is certainly less of a challenge in larger companies, where it is also easier to conclude collective agreements. Also, as interviewees in the four countries explained, the mere existence of a trade union in company is no guarantee that a collective agreement will be concluded. Moreover, it is often the case that several trade unions operate at company level, and it can complicate the conclusion of collective agreements if they cannot reach agreement about the content of bargaining.

Table 9 Trends in Percentage Rates of Trade Union Density

	Slovenia	Slovakia	Czech Republic	Poland
1993	58.0	67.3	64.4	28.8
1994	60.2	64.2	51.5	27.2
1995	50.5	56.1	43.5	20.2
1996	48.8	47.8	39.5	20.4
1997	44.1	42.0	36.9	20.4
1998	42.7	36.2	32.1	20.5
1999	40.4	34.2	30.0	20.5
2000	41.6	32.3	27.2	17.5
2001	40.8	30.5	23.6	15.5
2002	44.7	27.4	22.2	14.1
2003	43.7	26.1	22.3	18.8
2004	40.1	23.6	21.0	19.0
2005	37.1	22.8	19.7	18.1
2006	31.4	20.6	18.7	16.3
2007	29.0	18.8	17.9	15.6
2008	26.6	17.2	17.4	n/a
2009	26.3	16.0	17.2	14.6
2010	25.0	15.2	16.6	n/a
2011	23.1	14.1	15.8	13.6
2012	22.0	13.6	14.3	12.7
2013	21.2	13.3	12.7	n/a
2014	n/a	n/a	n/a	n/a

Source: ICTWSS database 5.1 (Visser 2016).

In order to fully grasp the regulatory nature and importance of company-level collective agreements, the analysis that follows in this chapter focuses on several points. Section 2 examines relevant aspects of company collective agreements in the four countries. In the first place, it explains company-level collective agreement in the four countries, including its definition, content and articulation with the other standard-setting sources (section 2.1). In addition, the parties to collective bargaining are described (section 2.2). The issues not covered by the previous sections are looked at briefly in section 2.3 (collective bargaining procedure, duration and the question as to whom collective agreements apply). Section 2.4 deals with company-level topics which do not arise from collective bargaining but which are important for understanding standard-setting processes at company level: the role of works councils and the role of unilateral standard-setting by employers. Section 3 contains comparative analysis of the traits presented, while section 4 provides concluding remarks on this chapter.

2 FOUR COUNTRIES: OVERVIEW OF LEGAL AND INSTITUTIONAL FRAMEWORK

As already noted in this chapter, there is no comprehensive dataset on company-level collective agreements in CEE, since there is no legal obligation in the four countries to register them. The comparative analysis of the content and functions of company-level collective agreements in this section is limited to knowledge gained from existing studies, combined with information from the interviews. Chapter 6 has already presented some characteristics of the legal framework in the four countries that can be extended to this chapter. Thus, the following lines will not fully reiterate information from Chapter 6, particularly regarding details on how the legal provisions pertaining to the four countries relate to the content (substance) and bargaining scope of collective agreements.

2.1 Explaining Company Collective Agreements

2.1.1 *Definition and Origin*

2.1.1.1 *Slovenia*

As explained in Chapter 6, the existing legal framework, anchored under the 2006 Act on Collective Agreements, defines no levels at which collective bargaining may take place in Slovenia, in this way leaving social partners free to negotiate at levels they decide. Thus, unlike the other three countries, in Slovenia there is no legally defined concept of company collective agreement. The legal framework which had existed before 2006, however, delineated collective bargaining at cross-sectoral, sectoral and company level.[680] It has already been demonstrated in this study (Chapter 6) that the Slovenian model of post-transitional transformation focused on centralised collective bargaining structures.[681] However, today's processes at company level can be linked to the legacies of self-management, which represented a pervasive paradigm of the pre-1990s socialist system. Within that system, the 'socialist' companies and their employees operated with a certain level of autonomy – Stanojević noted that the economy was based on large and labour intensive companies which enjoyed semi-autonomous market status.[682] Employees were considered owners of the means of production and could adopt different forms of self-management enactments through which they established their working conditions.[683] Yet, this self-management regulatory style was not fully autonomous, because, as Slovenian scholar Končar has noted,

---

680. The Act on Basic Rights of Employment Relationship of 1989 and the Employment Relationship Act of 1990.
681. Chapter 6, section 2.
682. Stanojević, M., 'The Rise and Decline of Slovenian Corporatism: Local and European Factors', *Europe-Asia Studies*, 2012, vol. 64, no. 5, pp. 860–862.
683. *See* Končar, P., 'Changes and Adaptations of Labour Law and Industrial Relations in Slovenia' in R. Blanpain and L. Nagy (eds), *Labour Law and Industrial Relations in Central and Eastern*

the role of self-management enactments was mainly to execute what had been already determined by legislation and, as such, they did not emanate from the autonomous will of employees.[684]

Even though the cornerstone of industrial relations is to be found at sector level today, the relevance of company level cannot be dismissed, especially having in mind a visible trend towards decentralisation of industrial relations.[685] Company is the locus for standard setting that is more appropriately tailored to the needs of companies, and it is the level at which the actual rights and conditions of work are decided.

There are no official data about the number of collective agreements concluded at company level in Slovenia. According to the interviewees, there is an evident contrast between collective bargaining practices in differently sized companies: all large companies and most of the medium-sized companies have collective agreements. Interviewees reported that most multinational companies have concluded company collective agreements, especially those with European-rooted funds. The probability of company collective agreements being concluded in smaller and medium-sized companies is considerably reduced.

2.1.1.2 Slovakia

As the previous chapter demonstrated, the Slovak legal framework delineates 'enterprise-level collective agreements' and 'higher-level collective agreements', which were introduced by the 1991 Act on Collective Bargaining. The law sets out that enterprise-level collective agreements are those concluded between trade union and the employer, but provides no further designation of these agreements. In principle, these collective agreements are more important standard-setting instruments in industrial relations than sectoral (higher-level) collective agreements, particularly when it comes to regulating wages and working time.[686] As explained during the interviews, collective bargaining is more likely to take place in bigger companies, and as is the case with Slovenia, it is considerably reduced in smaller and medium companies.

2.1.1.3 The Czech Republic

As has already been presented in the previous chapter, the legal framework in the Czech Republic acknowledges the concept of 'enterprise-level collective agreement'.

Europe (from Planned to Market Economy), Bulletin of Comparative Labour Relations, no. 31, The Hague, Kluwer Law International, 1996, pp. 157–158. For more sources on self-management, *see* fn 162.
684. *Ibid.*, pp. 157–158, also noting that the Slovenian self-management system was rather different from the other CEE countries, yet, equally inefficient.
685. As already noted in Chapter 6 (*see* section 2.1), decentralisation has been visible since the past decade, and particularly in the recent economic and financial crisis *see* Kanjuo Mrčela, A., *Living and working in Slovenia – Collective Bargaining* Dublin, Eurofound, 2017; Stanojević, M. and Kanjuo Mrčela, A., 'Slovenia at the Crossroads: Increasing Dependence on Supranational Institutions and the Weakening of Social Dialogue', *European Journal of Industrial Relations*, 2016, vol. 1, no. 14, pp. 1–14.
686. Czíria, L., *Living and Working in Slovakia*, Dublin, Eurofound, 2017.

The law recognises that these agreements are concluded between a trade union and an employer, but it does not provide further designation. Scholarship has explained that this type of collective agreement does not necessarily cover an entire enterprise, and that it is possible to have more than one such agreement under a single employer.[687] It has also been underlined that it is possible to conclude a group-undertaking collective agreement involving more than one employer (e.g., in the case of holdings).[688] In the Czech Republic, standards are set predominantly at company level. Nevertheless, as in the other CEE countries, company-level collective bargaining remains the province of certain parts of the economy, as it is mainly the bigger companies that have collective agreements. For example, in the metals sector, the interviewees have reported that the coverage rates of company collective agreements is approximately 65% – a stark contrast with the 10% coverage rate of higher-level collective agreement in this sector.

The post-1990s industrial relations focused on the company as the principal unit of decision-making.[689] Collective bargaining rates were marginal in the pre-transitional federal country of Czechoslovakia, but, to some extent, the legacies of that era have predetermined the current industrial relations landscape. Some form of company collective bargaining had been in existence in the pre-1990s Czechoslovakia – trade unions in companies were able to sign different types of collective accords with management.[690] These agreements were not autonomous, though, as their content was greatly restricted by the administrative regulations in place at the time.

2.1.1.4 Poland

Polish law recognises the notion of 'single-enterprise collective agreements' which, according to the Labour Code, are concluded between an employer and the trade unions operating within the enterprise. In Poland, these collective agreements represent the main collective standard-setting method. The focus of Polish industrial relations on single-enterprise agreements can be otherwise linked to specific legacies and to the type of economic transformation undertaken in the past two decades. Poland had already started economic transformation by the 1980s – well before the other CEE countries.[691] As explained by Sewerynski, these early reforms were notable for

---

687. Pichrt, J. and Štefko, M., 'Czech Republic' in R. Blanpain and F. Hendrickx (eds), *International Encyclopaedia for Labour Law and Industrial Relations*, The Hague, Kluwer Law International, 2015, p. 257.
688. Ibid.
689. Pollert, A., 'The Transformation of Trade Unionism in the Capitalist and Democratic Restructuring of the Czech Republic', *European Journal of Industrial Relations*, 1997, vol. 3, no. 2, p. 207.
690. Deak explained that these collective accords had the aim of ensuring social and economic development of the organisation and fixing the standards of employees as well as regulating their mutual cooperation, see Deak, L., 'Customary International Labour Laws and Their Application in Hungary, Poland and the Czech Republic' *Tulsa Journal of Comparative and International Law*, 1994, vol. 2, no. 1, p. 40; also, Myant, M., 'Czech and Slovak Trade Unions', *Journal of Communist Studies*, 1993, vol. 9, no. 4, p. 61.
691. On this topic, Florek noted that Poland started searching for the new labour relations model seven years earlier than the other CEE countries, and that the pre-transitional economic crisis started earlier in Poland, see Florek, L., 'Problems and Dilemmas of Labour Relations in Poland', *Comparative Labour Law Journal*, 1992, vol. 13, p. 112.

encouraging company collective bargaining by allowing far-reaching autonomy to plant organisations, and by opening up possibilities for company-level bargaining in state-owned enterprises by the Act on Workers' Self-Management in State-Owned Enterprises of 1981.[692] Company standard setting was further encouraged with a law adopted in 1984, which introduced the possibility of negotiating wages at company level. These developments led to the adoption of a law in 1986 which delineated collective bargaining at multi-enterprise and enterprise level.[693] This legislative framework, adopted in the 1980s, together with the policy choices made in the 1990s, as described in Chapter 2, played a major role in designating the company as the main locus of collective bargaining in modern industrial relations in Poland.

2.1.2 Content of Company-Level Agreements and Articulation with Other Standard-Setting Sources

2.1.2.1 Slovenia

There is a lack of comprehensive empirical data on the content of company collective agreements, and available studies have been able to present only their general descriptions. The earlier study on Slovenian industrial relations demonstrated that, in general, company collective agreements regulate similar matters as agreements at sectoral level.[694] This study also demonstrated that collective agreements at different levels do not differ much on the subjects they regulate, but mainly with respect to the scope of the rights and benefits of the employees. The most frequent items regulated in company collective agreements are wages and different types of benefits.[695] There is no comprehensive data on the content of company collective agreements in the recent crisis period – another recent study has only confirmed the decentralisation trend in Slovenia, including the greater powers that employers have at company level, more flexibility in the workplace and the lowered capacity of trade unions at local levels to protect employees.[696]

The previous chapter noted that the principles of favourability and the vertical hierarchy of rules are the building blocks of the relationship between standard-setting norms at different levels in Slovenia and in the other three CEE countries. Thus,

---

692. Sewerynski, M., 'Development of the Collective Bargaining System in Poland after the Second World War', *Comparative Labour Law Journal*, 1993, vol. 14, pp. 452–455.
693. Ibid., pp. 458–460.
694. Natlacen, M.P., 'The Evolving Structure of Collective Bargaining in Europe: National Report of Slovenia', Project VS/2003/0219 – SI2.359910, European Commission and University of Florence, 2004.
695. Ibid.
696. Stanojević, M. and Kanjuo Mrčela, A., 'Social Dialogue During the Economic Crisis: The Impact of Industrial Relations Reforms on Collective Bargaining in the Manufacturing Sector: Slovenia', Project: *The Impact of Industrial Relations Reforms on Collective Bargaining in the Manufacturing Sector*, Brussels, European Commission, 2014, pp. 17, 23, 35, 42; Stanojević, M. and Kanjuo Mrčela, A., 'Slovenia at the Crossroads: Increasing Dependence on Supranational Institutions and the Weakening of Social Dialogue', *European Journal of Industrial Relations*, 2016, vol. 1, no. 14, pp. 1–14.

Chapter 7: Company Level

company collective agreements should respect the terms and conditions in sectoral (or cross-sectoral) collective agreement and statutory law and may not set less favourable rules for employees than these sources of regulation. The previous chapter has already explained that opening clauses in the sectoral collective agreements, allowing deviation from the sectoral standard by setting less favourable conditions for employees at company-level collective agreements, are legally allowed in Slovenia. However, there are no clear data about the frequency of their use, although scholars have noticed their increased application during the recent economic and financial crisis period.[697]

2.1.2.2 Slovakia

Earlier studies have demonstrated that enterprise-level collective agreements cover similar topics as higher-level collective agreements, particularly wages and conditions of employment.[698] The interviewees in Slovakia explained that although these collective agreements usually cover the same type of issues as higher-level agreements, they represent an important tool for specifying rights and conditions and are the level at which the 'real agreement' on wages and remuneration can be reached. Also, the interviewees explained that sectoral collective agreements ('higher-level agreements' in Slovakia) tend to have a more general nature, and often only restate the provisions of labour laws. A study performed in the metals sector demonstrated that there is actually only a weak link between collective bargaining at the sectoral and company levels – both levels play an important role, but lack mutual coordination, as company collective agreements are often negotiated before agreements at sectoral level.[699] There is no clear empirical evidence on the effects which the crisis had on company-level collective bargaining. The available data only generally suggest that company collective bargaining gained an increased role.[700]

Principles of favourability and top-down hierarchy are also relevant here – enterprise-level collective agreements may only upgrade the provisions of higher-level collective agreements and the statutory labour law to the benefit of employee. Also, employment contracts may not define less favourable rights for employees than collective agreements or statutory labour law. The previous chapter showed that the relationship between norms at different levels is top-down – it is not possible to include opening clauses or similar clauses which would allow less favourable rights to be negotiated at company level. This opportunity existed in Slovakia for only a short time

---

697. Stanojević and Kanjuo Mrčela 2014, p. 33, particularly in the area of working time.
698. A survey performed by Research Institute of Labour, Social Affairs and Family (RILSAF) in 2000, as interpreted by Czíria, L., *Collective Bargaining Procedures, Structures and Scope*, Dublin, Eurofound, 2002. *See also* a report by Handiak, who noted that the main issues are wages and remuneration related conditions, in Handiak, P., 'The Evolving Structure of Collective Bargaining in Europe: National Report of Slovakia' Study VS/2003/0219SI2–359910, European Commission and University of Florence, 2004, p. 14.
699. Brngálová, B. and Kahancová, M., 'Governing the Metal Sector in Slovakia: Socio-Economic and Policy Context, Industrial Relations and the Challenge of Flexibility and Security', FP7 GUSTO Working Paper 6.20, 2013, p. 26.
700. Czíria, L., *Slovakia: Impact of the Crisis on Industrial Relations*, Dublin, Eurofound, 2013b.

during the crisis period (these provisions were promulgated in 2011 and rescinded in 2012),[701] but it was never availed of in practice.

2.1.2.3 The Czech Republic

Similarly to Slovakia, enterprise-level collective agreements in the Czech Republic cover the same or similar topics as higher-level collective agreements, but they offer solutions more appropriately tailored to local needs, particularly with respect to wages and different elements of pay.[702] In fact, the company is the cornerstone and the most developed collective bargaining level in the Czech Republic, but there is a lack of comprehensive and accurate empirical data on the content of these agreements. At the same time, there is also a lack of empirical data on the effects which the crisis has had on enterprise-level collective bargaining. Yet, the interviewees from the construction sector explained that the crisis affected the stipulation of wage increases at company level.

The principles of favourability and vertical hierarchy determine the relationship between legal rules at different levels in the Czech Republic, too. However, as the previous chapter has explained, derogation clauses which would allow setting less favourable conditions at the company level than the higher-level agreements are virtually non-existent and have no practical importance. In addition, the legal framework for these derogations is restrictively set. Therefore, in practice, enterprise-level collective agreement may only improve rights established by higher-level agreement.

2.1.2.4 Poland

Despite the general lack of comprehensive empirical data, an earlier study suggested that single-enterprise collective agreements first and foremost regulate wages, as well as working time and social benefits, while other topics are of less relevance.[703] The available evidence suggests that the crisis did not substantially change the collective bargaining landscape in Poland, although some deterioration of enterprise-level collective bargaining is visible.[704] A similar narrative has been given by respondents at the interviews, who added that the level of protection contained in the single-enterprise collective agreements usually do not much exceed the provisions of the Labour Code:

> The general position that employers present is: we are willing to sign collective agreement if its conditions don't exceed Labour Code regulations, meaning they are not more favourable for employees than Labour Code. Thus, signing a

---

701. As explained in Chapter 6, section 2.3.
702. This was demonstrated in an earlier study, Hála, J., Kroupa, A., Mansfeldova, Z., Kux, J., Vaskova, R. and Pleskot, I., *Development of Social Dialogue in the Czech Republic*, RILSA, 2002. Similar arguments can be found in: Tomes, I., 'The Evolving Structure of Collective Bargaining in Europe: National Report of the Czech Republic', Project VS/2003/0219-SI2.359910, European Commission and University of Florence, 2004, pp. 10–14.
703. Towalski, R., *Single-Establishment Bargaining in 2003 Examined*, Dublin, Eurofound, 2004a.
704. Czarzasty, J., *Poland: Impact of the Crisis on Industrial Relations*, Dublin, Eurofound, 2013b.

collective agreement has absolutely no sense as the whole idea of collective bargaining is that it provides regulations that exceed Labour Code in favour of employees.

The principles of favourability and vertical hierarchy rule the relationship between legal norms at different levels. Thus, the single-enterprise collective agreements may only improve standards set by multi-enterprise agreements and statutory legal regulation. Opening clauses or clauses with similar functions do not exist in Polish law. However, it is possible to suspend the application of collective agreement, in its entirety or partially, at any level, including enterprise level. These rules were introduced in 2002 and allow suspension for up to three years, the condition being that the employer is experiencing financial difficulty.[705] The Labour Code specifies that the decision on suspension should be taken jointly by the parties to the collective agreement, and if no trade union operates, the decision should be taken by representatives of employees in the company. Thus, one may note that this decision represents some form of a collective accord. However, minimum statutory rights must be respected, because suspension may not be used to diminish employees' rights that are anchored in the Labour Code. There is no comprehensive data on the use of these clauses in Poland, which would provide a relevant insight into industrial relations in that country, although the available data show that their use has been in decline in the recent years.[706]

2.2 Collective Bargaining Parties

2.2.1 Who Can Conclude Collective Agreements?

2.2.1.1 Slovenia

In Slovenia, only trade unions can sign collective agreements. Other forms of employee organisations at workplace level, such as works councils, cannot be parties to collective agreements. The 2006 Act on Collective Agreements stipulates that if more than one trade union operates in the workplace, a bargaining team can be formed, in which case each trade union participating in the collective bargaining will be considered a signatory to the concluded agreement. According to the Act on Trade Union Representativeness of 1993, in order to become representative, and therefore to be able to sign company collective agreements, trade unions need to fulfil a set of qualitative criteria: to be independent from the state and employer, to have existed for at least six months, to be democratic in character and to have their own funding. Also, at company level the trade union should fulfil one quantitative condition – it must have a membership of at least 15% of the company's employees.

---

705. Gardawski, J., *More Flexible Labour Code Comes into Force*, Dublin, Eurofound, 2003.
706. For example 176 times in 2004, *see* Towalski, R., *Collective Agreements in 2004 Examined*, Dublin, Eurofound, 2004b. According to recent data from Eurofound, the number of suspensions decreased from 130 in 2010 to 74 in 2013; *see* Czarzasty, J. and Mrozowicki, A., *Living and Working in Poland – Collective Bargaining*, Dublin, Eurofound, 2017.

2.2.1.2 Slovakia

Collective agreements are concluded only by trade unions, as other forms of employee representation cannot be their parties. According to the legal rules on collective bargaining, when more than one trade union operates at company level, they should first try to reach an agreement about their representation – if such accord cannot be reached in fifteen days, the decision of the trade union with the highest membership will be considered decisive. There are no rules on representativeness in Slovakia. Such legal rules were only in existence for a short while during the crisis period, when an amendment of the Labour Code in 2011 stipulated that at least 30% of employees in the company should be members of a representative trade union (this provision was rescinded in January 2013, before it was even applied in practice).[707] This amendment has been interpreted as controversial by the interviewees – even though the rule applied only to newly established trade unions, the 30% threshold was seen as high, and also as not compatible with the ILO framework. At the same time, the interviewees saw this provision as possibly detrimental to company collective bargaining, because most companies lack already a trade union, and the largest part of some sectors consists of small companies only, where such a high threshold is difficult to reach.

2.2.1.3 The Czech Republic

As in the other countries examined in this study, in the Czech Republic collective agreements are concluded only by trade unions. Any other types of employee representation may not engage in collective bargaining. When more than one trade union operates in a workplace, the Labour Code specifies that the employer should negotiate collective agreement with all the trade unions. According to the Labour Code, the unions are supposed to act jointly and in mutual consent, unless they agree differently amongst themselves about representation. This legal solution resulted from the Constitutional Court ruling of 2008 which repealed the earlier rule that an employer should negotiate with the largest trade union when no mutual consent is reached.[708] Moreover, it should be noted that a general feature of the Czech legal framework is the lack of rules on representativeness at any level. Differing from the Slovaks, the Czech policy makers have never attempted to introduce criteria for representativeness.

2.2.1.4 Poland

The parties to single-enterprise agreements in Poland are the employer and the trade union organised at company level. As in the other three countries, only trade unions may conclude collective agreements. As underlined by several interviewees, quite

---

707. Act no 361/2012 Coll.
708. Constitutional Court intervened in several areas with this ruling, repealing in total eleven provisions of the Labour Code (version of 2006 – Act no 262/2006). This ruling was interpreted as weakening the overall trade union position, see Hála, J. and Verveková, S., *Unions Claim Court's Repeal of Labour Code Will Diminish Trade Union Role*, Dublin, Eurofound, 2008.

often in Poland several trade unions co-exist at the workplace. Because this can render the conclusion of collective agreement difficult, the law provides the possibility of all trade unions which operate at the workplace negotiating jointly. Negotiations can also be conducted with a few of the trade unions only, but in this case, at least one of them should fulfil the representativeness criteria. The Labour Code specifies conditions which trade unions must fulfil to be considered representative at this single-enterprise level:

- If a trade union belongs to a multi-enterprise representative trade union, it should employ at least 7% of employees in the company.
- If a trade union does not belong to a multi-enterprise trade union, it should employ at least 10% of employees.
- If none of the trade unions fulfil these criteria, then the representative union will be considered to be the one employing the highest number of employees.

The topic of trade union representativeness is particularly relevant for the pluralistic and fragmented industrial relations in Poland; the trade unions with whom the interviews were conducted considered the topic of representativeness particularly problematic. They pointed out that the problem of concluding single-enterprise collective agreement is not so much related to the plurality of trade unions, as it is to the fact that these trade unions are too small to be representative. Interviewees have also reported cases of 'yellow' trade unions. According to one of the interviewees from the trade union side, there are examples of the employers unofficially financing and supporting such 'yellow' trade unions, with the aim of influencing the collective bargaining outcomes.

2.2.2 Organisation of Trade Unions and Competences

2.2.2.1 Slovenia

There are no official data about the number of trade union organisations set up at company level. Trade unions are established pursuant to the Employment Relationship Act, without any specific legal restrictions. The trade unions negotiate collective agreements and share information and consultation rights together with the works councils (the division of their responsibilities is defined within the Employment Relationship Act).

2.2.2.2 Slovakia

The legal framework embodied in the Act on the Association of Citizens of 1990 contains no specific restrictions on the trade union set up. The trade unions can mostly be found in medium or large enterprises, as it is difficult to set up unions in smaller companies. The Labour Code defines the rights of trade unions in the workplace, which, in addition to collective bargaining, includes a range of information and consultation powers and the supervision of the application of health and safety provision at the workplace. These trade union rights have been significantly curbed in comparison with the previous communist period. The communist trade union prerogatives, anchored under the 1965 Labour Code, were relatively broad, including the powers of trade unions to define working time, holidays and other aspects of working life.[709] This argument should however be nuanced – the communist trade unions were not fully autonomous organisations, they were instruments of the communist party and the employees did not have the right to join the organisation of their choosing.[710]

2.2.2.3 The Czech Republic

In the past two decades, the legal basis for establishing trade unions in the Czech Republic has been the 1990 Act on the Association of Citizens, enacted in the former state of Czechoslovakia. Since 2014, trade unions can be established only pursuant to the Civil Code.[711] As in Slovakia, there are no specific legal restrictions concerning trade union establishment. The only legal condition which has been recently introduced is that a trade union should have as its members at least three employees.[712] As respondents explained in interviews, this provision has been enacted as a form of legal insurance that a trade union can exist and be active in the workplace.

The trade union landscape in the Czech Republic has been characterised as fragmented, which originates in the legacies from the former communist period when the enterprise was the main sphere of operation for trade unions.[713] The fragmentation was further underpinned by the very nature of the transitional process – the focus of the 1990s reforms was on enterprise and on enhancing trade union decentralisation. The focus on decentralisation reflected a deliberate rejection of the former centralised system and marked a return to individualism and freedoms, also giving a substantial leeway to local trade unions.[714] The trade unions starting to operate at enterprise level were small and either had disassociated from the previously established unions at a higher level or had emerged from scratch, but the principle 'one workplace, one union' was maintained.[715]

Today, according to estimated data obtained during the interviews, around 30% of companies have trade unions. As with the other countries of CEE, trade union

---

709. Majtan, B., 'The Labour Code in the Republic of Slovakia', *Employee Relations*, 2005, vol. 27, no. 6, p. 605; also, Deak 1994, p. 40 and Belina, M., 'Labour Law and Industrial Relations in the Czech Republic' in R. Blanpain and L. Nagy (eds), *Labour Law and Industrial Relations in Central and Eastern Europe (from Planned to Market Economy)*, Bulletin of Comparative Labour Relations, no. 31, The Hague, Kluwer Law International, 1996, pp. 85-107.
710. Deak 1994, p. 40.
711. In effect from 1 January 2014.
712. Pichrt and Štefko 2015, p. 252.
713. Myant, M., 'Trade Unions in the Czech Republic', Report 115, Brussels, ETUI, 2010; Pollert 1997, p. 207.
714. Myant, M. and Smith, S., 'Czech Trade Unions in Comparative Perspective', *European Journal of Industrial Relations*, 1999, vol. 5, no. 3, p. 267 and pp. 265-285; also Myant 2010, p. 16; and Pollert 1997.
715. Myant 2010, p. 12.

organisation is more likely to be found in the larger than in the medium or small companies that predominate in some sectors (construction sector, e.g.). It should be stressed that the presence of a trade union in the workplace does not automatically lead to the conclusion that a collective agreement will be concluded. For example, available data suggest that around 23% of employees working in companies with trade unions were not covered by any company collective agreement in 2009.[716]

The rights of trade unions are defined in the Labour Code. Apart from the rights to collective bargaining, trade unions may also enjoy rights of co-decisions as in many instances the Labour Code requires the trade union's consent (e.g., regarding the dismissals of employees).[717] The trade unions also have rights of information and consultation, which are shared with works councils (e.g., employers have an obligation to inform their employees on wage related issues or to consult them on various items).

2.2.2.4 Poland

The current picture of trade unionism in Poland is labelled as 'competitive pluralism',[718] due to its fragmented and pluralised traits. This pluralisation and fragmentation, which appears in the form of a number of small trade union organisations operating in companies, and often not affiliated to any central organisation, has been emerging since the early period of economic transformation. Respondents at interviews explained that trade unions in companies rarely coordinate their activities with sectoral trade unions, and that trade union associations cannot control the outcome of single-establishment collective bargaining. According to available data, 55% of the total workforce in Poland is employed in companies where there is no trade union presence.[719] The current trade union landscape originates in the legacies from the 1980s, when the trade union movement, Solidarity, famous for its engagement in anti-communist activities, was established. Legislation allowing trade unionism appeared earlier in Poland than in the other CEE countries. As the result of massive social unrest, on 25 September 1981 the Act on Workers' Self-Management in State-Owned Enterprises was passed, well known for establishing the principle of employee decision-making in public enterprises.[720] In December 1981, martial law was passed, aiming to lessen the influence of political opposition; it resulted in the banning of Solidarity's activities and a ban on all the trade unions which operated at that time.[721] In 1982, a new law had been passed enabling the formation of 'new' trade unions,

---

716. Data from trade union confederation ČMKOS for 2009; *see* Myant 2010, p. 20.
717. Pichrt and Štefko 2015, pp. 242–243; Pichrt, J., 'Czech Republic: European Works Council Country Report' in R. Blanpain and F. Hendrickx (eds), *International Encyclopaedia for Labour Law and Industrial Relations*, The Hague, Kluwer Law International, 2010, p. 18.
718. Gardawski, J., Mrozowicki, A. and Czarzasty, J., *Trade Unions in Poland*, Brussels, ETUI, 2012, p. 11.
719. According to data presented in Hajn, Z. and Mitrus, L., 'Poland' in R. Blanpain and F. Hendrickx (eds), *International Encyclopaedia for Labour Law and Industrial Relations*, The Hague, Kluwer Law International, 2016, p. 244.
720. Florek 1992, p. 124; also, *see* Matey, M., 'The Prospects for Labor Law Reform in Poland', *Northwestern Journal of International Law & Business*, 1986, vol. 7, pp. 621–622.
721. Sewerynski 1993, p. 453.

while the existing trade unions had been declared illegal (including Solidarity, which continued working 'underground').[722] This 1982 Act on Trade Unions paved the way for a decentralised trade union structure in Poland by encouraging the autonomy of company-level trade unions. The law reflected the intention of the authorities, afraid of any political engagement and opposition on the side of trade unions, to avoid the formation of any new Solidarity-like union in the near future.[723] As the Polish scholar Sewerynski has noted, the 1982 law, which remained valid until the early 1990s, significantly weakened the trade union picture in Poland, because it allowed their formation at workplace level only, and one trade union per each workplace only.[724] As a consequence, new trade unions were formed in a small percentage of workplaces only and operated in conflict with the underground organisation of Solidarity.[725]

Following the demise of communism, in 1991 an amendment to the Act on Trade Unions allowed free trade union establishment in Poland. The trade union organisation was made free and independent from the state and employers, and it was possible to set up several unions in one workplace.[726] This Act also represented a transposition of the ILO-based freedom of association into Polish national law.[727] According to this law, as few as ten employees can form a trade union, but in practice, as explained throughout the interviews, their set up is a rather challenging task. As the interviews revealed, trade unions are usually found in the companies that had been state-owned in the communist period and had been subsequently privatised. These companies had practised some limited form of collective bargaining during the communist period and had therefore developed to some extent a collective bargaining culture. However, the interviewees explained that it is rather difficult to find a trade union in a company that had been organised from scratch in the post-communist period – the major reason is the lack of willingness on the employers' side to support their set-up. They also said that the probability of finding a trade union in companies with foreign capital and multinationals is higher. The interviewees claim that setting up a trade union in smaller companies, with less than twenty employees is often 'virtually impossible', which is the case, for example, in the construction sector.

The trade unions engage in collective bargaining and enjoy a variety of information and consultation rights and rights of codetermination. The information and consultation rights are shared with works councils.

---

722. Ibid.
723. On origins of the 1982 law, see Gardawski et al. 2012, Matey 1986, Sewerynski 1993.
724. Sewerynski 1993, p. 453.
725. Ibid.
726. Sewerynski, M., 'Changes in Polish Labour Law and Industrial Relations during the Period of Post-Communist Transformation' in R. Blanpain and L. Nagy (eds), *Labour Law and Industrial Relations in Central and Eastern Europe (from Planned to Market Economy)*, Bulletin of Comparative Labour Relations, no. 31, The Hague, Kluwer Law International, 1996, p. 95.
727. Ibid.

2.3 Other Issues

2.3.1 Procedure of Collective Bargaining

The collective bargaining procedure is uniformly prescribed for collective agreements concluded at any level in all four countries. Thus, this section will not reiterate what has already been said about this topic in Chapter 6. However, specific characteristics of the Polish legal framework will be mentioned again at this point, given their particular relevance for company collective bargaining. Differing from the provisions of the other three countries, the Polish Labour Code does not impose a general obligation on the bargaining party to reply to the written proposal, a process which would normally herald the beginning of the collective bargaining procedure. However, the Polish Labour Code sets out the conditions under which the bargaining party (usually the employer) may not refuse to enter into collective bargaining: when the employees are not covered by any agreement, when the bargaining is aimed at amending the current collective agreement to address the difficult economic situation of employer or employees, and when the bargaining proposal has been issued prior to the expiry of the current agreement. The Polish Labour Code furthermore sets out the obligation of parties to bargain in good faith and provides a definition of it – trade unions may only issue 'justified demands' in line with the financial capacities and economic situation of the employer. For employers, bargaining in good faith means that they should respect the interests of the employees not covered by the agreement. The Labour Code also explicitly lays down the obligation of the employer to disclose information on the economic situation to employees, but only when 'necessary to hold responsible negotiations'.

2.3.2 Duration

In *Slovenia*, the company collective agreement may be concluded for a definite or indefinite period, whilst in the latter case it may be cancelled provided six months' notice is given. In *Slovakia*, collective agreements usually last for one year, unless otherwise specified by the parties to its provisions. In the *Czech Republic*, unless differently stipulated by the parties, collective agreements will last for up to one year. In *Poland*, the Labour Code stipulates that if the agreement has not been concluded for a definite period, a notice period of three months will apply.

2.3.3 To Whom Does the Company Collective Agreement Apply?

In the four countries, the concluded company-level agreement binds all employees in the company, regardless of whether they are trade union members.

2.4 Beyond Collective Bargaining

2.4.1 Employers' Unilateral Standard-Setting

2.4.1.1 Slovenia

Individual employers in Slovenia can define rules and conditions of work and employment unilaterally in *general acts* which are regulated by the Employment Relationship Act.[728] In particular, if no trade union operates at the workplace, the general acts can regulate matters which would be otherwise covered by collective agreements. However, general acts cannot lower the conditions or reduce the rights of employees that have been guaranteed in the existing applicable collective agreements and statutory legal regulation. The adoption of such general acts is subject to certain conditions: before laying down the rules, the employer should consult the trade unions and works councils operating at the workplace. If no such employees' representatives operate (which may be the case in smaller companies), the employer is obliged to consult the employees.

2.4.1.2 Slovakia

The employer can issue several forms of internal regulation at the level of the workplace. The provisions of these unilateral acts must conform to the provisions of the Labour Code – they may not contain provisions which are less favourable to the employees than those laid down by collective agreements and statutory labour law. One of such unilateral acts can be *work rules* which specify the rules and conditions of the Labour Code in line with the specific conditions at the workplace. These work rules can be issued, however, only with the prior consent of the employee representatives.

2.4.1.3 The Czech Republic

According to the Labour Code, the employers may engage in two different types of unilateral standard-setting at the workplace. The first relates to *internal regulations*, which may specify wages and remuneration, but cannot contain provisions contrary to the applicable collective agreements and statutory labour laws. These provisions are issued for a least a year. The second type of unilateral acts is the *work rules* which detail the provisions of the labour laws in line with the specific conditions at the workplace. The Labour Code explicitly notes that if a trade union is present in the company, the employer can issue or alter these work regulations only with the prior written consent

---

728. Article 10 of the Employment Relationship Act adopted in 2013.

Chapter 7: Company Level

of the trade union organisation. However, there are no legal rules in place asking for prior consent or consultation with employees or employees' representatives when no trade union is present in the company. With respect to the internal regulations, there is no obligation whatsoever on the employer to consult or obtain consent, even when a trade union operates at the workplace.

2.4.1.4 Poland

The employers can issue two types of unilateral acts. The first is *work regulations* which, in the absence of collective agreement, regulate working conditions in companies with more than twenty employees. The Labour Code broadly specifies that work regulations can cover items such as health and safety, methods of payment of remuneration, and working time. Work regulations can even deal with mass dismissals.[729] Work regulations are agreed between an enterprise trade union and the employers – but, if there is no trade union in a company, these regulations can be issued unilaterally by the employer without any further consultation, according to the Labour Code. The second type is *remuneration regulations,* also regulated in the Labour Code. The employer is obliged to adopt these regulations in companies with at least twenty employees if the company is not covered by any collective agreement. These regulations may determine remuneration for work and work-related benefits. If there is a trade union within the enterprise, then these regulations must also be agreed with the union. However, according to the Labour Code, there is no obligation on the employer to consult or obtain the consent of the employees or their representatives when no trade union operates at the workplace.

2.4.2 Other Forms of Employee Representation: Works Councils

2.4.2.1 Slovenia

The legal basis for works councils is the Act on Participation of Workers, adopted in 1993, and subsequently amended in 2007. This Act, which was styled after the German model of codetermination, provides rights of information and consultation to works councils.[730] Thus, unlike the other three CEE countries, where their introduction resulted from the implementation of the EU *acquis* – as will be explained below – in Slovenia works councils were formed in the early 1990s. In support of its accession to

---

729. As demonstrated by an earlier study, *see* Sewerynski, M., 'The Evolving Structure of Collective Bargaining in Europe: National Report of Poland', Project VS/2003/0219-SI2.359910, European Commission and University of Florence, 2004b, p. 11.
730. Končar 1996, p. 171.

the EU, Slovenia implemented the relevant EU *acquis* in 2002,[731] but, available data shows no significant impact of it on industrial relations.[732]

Slovenia has a comparatively more pronounced institutional legacy of works councils than the other three countries, because the self-management style of socialism in the former country of Yugoslavia helped Slovenia to hone a tradition of employee involvement. As explained in this study, the self-management paradigm centred on the idea of employees being the owners of the means of production and deciding collectively on all the relevant aspects of company's life.[733] The workers, organised through several bodies, managed to enjoy a certain level of autonomy in decision-making. One of the most prominent forms of these bodies which could sign agreements and accords regulating the operation of the enterprise and its working conditions were 'basic organisations of associated labour'.[734] Today, works councils, which are directly elected by employees, may be established in enterprises with more than twenty employees, while smaller companies may have a worker trustee. In Slovenia, works councils can coexist alongside trade unions. Slovene scholar Vodovnik reported that, initially, the introduction of works councils was well received by trade unions, but shortly afterwards, the unions began to see them as competitors.[735] According to some estimates, there are works councils in around 20% of companies, mostly in large companies.[736] They cannot conclude collective agreements or any other type of binding agreements. Their powers are restricted to information and consultation, and these powers are shared with trade unions.[737] In addition, works councils may also enjoy rights of joint consultation and co-decision in certain cases.[738] The powers of works councils have also been discussed before the Constitutional Court, which in 2009 affirmed their rights in companies where no trade union operates.[739]

---

731. The Council Directive 94/45/EC on the establishment of a European Works Council or a procedure in Community-scale undertakings and Community-scale groups of undertakings for the purposes of informing and consulting employees was transposed in 2002. Directive 2002/14/EC of the European Parliament and of the Council establishing a general framework for informing and consulting employees in the European Community was transposed in 2007.
732. Pavlin, S., *Slovenia: The Impact of the Information and Consultation Directive*, Dublin, Eurofound, 2009.
733. *See* Chapter 2, section 3.
734. Concise classification and explanation of these self-management bodies can be found in Warner, M., 'Yugoslav "Self-Management" and Industrial Relations in Transition' *Industrial Relations Journal*, 1990, vol. 21, no. 3, pp. 209–220.
735. Vodovnik, Z., 'Slovenia' in R. Blanpain (ed.), *The Actors of Collective Bargaining*, Bulletin of Comparative Labour Relations, no. 51, The Hague, Kluwer Law International, 2004, p. 238.
736. Plachtej, B., *Slovenia: EIRO CAR on the Effect of the Information and Consultation Directive on Industrial Relations in the EU Member States Five Years After its Transposition*, Dublin, Eurofound, 2011.
737. *See* Vodovnik, Z. and Korpič-Horvat, E. 'Slovenia' in R. Blanpain and F. Hendrickx (eds), *International Encyclopaedia for Labour Law and Industrial Relations*, The Hague, Kluwer Law International, 2015, p. 306.
738. *Ibid.*
739. Plachtej 2011.

2.4.2.2 Slovakia

Works councils were formally introduced in the Slovak legal system in the early 2000s, with the implementation of the relevant EU directives.[740] Until 1959, certain forms of works councils had been in existence, which had the powers to protect the interests of employees by negotiating relevant aspects of work and employment.[741] After 1959, trade unions became the only possible form of employee representation, and works councils were reintroduced only in the early 2000s.[742] In reality, the introduction of works councils has not been welcomed by trade unions – they were perceived as competition. At the beginning, works councils could not operate in parallel to trade unions, but since 2003, trade unions and works councils may coexist in a company. According to estimates, there are works councils in only around 17% of companies.[743] They can be set up in companies with more than fifty employees, while in smaller companies it is possible to have works trustees, with the same type of responsibilities. Under the Labour Code, works councils enjoy information and consultation rights. They may also engage in joint decision-making with the employer and perform inspection activities at the workplace, but the division of competences, in principle, favours trade unions. According to the Labour Code provisions, if both trade union and works council operate at the workplace, it is the trade union that will have the right to collective bargaining, joint decision-making, receiving information and inspection activities. Nevertheless, the division of competences between the works councils and the trade unions have changed a few times in the past decade. In a nutshell, the trade unions have always had more rights at the workplace, including the right to collective bargaining and co-decision-making.[744]

2.4.2.3 The Czech Republic

The institutional legacies of works councils have been briefly mentioned above in relation to the Slovakian example. In the post-transitional context, works councils were

---

740. With the Labour Code, amendment No 311/2001 which entered into force in 2002 (with the effect as of May 2004, following Slovakia's membership of the EU) the Council Directive 94/45/EC on the establishment of a European Works Council or a procedure in Community-scale undertakings and Community-scale groups of undertakings for the purposes of informing and consulting employees was implemented. Directive 2002/14/EC of the European Parliament and of the Council establishing a general framework for informing and consulting employees in the European Community, was implemented with the Act 210/2003 which came into force on 1 July 2003.
741. The historical overview provided in Munkova, M., *Law on Employee Participation Amended*, Dublin, Eurofound, 2003.
742. *Ibid.*, however, with a short period from 1988–1990 when the specific form of 'socialist self-administrations' consisting of all company employees was made available.
743. Eurofound data from 2011, *see* Czíria, L., *Slovakia: Survey Charts Fall in Union Representation, Bargaining and Member Benefits*, Dublin, Eurofound, 2012.
744. Czíria, L., 'Collective Bargaining and Balanced Recovery: The Case of the Slovak Republic', Bratislava, Institute for Labour and Family Research, 2013a, p. 5; *see also* https://www.worker-participation.eu/National-Industrial-Relations/Countries/Slovak-Republic/Workplace-Representation.

officially introduced in the Czech Republic in 2000, following the implementation of the EU Directive on European Works Council 94/45/EC.[745] The interviewees claimed that their introduction was problematic given that the country lacked a tradition of such bodies. The interviewees also explained that this particular way of giving employees a voice in the workplace has not spread widely. Today, works councils can be established in companies with more than twenty-five employees. Initially, the Labour Code did not allow the coexistence of works councils and trade unions (this was a Czech model which was also adopted in the other CEE countries). Following a ruling of the Constitutional Court in 2008, works councils were eventually enabled in workplaces with trade unions.[746] As is the case in the other three CEE countries, works councils may not engage in collective bargaining, and their role is limited to information and consultation rights, a role which is also shared with the trade unions. As explained by Czech scholar Pichrt, the statutory legal regulation provides trade unions with broader powers, not only regarding collective bargaining (as a competence solely of trade unions), but also regarding information and consultation rights and rights of co-decision.[747]

2.4.2.4 Poland

Polish works councils have a certain legacy: some form of these bodies had been in existence in the 1950s.[748] These 'socialist' works councils were replaced by the works councils which could be formed in state-owned enterprises, pursuant to the Act on Workers' Self-Management in State-Owned Enterprises of 1981.[749] Subsequently, with the transposition of the relevant EU laws in the 2000s, they could be formed in private sector companies, too. Thus, today works councils can be formed on the basis of two different legal acts: (i) The Act on Workers' Self-Management in State-Owned Enterprises of 1981, thus in the state-owned (public) sector; or (ii) The 2006 Act on Information and Consultation, which implemented the respective EU Directive on Information and Consultation 2002/14/EC, allowing works councils in the private sector.[750]

---

745. Pichrt and Štefko 2015, p. 237. Furthermore, the Directive 2002/14/EC of the European Parliament and of the Council establishing a general framework for informing and consulting employees in the European Community was implemented in 2006 (with the effects from 1 January 2007).
746. Pichrt and Štefko 2015, pp. 238–240.
747. Pichrt, J., 'Czech Republic: European Works Council Country Report' in R. Blanpain and F. Hendrickx (eds), *International Encyclopaedia for Labour Law and Industrial Relations*, The Hague, Kluwer Law International, 2010, p. 18.
748. Federowicz, M. and Levitas, A., 'Poland: Councils under Communism and Neoliberalism' in J. Rogers and W. Streeck (eds), *Works Councils: Consultation, Representation and Cooperation in Industrial Relations*, Chicago, The University of Chicago Press, 1995, p. 289.
749. *Ibid.*, pp. 293–294.
750. It is also relevant to add that the Council Directive 94/45/EC on the establishment of a European Works Council or a procedure in Community-scale undertakings and Community-scale groups of undertakings for the purposes of informing and consulting employees was implemented in Poland in 2002.

The 2006 Act allows works councils to be established in private companies with more than fifty employees. These works councils have information and consultation rights only and may not conclude collective agreements. Initially, works councils could be established only in workplaces where no trade union operated, but since the Constitutional Court's ruling of 2008, they can coexist with trade unions in workplaces.[751] They are not widespread in Poland, for the reasons which include great number of small enterprises in the Polish economy where setting up works council is difficult, and reluctance of employers to support workers involvement.[752] It is noteworthy to add that this reluctance was the reason that works councils were introduced in the private sector only in the mid-2000s. Additional reason why works councils did not gain more popularity, as interviewees explained, is because the trade unions were fiercely opposed to their instigation, perceiving them as competition. A possible additional explanation lies in the fact that the policy makers were reluctant to introduce works councils to the private sector due to their stances against the privatisation policies.[753] As the result, the possibility of establishing works councils in those companies which were undergoing the privatisation process was excluded in 1993.[754] The 2006 Act, which eventually allowed their formation in the private sector, was adopted after a lengthy debate, where the most discussed items were the powers of works councils, the model for their election processes, and whether the 'Czech model' of a single-representation channel should be adopted.[755]

3 COMPARATIVE OVERVIEW: COMPANY COLLECTIVE AGREEMENTS AND THE COMPANY AS THE LOCUS OF STANDARD SETTING IN CEE

3.1 Introduction: Explaining the Legal and Institutional Framework for Company Standard Setting

The company evolved as the predominant level for standard setting in CEE for a few reasons. In the first place, as outlined in section 2 of this chapter, the company has been perceived in CEE countries as the most appropriate venue to deliver tailor-made decisions for employees. At the same time, the focus on the company was vital in order to facilitate competitiveness and adjustments to market demands – 'flexibility' became

---

751. Meardi, G., *Social Failures of EU Enlargement: A Case of Workers Voting with Their Feet*, New York, Routledge, 2012a, p. 34.
752. Gardawski et al. 2012, p. 25.
753. Flanagan, R., 'Institutional Reformation in Eastern Europe', *Industrial Relations*, 1998, vol. 37, no. 3, p. 349; Cox, T.M. and Mason, B., 'Trends and Developments in East Central European Industrial Relations', *Industrial Relations Journal*, 2000b, vol. 31, no. 2, p. 101.
754. Cox and Mason, 2000b, p. 101.
755. As summarised by Czarzasty, J. and Towalski, R., *Information and Consultation Bill Adopted*, Dublin, Eurofound, 2006.

the catchphrase of CEE economies,[756] and the company has become the locus for developing new mechanisms of industrial relations.[757]

However, a number of issues made a development of legal and institutional framework particularly challenging at this level. Likewise, while the development of SMEs represented an important element of post-transitional economic restructuring, there is a lack of trade union presence in these companies. [758] It is not easy to find tailor-made provisions for SMEs, especially as labour laws in CEE, as the legacy of the communist system, are based on the tacit assumption that large companies are the dominant mode of work organisation. [759] Additionally, the change in the ownership structures, resulting from the privatisation, has in the first instance affected company-level processes, questioning the ways in which the labour standards are set.[760] On top of this, the practice of concluding collective agreements in newly formed private companies did not become widely institutionalised with the privatisation process.[761] Moreover, the decreasing trade union density rates contribute to weakening trade unions at this level and shifting the powers to employers. Bearing in mind all the arguments listed, collective bargaining at company level in CEE can be rightfully described, as Pollert notes, as 'an amorphous term' especially having in mind unorganised labour and powerful management.[762]

How can the legal framework for company collective agreements in the four countries be best explained? The practices of European countries differ and it is not possible to identify a 'golden' formula for what a legal framework should look like. Despite the national variations, in continental European countries, company-level agreements do represent a relevant locus for standard setting, but are also part and parcel of the multi-level system. Thus, in explaining these agreements it is first and foremost critical to understand the role they play in a broader system. With the

---

756. Bronstein, A., 'Trends and Challenges of Labour Law in Central Europe' in J.D.R. Craig (ed.), *Globalisation and the Future of Labour Law*, Cambridge, Cambridge University Press, 2006, p. 197.
757. As explained by Vickerstaff, S.A. and Thirkell, J.E.M., 'Instrumental Rationality and European Integration: Transfer or Avoidance of Industrial Relations Institutions in Central and Eastern Europe?', *European Journal of Industrial Relations*, 2000, vol. 6, no. 2, p. 241, citing Neumann, L., 'Circumventing Trade Unions in Hungary: Old and New Channels of Wage Bargaining', *European Journal of Industrial Relations*, vol. 3, no. 2, 1997, pp. 183–202.
758. *See* Miklos, I., Kirov, V. and Makó, C., 'Labour Relations, Collective Bargaining and Employee Voice in SMEs in Central and Eastern Europe', *Transfer: European Review of Labour and Research*, 2007, vol. 12, no. 4, pp. 95–113. Yet the problem of employee representation and collective bargaining in SMEs is not restricted to CEE; for more information, *see* Biagi, M., 'Labour Law in Small and Medium-Sized Enterprises: Flexibility or Adjustment?', *Comparative Labour Law Journal*, 1994, vol. 16, pp. 439–466.
759. This argument was particularly underlined by Bronstein 2006, pp. 200–201.
760. Aguilera and Dabu particularly argued that privatisation was one of the factors which brought the issue of labour governance at the forefront at the enterprise level in CEE, *see* Aguilera, R.V. and Dabu, A., 'Transformation of Employment Relations Systems in Central and Eastern Europe', *Journal of Industrial Relations*, 2005, vol. 47, no. 1, pp. 16–42.
761. Vaughan-Whitehead, D., *EU Enlargement versus Social Europe? The Uncertain Future of the European Social Model*, Cheltenham, Edward Elgar, 2003, pp. 241–243.
762. Pollert, A., 'Ten Years of Post-Communist Central Eastern Europe: Labour's Tenuous Foothold in the Regulation of the Employment Relationship', *Economic and Industrial Democracy*, 2000, vol. 21, no. 2, p. 186.

persisting trend of downward decentralisation in Europe, collective agreements at sectoral and company level have been subject to substantial changes. Sectoral collective agreements have been providing leeway for a more substantial arrangements to be made at company level, which are more responsive to local needs. The opening up of regulatory space for company level has also changed the function of sectoral collective agreements – they are less concerned with prescribing standard levels, but rather with setting minimum levels in a sector, as noted by Visser.[763] Consequently, company collective agreements have become instruments for fine-tuning working conditions in line with the needs of companies. Being part of a broader system, company collective agreements remain connected to the other standard-setting levels with the logic of top-down and bottom-up processes, as explained by Marginson and Sisson.[764] Within *the top-down* processes, the company collective agreements derive their powers from collective agreements concluded at sectoral and cross-sectoral levels, which determine their scope and function. Within the *bottom-up* processes, as Marginson and Sisson note, sectoral collective agreements in some countries are periodically and regularly reviewed and altered to reflect company-level dynamics.[765] In explaining the mechanisms which connect the company level to the other levels, it is relevant to reiterate what has been said in Chapter 1, that the checks and balances which in various forms may exist in the model of articulated multi-employer bargaining are crucial for defending the system against uncontrolled decentralisation.[766] Sectoral collective agreements can have the role of checks and balances, since they prescribe conditions for company collective bargaining and set sector-wide standards. The extent to which sectoral collective agreements may perform this role varies. Different scenarios postulated by Marginson and Sisson have been presented in the previous Chapter 6, which involve different degrees of what these authors termed the 'hollowing-out' of sectoral collective agreements – the process which is corollary and taking place at the expense of expanding the scope of company-level standard setting.[767]

The focus of the following sections will not only be on scrutinising about how CEE company collective agreements are connected to sector and other levels. Bearing in mind the lack of collective bargaining tradition in CEE, it will also be necessary to check whether the basic postulates related to social partners and collective bargaining are in place in the four countries. In this respect, it is useful to underline that one of the purposes of collective bargaining regulation is workplace democracy. As explained by Davidov, the quest for workplace democracy is justified by inequalities in bargaining powers at the workplace level and the democratic deficit which is inherently built into the employment relationship.[768] Therefore, 'joining forces' and redeeming bargaining

---

763. *See* Visser, J., 'The Rise and Fall of Industrial Unionism', *Transfer: European Review of Labour and Research*, 2012, vol. 18, no. 2, p. 139.
764. Marginson, P. and Sisson, K., *European Integration and Industrial Relations: Multi-Level Governance in the Making*, Basingstoke, Palgrave Macmillan, 2006, p. 166.
765. As it is the case in Germany and Italy, *see* Marginson and Sisson, *ibid.*, p. 166.
766. *See* Chapter 1, section 4.
767. Margison and Sisson 2006, p. 165. On scenarios postulated by Marginson and Sisson, *see* Chapter 6, section 3.2.
768. Davidov, G., 'Collective Bargaining Laws: Purpose and Scope', *The International Journal of Comparative Labour Law and Industrial Relations*, 2004, vol. 20, no. 1, p. 84.

powers is vital for the individual employees to take part in decision-making on the matters which are of direct concern for them.[769] With workplace democracy in mind, Davidov delineated two distinct attributes of collective bargaining: (a) it subjects the employer to the rule of law and prevents arbitrariness in decision-making; (b) it also provides the employees with a 'voice', enabling them to engage in decision-making.[770] In a similar fashion, Ewing underlined the salience of rule of law for observing workplace democracy, as an instrument protecting from the arbitrary exercise of power. Ewing postulated three guiding principles which rule the relationship between rule of law and workplace democracy:

> the relationship between employer and worker should be governed by *clear rules*; the rules governing the employment relationship should be *comprehensive in their coverage* unless there are rational grounds for discriminating between different groups of workers; the rules governing the employment relationship *should not confer unnecessary discretionary power on management*; and any such discretionary powers should be fair, consistent and rational in their application (emphasis added).[771]

These 'workplace democracy' principles will be taken into account when assessing the legal provisions from the four countries.

3.2 Company Collective Agreements: Notion and Articulation

Based on the overview of the legal framework in the previous section, as well as discussion performed in Chapter 6, it can be argued that the focus of CEE laws has been the company level since the beginning of the 1990s. This legal focus on the company emerged from the general orientation of the post-transitional systems towards decentralisation. At the same time, it represented a shift from the previous system of state centralisation, and a result of the process of democratisation[772] and newly founded freedoms and private property. At any rate, this is evident in Poland, the Czech Republic and Slovakia where the concept of collective agreements concluded at the company level (known as single-enterprise or enterprise agreements in these countries) were legally contrasted against the 'other' types of collective agreements (multi-enterprise or higher-level collective agreements). This delineation was already in place in the early 1990s and has remained unchanged in these countries. Slovenia represents a somewhat a specific case in that its laws initially specified demarcation of the collective bargaining levels at company, sectoral and cross-sectoral level, but, as demonstrated in the previous chapter, the Slovenian Act on Collective Agreements of 2006 removed reference to specific collective bargaining levels. In Poland, Slovakia and the Czech Republic, the law does not specify the meaning of *single-enterprise or*

---

769. *Ibid.*, 84.
770. *Ibid.*, pp. 85–86.
771. Ewing, K.D., 'Democratic Socialism and Labour Law', *Industrial Law Journal*, 1995, vol. 24, no. 2, p. 119.
772. Iankova, E.A., *Eastern European Capitalism in the Making*, Cambridge, Cambridge University Press, 2002, p. 17.

enterprise collective agreements. Instead, these agreements are defined by the parties that can conclude them, but it is not clear if they should refer to the entire company or to part of it, and whether more than one agreement can be concluded at the company level.

What is the role of CEE company collective agreements and what position do they occupy in the multi-level system? Unfortunately, the general lack of comprehensive data on the content of these agreements prevents reasonable assessment. The previous section of this chapter demonstrated that, in principle, company-level agreements in the four countries cover the same or similar matters as any existing collective agreements at higher levels, but their role is to specify rights and conditions in line with the company or workplace environment. During the interviews in Slovakia, the Czech Republic and Poland, respondents claimed that company-level collective agreements are a more prominent source of workplace standards than sectoral collective agreements. This claim was confirmed during interviews in Slovenia, too, although there the interviewees also emphasized the relevance of the sector. Generally, in all four countries, the significance of company-level bargaining was particularly underlined in relation to wages and different forms of remuneration. As long as there are company collective agreements (bearing in mind the relatively modest coverage rates presented in Table 8 of this chapter), they represent the 'real' locus of standard setting in the four countries.

Yet there is an issue which was explained in the previous chapter and which remains valid when discussing company collective agreements. In all four countries, the substantive scope of collective agreements (sectoral *and* company) has been affected by a gradual transformation in the style of statutory regulation. This involved the transformation from a style which regulates all relevant aspects of work in a comprehensive and mandatory manner to one which postulates minimum substantive rights and further encourages collective bargaining.[773] As explained in this study already, it was only in the 2000s that the four CEE countries formally inserted legal rules claiming the freedom of social partners to negotiate on any matters. However, the statutory legal regulation remains comprehensive in these countries, particularly in Poland and the Czech Republic, as explained by interviewees. Therefore, one may question the extent to which such process of gradual transformation has been fully accomplished in these two countries. The issue which emanates is that the comprehensive regulatory style demotivates social partners from collective bargaining as they often see no added value in negotiating over matters that have already been stipulated in law.

To fully judge company collective agreements one has to take into consideration their articulation with the other sources of standard setting. The legal frameworks presented in section 2 are based on *rigid* top-down articulation between different sources, anchored by the favourability principle. The rigidity is reflected in the legal framework discouraging the option of stipulating less favourable employees' standards and rights at company level than those at other levels. It is further accentuated by the

---

773. As explained in Chapter 3 (section 4.2) and in Chapter 6 (section 3.1.2).

fact that the Labour Codes tend to regulate matters in a comprehensive and detailed manner, in this sense predetermining the content of collective agreements. One respondent from the interviews in the Czech Republic has even claimed that individual employers see no point in allowing the possibility of opening clauses or clauses with a similar function, as the law provides them with the opportunity to avoid collective bargaining altogether and to simply resort to internal regulation at company level.[774]

With these arguments in mind, how can the connection between company-level agreements and sectoral agreements be explained? Both cover the same or similar issues, yet it is useful to recall that sectoral collective agreements, where concluded, often set low standards, frequently reiterating statutory labour provisions. As an extension of what has been explained on this topic in Chapter 6,[775] it should be added that sectoral collective agreements thus represent a weak authority over company-level agreements – the sector level encourages a wide variation in company-level solutions, being only weakly 'controlled' from above.

Nevertheless, when speaking about articulation, certain variations among the countries can be observed. These variations have been already discussed in Chapter 6. It has been observed that Slovenia's system resembles the normative model of articulated multi-employer bargaining set out in in Chapter 1 most, while Poland resembles it least. In addition to what has been presented before, a specific case is the legal possibility in Poland of allowing the suspension of the collective agreement (at any level). When suspension is activated, it is no longer possible to speak about articulation, as the logic of the multi-level system becomes frustrated in these cases. If Polish single-enterprise agreements are suspended (having in mind that there are not many multi-enterprise agreements in Poland), employees will, in most cases, derive rights directly from statutory legal rules or from internal regulation by employers where applicable.

3.3 Parties to Company Collective Agreements

In comparative labour law systems, the right to be a party to company collective agreement is sometimes restricted to trade unions, but on occasion it can also be granted to works councils or even to a few employees.[776] The legal rules on representativeness may also vary. Many countries legally require trade unions to be representative if they are to be permitted to sign collective agreements; the quantitative threshold that trade unions must fulfil varies between 10% and 65% of employees.[777] The ILO framework allows – but does not oblige – countries to establish rules on representativeness. Nevertheless, the ILO rules contain no closer guidance on this point, but only require trade unions to be independent, to be able to organise their

---

774. As already mentioned in relation to articulation, *see* Chapter 6 (section 2.3).
775. *See* Chapter 6, section 3.2.
776. As noted by Jacobs, A., 'Article 11 ECHR: the Right to Bargain Collectively', in F. Dorssemont, K. Lörcher and I. Schömann (eds), *The European Convention on Human Rights and the Employment Relation*, Oxford, Hart Publishing, 2013, p. 316.
777. *Ibid.*, pp. 318–319. Jacobs also reported that in one case the ILO bodies considered the threshold of one-third of workers to be too high.

activities without interference from the public authorities and to be independent from employers' associations.[778] The ILO rules also require any criteria for representativeness to be based on objective and pre-established conditions in order to avoid bias or abuse.[779]

Before commenting on the legal rules of the four CEE countries, it is important to reiterate two salient points. First, the issue of declining trade union membership rates in CEE is most evident at company level, hindering the formation of basic trade unions. Second, there is a problem in the lack of trade union presence in the otherwise prevailing SMEs across the CEE economies. This problem has been identified and warned of in the literature.[780] The previous section demonstrated that rules on setting up trade unions were established early on in the transitional period, and while rules on representativeness are in place in Slovenia and Poland, the Czech Republic and Slovakia still struggle to establish them. Slovenian and Polish rules set no restrictive conditions, but the Slovakian '30 percent rule', explained in section 2.2.1 and which was in force for a short period, could be interpreted as restrictive.[781]

Inter-union rivalry represents a specific issue which has been documented elsewhere as common in CEE countries.[782] It was also deemed particularly relevant during the interviews in the Czech Republic and Poland. The previous section suggested that the legal framework struggles to identify in a *clear* manner who should be the collective bargaining party on the employees' side when more than one trade union exists in the workplace. The Czech, Slovak and Polish legal frameworks, especially, provide a complex set of rules for these situations. However, in some instances, when laws require trade unions to cooperate and reach joint agreement about their representation, as in Slovenia and the Czech Republic, it is unclear what should happen if they fail to reach such an agreement.

3.4 Procedure

Here only a short commentary can be made about the Polish Labour Code, which seems to be comparatively more protective of the employers' interests than do the provisions in the other three countries. This observation stems from the legal obligation of trade unions to refrain from making demands which exceed the employers' financial capacity and the limitation of the employers' obligation to disclose information on their financial situation.

---

778. ILO Freedom of Association and Protection of the Right to Organise Convention No 87, 1948 and Right to Organise and Collective Bargaining Convention, No 98, 1949, as reported by Gernigon, B., Odero, A. and Guido, H., 'ILO Principles Concerning Collective Bargaining' *International Labour Review*, 2000b, vol. 139, no. 1, pp. 37–38.
779. As reported by Jacobs 2013, p. 320.
780. Vaughan-Whitehead 2003, p. 242.
781. This was also mentioned by the interviewees in Slovakia.
782. As noted by Pollert 2000, pp. 194–195.

3.5 Beyond Collective Bargaining

3.5.1 *Works Councils*

Despite the fact that some form of works councils had been in existence in CEE during the previous communist period, as demonstrated in section 2.4.2 of this chapter, their formal instigation in the post-transitional period has taken place relatively recently. They were also introduced in CEE as a part of the social *acquis* which the candidate countries were supposed to transpose and implement prior to becoming the EU members. However, the role of the EU seems to have been limited, as noted by Meardi,[783] and works councils remained weak and insignificant in the overall industrial relations landscape of CEE. Meardi noted that the transfer of information and consultation rights from the EU *acquis* unfortunately did not lead to significant improvements in industrial relations in CEE; what the EU has neglected is that works councils have been successfully introduced only in those European countries which already had strong organised labour.[784] The general antagonism of trade unions (and even employers) to works councils, attested to by the interviewees in the four countries, was the reason that the Czech Republic initially allowed them only in companies where no trade union operated, and this model was adopted in other countries in the early 2000s.[785] As the previous sections have demonstrated, this 'Czech model' was subsequently modified in the selected countries – today the four countries allow the coexistence of trade unions and works councils in the same workplace.

In comparative labour law systems, works councils can, in principle, be granted certain standard-setting powers by being allowed to conclude some form of collective accords.[786] In CEE this has not been the case, and, in all likelihood, it will not occur in the near future. Because of the general reluctance to have works councils, in the four countries they are not provided with any legal possibility of engaging in collective bargaining and standard setting. The previous section has noted that they enjoy information and consultation rights, and that these rights are usually shared with trade unions. However, examining the four countries' legal provisions gives the overall impression that there is no necessarily clear demarcation of the responsibilities between trade unions and works councils in the four countries. For example, the Polish Labour Code makes no reference to works councils, and instead, their powers are regulated by the Polish 2006 Act on Information and Consultation.

3.5.2 *Managerial Powers: Individualisation of Terms and Conditions of Work*

The unilateral standard-setting role of employers represents a significant source of rights for employees in CEE. This can be concluded from the industrial relations data

---

783. Meardi 2012a, pp. 32–33.
784. *Ibid.*
785. *Ibid.*
786. Jacobs provides example of the Netherlands and Germany, where in principle, works councils can bargain on specific issues, *see* Jacobs 2013, p. 316.

presented in Table 1 (Chapter 1): low coverage rates of company agreements, combined with the low coverage of collective agreements at other levels in CEE (with the exception of Slovenia). For the majority of the workforce, the source of the rights and conditions at the workplace resides in statutory labour law only. Internal rules, therefore, may be useful to mimic the function of collective agreements in the sense of specifying and interpreting labour law in line with the requirements of the workplace. This is most likely to take place in SMEs: traditionally having no attachment to collective bargaining, their focus is shifting to more pronounced unilateral managerial powers.[787] However, the issue described is not restricted to small companies as internal rules may also be issued in larger companies. In fact, in countries such as Poland, internal regulation may not be issued in companies with less than twenty employees, where the rules and conditions are therefore most likely to be decided only on the basis of the individual employment relationship.

The salience of unilateral acts as standard-setting mechanism within the overall regulatory framework results from the general orientation of industrial relations in CEE towards the decentralisation and fragmentation. In these countries the lack of a centralised framework suits employers, and the system favour the emergence of managerial elites dominating at enterprise level.[788] Weak labour and powerful employers' prerogatives shift the focus away from collective bargaining and drive it towards *the individual relationship* between employer and employee. The standards are no longer prescribed in collective agreements, but by unilateral acts and individual employment contracts. It has been observed by Pollert, based on the example of the Czech Republic, that such a trend towards individualisation has been fostered since the early 1990s because the reforms were focused on strengthening company identity, rather than collective voice.[789] Vickerstaff and Thirkell describe that reinforced autonomy of enterprise and shifting the powers to hands of managers fragments labour relations system within each country.[790] However, taking into consideration the general industrial relations landscape in CEE, especially at company level, it is doubtful if such a trend is welcome from the point of view of the institutionalisation of collective bargaining in CEE. It is, nevertheless, a positive development that the legal framework in each of the four countries contains rules which, in line with Ewing's postulates on workplace democracy, control the prerogatives of the employer and also restrict the

---

787. Bluhm, K., 'Resolving Liberalisation Dilemma: Labour Relations in East-Central Europe and the Impact of European Union' in M.A. Moreau and M.E. Blas-López (eds), *Restructuring in the New EU Member States: Social Dialogue, Firms Relocation, and Social Treatment of Restructuring*, Brussels, Peter Lang, 2008, p. 68.
788. Martin, likewise, noted that the CEE countries developed 'managerial capitalism' aimed at accommodating managerial elites which dominate at enterprise level, *see* Martin, R., 'Politicised Managerial Capitalism: Enterprise Structures in Post-Socialist Central and Eastern Europe', *Journal of Management Studies*, 2002, vol. 39, no. 6, p. 833. See also Martin, R., *Constructing Capitalisms: Transforming Business Systems in Central and Eastern Europe*, Oxford, Oxford University Press, 2013.
789. Pollert, A., 'Labour and Trade Unions in the Czech Republic, 1989-2000' in S. Crowley and D. Ost (eds), *Workers after Workers' State: Labour and Politics in Postcommunist Eastern Europe*, Oxford, Rowman and Littlefield, 2001, pp. 25–26.
790. Vickerstaff and Thirkell 2000, p. 241.

employer's ability to act arbitrarily.[791] In all the four countries, likewise, the law often asks for prior consultation with trade unions, works councils or employees before internal regulations can be issued.

4 CONCLUSIONS

4.1 Notes on Development

In the communist period, collective bargaining has been rather limited and the trade union's role has been the one of protecting employees and facilitating achievement of the centrally administered goals.[792] The membership rates were high. Since trade unions administered a significant portion of employees' benefits, such as housing and holidays, they were even labelled as 'servicing machines'.[793] Accordingly, communist companies were considered as not only economic but also social institutions, due to their pronounced social and welfare functions.[794] The transition from communism to an open market economy involved the transformation of trade union functions, and companies merely lost the social component. This change seems to have impacted on trade unions first and foremost at company level, given the emphasis of post-transitional industrial relations on localised standard setting, as well as the need for trade unions to continue to present membership as an attractive option.

In order to explain which factors were crucial for building a legal framework at company level, following the analytical framework based on Bohle and Greskovits' delineation (Chapter 2), one may conclude the following. Of all CEE countries, *Slovenia's* legacy seems to have played the greatest role – the legacy of self-management helped this country hone a tradition of employee involvement in decision-making. However, the Slovenian post-transitional reforms, as already explained in this study, have been more focused on centralised collective bargaining levels and the company seem not have been a priority of policy reforms. The *Polish* example serves as a contrast to the Slovenian model. The legal framework encouraging collective bargaining at single-enterprise level, embodied in the aforementioned 1982 Act on Trade Unions and the 1981 Act on Workers' Self-Management in State-Owned Enterprises, started emerging before the official commencement of the transitional period. This legal framework enabled trade unions and works councils to be formed in Poland. Since the 1990s, the Polish transformation has been focused on the enterprise: the legal framework, created in the 1980s, paved the way for the company to occupy a dominant position in the current system. This argument is complementary to the one postulated in Chapter 6, where it was stated that development at sector and

---

791. Ewing 1995.
792. As explained by Flanagan 1998, p. 338.
793. As labelled by Ost, D., 'The Weakness of Strong Social Movements: Model of Unionism in the East European Context', *European Journal of Industrial Relations*, 2002, vol. 8, no. 1, p. 37.
794. Ost, D. and Weinstein, M., 'Unionists against Unions: Toward Hierarchical Management in Post-Communist Poland', *East European Politics and Societies*, 1999, vol. 13, no. 1, p. 2.

cross-sector levels was not a priority of policy reforms.[795] *The Czech Republic and Slovakia* share common legacies. Anchored by the 1965 Labour Code, under the communist regime the trade unions nominally enjoyed wide powers: they could determine wages and working conditions and participate in the management of the company. After the demise of the common state, both countries started developing their own labour laws. As suggested in the previous chapter, the basic difference between the Slovak and Czech system is that transitional policy making in the Czech Republic was comparatively more influenced by neoclassical market ideas and was more oriented towards company standard setting than the one in Slovakia.[796]

4.2 Assessing the Legal Framework for Company Collective Bargaining

As already outlined in Chapter 6 (section 3.1.1), in the early 1990s, the laws of Slovakia, the Czech Republic and Poland postulated the company as the main tenet of their collective bargaining systems. This conclusion can be reached primarily on the basis of the delineation of enterprise-level and multi-enterprise or higher-level agreements in these countries. Yet, the extent to which these countries today manage to support and promote meaningful collective bargaining at company level is subject to further debate. In line with the analytical remarks postulated in Chapter 3 (section 2.2), one can observe the active involvement of both institutionalisation and market narrative in shaping the company collective agreement in these countries.

Although these laws put the company at the forefront of legal transformation in the early 1990s, there remains the impression that, during the past two decades, *the institutionalisation of company collective bargaining has not been a greater policy priority, overall, than the other (centralised) collective bargaining levels*. Two major factors give rise to such an impression. *First*, as this chapter has demonstrated, the policy makers defined the most important elements of company collective bargaining in the early 1990s, but the subsequent legal amendments were not specifically aimed at promoting the company to any greater extent than any other collective bargaining level. Subsequent legal amendments of the past two decades were concerned, almost by default, with the issue of rivalry between trade unions, and rivalry between trade unions and works councils. Yet further refinement of the concept of the company collective agreement, with elements which could enhance company collective bargaining, was not a specific policy priority. For example, today it still remains unclear whether single-enterprise or enterprise collective agreements can be concluded for a part of the company only. Also, in countries such as the Czech Republic and Slovakia, there are no legal rules about trade union representativeness at this level. *Second*, company collective bargaining still faces major challenges which the law has not managed to address. It is striking that, because of the limited coverage rates of company agreements, a substantial proportion of the labour market in the countries examined – with the exception of Slovenia – still remains outside the collective

---

795. *See* Chapter 6, section 4.
796. *See* Chapter 6, section 4; Chapter 2, section 3.

bargaining system. Additionally, negotiated standard setting in small companies still represents a major challenge for these countries, as the laws contain no tailor-made solutions for collective standard setting in these companies.

The market narrative has played a visible role at company level. In the first place, as discussed in section 3.4 of this chapter, in Poland the collective bargaining procedure is formulated in a way which protects the employers' side from excessive financial demands on the trade union side. On a more general level, the market narrative is visible through several aspects in the four CEE countries, which overall undermine the efforts of institutionalisation of company collective bargaining. First, there is a visible shift from collective bargaining to the internal regulation, which represents an alternative to collective agreements in these countries and which somewhat undermines the collective bargaining role of trade unions. Second, internal regulation is often decided unilaterally, without any involvement of the employee side: as explained in section 2.4.1., in the Czech Republic and Poland, if no trade union is present in the company, the employer has no obligation to consult employees or their representatives. This substantially strengthens the powers of employers. Third, another example of market narrative occurs when the internal regulation is not a viable option in law. For example, in Poland, internal regulation cannot be used in small companies (below twenty employees), where conditions of work can be therefore determined only by individual negotiations between an employee and employer. Here we may observe a visible shift from collective to individual standard setting.

The observations made raise the question of whether and how the law can promote company collective bargaining in a more functional manner. Although no universal answer can be provided to that question, it is obvious that, following the analytical framework of 'workplace democracy' postulated in section 3.1 of this chapter, more *clarity* could be provided at company level. Clarity would be especially beneficial with regard to the collective bargaining procedure, particularly when more than one trade union operates at the workplace (as in Slovenia and the Czech Republic). As has been noted, in many instances, there are no clear legal rules on how to resolve the deadlock that arises when several trade unions disagree on collective representation. More clarity on the delineation between the competences of trade union and works councils could also be provided. In Slovakia and the Czech Republic, legal rules do not call for any representativeness criteria. In Poland, collective bargaining procedure could be more detailed, and more balanced in relation to trade unions. None of the four countries has any rules on employee representation in small and medium companies. While this is an issue common to many European countries, a way of addressing it could be, for example, the introduction of alternative types of employee representation in these companies, and a review of the ways in which the actual number of employees is calculated in any company.[797]

---

797. The 'underrepresentation' is a common problem to many countries, as acknowledged by Biagi. An overview of ways how different legal systems address SMEs has been provided in Biagi 1994 and Biagi, M., 'Employee Representation in Small and Medium-Sized Enterprises: A Comparative Overview', *Comparative Labour Law Journal*, 1992, vol. 13, no. 3, pp. 257–272.

On a final note, certain features of the four countries observed in this chapter seem to create resistance to the suggested model of articulated multi-employer bargaining, explained in Chapter 1. The first of these is the legal possibility of collective agreements being *suspended* (in Poland), and the second is the emphasis on internal regulation in all four countries (but particularly notable in Poland and the Czech Republic). It is a positive development that laws usually require some form of trade union or employees' consent in these situations (though with some exceptions to this, as explained above). Yet, at the same time, both suspension and internal regulation drive the process of standard setting further from the model of *negotiated* outcomes and generally undermine the role of trade unions at the company level.

CHAPTER 8
Conclusions

1 INTRODUCTION

This study has scrutinised the legal and institutional framework for collective bargaining in the four CEE countries and the ways in which it has been developing in the past two decades. Two research questions were formulated. Within the first research question, the study analysed the extent to which the four selected countries support and promote collective bargaining at different levels. The second research question was dedicated to exploring the development of the legal and institutional framework of rules for collective bargaining, including the role which the EU played in this respect.

This chapter aims at discussing the research findings and providing concluding thoughts on these research questions, and it is structured in the following manner. Section 2 presents a brief summary of findings by chapter. Section 3 aims at providing interpretations of the findings, first, by linking back to the proposed normative model (subsection 3.1) and second, by sketching an answer to the two research questions. Section 4 outlines the limits of the study, outlook and some challenges for the future research.

2 SUMMARY OF FINDINGS OF THE STUDY

Starting from the existing legal scholarship which in a somewhat ad hoc and non-comprehensive manner studied the collective bargaining laws in CEE,[798] this study attempted to provide a comprehensive comparative study of the legal and institutional framework for collective bargaining in the systems selected. With a view to reflecting the most pressing concerns of industrial relations – decentralised and underdeveloped systems of collective bargaining and weak social partners – the research was framed with the intention of interpreting the law in the context of the industrial relations

---
798. As presented in section 3.2 of Chapter 1.

setting. The study was deliberately designed to reflect CEE countries having different industrial relations models. As explained in Chapter 1, comparatively, Slovenia has the most centralised model of collective bargaining and Poland has one of the least centralised models. Slovakia and the Czech Republic come somewhere in-between – Slovakia has a reasonably developed centralised collective bargaining system, more so than the Czech Republic.

To be able to scrutinise the legal and institutional frameworks, the study designed in *Chapter 1* a *normative model of articulated multi-employer bargaining*. In industrial relations terms, this model reflects the reality of most of the European countries. To the greatest extent possible, the legal traits and principles of the model have been postulated and explained in that chapter. It has been explained that the proposed normative model is based on the standard-setting role of social partners, and also on the complementarity between collective agreements and statutory law, as the two different sources of standard setting (section 4.3). Moreover, Chapter 1 presented three major analytical elements of this model (section 4.3):

(1) The role of law should be observed as the one of supporting and promoting collective bargaining and the conclusion of collective agreements (auxiliary role).[799] Moreover, it is expected from labour law to protect employees – the statutory legal rules should set out legal minima that can be further upgraded and elaborated in collective agreements. Apart from protective role, law should also facilitate economic objectives (such as supporting productivity, efficiency and competiveness).

(2) In such a model, collective agreements perform more than one function: Supiot claimed that collective agreements can be instruments of flexibilisation and company management, or they can implement legal regulations or perform legislative functions.[800] Bruun claimed that collective agreements can have regulatory, flexibility or management functions.[801] Sectoral collective agreements play a particular role in most of the European countries – they tend to be predominantly concerned with providing rules and conditions for company-level bargaining, rather than setting universal substantive standards for a specific sector.[802]

(3) The suggested normative model rests on procedural mechanisms ensuring complementarity between various sources of standard setting (collective agreements and statutory legal rules). The aim of these mechanisms is to provide checks and balances against uncontrolled decentralisation.

---

799. As explained by Kahn Freund, *see* Chapter 1, section 4.3; based on Davies, P. and Freedland, M., *Kahn Freund's Labour and the Law*, 3rd edition, London, Stevens & Sons, 1983.
800. Supiot, A., *Beyond Employment: Changes in Work and the Future of Labour Law in Europe*, Oxford, Oxford University Press, 2001, pp. 97–100.
801. Bruun, N. 'The Autonomy of Collective Agreement' in R. Blanpain (ed.), *Collective Bargaining, Discrimination, Social Security and the European Integration*, Bulletin of Comparative Labour Relations, no. 48, The Hague, Kluwer Law International, 2003, p. 9.
802. Visser, J., 'Beneath the Surface of Stability: New and Old Modes of Governance in European Industrial Relations', *European Journal of Industrial Relations*, 2005, vol. 11, no. 3, p. 297.

Chapter 8: Conclusions

As Chapters 2 and 3 demonstrated, labour law reforms in these countries did not take place in isolation, but within the wider political, social, economic and industrial relations context. *Chapter 2*, drawing on a non-legal approach and the existing theoretical knowledge explaining capitalism, welfare and industrial relations, provided country-specific explanations of that context. After presenting the existing theoretical framework and approaches in relation to the CEE countries, this chapter concluded that the peculiar style of economic reforms undertaken in the 1990s underpinned decentralisation of industrial relations in these countries. This conclusion is more evident in the CEE countries that opted for a non-gradual, shock therapy style of macroeconomic reforms.[803] Chapter 2 particularly highlighted theoretical observations postulated by Bohle and Greskovits, and factors which these authors considered crucial for explaining the post-transitional framework of CEE (policies, including legacies, and external factors).[804] The following country elements were highlighted. In many aspects, Slovenia resembles continental European countries and it is the only country from the group selected which can be labelled as a coordinated market economy (section 3.1).[805] Despite resolute market orientation which was pertinent until 2006,[806] Slovakia has developed a more centralised collective bargaining structure and a better organised central representation of social partners[807] than the Czech Republic. Czech industrial relations have developed with a pronounced pro-market policy orientation, fragmented trade unions and inconsistent support towards social dialogue.[808] Polish industrial relations developed alongside the resolute liberalisation of the economy and the state has provided only a modest support for social dialogue and collective bargaining.[809]

Chapter 3 explained national responses to the challenges surrounding labour law transformation in the four countries. In an effort to group the factors of transformation, this chapter built on the elements postulated by Bohle and Greskovits (initially presented in Chapter 2):[810] policy choices (support for the legal and institutional framework for collective bargaining), labour law legacies and external influences. In an effort to detect the guiding paradigm of labour law transformation in CEE, this chapter identified *institutionalisation* and *market* narratives. Whereas the institutionalisation narrative entailed a long-term process of building legal and institutional framework which guarantees free and voluntary collective bargaining, the market narrative

---

803. As underlined in section 4 of Chapter 2.
804. Bohle, D. and Greskovits, B., 'Neoliberalism, Embedded Neoliberalism and Neocorporatism: Towards Transnational Capitalism in Central-Eastern Europe', *West European Politics*, 2007, vol. 30, no. 3, pp. 443–466.
805. CMEs, according to VoC classification, explained in section 2.1 of Chapter 2.
806. So-called Dzurinda era, as explained in section 3.2 of Chapter 2.
807. Duman, A. and Kureková, L., 'The Role of State in Development of Socio-Economic Models in Hungary and Slovakia: the Case of Industrial Policy', *Journal of European Public Policy*, 2012, vol. 19, no. 8, p. 1217 and Kahancová, M., 'From Bargaining to Advocacy: A Trade-off Between Improved Working Conditions and Trade Union Fragmentation in Slovakia' in M. Bernaciak and M. Kahancová (eds), *Innovative Union Practices in Central-Eastern Europe*, Brussels, ETUI, 2017, p. 180.
808. *See* section 3.3 of Chapter 2.
809. *See* section 3.4 of Chapter 2.
810. Bohle and Greskovits 2007.

entailed a process of restoring contractual freedoms[811] and ensuring that labour law provisions facilitate, rather than hinder economic growth (section 2.2). This chapter (section 2.2) underlined that the market narrative has been often confused with outright deregulation. Inspired by the belief that free market should govern labour, market narrative in this way paved the way for the unfettered freedom of employers at local levels and rendered the narrative of institutionalisation difficult in CEE.[812]

After presenting country-specific traits, Chapter 3 reached the following conclusions. The process of creating the legal and institutional framework for collective bargaining was gradual in the four countries, although the basic pieces of law were introduced in the early 1990s. The content of collective agreements has been changing in line with the evolving legal framework, which allowed gradual broadening of their regulatory space in the past two decades. However, the chapter also underlined that in some countries (in particular, Poland and the Czech Republic) the law still consists of comprehensive and all-encompassing mandatory regulation of work and employment, which undermines the substantive scope of collective agreements – the items which the social partners can negotiate about are already prescribed within statutory regulation (section 4). This represents a legacy of the previous communist period, when collective agreements played only a marginal role, while work and employment were regulated by coercive and all-encompassing statutory legal rules and administrative regulations. Furthermore, this chapter noted that collective agreements and labour laws have made a transition from the sphere of public law to that of private law in the past two decades. Yet, such a transition has been slower in some countries – in Slovakia and the Czech Republic, labour law retained its predominantly public character during the 1990s (section 4.1). Chapter 3 also highlighted that labour law transformation was marked by country-specific legacies. In particular, Slovenia's socialist self-management paradigm deserves mentioning because it enabled some form of employees' standard setting even before the 1990s. Moreover, the Polish legislation of the 1980s has been notable for postulating the enterprise as the basic tenet of standard setting, paving the way towards the decentralised industrial relations found in modern Poland.

Chapter 4 demonstrated that the EU has played only an indirect role in building the legal and institutional framework for collective bargaining in the past two decades. This chapter showed that the EU aimed at enhancing collective bargaining structures at all possible levels during the accession process. However, by using the approach of Europeanisation, this chapter demonstrated that the EU could not impose the desired changes – the conditionality mechanism was undermined by the low political salience of social issues during the accession process and the EU also lacked a precise 'message' about what the legal framework should look like in CEE (section 2.3). Moreover, after the recent economic and financial crisis period, the mechanism for rule transfer and the normative and ideological underpinnings of the EU role has changed. With the recent

---

811. Kollonay Lehoczky, C., 'European Enlargement: A Comparative View of Hungarian Labour Law' in G.A. Bermann and K. Pistor (eds), *Law and Governance in an Enlarged European Union*, Oxford, Hart Publishing, 2004, pp. 210–212.
812. Section 2.2 of Chapter 2.

Chapter 8: Conclusions

crisis, there has been no visible incentive for the EU to influence the improvement of the centralised collective bargaining structures in CEE. On the contrary, many of the 'crisis packages' the EU issued during the financial crisis era emphasized the need for further decentralisation of bargaining towards company level. In this respect 'Europeanisation' became a somewhat ambivalent and even confusing message that did not contribute to the strengthening of collective bargaining structures in CEE countries.

The second part of the study investigated collective bargaining, and, where applicable, other forms of standard setting at the national, sectoral and company levels. *Chapter 5* demonstrated that there is a weak link between what is discussed in tripartite institutions and collective agreements. The tripartite bodies have a consultative role only and may not issue legally binding decisions. Social pacts, with the exception of Slovenia, have a poor track record, and as such, do not have tangible impact on collective bargaining.[813] Another exception is the Polish social pact of 1993, which has contributed towards a decentralised landscape, by emphasising the regulatory powers of the enterprise.[814] The chapter found that the limited tripartite outcomes in CEE may not be linked to restrictively or ill-defined tripartite competences. There are notable exceptions to this general observation. As the Slovak and Czech examples demonstrated, in certain periods the competences of tripartite bodies did not allow agreements to be reached. Nevertheless, these exceptions were temporary (as described in section 2) – the Czech tripartite statute narrowed down the competences of the tripartite body from agreement reaching to consultation in 1995, restoring them in 1997. In Slovakia, the 2004 tripartite statute, which was valid until 2007, narrowly defined the competences of the tripartite body, not allowing it to reach agreements.

Chapter 6 examined sectoral collective agreements. What is common to the countries examined is the lack of a precise meaning of 'sector' and 'sectoral collective agreement'. Legally, it remains unclear how the Polish 'multi-enterprise' and Czech and Slovak 'higher-level' agreements actually relate to sector level agreements. Moreover, these collective agreements have a modest regulatory role – where they exist, they usually set a low sectoral minimum, encouraging substantive variation at company level (*see* section 3.2). The instrument for the extension of collective agreements is in place in the four countries, but it is not regularly applied in practice. With some country variations (presented in Table 7), derogations to the detriment of employees *in peius* are generally discouraged.

Slovenia somewhat represents an exception to this general picture – the pre-2006 legal framework defined levels at which collective bargaining may take place. The 2006 legal reform deleted the reference to the bargaining levels, but by that year, collective bargaining practices had already been firmly set at sectoral level. Slovenian statutory law stimulates the sectoral level by suggesting that some matters be more closely

---

813. As explained in section 2 of Chapter 5. In particular, centralised collective bargaining, according to Stanojević, represented an implementation mechanism for the income policies defined in social pacts in Slovenia, *see* Stanojević, M., 'Social Pacts in Slovenia: Accommodation to the EMU Regime and the Post-Euro Development', *Warsaw Forum of Economic Sociology*, 2011, vol. 2, no. 1, p. 108.
814. As explained in section 2.4 of Chapter 5. This was the 1993 Pact on State-Owned Enterprises in the Restructuring Process.

regulated in sectoral collective agreements (section 2.2). Extensions of collective agreements are regularly exercised in Slovenia, and it is possible to derogate from the statutory laws to the detriment of employees (sections 2.3 and 2.5). Slovakia and the Czech Republic have a similar legal framework in place. These two countries contain no clear definition of sectoral collective agreement, and no rules of representativeness at this level. Yet, two important differences delineate the two countries. First, until 2014, Slovak laws prescribed more restrictive conditions for collective agreements extensions than the rules in the Czech Republic (at certain times, individual employers' consent has been a factor rendering extensions virtually impossible in Slovakia, as described in section 2.5). As shown in Chapter 6, Slovak legal rules on extensions were relaxed in 2014 – yet it remains to be seen if these conditions will be subject to changes in the future. Second, Slovak rules prescribe no possibility of derogation from statutory legal rules *in peius*, unlike the Czech rules, which allow some limited opportunities in that respect (section 2.3). Polish laws have not been designed with the sector in mind. Apart from the lack of definition of sector, the rules on extension of collective agreements are restrictively defined, and there is no possibility of derogation to the detriment of employees in Poland. Yet, Polish law is specific for allowing the suspension of collective agreements (section 2.3).

Chapter 6 has also demonstrated that the role of policies, in various degrees and forms, was decisive for shaping the sector as a locus of standard setting in the four countries. The model of reforms pursued in Poland, likewise, was focused on the company as the main tenet of policies. Slovenia's policies were tailored with the mindset of gradual reforms: in this study the gradualism philosophy, which was leading the industrial relations reforms,[815] was observed as a powerful determinant of legal reforms. When it comes to Slovakia and the Czech Republic, initial legal reforms postulated the company as the main tenet of collective bargaining. Later on, Slovakia's industrial relations managed to develop more prominent standard setting at sectoral level. Yet, after more than two decades, Slovakia's laws provide fewer stimuli for sectoral collective bargaining than the Czech Republic. How can the difference between the two countries be explained? As this study underlined, in Slovakia, the social partners on both sides have more pronounced centralised capacities and representation, as well as more coordinated structures for industrial relations.[816] In contrast, Czech trade unions are fragmented and decentralised.[817] This study understands that the comparatively more developed sectoral structures which exist in Slovakia, cannot, therefore, be ascribed to law.

During the interviews, the company was highlighted as the most important locus for standard setting. Nevertheless, *Chapter 7* demonstrated that standard setting at company level is not fostered by the legal systems more than any other level. Company level is not clearly designated in the laws of Slovakia, the Czech Republic and Poland:

---

815. Crowley, S. and Stanojević, M., 'Varieties of Capitalism, Power Resources, and Historical Legacies: Explaining the Slovenian Exception', *Politics & Society*, 2011, vol. 39, no. 2, pp. 268-295.
816. As underlined by Duman and Kureková 2012, p. 1217 and Kahancová 2017, p. 180.
817. *See* Myant, M., 'Trade Unions in the Czech Republic', Report 115, Brussels, ETUI, 2010.

here it is not clear if company collective agreements refer to the entire company or part of it. Slovenia contains no designation of company collective agreements at all. In the countries examined, complicated and sometimes unclear set of rules are in place when more than one trade union operates at company level (the latter is specifically the case in Slovenia and the Czech Republic).[818] Moreover, in the countries researched, internal employers' regulation is considered an alternative to collective bargaining, which diminishes the collective bargaining role of trade unions. The laws usually prescribe that employers should consult trade unions or employees' representatives before issuing the internal regulation. Yet, as evidenced in Chapter 7, there are examples where no such employer's obligation exists (in particular, in the Czech Republic and Poland, *see* section 2.4.1). Sometimes internal rules cannot be issued and standards can be decided on an individual basis only – this is the case in small companies in Poland.

This chapter has also demonstrated that the role of policies and legacies, to varying degrees and in various forms, shaped standard setting at company level. Slovenia's post-transitional framework has focused rather on the sector as the main locus of standard setting, but one may note that the legacy of self-management helped this country to hone a tradition of employee involvement in company decision-making. Hence, works councils developed in Slovenia earlier than in the other CEE countries – already by the early 1990s (section 2.4.2). Slovakia and the Czech Republic have had some modest legacy of company level collective bargaining in the communist period (section 2.1.1) and the post-transitional industrial relations particularly focused on enterprise as the principal decision-making unit (especially in the Czech Republic).[819] The Polish post-transitional framework emerged from the 1980s legislation, which postulated the company as the main standard-setting level (section 2.1.1).

3 INTERPRETING THE FINDINGS

3.1 Normative Model of Articulated Multi-employer Bargaining

3.1.1 Country Variations

How do the four countries fare with respect to the proposed normative model of articulated multi-employer bargaining? *Polish laws* resemble the proposed model the least. As explained in Chapter 6, the sector is the missing level in Poland, not only in practice (bearing in mind the marginal coverage of multi-enterprise agreements), but

---

818. As argued in section 2.2.1., in Slovenia, a bargaining team is formed when more than one trade union operates in a company, but law contains no further rules on collective bargaining procedure if no such team can be formed. Similarly, in the Czech Republic, when more than one trade union exists in a company, they are supposed to act jointly (or to agree on a specific type of representation) when engaging in collective bargaining – yet, no further specification is offered in law on collective bargaining procedure if these trade unions cannot agree on representation.
819. As demonstrated in section 2.1.1. *See also* Pollert, A., 'The Transformation of Trade Unionism in the Capitalist and Democratic Restructuring of the Czech Republic', *European Journal of Industrial Relations*, 1997, vol. 3, no. 2, p. 207.

also in law. The articulation between different sources is rather rigid – Polish single-enterprise collective agreements may not derogate *in peius* from the rights postulated at other (higher) bargaining levels and statutory law. While it is possible to suspend an application of a collective agreement for a temporary period, Chapter 7 underlined that such a mechanism actually represents a negation of articulation – suspension annuls the possibility of standard setting at a certain level.[820] The articulating mechanisms play the role of facilitating the relationship between standard setting at different levels, but suspension has no such effect. If a multi-enterprise agreement is suspended, the link between the company level and statutory law will be annulled. If single-enterprise agreement is suspended (taking into account the marginal relevance of multi-employer agreements in Polish industrial relations), employees might cease to be covered by any collective agreement. Furthermore, in Poland, there is no legal solution in place to protect employees in SMEs where they are exposed to trends towards individualisation and to fragmentation of standard setting. According to the Labour Code, the employer is not obliged to issue internal regulation to regulate working conditions for employees in companies with less than twenty employees (section 2.4.1 of Chapter 7). As underlined by the interviewees in Warsaw, Polish laws have not been designed with the sector level in mind and there have been no efforts to generate any meaningful standard setting at this level. The resurgence of sector in the law is scarcely imaginable, nor, in the future, its appearance in practice. In fact, one of the interviewees pointed out that:

> if we meet in 5-10 years' time, there will be no sectoral agreements at all in Poland. The reason is that decentralisation is a European trend and there is no pressure from Western Europe to build sectoral structures. Also, there will be no power on the side of Polish trade unions to force their signing.

At the other end of the spectrum, Slovenia's legal framework is the one which resembles the proposed normative model the most. Even though a certain trend to decentralisation has been visible in Slovenian industrial relations since the mid-2000s,[821] the legal framework created in 2006 may not be interpreted as restricting collective bargaining at sectoral or cross-sectoral levels. The sector is promoted in law in several ways. The law stipulates rules on the extension of collective agreements, and these provisions are regularly exercised. Statutory laws often encourage regulation of certain items via sectoral collective agreements (section 2.2 of Chapter 6). The articulation between sources at different levels is facilitated with the mechanism of derogation described in Chapter 6, allowing derogation to the detriment of employees and the stipulation of opening clauses in sectoral collective agreements. Yet, Slovenian industrial relations have not been immune to decentralisation pressures during the recent crisis period.[822]

Czech and Slovakian laws share a common legal legacy and have legal frameworks which largely resemble each other. Yet, in line with the previously mentioned

---

820. *See* Chapter 7, section 3.
821. As observed in Chapter 1 (Table 2) and Chapter 4 (Table 3).
822. Kanjuo Mrčela 2017, Stanojević and Kanjuo Mrčela 2016.

observations, Slovakian laws resemble the proposed normative model less, despite the fact that centralised standard setting is more pronounced than in the Czech Republic. However, the number and content of legal amendments in the recent years show that both the Czech and Slovak legal systems are still in flux. In fact, some of the recent legal amendments have encouraged the idea of sector level bargaining, showing that these two countries could potentially move closer to the proposed normative model in future. Slovakia lifted the condition of employers' consent on extensions in 2014.[823] And in recent years, Czech laws have introduced salient elements which support sector level collective bargaining – despite giving up the membership of employers' associations, individual employers should remain bound by relevant collective agreements. Also, since 2014, the legal basis on which the Czech employers' associations are set up has been changed, ensuring that collective bargaining remains within the remit of their activities.[824] However, there are other areas where further improvements could facilitate more meaningful sectoral collective bargaining in both countries and lead them towards the proposed normative model. For example, this could be by encouraging different forms of derogations *in peius*, controlled by provisions at sectoral (higher-level) agreements. Rules on extensions could be made more relaxed in the Czech Republic. Neither country has rules on the representativeness of social partners at this level – such rules could facilitate more legitimate collective bargaining.

3.1.2 The Legal Architecture of the Normative Model: Three Analytical Elements

As suggested in Chapter 1, the normative model consists of three major analytical elements, on which the following lines will reflect to in relation to the four CEE countries:

(a) In the CEE countries, *the auxiliary role* of the statutory laws is not fully developed. The auxiliary role of the state – the state promoting collective bargaining at all levels and ensuring that trade union interests are protected – has been missing, in various forms and degrees. After the analysis in the second part of the study has been performed, it is evident that, in several instances, laws could support and stimulate collective bargaining in a more meaningful manner. For example, law could stimulate sectoral collective bargaining by facilitating extensions of collective agreements or by enforcing rules on social partners' representativeness. Furthermore, this observation leads to the question whether collective agreements have emerged as autonomous standard-setting sources in CEE. Sciarra has written that 'the autonomy of a collective bargaining system is measured comparatively in

---
823. As described in Chapter 6, section 2.5.
824. As described in Chapter 6, section 2.4.

relation to the degree of incisiveness exhibited by statute law'.[825] Judging the CEE laws from this premise, one may conclude that collective agreements, after more than two decades, have not fully emerged as the autonomous standard-setting source. A major reason behind this is that the statutory law still exhibits a great influence on collective agreements by exerting control over their substance. By providing a comprehensive and detailed mandatory regulation of substantive conditions of work, instead of providing only minimum rules, the laws do not stimulate conclusion of collective agreements. This observation, which was made in Chapter 3, has been particularly underlined by the interviewees in Poland and the Czech Republic.[826] Moreover, this study also revealed that in Slovakia the statutory law exhibits great influence on collective agreements, as they often replicate the provisions of statutory laws.[827] In Slovenia, such statutory influence seems to have had the least impact on collective agreements.

(b) Corollary to the described regulatory style of statutory laws is the *limited role and function of collective agreements in CEE*. Company collective agreements in CEE, in principle, play a more meaningful role than sectoral collective agreements – they are usually employed to specify the terms and conditions of statutory laws and sectoral collective agreements.[828] The role of sectoral collective agreements is far less ambitious. As demonstrated in Chapter 6 sectoral collective agreements concluded in the four countries have a low regulatory role, given that they embody only a slight upgrade from those standards prescribed in law.[829] In addition, in Slovenia, the implementing function of sectoral collective agreements – the role of these agreements in substantiating the terms and conditions of statutory law (which prescribe only general and broad terms) – seems to be more pronounced than in the other three countries. But, a general impression which emanates from the four countries is that broadening the scope of collective agreements – by allowing them to stipulate more thematic elements and areas and making them substance-wise less dependent on law – would facilitate more meaningful collective bargaining and expand the roles and functions of collective agreements. Here it is useful to go back to the postulates of collective agreements, presented in Chapter 1 and the delineation of Supiot's functions of collective agreements.[830] Sectoral collective agreements in CEE could be employed, for example, as instruments of flexibility in the sense understood by Supiot, by expanding the legal possibilities of setting less favourable rules for employees (derogation *in peius*) and allowing stipulation of different

---

825. Sciarra, S., 'The Evolution of Collective Bargaining: Observations on a Comparison in the Countries of the European Union', *Comparative Labour Law and Policy Journal*, 2007, vol. 29, p. 7, as quoted in Chapter 3, section 4.2.
826. *See* Chapter 3, section 4.2.1.
827. *See* Chapter 6, section 2.2.
828. *See* Chapter 7, section 2.1.2.
829. *See* Chapter 6, sections 2.2, 3.1.2 and 3.2.
830. Section 4.3 of Chapter 1; *see* Supiot 2001, pp. 97–100.

types of derogation clauses.[831] Also, company collective bargaining could be made more meaningful if collective agreements were used more as company management tools. Allowing company collective agreements to expand and to regulate more elements of company organisation would be a welcome development to offset the trend to individualisation described in Chapter 7. However, none of these transformations in the functions of collective agreements can be performed without ensuring that the issues related to the organisation and capacities of social partners at distinct levels are addressed. For the sectoral level, the issue of employers' capacities seems to be the most topical – while trade unions often claim they have no negotiating partner, employers' associations need an incentive to engage in sectoral bargaining. At the company level, the key challenge is to empower trade unions. Currently the company trade unions may perform a salient consulting role before the unilateral employers' acts are issued, but the focus of trade union activities should be more on collective bargaining.[832] In addition, improving employee representation, particularly in smaller enterprises, represents a distinct challenge in CEE.

(c) When it comes to *articulation*, this study has explained that the four countries rest on a rigid top-down ordering, which dictates that collective agreements at lower hierarchical levels may only set more favourable conditions for employees. While there are some important exceptions – the Slovenian system is notably the least rigid (as depicted in Chapters 6 and 7), the legal systems presented generally discourage deviations. This argument was repeated several times during the interviews in the four countries as a problematic trait, which demotivates collective bargaining, particularly on the side of employers. A specific example is the possibility to suspend collective agreements under Polish law, which by its nature upsets the multi-level standard-setting scheme and articulation between different levels.

3.2 Sketching Answers to the Research Questions

A general picture emanating from this study is that in many instances the law has provided a pretext for the trend towards decentralised collective bargaining and, likewise, that it has not always provided a stimulus for sectoral and cross-sectoral collective bargaining. Thus, *regarding the first research question*, one may conclude that the laws could, in a more resolute manner, support and promote collective bargaining at all levels. This, of course is both a legislative and political matter. As demonstrated in the second part of the study, the laws provide no clear designation of either sectoral or company collective agreements in the four countries. To sum up the

---

831. This would lead to what Supiot called 'negotiated flexibilisation', *ibid.*, p. 98.
832. The legal framework on unilateral employers' acts in the four countries has been explained in Chapter 7, section 2.4.1.

most prominent elements depicted in the second part of the study; except in Slovenia, the rules on the extension of collective agreements are restrictive and cannot be easily put into practice. The rules on representativeness are missing in Slovakia and the Czech Republic. The articulation between the different standard-setting levels is rigid overall and deprives social partners from incentives to engage in collective bargaining. Nevertheless, although these systems are decentralised, the study did not find that the four countries' laws offer more resolute support to company level. In fact, company level faces a set of distinct challenges, which, as elaborated in Chapter 7, underpin the individualisation of standard setting and the shift to employers' powers. In particular, laws could support collective bargaining at company level, as discussed in Chapter 7, for example, by clarifying the collective bargaining procedure when more than one trade union operates at the company level.

The above observations represent general remarks, but there are remarkable country variations. These variations can be summarised as follows. *Slovenia* is an exceptional example for obvious reasons – it not only has the most developed centralised collective bargaining structure, but also has a legal system that supports and promotes collective bargaining at any level. At the other end of the spectrum, *Polish laws* have not been designed to underpin centralised (sectoral or cross-sectoral) collective bargaining as the predominant locus for standard setting. In fact, Polish laws are very much company-centred, rather than sector-centred. *Slovakia* and the *Czech Republic* have rather similar legal frameworks. Surprisingly, whereas Slovakia has comparatively more developed sectoral collective bargaining, in comparison, its laws do not provide a more stimulating climate for collective bargaining at sectoral level than the Czech laws. The major difference between Slovakian and Czech laws lies in the approach to the extension of collective agreements and the legal possibilities for derogation to the detriment of employees *in peius*.[833]

When it comes to the second research question, the study has found that the laws of the countries selected have experienced slow and gradual transformation: the legal transformation which began in the early 1990s formally instigated basic rights and freedoms, but this represented only the beginning of reform. In the subsequent years, legal frameworks were reshaped, slowly and steadily introducing free and voluntary collective bargaining. In fact, this study demonstrated that none of the CEE systems examined were based on free and voluntary collective bargaining at any time in the 1990s. The most prominent legal reforms took place only in the mid-2000s. The recent crisis period did not bring any substantial change in the existing legal and institutional frameworks in the four countries. Exceptionally, some changes were envisaged in Slovakia (regarding the collective agreements' extensions, opening clauses and trade union representativeness),[834] but most of these innovations were only short-lived.

The study has found that the legal transformation was shaped in a national-specific mix of policy choices and the path-dependant role of legacies originating from the previous communist setting. The role of the EU in shaping these laws has been only indirect and rather limited. *Regarding Slovenia*, this study argued that the philosophy

---

833. As explained in Chapters 6 and 7.
834. *See* Chapter 6, sections 2.5 and 2.3, and Chapter 7, section 2.2.1.

of gradualism facilitated the transformation of both industrial relations and law, particularly by facilitating the evolvement of three generations of collective agreements.[835] The 2006 Act on Collective Agreements enabled full implementation of freedom of association, but industrial relations developed at sectoral level even before this Act entered into force. Yet, some elements of the pre-2006 legal framework were vital for establishing the collective bargaining practices at sectoral level, in particular the mandatory membership of the Chamber of Commerce and Industry and the mandatory nature of collective agreements (Chapter 3, section 3.1). *Polish laws* have not developed with the sector in mind. As already mentioned in this chapter, the laws enacted in the 1980s paved the way for decentralised collective bargaining by emphasising the company level.[836] Moreover, the 1993 tripartite social pact further highlighted decision-making at company level.[837] The interviewees in Poland claimed that the sector was not a policy priority in the past two decades. When it comes to the *Czech Republic*, this study found evidence of the company being the main tenet of policies in the post-transitional framework.[838] Some form of company collective bargaining had been in existence in pre-1990s Czechoslovakia, because company trade unions could sign different types of collective accords with management.[839] Yet, post-transitional *Slovakia* managed to build more reasonably developed sectoral structures compared with the decentralised and fragmented Czech trade unions, thanks to the well-organised centralised representation of social partners.[840]

This study claims that *institutionalisation and market narrative* shaped the process of labour law transformation in CEE. As evidenced in the second part of the study, the process of institutionalisation has been developing slowly and gradually: collective agreements have been slowly widening their substantive scope and changing their legal nature. It can be claimed that the process of institutionalisation has not been fully accomplished in CEE, as the auxiliary role has not fully developed and collective agreements may undergo further transformation in future. Market narrative has been often translated into outright decentralisation. This is most evident at company level, as Chapter 7 demonstrated: here the lack of support for company collective bargaining translated into trends in the individualisation of standard setting and diminution of the role of trade unions. The overall impression is that the market narrative has played the most resolute role in Polish legal transformation, but it has also been present in the other countries examined, particularly in the Czech Republic and Slovakia.

---

835. The three generations were postulated by Vodovnik and Korpič-Horvat, 2015, pp. 278–279, *see* Chapter 3 (section 3.1) and Chapter 6. On gradualism in Slovenian industrial relations, *see* Crowley and Stanojević 2011.
836. *See* Chapter 3, section 3.4. *See also* Chapter 7, section 2.1.
837. 1993 Pact on State-Owned Enterprises in the Restructuring Process, *see* Chapter 5, section 2.4.
838. *See* Chapter 7, section 2.1.1, based on Pollert 1997, p. 207.
839. *See* Chapter 7, section 2.1.1, based on Deak, L., 'Customary International Labour Laws and Their Application in Hungary, Poland and the Czech Republic', *Tulsa Journal of Comparative and International Law*, 1994, vol. 2, no. 1, p. 40; also, Myant, M., 'Czech and Slovak Trade Unions', *Journal of Communist Studies*, 1993, vol. 9, no. 4, pp. 59–84.
840. Comparatively stronger central organisation of Slovak social partners was also acknowledged in: Duman and Kureková 2012, p. 1217 and Kahancová 2017, p. 180.

On a final note, there are important observations which stem from the answers provided to the two research questions. This study has highlighted the role of law in facilitating meaningful collective bargaining in CEE. It is clear that CEE collective bargaining is facing a number of challenges for which solutions cannot be found in law; the most pressing being the declining trade union density rates and the general lack of a collective bargaining culture. Notwithstanding these issues, the aim of the study was to emphasise that the transformation of industrial relations in CEE prompts careful appraisal of the legal frameworks – the main rationale for such appraisal is that laws enabling social partners to bargain collectively have emerged only relatively recently. A legal framework facilitating free and voluntary organisation of social partners and collective bargaining is a necessary prerequisite for meaningful collective bargaining, but it is not its guarantee.

With the described regulatory style of statutory labour laws, the state in CEE clearly performs a protective function – given the weaknesses on the side of social partners, these countries have opted to provide more extensive statutory regulation, rather than to have standards prescribed by collective agreement. This observation has been already made in Chapter 3.[841] Yet, this regulatory style can be also seen as a legacy from the communist times, when the statutory legislation was rather comprehensive and all-encompassing. The culture of collective bargaining, on the other hand, is still young in post-communist CEE. This protective function has rendered the *institutionalisation* of collective agreements slow in post-transitional terms, because collective agreement in these countries could not formally regulate any matter social partners wished until the last decade.[842]

One may also claim that the protective function described facilitates *market narrative*.[843] As this study has demonstrated in its second part, the legal ordering of these countries is peculiar in the way it facilitates market narrative in CEE: whilst the collective bargaining system is labelled as decentralised, the predominant and most powerful source of standards remains centralised at the statutory level. Such centralisation of regulation translates into poor regulatory power and poor scope for collective agreements, a lack of incentive on the employers' side to engage in collective bargaining and in tension over the regulation of matters via employers' prerogatives (through unilateral standard-setting or even individual bargaining) rather than collective bargaining.

---

841. As mentioned in that chapter (section 5), this situation created a 'liberalisation dilemma' in these countries, because the retreat of the state in these countries could generate the effect of strengthening managerial unilateralism, see Bluhm, K., 'Resolving Liberalisation Dilemma: Labour Relations in East-Central Europe and the Impact of European Union', in M.A. Moreau and M.E. Blas-López (eds), *Restructuring in the New EU Member States: Social Dialogue, Firms Relocation, and Social Treatment of Restructuring*, Brussels, Peter Lang, 2008, p. 60.
842. As Chapter 3 (section 4.2.1) demonstrated, the legal provisions formally allowing social partners to negotiate on any matters they wish have been introduced in these countries in the 2000s.
843. As postulated in Chapter 3, section 2.2.

4 LIMITS, OUTLOOKS AND FUTURE CHALLENGES

A limitation of this study is the general lack of comprehensive and reliable industrial relations data on collective agreements in CEE. This holds particularly for collective agreements at company level, because there is no legal obligation to register them in none of these countries. More detailed empirical data, particularly on the content of collective agreements (at any level), but also on their number and coverage, could lead to a more objective assessment of the labour law transformation in CEE. It would be particularly useful to monitor how the function of collective agreements has evolved in line with the changes (liberalisation) of the substantive legal framework. Further research providing synergy between legal and industrial relations approaches could provide more insights into the functions and nature of the CEE collective agreements, and it could more comprehensively pinpoint areas where laws could provide more support for collective bargaining.

This study has designed a normative articulated multi-employer bargaining model as a legal benchmark against which CEE laws have been scrutinised. To the fullest extent possible, this study has pointed out shortcomings and pinpointed areas where the legal framework could be enhanced in order to facilitate collective bargaining. However, this study did not offer concrete solutions to the issues identified: this could be the task of further research. Likewise, it would be useful to study the laws of the EU Member States with a view to exploring different models of legal regulation and providing solutions to particular issues. Such a comparative perspective could investigate, for example, how different Member States deal with the issues related to employee representation in small companies, how they use instruments the extension of collective agreements, or what kind of models of derogation *in peius* and mechanisms of articulation could be considered attractive for CEE countries.

Bibliography

Aguilera, R.V. and Dabu, A., 'Transformation of Employment Relations Systems in Central and Eastern Europe', *Journal of Industrial Relations*, 2005, vol. 47, no. 1, pp. 16–42.

Aslund, A., *How Capitalism Was Built: The Transformation of Central and Eastern Europe, Russia and Central Asia*, Cambridge, Cambridge University Press, 2007.

Avdagic, S. and Crouch, C., 'Organised Economic Interests: Diversity and Change in an Enlarged Europe' in P.M. Heywood, E. Jones, M. Rhodes and U. Sedelmeier (eds), *Developments in European Politics*, Basingstoke, Palgrave Macmillan, 2006, pp. 196–215.

Avdagic, S., 'State-Labour Relations in East Central Europe: Explaining Variations in Union Effectiveness', *Socio-Economic Review*, 2005, vol. 3, pp. 25–53.

Avdagic, S., 'The Conditions for Pacts: A Fuzzy-Set Analysis of the Resurgence of Tripartite Concertation' in S. Avdagic, M. Rhodes and J. Visser (eds), *Social Pacts in Europe: Emergence, Evolution, and Institutionalisation*, Oxford, Oxford University Press, 2011.

Avdagic, S., 'Tripartism and Economic Reforms in Slovenia and Poland' in L. Fraile (ed.), *Blunting Neoliberalism: Tripartism and Economic Reforms in the Developing World*, Basingstoke, Palgrave Macmillan, 2010a, pp. 39–84.

Avdagic, S., 'When Are Concerted Reforms Feasible? Explaining the Emergence of Social Pacts in Western Europe', *Comparative Political Studies*, 2010b, vol. 43, no. 5, pp. 628–657.

Baccaro, L. and Howell, C., 'A Common Neoliberal Trajectory: The Transformation of Industrial Relations in Advanced Capitalism', *Politics & Society*, 2011, vol. 39, no. 4, pp. 521–563.

Bailey, D. and de Propris, L., 'A Bridge Too Phare? EU Pre-Accession Aid and Capacity-Building in the Candidate Countries', *Journal of Common Market Studies*, 2004, vol. 42, no. 1, pp. 77–98.

Barancová, H. and Olšovská, A., 'Slovakia' in R. Blanpain and F. Hendrickx (eds), *International Encyclopaedia for Labour Law and Industrial Relations*, The Hague, Kluwer Law International, 2014.

Barancová, H., 'Labour Law in the Slovak Republic, Present Situation and Future Trends' in R. Blanpain and L. Nagy (eds), *Labour Law and Industrial Relations in Central and Eastern Europe (from Planned to Market Economy)*, Bulletin of

Comparative Labour Relations, no. 31, The Hague, Kluwer Law International, 1996, pp. 139–156.

Barnard, C., 'EU Employment Law and the European Social Model: The Past, the Present and the Future', *Current Legal Problems*, 2014, vol. 67, no. 1, pp. 1–39.

Bekker, S. and Klosse, S., 'EU Governance of Economic and Social Policies', *European Journal of Social Law*, 2013, vol. 2, pp. 103–120.

Bekker, S. and Palinkaš, I., 'The Impact of the Financial Crisis on EU Economic Governance: A Struggle Between Hard and Soft Law and Expansion of the EU Competences?', *Tilburg Law Review*, 2012, vol. 17, pp. 360–366.

Belina, M., 'Labour Law and Industrial Relations in the Czech Republic' in R. Blanpain and L. Nagy (eds), *Labour Law and Industrial Relations in Central and Eastern Europe (from Planned to Market Economy)*, Bulletin of Comparative Labour Relations, no. 31, The Hague, Kluwer Law International, 1996, pp. 85–107.

Bercusson, B., *European Labour Law*, 2nd edn, Cambridge, Cambridge University Press, 2009.

Berdnarik, R., 'Slovakia: Extension of Multi-Employer Collective Agreements Marks a Turning Point', Dublin, Eurofound, 2015, available at: http://www.eurofound.europa.eu/observatories/eurwork/articles/working-conditions-industrial-relations/slovakia-extension-of-multi-employer-collective-agreements-marks-a-turning-point (accessed 1 December 2017).

Bernaciak, M., 'Social Dialogue Revival or "PR Corporatism"? Negotiating Anti-Crisis Measures in Poland and Bulgaria', *Transfer: European Review of Labour and Research*, 2013, vol. 19, no. 2, pp. 239–251.

Biagi, M., 'Changing Industrial Relations' in M. Biagi and M. Tiraboschi (eds), *Marco Biagi: Selected Writings*, The Hague, Kluwer Law International, 2003.

Biagi, M., 'Employee Representation in Small and Medium-Sized Enterprises: A Comparative Overview', *Comparative Labour Law Journal*, 1992, vol. 13, no. 3, pp. 257–272.

Biagi, M., 'Labour Law in Small and Medium-Sized Enterprises: Flexibility or Adjustment?', *Comparative Labour Law Journal*, 1994, vol. 16, pp. 439–466.

Blanpain, R., *European Labour Law*, 11th edn, Alphen aan den Rijn, Kluwer Law International, 2008.

Bluhm, K., 'Resolving Liberalisation Dilemma: Labour Relations in East-Central Europe and the Impact of European Union', in M.A. Moreau and M.E. Blas-López (eds), *Restructuring in the New EU Member States: Social Dialogue, Firms Relocation, and Social Treatment of Restructuring*, Brussels, Peter Lang, 2008, pp. 59–79.

Bohle, D. and Greskovits, B., 'Neoliberalism, Embedded Neoliberalism and Neocorporatism: Towards Transnational Capitalism in Central-Eastern Europe', *West European Politics*, 2007, vol. 30, no. 3, pp. 443–466.

Bohle, D. and Greskovits, B., 'Slovakia and Hungary: Successful and Failed Euro Entry Without Social Pacts' in P. Pochet, M. Keune and D. Natalie (eds), *After the Euro and Enlargement: Social Pacts in the EU*, Brussels, ETUI, 2010, pp. 345–369.

Bohle, D. and Greskovits, B., 'Varieties of Capitalism and Capitalism "tout court"', *European Journal of Sociology*, 2006, vol. 50, no. 3, pp. 355–386.

Bibliography

Bohle, D. and Greskovits, B., *Capitalist Diversity on Europe's Periphery*, Ithaca, Cornel University Press, 2012.

Bohle, D., 'Trade Unions and the Fiscal Crisis of the State', *Warsaw Forum of Economic Sociology*, 2011, vol. 2, no. 1, pp. 89–105.

Brngálová, B. and Kahancová, M., 'Governing the Metal Sector in Slovakia: Socio-Economic and Policy Context, Industrial Relations and the Challenge of Flexibility and Security', FP7 GUSTO Working Paper 6.20, 2013.

Bronstein, A., 'Trends and Challenges of Labour Law in Central Europe' in J.D.R. Craig (ed.), *Globalisation and the Future of Labour Law*, Cambridge, Cambridge University Press, 2006, pp. 191–214.

Bruun, N., 'The Autonomy of Collective Agreement' in R. Blanpain (ed.), *Collective Bargaining, Discrimination, Social Security and the European Integration*, Bulletin of Comparative Labour Relations, no. 48, The Hague, Kluwer Law International, 2003, pp. 1–49.

Bruun, N., Lörcher, K. and Schömann, I. (eds), *The Economic and Financial Crisis and Collective Labour Law in Europe*, Oxford, Hart Publishing, 2014.

Buchen, C., 'Estonia and Slovenia as Antipodes' in D. Lane and M. Myant (eds), *Varieties of Capitalism in Post-Communist Countries*, Basingstoke, Palgrave Macmillan, 2007, pp. 65–89.

Bulla, M., Czíria, L. and Kahancová, M., 'Impact of Legislative Reforms on Industrial Relations and Working Conditions in Slovakia', ILO Background Study, 2013 (unpublished).

Calmfors, L. and Driffill, J., 'Bargaining Structure, Corporatism and Macroeconomic Performance', *Economic Policy*, 1988, vol. 3, no. 6, pp. 13–61.

Casale, G., 'Evolution and Trends in Industrial Relations in Central and Eastern European Countries', *The International Journal of Comparative Labour Law and Industrial Relations*, 2003, vol. 19, no. 1, pp. 5–32.

Casale, G., 'Experiences of Tripartite Relations in Central and Eastern European Countries', *The International Journal of Comparative Labour Law and Industrial Relations*, 2000, vol. 16, no. 2, pp. 129–142.

Casale, G., Kubinková, M. and Rychly L., 'Social Dialogue – The Czech Success Story', Working Paper no. 4, Geneva, International Labour Office, 2001.

Cerami, A. and Vanhuysse, P., 'Introduction: Social Policy Pathways, Twenty Years after the Fall of the Berlin Wall' in A. Cerami and P. Vanhuysse (eds), *Post-Communist Welfare Pathways – Theorising Social Policy Transformations in Central and Eastern Europe*, Basingstoke, Palgrave Macmillan, 2009, pp. 1–14.

Chirico, F. and Larouche, P., 'Conceptual Divergence, Functionalism, and the Economics of Convergence' in S. Prechal and B. Roermund (eds), *The Coherence of EU Law: The Search for Unity in Divergent Concepts*, Oxford, Oxford University Press, 2008, pp. 463–494.

Collins, H. 'Contractual Autonomy', in A. Bogg, C. Costello, A.C.L. Davies and J. Prassl (eds), *The Autonomy of Labour Law*, Oxford, Hart Publishing, 2015, pp. 45–71.

Cook, L.J., 'More Rights, Less Power: Labour Standards and Labour Markets in East European Post-Communist States', *Studies in Comparative International Development*, 2010, vol. 45, no. 2, pp. 170–197.

Countouris, N. and Freedland M. (eds), *Resocialising Europe in a Time of Crisis*, Cambridge, Cambridge University Press, 2013.

Coutu, M., Le Friant, M. and Murray, G., 'Broken Paradigms: Labour Law in the Wake of Globalisation and the Economic Crisis', *Comparative Labour Law and Policy Journal*, 2013, vol. 34, pp. 565–584.

Cox, T.M. and Mason, B., 'Interest Groups and the Development of Tripartism in East Central Europe', *European Journal of Industrial Relations*, 2000a, vol. 6, no. 3, pp. 325–347.

Cox, T.M. and Mason, B., 'Trends and Developments in East Central European Industrial Relations', *Industrial Relations Journal*, 2000b, vol. 31, no. 2, pp. 97–114.

Crouch, C., *Industrial Relations and European State Traditions*, Oxford, Oxford University Press, 1993.

Crowley, S. and Stanojević, M., 'Varieties of Capitalism, Power Resources, and Historical Legacies: Explaining the Slovenian Exception', *Politics & Society*, 2011, vol. 39, no. 2, pp. 268–295.

Crowley, S., 'Explaining Labor Weakness in Post-Communist Europe: Historical Legacies and Comparative Perspective', *East European Politics and Societies*, 2004, vol. 18, no. 3, pp. 394–429.

Czarzasty, J. and Mrozowicki, A., 'Living and Working in Poland – Collective Bargaining', Dublin, Eurofound, 2017, available at: https://www.eurofound.europa.eu/country/poland#collective-bargaining, (accessed 1 December 2017).

Czarzasty, J. and Towalski, R., 'Information and Consultation Bill Adopted', Dublin, Eurofound, 2006, available at: http://www.eurofound.europa.eu/observatories/eurwork/articles/information-and-consultation-bill-adopted (accessed 1 December 2017).

Czarzasty, J., 'Poland: Impact of the Crisis on Industrial Relations', Dublin, Eurofound, 2013, available at: http://www.eurofound.europa.eu/observatories/eurwork/comparative-information/national-contributions/poland/poland-impact-of-the-crisis-on-industrial-relations (accessed 1 December 2017).

Czarzasty, J., 'Poland: National-Level Tripartite Social Dialogue Back on Track', Dublin, Eurofound, 2015, available at: http://www.eurofound.europa.eu/observatories/eurwork/articles/industrial-relations/poland-national-level-tripartite-social-dialogue-back-on-track (accessed 1 December 2017).

Czarzasty, J., *Capacity Building for Social Dialogue in Poland*, Dublin, Eurofound, 2006.

Czíria, L., '2002 Annual Review for Slovakia', Dublin, Eurofound, 2003c, available at: http://www.eurofound.europa.eu/observatories/eurwork/articles/2002-annual-review-for-slovakia (accessed 1 December 2017).

Czíria, L., 'Collective Bargaining and Balanced Recovery: The Case of the Slovak Republic', Bratislava, Institute for Labour and Family Research, 2013a, retrieved from http://www.ivpr.gov.sk/IVPR/images/IVPR/2013/collective.pdf (accessed 1 December 2017).

Czíria, L., 'Collective Bargaining Procedures, Structures and Scope', Dublin, Eurofound, 2002, available at: http://www.eurofound.europa.eu/observatories/

eurwork/articles/collective-bargaining-procedures-structures-and-scope (accessed 1 December 2017).

Czíria, L., 'Employers Oppose New Collective Agreement Extension Rules', Dublin, Eurofound, 2008, available at: http://www.eurofound.europa.eu/observatories/eurwork/articles/employers-oppose-new-collective-agreement-extension-rules (accessed 1 December 2017).

Czíria, L., 'Government Plans Changes to Collective Bargaining Laws', Dublin, Eurofound, 2010, available at: http://www.eurofound.europa.eu/observatories/eurwork/articles/industrial-relations/government-plans-changes-to-collective-bargaining-laws (accessed 1 December 2017).

Czíria, L., 'Legislation Amended to Extend Collective Agreements', Dublin, Eurofound, 2007b, available at: http://www.eurofound.europa.eu/observatories/eurwork/articles/legislation-amended-to-extend-collective-agreements (accessed 1 December 2017).

Czíria, L., 'Living and Working in Slovakia', Dublin, Eurofound, 2017, available at: https://www.eurofound.europa.eu/country/slovakia#actors-and-institutions (accessed 1 December 2017).

Czíria, L., 'New Rules Adopted for Tripartite Social Dialogue', Dublin, Eurofound, 2005, available at: https://www.eurofound.europa.eu/fr/observatories/eurwork/articles/new-rules-adopted-for-tripartite-social-dialogue (accessed 1 December 2017).

Czíria, L., 'Slovakia: An Example of 'Emancipated' Sectoral Social Dialogue?', in Y. Ghellab and D. Vaughan-Whitehead (eds), *Sectoral Social Dialogue in Future EU Member States: The Weakest Link*, Budapest, ILO, 2003a.

Czíria, L., 'Slovakia: Impact of the Crisis on Industrial Relations', Dublin, Eurofound, 2013b, available at: http://www.eurofound.europa.eu/observatories/eurwork/comparative-information/national-contributions/slovakia/slovakia-impact-of-the-crisis-on-industrial-relations (accessed 1 December 2017).

Czíria, L., 'Slovakia: Survey Charts Fall in Union Representation, Bargaining and Member Benefits', Dublin, Eurofound, 2012, available at: https://www.eurofound.europa.eu/observatories/eurwork/articles/working-conditions-industrial-relations/slovakia-survey-charts-fall-in-union-representation-bargaining-and-member-benefits (accessed 1 December 2017).

Czíria, L., 'Tripartism Examined', Dublin, Eurofound, 2003b, available at: https://www.eurofound.europa.eu/it/observatories/eurwork/articles/tripartism-examined (accessed 1 December 2017).

Czíria, L., *Capacity Building for Social Dialogue at Sectoral and Company Level-Slovakia*, Dublin, Eurofound, 2007a.

Czíria, L., *Capacity Building for Social Dialogue in Slovakia*, Dublin, Eurofound, 2006.

Davidov, G. and Langille, B., 'The Contribution of Labour Law to Economic and Human Development' in G. Davidov and B. Langille (eds), *The Idea of Labour Law*, Oxford, Oxford University Press, 2011.

Davidov, G., 'Collective Bargaining Laws: Purpose and Scope', *The International Journal of Comparative Labour Law and Industrial Relations*, 2004, vol. 20, no. 1, pp. 81–106.

Davidov, G., Freedland, M. and Kountouris, N., 'The Subjects of Labor Law: "Employees" and other Workers' in M.W. Finkin and G. Mundlak (eds), *Comparative Labor Law*, Cheltenham, Edvard Elgar, 2015, pp. 115–131.

Davies, P. and Freedland, M., *Kahn Freund's Labour and the Law*, 3rd edn, London, Stevens & Sons, 1983.

De la Porte, C. and Heins, E., 'A New Era of European Integration? Governance of Labour Market and Social Policy since the Sovereign Debt Crisis', *Comparative European Politics*, 2015, vol. 13, pp. 8–28.

Deacon, B., 'Developments in East European Social Policy' in C. Jones (ed.), *New Perspectives on the Welfare State in Europe*, London, Routledge, 1993.

Deacon, B., 'Eastern European Welfare States: The Impact of the Politics of Globalisation', *Journal of European Social Policy*, 2000, vol. 10, no. 2, pp. 146–161.

Deak, L., 'Customary International Labour Laws and Their Application in Hungary, Poland and the Czech Republic', *Tulsa Journal of Comparative and International Law*, 1994, vol. 2, no. 1, pp. 1–44.

Deakin, S. and Wilkinson, F., 'Rights vs Efficiency? The Economic Case for Transnational Labour Standards', *Industrial Law Journal*, 1994, vol. 23, no. 4, pp. 289–310.

Drahokoupil, J. and Myant, M., 'Labour's Legal Resources After 2004: The Role of the European Union', *Transfer: European Review of Labour and Research*, 2015, vol. 21, no. 3, pp. 327–341.

Duman, A. and Kureková, L., 'The Role of State in Development of Socio-Economic Models in Hungary and Slovakia: the Case of Industrial Policy', *Journal of European Public Policy*, 2012, vol. 19, no. 8, pp. 1207–1228.

Esping-Andersen, G., *Three Worlds of Welfare Capitalism*, New Jersey, Princeton University Press, 1990.

Esping-Andersen, G., *Welfare States in Transition: National Adaptations in Global Economies*, London, SAGE, 1996.

European Commission, *Communication 'Europe 2020 – A Strategy for Smart, Sustainable and Inclusive Growth'* COM(2010)2020, Luxembourg, Office for Official Publications of the European Commission, 2010.

European Commission, *Industrial Relations in Europe 2002*, Luxembourg, Office for Official Publications of the European Communities, 2002.

European Commission, *Industrial Relations in Europe 2012*, Luxembourg, Publications Office of the European Union, 2013.

European Commission, *Industrial Relations in Europe 2014*, Luxembourg, Publication Office of the European Union, 2015.

European Commission, *White Paper – European Social Policy: A Way Forward for the Union*, COM(1994)333, Luxembourg, Office for Official Publications of the European Commission, 1994.

Ewing, K.D., 'Democratic Socialism and Labour Law', *Industrial Law Journal*, 1995, vol. 24, no. 2, pp. 103–132.

Fahlbeck, R., 'Collective Agreements: A Crossroad between Public Law and Private Law', *Comparative Labour Law Journal*, 1987, vol. 3, no. 2, pp. 268–295.

Federowicz, M. and Levitas, A., 'Poland: Councils under Communism and Neoliberalism', in J. Rogers and W. Streeck (eds), *Works Councils: Consultation, Representation and Cooperation in Industrial Relations*, Chicago, The University of Chicago Press, 1995, pp. 283–312.

Feldmann, M., 'Coalitions and Corporatism: The Slovenian Political Economy and the Crisis', *Government and Opposition*, 2014, vol. 49, no. 1, pp. 70–91.

Feldmann, M., 'Emerging Varieties of Capitalism in Transition Countries: Industrial Relations and Wage Bargaining in Estonia and Slovenia', *Comparative Political Studies*, 2006, vol. 39, no. 7, pp. 829–854.

Fenger, H.J.M., 'Welfare Regimes in Central and Eastern Europe: Incorporating Post-Communist Countries in a Welfare Regime Typology', *Contemporary Issues and Ideas in Social Sciences*, 2007, vol. 3, no. 2.

Ferner A. and Hyman R., 'Introduction: Industrial Relations in the New Europe – Seventeen Type of Ambiguity', in Ferner A. and Hyman R. (eds), *Industrial Relations in the New Europe*, Blackwell, Oxford, 1992.

Fisher, S., Gold, J. and Haughton, T., 'Slovakia's Neoliberal Turn', *Europe-Asia Studies*, 2007, vol. 59, no. 6, pp. 977–998.

Flanagan, R., 'Institutional Reformation in Eastern Europe', *Industrial Relations*, 1998, vol. 37, no. 3, pp. 337–357.

Florek, L., 'Problems and Dilemmas of Labour Relations in Poland', *Comparative Labour Law Journal*, 1992, vol. 13, pp. 111–128.

Freedland, M. and Kountouris, N., *The Legal Construction of Personal Work Relations*, Oxford, Oxford Monographs on Labour Law, 2011.

Freedland, M., 'Otto Kahn-Freund, the Contract of Employment and the Autonomy of Labour Law', in A. Bogg, C. Costello, A.C.L. Davies and J. Prassl (eds), *The Autonomy of Labour Law*, Oxford, Hart Publishing, 2015, pp. 29–44.

Gardawski, J. and Meardi, G., 'Keep Trying? Polish Failures and Half – Successes in Social Pacting', *Warsaw Forum of Economic Sociology*, 2010, vol. 1, no. 2, pp. 69–90.

Gardawski, J., 'More Flexible Labour Code Comes into Force', Dublin, Eurofound, 2003, available at: http://www.eurofound.europa.eu/observatories/eurwork/articles/more-flexible-labour-code-comes-into-force (accessed 1 December 2017).

Gardawski, J., 'OPZZ and Four Employers' Confederations Sign Bipartite Agreement', Dublin, Eurofound, 2004, available at: http://www.eurofound.europa.eu/eiro/2004/01/feature/pl0401108f.htm (accessed 1 December 2017).

Gardawski, J., 'The Development of the National Tripartite Commission', Dublin, Eurofound, 2002, available at: http://www.eurofound.europa.eu/observatories/eurwork/articles/the-development-of-the-national-tripartite-commission (accessed 1 December 2017).

Gardawski, J., Mrozowicki, A. and Czarzasty, J., *Trade Unions in Poland*, Brussels, ETUI, 2012.

Gernigon, B., Odero, A. and Guido, H., 'Collective Bargaining' in *Fundamental Rights at Work and International Labour Standards*, Geneva, ILO, 2000a.

Gernigon, B., Odero, A. and Guido, H., 'ILO Principles Concerning Collective Bargaining' *International Labour Review*, 2000b, vol. 139, no. 1, pp. 33–55.

Ghellab, Y. and Vaughan-Whitehead, D., *Sectoral Social Dialogue in Future EU Member States: The Weakest Link*, Budapest, ILO, 2003.

Glassner, V., 'Central and Eastern European Industrial Relations in the Crisis: National Divergence and Path-Dependent Change', *Transfer: European Review of Labour and Research*, 2013, vol. 19, no. 2, pp. 155–169.

Goetschy, J., 'Taking Stock of Social Europe: Is There Such a Thing as a Community Social Model?', in M. Jepsen and A. Serrano Pascual (eds), *Unwrapping the European Social Model*, Bristol, The Policy Press, 2006, pp. 47–72.

Goldin, A., 'Global Conceptualisations and Local Constructions of the Idea of Labour Law' in G. Davidov and B. Langille (eds), *The Idea of Labour Law*, Oxford, Oxford University Press, 2011, pp. 69–87.

Grabbe, H., *The EU's Transformative Power: Europeanisation through Conditionality in Central and Eastern Europe*, Basingstoke, Palgrave Macmillan, 2006.

Grdesic, M., 'Mapping the Paths of the Yugoslav Model: Labour Strength and Weakness in Slovenia, Croatia and Serbia', *European Journal of Industrial Relations*, 2008, vol. 14, no. 2, 133–151.

Guardiancich, I. and Pliszkiewicz, M., 'The Case of Poland' in I. Guardiancich (ed.), *Recovering from the Crisis Through Social Dialogue in the New EU Member States: The Case of Bulgaria, the Czech Republic, Poland and Slovenia*, Budapest, ILO, 2012, pp. 71–93.

Guardiancich, I., 'Slovenia: The End of a Success Story? When a Partial Reform Equilibrium Turns Bad', *Europe-Asia Studies*, 2016, vol. 68, no. 2, pp. 205–231.

Guardiancich, I., 'The Case of Slovenia', in I. Guardiancich (ed.), *Recovering from the Crisis Through Social Dialogue in the new EU Member States: The Case of Bulgaria, the Czech Republic, Poland and Slovenia*, Budapest, ILO, 2012, pp. 95–128.

Guardiancich, I., 'The Uncertain Future of Slovenian Exceptionalism', *East European Politics & Societies*, 2011, vol. 26, no. 2, pp. 380–399.

Hager, M.M., 'Constructing a New Liberal Capitalism: Czechoslovakian Labor Law in Transition', *American University International Law Review*, 1992, vol. 7, no. 3, pp. 503–528.

Hajn, Z. and Mitrus, L., 'Poland' in R. Blanpain and F. Hendrickx (eds), *International Encyclopaedia for Labour Law and Industrial Relations*, The Hague, Kluwer Law International, 2016.

Hajn, Z., 'Collective Labour Agreements and Contracts of Employment in Polish Labour Law', in M. Sewerynski (ed.), *Collective Agreements and Individual Contracts of Employment*, The Hague, Kluwer Law International, 2003, pp. 191–205.

Hála, J. and Kroupa, A., 'Council of Economic and Social Agreement Tightens Representativeness Criteria', Dublin, Eurofound, 2005, available at: http://www.eurofound.europa.eu/eiro/2005/03/feature/cz0503102f.htm (accessed 1 December 2017).

Hála, J. and Verveková, S., 'Unions Claim Court's Repeal of Labour Code Will Diminish Trade Union Role', Dublin, Eurofound, 2008, available at: http://www.eurofound.europa.eu/observatories/eurwork/articles/unions-claim-courts-repeal-of-labour-code-will-diminish-trade-union-role (accessed 1 December 2017).

Hála, J., 'Czech Republic – Developments in Social Partner Organisations: Employer Organisations', Dublin, Eurofound, 2010, available at: http://www.eurofound.europa.eu/observatories/eurwork/comparative-information/national-contributions/czech-republic/czech-republic-developments-in-social-partner-organisations-employer-organisations (accessed 1 December 2017).

Hála, J., 'Opposition to New Law on Union Plurality in Collective Bargaining', Dublin, Eurofound, 2007, available at: https://www.eurofound.europa.eu/de/observatories/eurwork/articles/opposition-to-new-law-on-union-plurality-in-collective-bargaining (accessed 1 December 2017).

Hála, J., Kroupa, A., Mansfeldova, Z., Kux, J., Vaskova, R. and Pleskot, I. 'Development of Social Dialogue in the Czech Republic', RILSA, 2002, available at: praha.vupsv.cz/fulltext/dialen.pdf (accessed 1 December 2017).

Hall, P.A., Soskice, P., 'An Introduction to Varieties of Capitalism' in A.P. Hall and P. Soskice (eds), *Varieties of Capitalism: The Institutional Foundations of Comparative Advantage*, Oxford, Oxford University Press, 2001.

Hancké, B., *Debating a Varieties of Capitalism: A Reader*, Oxford, Oxford University Press, 2009.

Hancké, B., Rhodes, M. and Thatcher, M., 'Introduction: Beyond Varieties of Capitalism', in B. Hancké, M. Rhodes and M. Thatcher (eds), *Beyond Varieties of Capitalism: Conflict, Contradictions, and Complementarities in the European Economy*, Oxford, Oxford University Press, 2007, pp. 3–38.

Handiak, P., 'The Evolving Structure of Collective Bargaining in Europe: National Report of Slovakia' Study VS/2003/0219SI2-359910, European Commission and University of Florence, 2004.

Hendrickx, F. and Giubonni, S., 'European Union Labour Law and the European Social Model: A Critical Appraisal' in M.W. Finkin and G. Mundlak (eds), *Comparative Labor Law*, Cheltenham, Edward Elgar, 2015, pp. 379–402.

Hendrickx, F., 'The Future of Collective Labour Law in Europe', *European Labour Law*, 2010, vol. 1, pp. 59–79.

Hepple, B. and Veneziani, B. (eds), *The Transformation of Labour Law in Europe: A Comparative Study of 15 Countries 1945-2004*, Oxford, Hart Publishing, 2009.

Hepple, B., 'Factors Influencing the Making and Transformation of Labour Law in Europe' in G. Davidov and B. Langille (eds), *The Idea of Labour Law*, Oxford, Oxford University Press, 2011, pp. 30–42.

Howell, C., 'The Changing Relationship Between Labour and the State in Contemporary Capitalism', *Law, Culture and the Humanities*, 2012, vol. 11, no. 1, pp. 6–16.

Iankova, E. and Turner, L., 'Building the New Europe: Western and Eastern Roads to Social Partnership', *Industrial Relations Journal*, 2004, vol. 35, no. 1, pp. 76–92.

Iankova, E.A., *Eastern European Capitalism in the Making*, Cambridge, Cambridge University Press, 2002.

Bibliography

Ignjatović, M., 'Slovenia: Wage Flexibility and Collective Bargaining', Dublin, Eurofound, 2009, available at: https://www.eurofound.europa.eu/observatories/eur work/comparative-information/national-contributions/slovenia/slovenia-wage-flexibility-and-collective-bargaining (accessed 1 December 2017).

Inglot, T., 'Czech Republic, Hungary, Poland and Slovakia: Adaptation and Reform of the Post-Communist "Emergency Welfare States"' in A. Cerami and P. Vanhuysse (eds), *Post-Communist Welfare Pathways – Theorising Social Policy Transformations in Central and Eastern Europe*, Basingstoke, Palgrave Macmillan, 2009, pp. 73–95.

Inglot, T., *Welfare States in East Central Europe, 1919–2004*, Cambridge, Cambridge University Press, 2008.

Jacobs, A., 'Article 11 ECHR: The Right to Bargain Collectively' in F. Dorssemont, K. Lörcher and I. Schömann (eds), *The European Convention on Human Rights and the Employment Relation*, Oxford, Hart Publishing, 2013, pp. 309–332.

Jacobs, A., 'Collective Labour Relations' in B. Hepple and B. Veneziani (eds), *The Transformation of Labour Law in Europe: A Comparative Study of 15 Countries 1945-2004*, Oxford, Hart Publishing, 2009, pp. 201–231.

Jacobs, A., 'Decentralisation of Labour Law Standard Setting and the Financial Crisis' in N. Bruun, K. Lörcher and I. Schömann (eds), *The Economic and Financial Crisis and Collective Labour Law in Europe*, Oxford, Hart Publishing, 2014, pp. 171–192.

Jepsen, M. and Serrano Pascual, A., 'Introduction' in M. Jepsen and A. Serrano Pascual (eds), *Unwrapping the European Social Model*, Bristol, The Policy Press, 2006a, pp. 1–24.

Jepsen, M., Serrano Pascual, A.S., 'The Concept of the ESM and Supranational Legitimacy-Building' in M. Jepsen and A. Serrano Pascual (eds), *Unwrapping the European Social Model*, Bristol, The Policy Press, 2006b, pp. 25–46.

Kahancová, M., 'Central and Eastern European Trade Unions after the EU Enlargement: Successes and Failures for Capacity Building', *Transfer: European Review of Labour and Research*, 2015, vol. 21, no. 3, pp. 343–357.

Kahancová, M., 'From Bargaining to Advocacy: A Trade-off Between Improved Working Conditions and Trade Union Fragmentation in Slovakia' in M. Bernaciak and M. Kahancová (eds), *Innovative Union Practices in Central-Eastern Europe*, Brussels, ETUI, 2017.

Kahancová, M., 'The Demise of Social Partnership or a Balanced Recovery? The Crisis and Collective Bargaining in Slovakia', *Transfer: European Review of Labour and Research*, 2013, vol. 19, no. 2, pp. 171–183.

Kahn-Nisser, S., 'Conditionality, Communication and Compliance: The Effect of Monitoring on Collective Labour Rights in Candidate Countries', *Journal of Common Market Studies*, 2013, vol. 51, no. 6, pp. 1–17.

Kahn-Nisser, S., 'External Governance, Convention Ratification and Monitoring: The EU, the ILO and Labour Standards in EU Accession Countries', *European Journal of Industrial Relations*, 2014, vol. 20, no. 4, pp. 383–398.

Kajankova, M., *Capacity Building for Social Dialogue at Sectoral and Company Level – the Czech Republic*, Dublin, Eurofound, 2007.

Bibliography

Kanjuo Mrčela, A. 'Living and Working in Slovenia – Collective Bargaining', Dublin, Eurofound, 2017, available at: http://www.eurofound.europa.eu/observatories/eurwork/comparative-information/national-contributions/slovenia/slovenia-working-life-country-profile (accessed 1 December 2017).

Kanjuo Mrčela, A. 'Slovenia: New Social Agreement 2015–2016', Dublin, Eurofound, 2015, available at: https://www.eurofound.europa.eu/observatories/eurwork/articles/industrial-relations/slovenia-new-social-agreement-2015-2016 (accessed 1 December 2017).

Keller, B. and Weber, S., 'Sectoral Social Dialogue at EU level: Problems and Prospects of Implementation', *European Journal of Industrial Relations*, 2011, vol. 17, no. 3, pp. 227–243.

Keune, M. and Marginson, P., 'Transnational Industrial Relations as Multi-Level Governance: Interdependencies in European Social Dialogue', *British Journal of Industrial Relations*, 2013, vol. 51, no. 3, pp. 473–497.

Keune, M. and Pochet, P., 'Conclusions: Trade Union Structures, the Virtual Absence of Social Pacts in the New Member States and the Relationship Between Sheltered and Exposed Sectors' in P. Pochet, M. Keune and D. Natalie (eds), *After the Euro and Enlargement: Social Pacts in the EU*, Brussels, ETUI, 2010, pp. 395–416.

Keune, M., 'Less Governance Capacity and More Inequality: The Effects of the Assault on Collective Bargaining in the EU' in G. Van Gyes and T. Schulten (eds), *Wage Bargaining Under the new European Economic Governance*, Brussels, ETUI, 2015, pp. 285–293.

Keune, M., 'The European Social Model and Enlargement' in M. Jepsen and A. Serrano Pascual (eds), *Unwrapping the European Social Model*, Bristol, The Policy Press, 2006, pp. 167–189.

King, L., 'Central European Capitalism in Comparative Perspective' in B. Hancké, M. Rhodes and M. Thatcher (eds), *Beyond Varieties of Capitalism: Conflict, Contradictions, and Complementarities in the European Economy*, Oxford, Oxford University Press, 2007, pp. 307–327.

King, L., 'Postcommunist Divergence: A Comparative Analysis of the Transition to Capitalism in Poland and Russia', *Studies in Comparative International Development*, 2002, vol. 37, no. 3, pp. 3–34.

Kohl, H. and Platzer, H.-W., 'The Role of the State in Central and Eastern European Industrial Relations: The Case of Minimum Wages', *Industrial Relations Journal*, 2007, vol. 38, no. 6, pp. 614–635.

Kohl, H., 'Convergence and Divergence – Ten Years since EU Enlargement', *Transfer: European Review of Labour and Research*, 2015, vol. 21, no. 3, pp. 285–311.

Kohl, H., 'Freedom of Association, Employees' Rights and Social Dialogue in Central and Eastern Europe and the Western Balkans: Results of a Survey of 16 Formerly Socialist Countries in Eastern Europe', Berlin, Friedrich Ebert Stiftung, 2009.

Kohl, H., Lecher, W. and Platzer, H.-W., 'Transformation, EU Membership and Labour Relations in Central Eastern Europe: Poland – Czech Republic – Hungary – Slovenia', *Transfer: European Review of Labour and Research*, 2000, vol. 6, no. 3, pp. 399–415.

Kollonay-Lehoczky, C., 'European Enlargement: A Comparative View of Hungarian Labour Law' in G.A. Bermann and K. Pistor (eds), *Law and Governance in an Enlarged European Union*, Oxford, Hart Publishing, 2004, pp. 209–238.

Kollonay Lehoczky, C., 'The Future of Labour Law: Insights from an East European Country', *European Labour Law Journal*, 2010, vol. 1, no. 1, pp. 33–43.

Končar, P., 'Changes and Adaptations of Labour Law and Industrial Relations in Slovenia' in R. Blanpain and L. Nagy (eds), *Labour Law and Industrial Relations in Central and Eastern Europe (from Planned to Market Economy)*, Bulletin of Comparative Labour Relations, no. 31, The Hague, Kluwer Law International, 1996, pp. 157–172.

Končar, P., 'EU v. National Industrial Relations Perspective: The Slovenian Perspective' in M. Ronnmar (ed.), *EU v. National Industrial Relations Perspective: Comparative and Interdisciplinary Perspectives*, Alphen aan den Rijn, Kluwer Law International, 2008, pp. 41–52.

Kovačić, H., 'Slovenia: Changes to Wage-Setting Mechanisms in the Context of the Crisis and the EU's New Economic Governance Regime', Dublin, Eurofound, 2014, available at: https://www.eurofound.europa.eu/observatories/eurwork/comparative-information/national-contributions/slovenia/slovenia-changes-to-wage-setting-mechanisms-in-the-context-of-the-crisis-and-the-eus-new-economic (accessed 1 December 2017).

Kroupa, A. and Hála, J., *Capacity Building for Social Dialogue in the Czech Republic*, Dublin, Eurofound, 2006.

Kroupa, A., 'Extension of Collective Agreements to Increase Sectoral Coverage', Dublin, Eurofound, 2006, available at: http://www.eurofound.europa.eu/observatories/eurwork/articles/extension-of-collective-agreements-to-increase-sectoral-coverage (accessed 1 December 2017).

Kubinková, M., 'Tripartism and Industrial Relations in the Czech Republic' in G. Casale (ed.), *Social Dialogue in Central and Eastern Europe*, Budapest, ILO, 1999, pp. 118–145.

Kyzlinkova, R., Lehmann, S., Pojer, P. and Veverková S. 'Living and Working in Czech Republic – Collective Bargaining', Dublin, Eurofound, 2017, available at: https://www.eurofound.europa.eu/country/czech-republic#collective-bargaining (accessed 1 December 2017).

Lado, M. and Vaughan-Whitehead, D., 'Social Dialogue in Candidate Countries: What For?', *Transfer: European Review of Labour and Research*, 2003, vol. 9, no. 64, pp. 64–87.

Lafoucriere, C. and Green, R., 'Social Dialogue as a Regulatory Mode of the ESM: Some Empirical Evidence from the New Member States' in M. Jepsen and A. Serrano Pascual (eds), *Unwrapping the European Social Model*, Bristol, The Policy Press, 2006, pp. 233–254.

Lane, D., 'Emerging Varieties of Capitalism in Former State Socialist Societies', *Competition & Change*, 2005, vol. 9, no. 3, pp. 221–241.

Lane, D., 'Post-State Socialism: A Diversity of Capitalisms?' in D. Lane and M. Myant (eds), *Varieties of Capitalism in Post-Communist Countries*, Basingstoke, Palgrave Macmillan, 2007, pp. 13–40.

Le Friant, M., 'Collective Autonomy: Hope or Danger?', *Comparative Labour Law and Policy Journal*, 2013, vol. 34, pp. 627–654.

Lendvai, N., 'EU Integration and Post-Communist Welfare: Catch-up Convergence Before and After the Economic Crisis' in I.E. Vural (ed.), *Converging Europe: Transformation of Social Policy in the Enlarged European Union and in Turkey*, Farnham, Ashgate, 2011, pp. 181–207.

Lindstrom, N., *The Politics of Europeanisation and Post-Socialist Transformations*, Basingstoke, Palgrave Macmillan, 2015.

Lo Faro, A., *Regulating Social Europe*, Oxford, Hart Publishing, 2000.

López-Santana, M., 'The Domestic Implications of European Soft Law: Framing and Transmitting Change in Employment Policy', *Journal of European Public Policy*, 2006, no. 4, pp. 481–499.

Lord Wedderburn, 'Labour Law: From Here to Autonomy?', *Industrial Law Journal*, 1987, vol. 16, no. 1, pp. 1–29.

Luzar, B. *Capacity Building for Social Dialogue at Sectoral and Company Level-Slovenia*, Dublin, Eurofound, 2007.

Machaliková, A., 'Tripartism in Slovak Republic' in G. Casale (ed.), *Social Dialogue in Central and Eastern Europe*, Budapest, ILO, 1999, pp. 288–304.

Mailand, M. and Due, J., 'Social Dialogue in Central and Eastern Europe: Present State and Future Development', *European Journal of Industrial Relations*, 2004, vol. 10, no. 2, pp. 179–197.

Majtan, B., 'The Labour Code in the Republic of Slovakia', *Employee Relations*, 2005, vol. 27, no. 6, pp. 603–612.

Marginson, P. and Meardi, G., 'European Union Enlargement and the Foreign Direct Investment Channel of Industrial Relations Transfer', *Industrial Relations Journal*, 2006, vol. 37, no. 2, pp. 92–110.

Marginson, P. and Sisson, K., *European Integration and Industrial Relations: Multi-Level Governance in the Making*, Basingstoke, Palgrave Macmillan, 2006.

Marginson, P., 'Coordinated Bargaining in Europe: From Incremental Corrosion to Frontal Assault?', *European Journal of Industrial Relations*, 2015, vol. 21, no. 2, pp. 97–114.

Marleau, V., 'Globalisation, Decentralisation and the Role of Subsidiarity in the Labour Setting' in J.R. Craig and M. Lynk (eds), *Globalisation And the Future of Labour Law*, Cambridge, Cambridge University Press, 2006, pp. 108–142.

Martin, R., 'Politicised Managerial Capitalism: Enterprise Structures in Post-Socialist Central and Eastern Europe', *Journal of Management Studies*, 2002, vol. 39, no. 6, pp. 823–839.

Martin, R., 'Segmented Employment Relations: Post-Socialist Managerial Capitalism and Employment Relations in Central and Eastern Europe', *The International Journal of Human Resource Management*, 2006, vol. 17, no. 8, pp. 1353–1365.

Martin, R., *Constructing Capitalisms: Transforming Business Systems in Central and Eastern Europe*, Oxford, Oxford University Press, 2013.

Matey, M., 'The Prospects for Labor Law Reform in Poland', *Northwestern Journal of International Law & Business*, 1986, vol. 7, pp. 621–632.

Bibliography

Meardi, G. and Trappman, V., 'Between Consolidation and Crisis: Divergent Pressures and Sectoral Trends in Poland', *Transfer: European Review of Labour and Research*, 2013, vol. 19, pp. 195-204.

Meardi, G., 'Industrial Relations after European State Traditions?', in L. Burroni, M. Keune and G. Meardi (eds), *Economy and Society in Europe: A Relationship in Crisis*, Cheltenham, Edward Elgar, 2012b, pp. 100-124.

Meardi, G., 'More Voice after More Exit? Unstable Industrial Relations in Central Eastern Europe', *Industrial Relations Journal*, 2007, vol. 38, no. 6, pp. 503-523.

Meardi, G., 'The Trojan Horse for the Americanisation of Europe? Polish Industrial Relations Towards the EU', *European Journal of Industrial Relations*, 2002, vol. 8, no. 1, pp. 77-99.

Meardi, G., *Social Failures of EU Enlargement: A Case of Workers Voting with Their Feet*, New York, Routledge, 2012a.

Miklos, I., 'Slovakia: A Story of Reforms', in W. Bienkowski, J. Brada and M. Radlo (eds), *Growth versus Security: Old and New EU Members – Quest for a New Economic and Social Model*, Basingstoke, Palgrave Macmillan, 2011, pp. 54-89.

Miklos, I., Kirov, V. and Makó, C., 'Labour Relations, Collective Bargaining and Employee Voice in SMEs in Central and Eastern Europe', *Transfer: European Review of Labour and Research*, 2007, vol. 12, no. 4, pp. 95-113.

Molina, O., 'Social Pacts, Collective Bargaining and Trade Union Articulation Strategies', *Transfer: European Review of Labour and Research*, 2008, vol. 14, no. 3, pp. 399-418.

Munkova, M., 'Law on Employee Participation Amended', Dublin, Eurofound, 2003, available at: http://www.eurofound.europa.eu/observatories/eurwork/articles/law-on-employee-participation-amended (accessed 1 December 2017).

Myant, M. and Smith, S., 'Czech Trade Unions in Comparative Perspective', *European Journal of Industrial Relations*, 1999, vol. 5, no. 3, pp. 265-285.

Myant, M., 'Czech and Slovak Trade Unions', *Journal of Communist Studies*, 1993, vol. 9, no. 4, pp. 59-84.

Myant, M., 'The Czech Republic: From 'Czech' Capitalism to 'European' Capitalism' in D. Lane and M. Myant (eds), *Varieties of Capitalism in Post-Communist Countries*, Basingstoke, Palgrave Macmillan, 2007, pp. 105-124.

Myant, M., 'The Impact of the Economic Crisis on Collective Bargaining in the Czech Republic', *Transfer: European Review of Labour and Research*, 2013, vol. 19, no. 2, pp. 185-194.

Myant, M., 'Trade Unions in the Czech Republic', Report 115, Brussels, ETUI, 2010.

Myant, M., Slocock, B. and Smith, S., 'Tripartism in the Czech and Slovak Republic', *Europe-Asia Studies*, 2000, vol. 52, no. 4, pp. 723-739.

Mykhenko, V., 'Strengths and Weaknesses of "Weak" Coordination: Economic Institutions, Revealed Comparative Advantages, and Socio-Economic Performance of Mixed Market Economies in Poland and Ukraine' in B. Hancké, M. Rhodes and M. Thatcher (eds), *Beyond Varieties of Capitalism: Conflict, Contradictions, and Complementarities in the European Economy*, Oxford, Oxford University Press, 2007, pp. 351-378.

Natali, D. and Pochet, P., 'The Evolution of Social Pacts in the EMU Era: What Type of Institutionalisation?', *European Journal of Industrial Relations*, 2009, vol. 15, no. 2, pp. 147–166.

Natlacen, M.P., 'The Evolving Structure of Collective Bargaining in Europe: National Report of Slovenia', Project VS/2003/0219 – SI2.359910, European Commission and University of Florence, 2004.

Neumann, L., 'Circumventing Trade Unions in Hungary: Old and New Channels of Wage Bargaining', *European Journal of Industrial Relations*, vol. 3, no. 2, 1997, pp. 183–202.

Nölke, A. and Vliegenthart, A., 'Enlarging the Varieties of Capitalism: The Emergence of Dependent Market Economies in East Central Europe', *World Politics*, 2009, vol. 61, no. 4, pp. 670–702.

Olney, S. and Rueda, M., *Convention No 154: Promoting Collective Bargaining*, Geneva, ILO, 2005.

Orenstein, M., 'The Czech Tripartite Council and Its Contribution to Social Peace', *Druzboslovne razprave*, 1994, vols 17–18, pp. 192–208.

Orenstein, M., 'Transitional Social Policy in the Czech Republic and Poland', *Czech Sociological Review*, 1995, vol. 3, no. 2, pp. 179–196.

Ost, D. and Weinstein, M., 'Unionists against Unions: Toward Hierarchical Management in Post-Communist Poland', *East European Politics and Societies*, 1999, vol. 13, no. 1, pp. 1–33.

Ost, D., '"Illusory Corporatism" Ten Years Later', *Warsaw Forum of Economic Sociology*, 2011, vol. 2, no. 1, pp. 19–49.

Ost, D., 'Illusory Corporatism in Eastern Europe: Neoliberal Tripartism and Postcommunist Class Identities', *Politics & Society*, 2000, vol. 28, no. 4, pp. 503–530.

Ost, D., 'The Weakness of Strong Social Movements: Model of Unionism in the East European Context', *European Journal of Industrial Relations*, 2002, vol. 8, no. 1, pp. 33–51.

Ost, D., *Defeat of Solidarity: Anger and Politics in Postcommunist Europe*, Cornell, Cornell University Press, 2005.

Ost, D., *Solidarity and the Politics of Anti-Politics: Opposition and Reform in Poland Since 1968*, Philadelphia, Temple University Press, 1990.

Paczynska, A., 'Confronting Change: Labor, State, and Privatisation' *Review of International Political Economy*, 2007, vol. 14, no. 2, pp. 333–356.

Paczynska, A., *State, Labor, and the Transition to a Market Economy – Egypt, Poland, Mexico, and the Czech Republic*, Pennsylvania, The Pennsylvania State University Press, 2009.

Parissaki, M. and Vega Vega, S., *Capacity Building for Social Dialogue at Sectoral and Company Level in the New Member States, Croatia and Turkey*, Dublin, Eurofound, 2008.

Pavlin, S., 'Slovenia: The Impact of the Information and Consultation Directive', Dublin, Eurofound, 2009, available at: http://www.eurofound.europa.eu/ob servatories/eurwork/comparative-information/national-contributions/slovenia /slovenia-the-impact-of-the-information-and-consultation-directive (accessed 1 August 2016).

Bibliography

Perez-Solorzano Borragan, N. and Smismans, S., 'The EU and Institutional Change in Industrial Relations in the New Member States' in S. Smismans (ed.), *The European Union and Industrial Relations: New Procedures, New Context*, Manchester, Manchester University Press, 2012, pp. 116–138.

Pichrt, J. and Štefko, M., 'Czech Republic' in R. Blanpain and F. Hendrickx (eds), *International Encyclopaedia for Labour Law and Industrial Relations*, The Hague, Kluwer Law International, 2015.

Pichrt, J., 'Czech Republic: European Works Council Country Report' in R. Blanpain and F. Hendrickx (eds), *International Encyclopaedia for Labour Law and Industrial Relations*, The Hague, Kluwer Law International, 2010.

Plachtej, B., 'Slovenia: EIRO CAR on the Effect of the Information and Consultation Directive on Industrial Relations in the EU Member States Five Years After its Transposition', Dublin, Eurofound, 2011, available at: http://www.eurofound.europa.eu/observatories/eurwork/comparative-information/national-contributions/slovenia/slovenia-eiro-car-on-the-effect-of-the-information-and-consultation-directive-on-industrial (accessed 1 December 2017).

Polanyi, K., *The Great Transformation: The Political and Economic Origins of Our Time*, Boston, Beacon Press, 1957.

Pollert, A., 'Labour and Trade Unions in the Czech Republic, 1989-2000' in S. Crowley and D. Ost (eds), *Workers after Workers' State: Labour and Politics in Postcommunist Eastern Europe*, Oxford, Rowman and Littlefield, 2001, pp. 13–36.

Pollert, A., 'Ten Years of Post-Communist Central Eastern Europe: Labour's Tenuous Foothold in the Regulation of the Employment Relationship', *Economic and Industrial Democracy*, 2000, vol. 21, no. 2, pp. 183–210.

Pollert, A., 'The Transformation of Trade Unionism in the Capitalist and Democratic Restructuring of the Czech Republic', *European Journal of Industrial Relations*, 1997, vol. 3, no. 2, pp. 203–228.

Pollert, A., 'Trade Unionism in Transition in Central and Eastern Europe', *European Journal of Industrial Relations*, 1999, vol. 5, no. 2, pp. 209–234.

Potucek, M., 'Accession and Social Policy: the Case of the Czech Republic', *Journal of European Social Policy*, 2004, vol. 14, pp. 253–266.

Potucek, M., 'Current Social Policy Developments in the Czech and Slovak Republics', *Journal of European Social Policy*, 1993, vol. 3, pp. 209–226.

Potucek, M., 'Metamorphoses of Welfare States in Central and Eastern Europe' in M. Seeleib-Kaiser (ed.), *Welfare State Transformations: Comparative Perspectives*, Basingstoke, Palgrave Macmillan, 2008, pp. 79–96.

Radaelli, C.M., 'The Europeanisation of Public Policy' in K. Featherstone and C.M. Radaelli (eds), *The Politics of Europeanisation*, Oxford, Oxford University Press, 2003, pp. 27–56.

Regini, M., 'Between Deregulation and Social Pacts: The Responses of European Economies to Globalization', *Politics & Society*, 2000a, vol. 28, no. 1, pp. 5–33.

Regini, M., 'The Dilemmas of Labour Market Regulation', in G. Esping-Andersen and M. Regini (eds), *Why Deregulate Labour Markets*, Oxford, Oxford University Press, 2000b, pp. 11–30.

Sajo, A., 'New Legalism in East Central Europe: Law as an Instrument of Social Transformation', *Journal of Law and Society*, 1990, vol. 17, no. 3, pp. 329-344.
Saxonberg, S. and Sirovatka, T., 'Neoliberalism by Decay? The Evolution of the Czech Welfare State', *Social Policy and Administration*, 2009, vol. 43, no. 2, pp. 186-203.
Schiek, D., 'The EU's Socio-Economic Model(s) and the Crisi(e)s – Any Perspectives?', in D. Schiek (ed.), *EU Economic and Social Model in the Global Crisis*, Farnham, Ashgate, 2013, pp. 1-22.
Schimmelfennig, F. and Sedelmeier, S., 'Governance by Conditionality: EU Rule Transfer to the Candidate Countries of Central and Eastern Europe', *Journal of European Public Policy*, 2004, vol. 11, no. 4, pp. 669-687.
Schimmelfennig, F. and Sedelmeier, U. (eds), *Europeanisation and Central and Eastern Europe*, Ithaca, Cornell University Press, 2005.
Schimmelfennig, F. and Sedelmeier, U., 'Introduction: Conceptualising the Europeanisation and Central and Eastern Europe' in F. Schimmelfennig and U. Sedelmeier (eds), *Europeanisation and Central and Eastern Europe*, Ithaca, Cornell University Press, 2005, pp. 1-28.
Schimmelfennig, F., Engert, S. and Knobel, H., 'The Impact of EU Political Conditionality' in F. Schimmelfennig and U. Sedelmeier (eds), *The Europeanisation of Central and Eastern Europe*, New York, Cornell University Press, 2005, pp. 29-50.
Sciarra, S., 'The Evolution of Collective Bargaining: Observations on a Comparison in the Countries of the European Union', *Comparative Labour Law and Policy Journal*, 2007, vol. 29, pp. 1-28.
Sewerynski, M., 'Changes in Polish Labour Law and Industrial Relations During the Period of Post-Communist Transformation' in R. Blanpain and L. Nagy (eds), *Labour Law and Industrial Relations in Central and Eastern Europe (from Planned to Market Economy)*, Bulletin of Comparative Labour Relations, no. 31, The Hague, Kluwer Law International, 1996, pp. 85-107.
Sewerynski, M., 'Development of the Collective Bargaining System in Poland after the Second World War', *Comparative Labour Law Journal*, 1993, vol. 14, pp. 441-477.
Sewerynski, M., 'Prospects for the Development of Labour Law and Social Security Law in Central and Eastern Europe in the Twenty-First Century', *Comparative Labour Law and Policy Journal*, 1997, vol. 18, pp. 182-203.
Sewerynski, M., 'The Evolving Structure of Collective Bargaining in Europe: National Report of Poland', Project VS/2003/0219-SI2.359910, European Commission and University of Florence, 2004b.
Sewerynski, M., 'Toward a New Codification of Polish Labour Law', *Comparative Labour Law and Policy Journal*, 2004a, vol. 26, pp. 55-96.
Sissenich, B., 'The Transfer of EU Social Policy to Poland and Hungary' in F. Schimmelfennig and U. Sedelmeier (eds), *The Europeanisation of Central and Eastern Europe*, New York, Cornell University Press, 2005, pp. 156-178.
Sissenich, B., *Building States Without Society: European Union Enlargement and the Transfer of EU Social Policy to Poland and Hungary*, Plymouth, Lexington Books, 2007.

Sisson, K. and Marginson, P., 'Coordinated Bargaining: A Process for Our Times?', *British Journal of Industrial Relations*, 2002, vol. 40, no. 2, pp. 197–220.

Skledar, S., 'Collective Bargaining Legislation Examined', Dublin, Eurofound, 2003, available at: http://eurofound.europa.eu/observatories/eurwork/articles/collective-bargaining-legislation-examined (accessed 1 December 2017).

Skledar, S., 'Government Wants Voluntary Membership of Chamber of Commerce and Industry', Dublin, Eurofound, 2005, available at: http://eurofound.europa.eu/observatories/eurwork/articles/government-wants-voluntary-membership-of-chamber-of-commerce-and-industry (accessed 1 December 2017).

Soskice, D., 'Wage Determination: The Changing Role of Institutions in Advanced Industrialised Countries', *Oxford Review of Economic Policy*, 1990, vol. 6, no. 4, pp. 36–61.

Sroka, J. *Capacity Building for Social Dialogue at Sectoral and Company Level – Poland*, Dublin, Eurofound, 2007.

Standing, G., 'Social Protection in Central and Easter Europe: A Tale of Slipping Anchors and Torn Safety Nets' in G. Esping-Andersen (ed.), *Welfare States in Transition: National Adaptations in Global Economies*, London, SAGE, 1996, pp. 225–255.

Stanojević, M. and Kanjuo Mrčela, A., 'Slovenia at the Crossroads: Increasing Dependence on Supranational Institutions and the Weakening of Social Dialogue', *European Journal of Industrial Relations*, 2016, vol. 1, no. 14, pp. 1–14.

Stanojević, M. and Kanjuo Mrčela, A., 'Social Dialogue during the Economic Crisis: The Impact of Industrial Relations Reforms on Collective Bargaining in the Manufacturing Sector: Slovenia', Project: *The Impact of Industrial Relations Reforms on Collective Bargaining in the Manufacturing Sector*, Brussels, European Commission, 2014.

Stanojević, M. and Klarič, M., 'The Impact of Socio-Economic Shocks on Social Dialogue in Slovenia', *Transfer: European Review of Labour and Research*, 2013, vol. 19, no. 2, pp. 217–226.

Stanojević, M. and Krašovec, A., 'Slovenia: Social Pacts and Political Exchange' in S. Avdagic, M. Rhodes, and J. Visser (eds), *Social Pacts in Europe: Emergence, Evolution, and Institutionalisation*, Oxford, Oxford University Press, 2011, pp. 232–258.

Stanojević, M. and Vehovar, U., 'Slovenia's Integration into the European Market Economy: Gradualism and Its Rigidities' in P. Leisink, B. Steijn and U. Veersma (eds), *Industrial Relations in the New Europe: Enlargement, Integration and Reform*, Cheltenham, Edward Elgar, 2007, pp. 81–114.

Stanojević, M., 'Avoiding Shock Therapy: Trade Unions' Role in the Transition to a Market Economy in Slovenia' in D. Dimitrova and J. Vilrokx (eds), *Trade Union Strategies in Central and Eastern Europe: Towards Decent Work*, Budapest, ILO, 2005, pp. 201–229.

Stanojević, M., 'Conditions for a Neoliberal Turn: The Cases of Hungary and Slovenia', *European Journal of Industrial Relations*, 2014, vol. 20, no. 2, pp. 97–112.

Stanojević, M., 'Social Pacts in Slovenia: Accommodation to the EMU Regime and the Post-Euro Development', *Warsaw Forum of Economic Sociology*, 2011, vol. 2, no. 1, pp. 107–135.

Stanojević, M., 'The Rise and Decline of Slovenian Corporatism: Local and European Factors', *Europe-Asia Studies*, 2012, vol. 64, no. 5, pp. 857–877.

Streeck W., 'National Diversity, Regime Competition, and Institutional Dead-Lock: Problems in Forming a European Industrial Relations System', *Journal of Public Policy*, 1992, vol. 12, pp. 301–330.

Supiot, A., *Beyond Employment: Changes in Work and the Future of Labour Law in Europe*, Oxford, Oxford University Press, 2001.

Swiatkowski, A.M., 'Are the Post-Socialists' Current Collective Bargaining Procedures Effective as a Means to Implement European Labour Law in Poland?', *Tilburg Foreign Law Review*, 2002, vol. 10, pp. 169–180.

Tomes, I., 'The Evolving Structure of Collective Bargaining in Europe: National Report of the Czech Republic', Project VS/2003/0219-SI2.359910, European Commission and University of Florence, 2004.

Towalski, R., 'Collective Agreements in 2004 Examined', Dublin, Eurofound, 2004b, available at: http://www.eurofound.europa.eu/observatories/eurwork/articles/collective-agreements-in-2004-examined (accessed 1 December 2017).

Towalski, R., 'Employers' Organisations Examined', Dublin, Eurofound, 2002, available at: http://www.eurofound.europa.eu/observatories/eurwork/articles/employers-organisations-examined-0 (accessed 1 December 2017).

Towalski, R., 'Single-Establishment Bargaining in 2003 Examined', Dublin, Eurofound, 2004a, available at: http://www.eurofound.europa.eu/observatories/eurwork/articles/single-establishment-bargaining-in-2003-examined (accessed 1 December 2017).

Towalski, R., 'Social Partners Sign Social Pact Declaration', Dublin, Eurofound, 2007, available at: http://www.eurofound.europa.eu/eiro/2007/02/articles/pl0702049i.htm (accessed 1 December 2017).

Towalski, R., 'Wage Formation: Poland', Dublin, Eurofound, 2009, available at: http://www.eurofound.europa.eu/observatories/eurwork/comparative-information/national-contributions/poland/wage-formation-poland (accessed 1 December 2017).

Trappman, V., *Fallen Heroes in Global Capitalism Workers and the Restructuring of the Polish Steel Industry*, New York, Palgrave Macmillan, 2013.

Traxler F., Blaschke S. and Kittel B., *National Labour Relations in Internationalised Markets*, Oxford, Oxford University Press, 2001.

Traxler, F. 'Collective Bargaining: Levels and Coverage', *Employment Outlook*, Paris, OECD, 1994.

Traxler, F., 'Bargaining (De)centralisation, Macroeconomic Performance and Control over the Employment Relationship', *British Journal of Industrial Relations*, 2003a, vol. 41, no. 1, pp. 1–27.

Traxler, F., 'Collective Bargaining in the OECD: Developments, Preconditions and Effects', *European Journal of Industrial Relations*, 1998, vol. 4, no. 2, pp. 207–226.

Traxler, F., 'Coordinated Bargaining: A Stocktaking of Its Preconditions, Practices and Performance', *Industrial Relations Journal*, 2003b, vol. 34, no. 3, pp. 194-209.

Traxler, F., 'Farewell to Labour Market Associations? Organised versus Disorganised Decentralisation as a Map for Industrial Relations' in F. Traxler and C. Crouch (eds), *Organised Industrial Relations in Europe: What Future?*, Aldershot, Avebury, 1995, pp. 3-19.

Traxler, F., 'National Pacts and Wage Regulation in Europe: A Comparative Analysis' in G. Fajertag and P. Pochet (eds), *Social Pacts in Europe: New Dynamics*, Brussels, ETUI/OSE, 2000, pp. 401-417.

Treib, O. and Falkner, G., 'Conclusions – The State of EU Standards in Central and Eastern European Practice' in G. Falkner, O. Treib and E. Holzleithner (eds), *Compliance in the Enlarged European Union: Living Rights or Dead Letters?*, Aldershot, Ashgate Publishing, 2008, pp. 157-182.

Trubek, D.M. and Mosher, J.S., 'New Governance, Employment Policy and the European Social Model' in J. Zeitlin and D.M. Trubek (eds), *Governing Work and Welfare in a New Economy: European and American Experiments*, Oxford, Oxford University Press, 2003, pp. 33-59.

Trubek, D.M. and Trubek, L.G., 'Hard and Soft Law in the Construction of Social Europe: the Role of the Open Method of Coordination', *European Law Journal*, 2005, vol. 11, no. 3, pp. 343-364.

Vaughan-Whitehead, D., 'Social Dialogue in EU Enlargement: Acquis and Responsibilities', *Transfer: European Review of Labour and Research*, 2000, vol. 3, pp. 387-398.

Vaughan-Whitehead, D., 'The European Social Model in Times of Crisis: An Overview', in D. Vaughan-Whitehead (ed.), *The European Social Model in Crisis: Is Europe Losing its Soul?*, Cheltenham, Edward Elgar, 2015, pp. 1-65.

Vaughan-Whitehead, D., 'The World of Work in the New EU Member States: Diversity and Convergence' in D. Vaughan-Whitehead (ed.), *Working and Employment Conditions in New EU Member States*, Geneva, ILO, 2005, pp. 1-43.

Vaughan-Whitehead, D., *EU Enlargement versus Social Europe? The Uncertain Future of the European Social Model*, Cheltenham, Edward Elgar, 2003.

Veneziani, B., 'Austerity Measures, Democracy and Social Policy in the EU' Austerity' in N. Bruun, K. Lörcher and I. Schömann (eds), *The Economic and Financial Crisis and Collective Labour Law in Europe*, Oxford, Hart Publishing, 2014, pp. 109-152.

Veneziani, B., The Intervention of the Law to Regulate Collective Bargaining and Trade Union Representation Rights in European Countries: Recent Trends and Problems', *Transfer, European Review of Labour and Research*, 1999, vol. 5, nos 1-2, pp. 100-135.

Verveková, S., 'The Case of the Czech Republic', in I. Guardiancich (ed.), *Recovering from the Crisis Through Social Dialogue in the New EU Member States: The Case of Bulgaria, the Czech Republic, Poland and Slovenia*, Budapest, ILO, 2012a, pp. 47-64.

Verveková, S., 'Trade Unions Abandoned Tripartite Talks', Dublin, Eurofound, 2012b, available at: http://www.eurofound.europa.eu/observatories/eurwork/articles/

industrial-relations/trade-unions-abandoned-tripartite-talks, (accessed 1 December 2017).

Verveková, S., 'Tripartite Agreement on Short-Term Anti-Crisis Measures', Dublin, Eurofound, 2010, available at: http://www.eurofound.europa.eu/observatories/eurwork/articles/industrial-relations/tripartite-agreement-on-short-term-anti-crisis-measures (accessed 1 December 2017).

Vickerstaff, S.A. and Thirkell, J.E.M., 'Instrumental Rationality and European Integration: Transfer or Avoidance of Industrial Relations Institutions in Central and Eastern Europe?', *European Journal of Industrial Relations*, 2000, vol. 6, no. 2, pp. 237–251.

Visser, J, 'Wage Bargaining Institutions – from Crisis to Crisis', No. 488, Directorate General Economic and Financial Affairs (DG ECFIN), European Commission, 2013.

Visser, J., 'Beneath the Surface of Stability: New and Old Modes of Governance in European Industrial Relations', *European Journal of Industrial Relations*, 2005, vol. 11, no. 3, pp. 287–306.

Visser, J., 'The Five Pillars of the European Social Model of Labor Relations' in J. Beckert, B. Ebbinghaus, A. Hassel and P. Manow (eds), *Transformationen des Kapitalismus: Schriftenreihe aus dem Max Planck Insititut für Gesellschaftsforschung Köln*, Frankfurt a/M: Campus Verlag, Band 57, 2006, pp. 315–336.

Visser, J., 'The Quality of Industrial Relations and the Lisbon Strategy' in European Commission, *Industrial Relations in Europe 2008*, Luxembourg, Publications Office of the European Union, 2009, pp. 45–73.

Visser, J., 'The Rise and Fall of Industrial Unionism', *Transfer: European Review of Labour and Research*, 2012, vol. 18, no. 2, pp. 129–141.

Visser, J., *The ICTWSS Database: Institutional Characteristics of Trade Unions, Wage Setting, State Intervention and Social Pacts in 51 Countries Between 1960 and 2014*, version 5.1, Amsterdam, Amsterdam Institute of Advanced Labour Studies, 2016.

Vodovnik, Z. and Korpič-Horvat, E., 'Slovenia' in R. Blanpain and F. Hendrickx (eds), *International Encyclopaedia for Labour Law and Industrial Relations*, The Hague, Kluwer Law International, 2015.

Vodovnik, Z., 'Slovenia' in R. Blanpain (ed.), *The Actors of Collective Bargaining*, Bulletin of Comparative Labour Relations, no. 51, The Hague, Kluwer Law International, 2004, pp. 231–240.

Warner, M., 'Yugoslav 'Self-Management' and Industrial Relations in Transition' *Industrial Relations Journal*, 1990, vol. 21, no. 3, pp. 209–220.

Weiss, M., 'Industrial Relations and EU Enlargement' in J.D.R. Craig (ed.), *Globalisation and the Future of Labour Law*, Cambridge, Cambridge University Press, 2006, pp. 169–190.

Weiss, M., 'The Future of Workers' Participation in the EU' in C. Barnard, S. Deakin and G. Morris (eds), *The Future of Labour Law: Libber Amicorum Bob Hepple QC*, Oxford, Hart Publishing, 2004, pp. 229–252.

Welz, C. and Kauppinen, T., *Social Dialogue and Conflict Resolution in the Acceding Countries*, Dublin, Eurofound, 2004.

Welz, C., *The European Social Dialogue under Articles 138 and 139 of the EC Treaty: Actors, Processes, Outcomes*, Alphen aan den Rijn, Kluwer Law International, 2008.

Wincott, D., 'The Idea of the European Social Model: Limits and Paradoxes of Europeanisation' in K. Featherstone and C.M. Radaelli (eds), *The Politics of Europeanisation*, Oxford, Oxford University Press, 2003, pp. 279–302.

Woolfson, C., 'Labour Standards and Migration in the New Europe: Post-Communist Legacies and Perspectives', *European Journal of Industrial Relations*, 2007, vol. 13, no. 2, pp. 199–218.

Woolfson, C., 'Working Environment and 'Soft Law' in the Post-Communist New Member States', *Journal of Common Market Studies*, 2006, vol. 44, no. 1, pp. 195–215.

Worker-participation data, ETUI, Brussels, available at: http://www.worker-participation.eu/National-Industrial-Relations/ (accessed 1 December 2017).

List of Interviewees

Slovenia

The following interviews were conducted in Ljubljana in January 2012:

Trade Unions

    Trade Union of Metal and Electro Industry of Slovenia (SKEI) – President.
    Svet Gorenjskih Sindikatov (SGS) – President.

Employers' Associations

    The Chamber of Commerce and Industry (GZS) – Chief Legal Officer.
    Association of Employers of Slovenia (ZDS) – Adviser to the Secretary General.
    Združenje Kovinske Industrije (Association of the Metal Industry, within the Chamber of Industry and Commerce) – President.

Ministry of Labour, Family, Social Affairs and Equal Opportunities

    Written answers provided to the questionnaire.

Slovakia

The following interviews were conducted in Bratislava in April 2012:

Trade Unions

    Energy and Chemical Sectors Trade Union Association (ECHOZ), which is associated to the trade union confederation KOZ SR – Joint meeting with the Adviser on Internal Relations, the Legal Specialist and the Economic Policy Specialist.
    Metalworkers' Trade Union Federation (OZ KOVO) – Joint meeting with the Vice President and the Legal Specialist.
    Integrated Trade Union Association (IOZ), which affiliates trade unions from different sectors, including construction – Regional Coordinator.

List of Interviewees

Employers' Associations

Association of Mechanical Engineering (ZSP SR) – Vice President.

Ministry of Labour, Social Affairs and Family

Head of the Department of Labour Relations.

The Czech Republic

The following interviews were conducted in Prague in April 2012:

Trade Unions

Czech-Moravian Confederation of Trade Union (ČMKOS) – Joint meeting with the Chief of the Legal Department and Wage Bargaining Specialist.
Czech Metalworkers' Federation (OS KOVO) – Joint meeting with Vice President and the Head of the Trade Union Policy Department.
Trade Union of Building Workers of the Czech Republic (OS STAVBA) – Collective Bargaining Specialist.

Employers' Associations

Confederation of Industry of the Czech Republic – Senior Expert.
Association of Building Entrepreneurs in the Czech Republic (SPS CZ) – Chief of the Legal Department.

Ministry of Labour and Social Affairs

Joint meeting with the Head of the Department for Collective Bargaining, Collective Bargaining Specialist and Wage Policy Specialist.

Poland

The following interviews were conducted in Warsaw in November 2012:

Trade Unions

NSZZ Solidarnosc, Legal Adviser (specialist in tripartite dialogue).
NSZZ Solidarnosc, Legal Adviser (specialist in branch and sectoral issues).
All-Poland Alliance of Trade Unions (OPZZ) – Director of the Department for International Co-Operation and European Integration.
Federation of Metalworking Trade Unions in Poland (KZZMP) – President.
ZZ Budowlani, trade union for the construction sector – Secretary General.

Employers' Associations

Polish Craft Association (ZRP) – Social Dialogue Specialist – Phone interview.

List of Interviewees

Ministry of Labour and Social Policy

Joint meeting with the Head of Division for International Cooperation; the Head of Division for Mediation; the specialists in Collective Agreements, National and Regional Social Dialogue, and International Cooperation.

An academic interview

Dr Jan Czarzasty, Warsaw School of Economics.

Index

A

Accession negotiations, 6, 93. *see also* EU enlargement
Acquis communautaire. see also social *acquis* & economic *acquis*
legal and institutional *acquis*, 87
All-Poland Alliance of Trade Union (OPZZ), 50, 116, 118, 126
Articulated multi-employer bargaining model, 9, 16–19, 22, 127, 168, 221
Articulation
    derogation *in peius (in peius)*, 14, 23, 96, 162, 211, 212, 214–216, 218, 221
    favourability principle, 141–144, 162, 197
    opening clauses/opt-out clauses, 23, 142–144, 162, 163, 164, 179, 181, 198, 214, 218
    top-down hierarchy, 22, 141–144, 162, 168, 179
August Agreement, 117
Austria, 123
Autonomy
    autonomous regulation, 19, 20, 57, 58, 63, 70
    collective autonomy, 19, 70, 74–75
    autonomy of labour law, 68
    autonomy of social partners, 74, 86, 94, 98, 133

B

Balcerowicz program, 32
Baltic countries, 37, 40, 42
Bohle and Greskovits' regimes, 34, 36–38, 43, 45, 47, 49, 51, 55, 167, 202, 209

C

Capacity building, 89, 94. *see also* Social partners
Capitalism in CEE, 34–39. *see also* Varieties of capitalism
Centralisation, 13, 14, 15, 16, 23, 35, 44, 51, 52, 56, 98, 107, 157, 196, 202, 209, 211, 218, 220
Chamber of Commerce and Industry (GSZ), 44, 45, 61, 150, 157, 161, 165, 166, 219
Checks and balances, 18, 23, 163, 195, 208
Civil Code
    Czech, 148, 165, 184
    Slovak, 68–69
CMEs. *see* Varieties of capitalism
Collective agreements. *see also* extensions of collective agreements
    contractual and normative parts, 138–141, 158
    definition, 69, 132–138, 175–178

Index

duration, 155–156, 187
emancipation, 67–75
function, 21, 22, 53, 58, 65, 67, 162, 201, 208, 216, 217, 221
nature, 21–22, 67–70
registration, 155–156
substantive scope (or content), 70–74, 76–77, 158–160, 138–144, 178–181
Collective autonomy. *see* autonomy
Collective bargaining. *see also* coordination of industrial relations
coverage, 5, 24, 41, 43, 96, 122, 160–161, 172
levels, 2, 4, 8, 9, 13, 17, 21, 94, 130, 132, 173, 196, 202, 203
multi-employer bargaining, 16–17
parties, 144–149, 165–167, 181–186
procedure, 156, 187
Collective self-determination, 74
Communism/communist systems, 13, 22, 31, 38, 44, 53, 57, 67, 68, 117, 147, 186, 194, 202
Competitive pluralism, 49, 185
Complementarity, 18, 19, 22, 161, 208
Concerted regulation model, 18
Conditionality, 90–94, 100, 210
Confederation of the Trade Unions of Slovak Republic (KOZ SR), 111, 146
Construction sector, 25, 180, 185, 186
Contract law, 68
Coordination, 17, 35, 37, 41, 46, 85, 122, 179
Copenhagen criteria, 87, 88
Crisis, economic and financial, 1, 7, 9, 11, 14, 22, 27, 38, 45, 47, 50, 54, 56, 64, 65, 77–100, 117–119, 123, 132, 158, 163, 179, 210
Cross-sectoral collective agreements in Slovenia, 108

Czech Republic
1991 Act on Collective Bargaining, 65, 72, 153
company collective agreements, 176–177
economic welfare and industrial relations trends, 47–48
labour law development, 64–65
sectoral collective agreements, 135–136
tripartism, 112–115
Czech-Moravian Confederation of Trade Unions (ČMKOS), 130, 147, 173

D

Decentralisation of collective bargaining/decentralised collective bargaining, 1–27, 13–16, 26, 33, 42, 51, 99, 100, 140, 172, 217, 219
organised and disorganised decentralisation, 14, 121, 130, 158, 162, 168
Delors, Jacques, 82
Deregulation, 18, 42, 51, 59, 64, 210
Derogation *in peius*. *see* Articulation
Dzurinda era, 46

E

Economic *acquis*, 94, 100
Emerging market economies, 35, 37
Employers' associations, 5, 17, 165–167
in Czech Republic, 112–114, 147, 148, 153–155, 168, 215
in Poland, 66, 115–118, 136, 149
in Slovakia, 63, 110, 146, 155, 168
in Slovenia, 145, 165
Enlargement, 1, 10, 79, 89, 92, 94. *see also* Accession negotiations
Enterprise-level collective agreements, 134–135, 176–177

Index

ESM. *see* European social model (ESM)
Estonia, 4, 24, 37
EU economic governance, 96–99
Eurofound, 24
European Commission, 3, 6, 82, 87–90, 97, 128
European Council, 10, 82, 83, 87, 97
European model of industrial relations, 81, 83
European Semester, 97, 98
European social dialogue, 80, 86, 87
European social model (ESM), 81–85
Europeanisation, 81, 89–95, 210, 211
Extensions of collective agreements, 150–154, 160–161

F

Favourability principle. *see* Articulation
Fico era, 46
Flexibility of labour markets, 65, 159
France, 14, 23, 68
Free market rationale, 59
Freedom of association, 13, 19, 59, 61, 63, 64, 75, 85–87, 146, 148, 160, 186, 219

G

Gdansk Agreement. *see* August Agreement
General Industrial Classification of Economic Activities (NACE), 151–155
Generations of collective agreements in Slovenia, 62, 76, 138, 219
Germany, 23, 35, 123, 162
Gradualism in Slovenia, 33, 49, 212, 219

H

Hard law, 85, 86, 98. *see also* soft law
Higher-level collective agreements
   in Czech Republic, 135, 153, 172, 177, 180, 196
   in Slovakia, 134, 139, 140, 142, 146, 151, 152, 155, 176, 179, 196
Hungary, 24, 38, 40, 42

I

ILO. *see* International Labour Organisation (ILO)
Individualisation, 200–202, 214, 217–219
Inflation, 31, 39, 49, 99, 104, 106
Information and consultation rights, 87, 92, 183, 184, 185, 186, 187, 189, 190, 191–193, 200
Institutionalisation of industrial relations, 58–59
International Labour Organisation (ILO), 8, 9, 19, 56, 59, 62, 69, 71, 74, 94, 123, 124, 145, 152, 157, 158, 160, 164–166, 182, 186, 198, 199
Italy, 14, 68, 120, 121, 164

K

Klaus, Václav, 32, 47, 48

L

Labour Code
   in Czech Republic, 46, 64, 65, 72, 140, 143, 144, 182, 185, 188, 203
   in Poland, 66, 67, 72, 73, 136, 141, 144, 149, 155, 156, 159, 177, 180, 181, 183, 187, 189, 199, 200
   in Slovakia, 63, 71–72, 96, 134, 135, 139, 140, 143, 182, 183, 184, 188
Labour laws
   auxiliary legislation, 20, 73, 208, 215
   factors pertinent to labour law transformation, 54–56
   nature, 19–21
   protective function, 20, 220
   regulatory legislation, 20

Index

Liberalisation
  dilemma, 43, 77
  of collective agreements, 73, 76, 138
  of industrial relations, 13, 43
LMEs. *see* Varieties of capitalism

M

Market narrative, 59, 60, 70, 100, 203, 204, 209–210, 219, 220
Metals sector, 25, 148, 149, 151, 154, 177, 179
Minimum standards/rights, 15, 20, 73
Multi-enterprise agreements, 136, 144, 154, 157, 168, 178, 181, 198, 213, 214
Multi-level system/framework, 19, 85, 120, 132, 194, 197, 198

N

NACE. *see* General Industrial Classification of Economic Activities (NACE)
Neocorporatism, 103
Neoliberalism/neoliberal, 32, 37–40, 43, 45–50, 60, 94, 107, 122
Netherlands, 14

O

Open method of coordination, 80
OPZZ. *see* All-Poland Alliance of Trade Union (OPZZ)

P

Pact on State-Owned Enterprises in the Restructuring Process, 115–117
Path dependency, 55
Poland
  company collective agreements, 177–178
  economic, welfare and industrial relations trends, 49–50
  labour law development, 65–67
  sectoral collective agreements, 136–138
  tripartism, 115–119
Private law, 67–70, 76, 153, 210
Privatisation, 31, 32, 33, 39, 43, 44, 60, 62, 115, 117, 121, 123, 134, 137, 138, 193, 194
Public law, 67–70, 210

R

Race to the bottom, 15, 18, 80
Regime competition, 79
Regional (tripartite) social dialogue, 112, 115, 119
Representativeness
  in Czech Republic, 113–114, 147–148
  in Poland, 116–117, 148–150
  in Slovakia, 110, 146–147
  in Slovenia, 106, 144–146
  models of, 166
Right to collective bargaining, 5, 21, 67, 74, 94, 96, 191
Round table agreement, 117
Rule of law, 87, 196
Rule transfer, 89, 90, 91, 100, 210

S

Self-management, 33, 44, 57, 58, 60, 76, 133, 166, 175, 176, 178, 185, 190, 192, 202, 210, 213
Shock therapy, 32, 44, 49, 51, 59, 209
Single-employer bargaining, 17, 171
Single-enterprise agreements, 163, 177, 182, 198, 214
Slovakia
  company collective agreements, 176
  economic, welfare and industrial relations trends, 45–47
  labour law development, 63–64
  sectoral collective agreements, 134–135, 139–140
  the 1991 Act on Collective Bargaining, 63, 134, 151, 176

Index

tripartism, 108–112
Slovenia
  company collective agreements, 175–176
  economic, welfare and industrial relations trends, 43–45
  labour law development, 60–63
  sectoral collective agreements, 132–134, 138–139
  the 2006 Act on Collective Agreements, 61–63, 71, 134, 139, 142, 145, 150, 154, 155, 157, 175, 181, 196, 219
  tripartism, 105–108
Small and Medium Enterprises (SMEs), 173, 194, 199, 201, 214
SMEs. *see* Small and Medium Enterprises (SMEs)
Social *acquis*, 9, 81, 85–88, 90–93, 99, 200
Social dialogue
  as an element of *acquis*, 9, 56, 79, 81, 85–88
  notion, 2
Social gap, 1, 18
Social learning, 90–92, 94, 100
Social pacts
  in Czech Republic, 114
  in Poland, 117–118
  in Slovakia, 110–111
  in Slovenia, 106–107
  notion and understanding, 119–123
Social partners. *see also* Autonomy & Capacity building
  capacity, 165
  free organisation, 59, 164
Soft law, 86. *see also* hard law
Solidarity, 33, 49, 50, 52, 66, 82, 115–118, 126, 185, 186
Spain, 14, 68, 120, 121
Subsidiarity, 69, 74, 75
Suspension of collective agreement, 144, 162–163, 198

T

Trade unions
  density, 3, 43, 147, 174, 194, 220
  fragmentation, 42, 49, 50, 52, 183–185, 209, 212, 219
  in Czech Republic, 147, 184–185
  in Poland, 149, 185–186
  in Slovakia, 146, 183–184
  in Slovenia, 144, 183
Tripartism
  committees (sectoral/tripartite), 119, 137, 151, 152
  in Czech Republic, 112–115
  in Poland, 115–119
  in Slovakia, 108–112
  in Slovenia, 105–108
  institutionalisation of, 123–125
  notion in CEE, 119–123

U

UK. *see* United Kingdom (UK)
Unemployment, 31, 39, 43, 49, 83, 95, 104, 106, 113
Unilateral standard-setting, 99, 174, 188–189, 200. *see also* individualisation
United Kingdom (UK), 13, 14, 35, 41, 68, 84, 86

V

Varieties of Capitalism, 34–35. *see also* LMEs & CMEs
Visegrad countries, 38, 40, 52

W

Wage
  in collective agreements, 178, 179, 180
  increases, 180
  inequalities, 38

Index

minimum wage, 77, 126, 160, 164
wage bargaining, 26, 41
wage setting, 84, 98, 99, 107
wage tariff, 164
Welfare regimes in CEE, 38-40

Working time, 15, 73, 77, 93, 132, 141, 176, 180, 184, 189
Workplace democracy, 195, 196, 201, 204
Works councils, 189-193, 200-202

BCLR - BULLETIN OF COMPARATIVE LABOUR RELATIONS

Vol. Author/Title/Year/ISBN

1. Roger Blanpain, *Individual Employment Contracts: Collective Agreements*, 1970.
2. Roger Blanpain, *Social Planning*, 1971 (ISBN 90-312-0018-2).
3. Roger Blanpain, *Guaranteed Income Funds*, 1972 (ISBN 90-312-0019-0).
4. Roger Blanpain, *Employee Participation at the Level of the Enterprise*, 1973 (ISBN 90-312-0020-4).
5. Roger Blanpain, *Vastheid van Betrekking: Staking en Bezetting*, 1974.
6. Roger Blanpain, *Labour Law and Industrial Relations (International Bibliography)*, 1975 (ISBN 90-312-0023-9).
7. Roger Blanpain, *Multinational Enterprises*, 1976 (ISBN 90-312-0024-7).
8. Roger Blanpain, *Worker's Participation in the European Company*, 1977 (ISBN 90-312-0044-1).
9. Roger Blanpain, *Women and Labour*, 1978 (ISBN 90-312-0077-8).
10. Roger Blanpain, *European Conference on Labour Law and Industrial Relations: Multinational Enterprises*, 1979 (ISBN 90-312-0091-3).
11. Roger Blanpain, *Job Security and Industrial Relations*, 1980 (ISBN 90-312-0147-2).
12. Roger Blanpain, Greg Bamber & Russell Lansbury, *Technological Change and Industrial Relations: An International Symposium*, 1983 (ISBN 90-312-0205-3).
13. Roger Blanpain, James Janssen van Raay & A. Moulty, *Worker's Participation in the European Community: The Fifth Directive*, 1984 (ISBN 90-654-4187-5).
14. Roger Blanpain, *Equality and Prohibition of Discrimination in Employment*, 1985 (ISBN 90-654-4215-4).
15. Roger Blanpain, *Restructuring Labour in the Enterprise: Law and Practice in France, F.R. of Germany, Italy, Sweden and the United Kingdom*, 1986 (ISBN 90-654-4283-9).
16. Roger Blanpain & E. Kassalow, *Unions and Industrial Relations: Recent Trends and Prospect: A Comparative Treatment*, 1987 (ISBN 90-654-4294-4).
17. Roger Blanpain & Marco Biagi, *Trade Union Democracy and Industrial Relations*, 1988 (ISBN 90-654-4394-0).
18. Roger Blanpain & Jelle Visser, *In Search of Inclusive Unionism*, 1990 (ISBN 90-654-4439-4).
19. Roger Blanpain, *Flexibility and Wages: A Comparative Treatment*, 1990 (ISBN 90-654-4461-0).

20. Roger Blanpain, Stephen Frenkel & Oliver Clarke, *Economic Restructuring and Industrial Relations in Industrialised Countries*, 1990 (ISBN 90-654-4488-2).
21. Roger Blanpain & Friedrich Fürstenberg, *Structure and Strategy in Industrial Relations*, 1991 (ISBN 90-654-4559-5).
22. Roger Blanpain, Amira Galin & Ozer Carmi, *Flexible Work Patterns and Their Impact on Industrial Relations*, 1991 (ISBN 90-654-4572-2).
23. Roger Blanpain, *Workers' Participation: Influence on Management Decision-Making by Labour in the Private Sector*, 1992 (ISBN 90-654-4600-1).
24. Roger Blanpain, Brian Brooks & Chris Engels, *Employed or Self-Employed*, 1992 (ISBN 90-654-4613-3).
25. Roger Blanpain & Tiziano Treu, *Industrial Relations Developments in the Telecommunications Industry*, 1993 (ISBN 90-654-4642-7).
26. Roger Blanpain & Marco Biagi, *Industrial Relations in Small and Medium Sized Enterprises*, 1993 (ISBN 90-654-4696-6).
27. Roger Blanpain & Marco Biagi, *Participative Management and Industrial Relations in a Worldwide Perspective*, 1993 (ISBN 90-654-4769-5).
28. Roger Blanpain, Jacques Rojot & Hoyt N. Wheeler, *Employee Rights and Industrial Justice*, 1994 (ISBN 90-654-4804-7).
29. Roger Blanpain & Ruth Ben-Israel, *Strikes and Lock-Outs in Industrialized Market Economies*, 1994 (ISBN 90-654-4841-1).
30. Roger Blanpain, Kazuo Sugeno & Yasuo Suwa, *The Harmonization of Working Life and Family Life*, 1995 (ISBN 90-411-0064-4).
31. Roger Blanpain & Laszio Nagy, *Labour Law and Industrial Relations in Central and Eastern Europe*, 1996 (ISBN 90-411-0298-1).
32. Roger Blanpain, *Labour Law and Industrial Relations in the European Union*, 1997 (ISBN 90-411-0527-1).
33. Taco Van Peijpe, *Employment Protection under Strain*, 1998 (ISBN 90-411-0528-8).
34. Roger Blanpain, Takashi Araki & Ryuichi Yamakawa, *The Process of Industrialization and the Role of Labour Law in Asia*, 1999 (ISBN 9-041-1104-7-X).
35. Roger Blanpain & Marco Biagi, *Non-standard Work and Industrial Relations*, 1999 (ISBN 90-411-1117-4).
36. Roger Blanpain, *Private Employment Agencies: The Impact of ILO Convention 181 (1997) and the Judgment of the European Court of Justice of 11 December 1997*, 1999 (ISBN 90-411-1118-2).
37. Roger Blanpain, *Multinational Enterprises and the Social Challenges of the XXIst Century: The ILO Declaration on Fundamental* Principles *at Work, Public and Private Corporate Codes of Conduct*, 2000 (ISBN 90-411-1280-4).
38. Roger Blanpain, Ryuichi Yamakawa & Takashi Araki, *Deregulation and Labour Law: In Search of a Labour Concept for the 21st Century*, 2000 (ISBN 90-411-1370-3).
39. Roger Blanpain, *The Council of Europe and the Social Challenges of the XXIst Century*, 2001 (ISBN 90-411-1543-9).

40. Roger Blanpain, *On-Line Rights for Employees in the Information Society, Use & Monitoring of E-Mail & Internet at Work*, 2002 (ISBN 90-411-1626-5).
41. Roger Blanpain, *The Evolving Employment Relationship and the New Economy: The Role of Labour Law & Industrial Relations*, 2001 (ISBN 90-411-1691-5).
42. Roger Blanpain, *Involvement of Employees in the European Union, Works Councils, Company Statute, Information and Consultation Rights*, 2002 (ISBN 90-411-1760-1).
43. Michele Colucci, *The Impact of the Internet and New Technologies on the Workplace: A Legal Analysis from a Comparative Point of View*, 2002 (ISBN 90-411-1824-1).
44. Roger Blanpain, *White Paper on the Labour Market in Italy: The Quality of European Industrial Relations and Changing Industrial Relations*, 2002 (ISBN 90-411-1841-1).
45. Roger Blanpain, Russell D. Lansbury & Young-Bum Park, *Impact of Globalisation on Employment Relations: A Comparison of the Automobile and Banking Industries in Australia and Korea*, 2002 (ISBN 90-411-1850-0).
46. Roger Blanpain & Antoine Jacobs, *Employee Rights in Bankruptcy: A Comparative-Law Assessment*, 2002 (ISBN 90-411-1942-6).
47. Roger Blanpain, Takashi Araki & Shinya Ouchi, *Corporate Restructuring and the Role of Labour Law*, 2003 (ISBN 90-411-1949-3).
48. Roger Blanpain, *Collective Bargaining, Discrimination, Social Security and European Integration*, 2003 (ISBN 90-411-2010-6).
49. Roger Blanpain & Luis Aparicio-Valdez, *Labour Relations in the Asia- Pacific Countries*, 2004 (ISBN 90-411-2239-7).
50. Roger Blanpain & Ronnie Graham, *Temporary Agency Work and the Information Society*, 2004 (ISBN 90-411-2252-4).
51. Roger Blanpain, *The Actors of Collective Bargaining: A World Report*, 2004 (ISBN 90-411-2253-2).
52. Roger Blanpain & Michele Colucci, *The Globalisation of Labour Standards: The Soft Law Track*, 2004 (ISBN 90-411-2303-2).
53. Roger Blanpain, Takashi Araki & Shinya Ouchi, *Labour Law in Motion: Diversification of the Labour Force & Terms and Conditions of Employment*, 2005 (ISBN 90-411-2315-6).
54. Roger Blanpain, *Smoking and the Workplace*, 2005 (ISBN 90-411-2325-3).
55. Roger Blanpain, *Confronting Globalization: The Quest for a Social Agenda*, 2005 (ISBN 90-411-2381-4).
56. Roger Blanpain, Thomas Blanke & Edgar Rose, *Collective Bargaining Wages in Comparative Perspective: Germany, France, the Netherlands, Sweden and the United Kingdom*, 2005 (ISBN 90-411-2388-1).
57. Roger Blanpain & Anne Numhauser-Henning, *Women in Academia & Equality Law: Aiming High - Falling Short?*, 2006 (ISBN 978-90-411-2427-6).
58. Roger Blanpain, *Freedom of Services in the European Union: Labour and Social Security Law: The Bolkestein Initiative*, 2006 (ISBN 978-90-411-2453-5).
59. Roger Blanpain, Frans Pennings & Nurhan Sural, *Flexibilisation and Modernisation of the Turkish Labour Market*, 2006 (ISBN 978-90-411-2490-X).

60. Roger Blanpain & Boel Flodgren, *Corporate and Employment Perspectives in a Global Business Environment*, 2006 (ISBN 978-90-411-2537-X).
61. Roger Blanpain, Shinya Ouchi & Takashi Araki, *Decentralizing Industrial Relations and The Role of Labor Unions and Employee Representatives*, 2007 (ISBN 978-90-411-2583-3).
62. Roger Blanpain, *European Framework Agreements and Telework: Law and Practice: A European and Comparative Study*, 2007 (ISBN 978-90-411-2560-4).
63. Roger Blanpain, Jim Kitay, Leanne Cutcher & Nick Wailes, *Globalization and Employment Relations in Retail Banking*, 2007 (ISBN 978-90-411-2620-1).
64. Roger Blanpain, Russell Lansbury, Jim Kitay, Nick Wailes & Anja Kirsch, *Globalization and Employment Relations in the Auto Assembly Industry: A Study of Seven Countries*, 2008 (ISBN 978-90-411-2698-6).
65. Roger Blanpain & Michele Tiraboschi, *The Global Labour Market: From Globalization to Flexicurity*, 2008 (ISBN 978-90-411-2722-8).
66. Roger Blanpain, Michele Colucci & Frank Hendrickx, *The Future of Sport in the European Union: Beyond the EU Reform Treaty and the White Paper*, 2008 (ISBN 978-90-411-2761-7).
67. Roger Blanpain, Linda Dickens, *Challenges in European Employment Relations: Employment Regulation, Trade Union Organization, Equality, Flexicurity, Training and New Approaches to Pay*, 2008 (ISBN 978-90-411-2771-6).
68. Roger Blanpain, Hiroya Nakakubo & Takashi Araki, *New Developments in Employment Discrimination Law*, 2008 (ISBN 978-90-411-2782-2).
69. Roger Blanpain, Andrzej Marian wiątkowski, *The Laval and Viking Cases: Freedom of Services and Establishment v. Industrial Conflict in the European Economic Area and Russia*, 2009 (ISBN 978-90-411-2850-8).
70. Roger Blanpain, William Bromwich, Olga Rymkevich, Silvia Spattini, *The Modernization of Labour Law and Industrial Relations in a Comparative Perspective*, 2009 (ISBN 978-90-411-2865-2).
71. Roger Blanpain, Juan Pablo Landa & Brian Langille, *Employment Policies and Multilevel Governance*, 2009 (ISBN 978-90-411-2866-9).
72. Roger Blanpain, European Works Councils; *The European Directive 2009/38/EC of 6 May 2009*, 2009 (ISBN 978-90-411-3208-6).
73. Roger Blanpain, William Bromwich, Olga Rymkevich & Silvia Spattini, *Labour Productivity, Investment in Human Capital and Youth Employment: Comparative Developments and Global Responses*, 2010 (ISBN 978-90-411-3249-9).
74. Greg J. Bamber & Philippe Pochet, *Regulating Employment Relations, Work and Labour Laws: International Comparisons between Key Countries*, 2010 (ISBN 978-90-411-3199-7). General Editor: Roger Blanpain.
75. Roger Blanpain, Desislava Nikolaeva Dimitrova, *Seafarers' Rights in the Globalized Maritime Industry*, 2010 (ISBN 978-90-411-3349-6).
76. Roger Blanpain, Hiroya Nakakubo & Takashi Araki, *Regulation of Fixed-Term Employment Contracts*, 2010 (ISBN 978-90-411-3356-4).

77. Roger Blanpain, William Bromwich, Olga Rymkevich & Iacopo Senatori, *Rethinking Corporate Governance*, 2011 (ISBN 978-90-411-3450-9).
78. Roger Blanpain & Frank Hendrickx, *Labour Law between Change and Tradition: Liber Amicorum Antoine Jacobs*, 2011 (ISBN 978-90-411-3424-0).
79. Roger Blanpain, Thomas Klebe, Marlene Schmidt & Bernd Waas, *Trade Union Rights at the Workplace*, 2012 (ISBN 978-90-411-3460-8).
80. Roger Blanpain, William Bromwich, Olga Rymkevich & Iacopo Senatori, *Labour Markets, Industrial Relations and Human Resources Management: From Recession to Recovery*, 2012 (ISBN 978-90-411-4004-3).
81. Roger Blanpain, Hiroya Nakakubo & Takashi Araki, *Systems of Employee Representation at the Enterprise: A Comparative Study*, 2012 (ISBN 978-90-411-4080-7).
82. Roger Blanpain & Frank Hendrickx, *Temporary Agency Work in the European Union and the United States*, 2013 (ISBN 978-90-411-4769-1).
83. Roger Blanpain, Toker Dereli, Y. Pınar Soykut-Sarıca & Aslı en-Tabaı, *Emerging Patterns of Work and Turkish Labour Market Challenges under Globalization: Readings on Labour and Employment Relations*, 2014
(ISBN 978-90-411-4983-1).
84. Roger Blanpain, Pablo Arellano Ortiz, Marius Olivier & Gijsbert Vonk, *Social Security and Migrant Workers: Selected Studies of Cross-border Social Security Mechanisms*, 2014 (ISBN 978-90-411-4770-7).
85. Roger Blanpain & Nikita Lyutov, *Workers' Representation in Central and Eastern Europe: Challenges and Opportunities for the Works Councils' System*, 2014 (ISBN 978-90-411-4746-2).
86. Roger Blanpain, Ulla Liukkunen & Chen Yifeng, *China and ILO Fundamental Principles and Rights at Works*, 2014 (ISBN 978-90-411-4984-8).
87. Roger Blanpain, *The Use of Languages and Employment Relations*, 2014 (ISBN 978-90-411-5606-8).
88. Roger Blanpain, Hiroya Nakakubo & Takashi Araki, *Protection of Employees' Personal Information and Privacy*, 2014 (ISBN 978-90-411-5608-2).
89. Roger Blanpain, Jan Wouters, Glenn Rayp, Laura Beke & Axel Marx, *Protecting Labour Rights in a Multi-polar Supply Chain and Mobile Global Economy*, 2015 (ISBN 978-90-411-5662-4).
90. Roger Blanpain & Stefania Marassi, *Globalization and Transnational Collective Labour Relations: International and European Framework Agreements at Company Level*, 2015 (ISBN 978-90-411-4748-6).
91. Roger Blanpain, Frank Hendrickx & Petra Herzfeld Olsson, *National Effects of the Implementation of EU Directives on Labour Migration from Third Countries*, 2016 (ISBN 978-90-411-6257-1).
92. Roger Blanpain, Frank Hendrickx & D'Arcy du Toit, *Labour Law and Social Progress: Holding the Line or Shifting the Boundaries?* 2016 (ISBN 978-90-411-6747-7).

93. Roger Blanpain & Frank Hendrickx, *Reasonable Accommodation in the Modern Workplace: Potential and Limits of the Integrative Logics of Labour Law*, 2016 (ISBN 978-90-411-6258-8).
94. Roger Blanpain, Frank Hendrickx & Bernd Waas, *New Forms of Employment in Europe*, 2016 (ISBN 978-90-411-6239-7).
95. Roger Blanpain, Frank Hendrickx, Hiroya Nakakubo & Takashi Araki, *The Notion of Employer in the Era of the Fissured Workplace: Should Labour Law Responsibilities Exceed the Boundary of the Legal Entity?*, 2017 (ISBN 978-90-411-8470-2).
96. Elena Sychenko, *Individual Labour Rights as Human Rights: The Contributions of the European Court of Human Rights to Worker's Rights Protection*, 2017 (ISBN 978-90-411-8629-4).
97. William Bromwich & Olga Rymkevich, *Improving Workplace Quality: New Perspectives and Challenges for Worker Well-Being*, 2017 (ISBN 978-90-411-8628-7).
98. Sarah De Groof, *Work-Life Balance in the Modern Workplace: Interdisciplinary Perspectives from Work-Family Research, Law and Policy*, 2017 (ISBN 978-90-411-8630-0).
99. Sylvaine Laulom, *Collective Bargaining Developments in Times of Crisis*, 2018 (ISBN 978-90-411-8999-8).
100. Frank Hendrickx & Valerio De Stefano, *Game Changers in Labour Law: Shaping the Future of Work*, 2018 (ISBN 978-90-411-9953-9).
101. Ivana Palinkaš, *The Legal and Institutional Framing of Collective Bargaining in CEE Countries: Between Europeanisation and Decentralisation*, 2018 (ISBN 978-90-411-9199-1).